How to Write
for the
World of Work

HOW TO WRITE FOR THE WORLD OF WORK

THIRD EDITION

THOMAS E. PEARSALL
University of Minnesota

DONALD H. CUNNINGHAM
Texas Tech University

HOLT, RINEHART AND WINSTON
New York   Chicago   San Francisco   Philadelphia
Montreal   Toronto   London   Sydney
Tokyo   Mexico City   Rio de Janeiro   Madrid

Library of Congress Cataloging in Publication Data

Pearsall, Thomas E.
  How to write for the world of work.

  Bibliography: p.
  Includes index.
  1. Commercial correspondence.   2. Business report
writing.   I. Cunningham, Donald H.   II. Title.
HF5721.P39 1986   808'.066651   85-13939

ISBN 0-03-002123-5

Holt, Rinehart and Winston
The Dryden Press
Saunders College Publishing

To Anne and Pat

We [teachers of writing] must concern ourselves, first and foremost, beyond all our other legitimate concerns, with the world's first expectation of us: producing in our students genuine competence in the sort of spoken and written language required for the world's work.

PREFACE

As in our second edition, we continue our use of the term *transactional writing* for the writing we describe in this book. We take the term from the report of a project of the Great Britain Schools Council, where it is defined as follows:

> This is language to get things done: to inform people . . . to advise or persuade or instruct people. Thus the transactional is used for example to record facts, exchange opinions, explain and explore ideas, construct theories; to transact business, conduct campaigns, change public opinion. Where the transaction (whatever it is we want to do with language) demands accurate and specific reference to what is known about reality, this need constitutes a demand for language in the transactional category.[1]

We have adopted the term for our book because its definition so well fits the kind of writing that is our subject: the writing that goes on in the world of work. We divide this writing into its two major components—correspondence and reports. In reports, we also cover oral reports. We break these components down into their day-to-day tasks, such as employment letters, customer relations letters, and recommendation reports. We tell as carefully and precisely as we can how to accomplish each of these tasks. We use real examples, most reproduced as they originally appeared in some work situation. Some we have modified slightly to make them more generally applicable. Although we have designed this book for the classroom, we want it to have the feel of the world where one day the classroom exercises will become the real thing.

Our audience remains the student who is being educated for a specific vocation or profession. We visualize that student as practical and industrious, willing to work when shown what needs to be done. This student already knows or will quickly see the need for good communication in an organization. Our purpose, as in previous editions, is to lead that student from the simpler forms of correspondence to the challenging complexity of writing tasks such as instructions, recommendation reports, and proposals.

We have made some significant revisions for this third edition. The major ones are these:

- Our most important revision has been an organizational one. We now begin with a Unit I that is now called "Basic Principles." In this unit we gather together those principles a writer needs to master whether writing letters or reports. We include chapters on the process of transactional writing, persuasion and scientific argument, and style and tone. Correspondence is covered in Unit II and reports in Unit III. Unit IV is the "Writer's Guide" where, in alphabetical order, we cover the major conventions writers need to know.

- We have changed our recommended documentation style, described in Chapter 9, "Basic Principles of Reports," from the style of the Modern Language Association to that of *The Chicago Manual of Style,* 13th edition. The *Chicago Manual* style, sometimes with slight modifications, is now the most commonly used style in scientific and technical writing. We have changed our own documentation to conform to the *Chicago Manual.* Also, we have gathered all our notes together in "Chapter Notes" on pages 446–449, both to clean up our pages and to provide an array of examples in one place.
- Chapter 9, "Basic Principles of Reports," has been reorganized to clarify the relationship between principles of document design and the format and formal elements of reports.
- Chapter 11, "Bibliographic Reports and Literature Reviews," has been updated and now emphasizes the importance of a good introduction in such reports.
- Graphics are emphasized even more than in previous editions, particularly in Chapter 12, "Mechanism Description," and Chapter 13, "Process Description."
- Chapter 16, "Recommendation Reports," is a new chapter. Using a student report as an example, it shows, first, how to find solutions to problems by following a path of practical logic and, second, how to report the solutions in a coherent, well-constructed report.

In addition to these major revisions, many smaller ones have been made. Older examples have been replaced with newer ones. More use has been made of student examples. More emphasis has been placed on the thinking and planning that goes into reports. Points that our reviewers and correspondents have had trouble with have been clarified. While making these changes, large and small, we have kept an eye on the length of our book. As in the past, we have aimed for concision.

An *Instructor's Manual* is available to accompany the text. It gives general suggestions for writing assignments and classroom activities, a detailed syllabus, and a list of further sources of information. The manual may be obtained through your local Holt representative or by writing the English Editor, College Department, Holt, Rinehart and Winston, 383 Madison Avenue, New York, NY 10017.

Acknowledgments

As in previous editions, we thank Professors Frederick H. MacIntosh of the University of North Carolina and John A. Walter of the University of

Texas. We thank Professor MacIntosh for his phrase "writing for the world's work," which in modified form has become part of our title. We thank him also for the passage we have set above this Preface, which expresses so well the obligation we feel as authors and teachers.[2] Professor Walter we thank again for his statement that "scientists and engineers are concerned, when they write, with presenting information to a specific body of readers for a specific purpose."[3] We think all writers in the world of work have these basic concerns. Our version of Professor Walter's statement—*transactional writing presents specific information to a specific audience for a specific purpose*— is stated and illustrated frequently throughout this book.

For this third edition, we thank the following reviewers for their candid and useful advice: O. Jane Allen, New Mexico State University; Michael Keene, University of Tennessee at Knoxville; Shannon Kiser, Shawnee State Community College; Allison McCormack, Miami University–Hamilton; Joan Sherman, Rutgers, The State University; and Thomas Warren, Oklahoma State University.

As always, we thank Anne Pearsall and Pat Cunningham for their love and understanding.

T.E.P
D.H.C.

CONTENTS

U N I T

I

C H A P T E R

1

THE PROCESS OF TRANSACTIONAL WRITING

The course for which you are reading this text may be called professional writing, technical writing, business writing, or, perhaps, simply Communication II. Whatever the title, because your instructor has chosen this book, the course will be about writing for the world of work. We refer to our subject as transactional writing.

Transactional writing is writing that links people together in the world of work. It links businessperson to businessperson, management to labor, business to government, engineer to technician, buyer to seller. It provides the records that industry and government need to function year by year. Basically, transactional writing consists of correspondence and reports. A look at our Table of Contents will suggest the variety: inquiry and response letters . . . customer relations letters . . . recommendation reports . . . proposals. Because reports must be made orally, we have included a section on this method of presentation as well.

Communication is important in the world of work. Certainly, ample evidence to support such a position has been gathered over the last 30 years or so. In 1957, a General Electric Company survey revealed that its engineering personnel ranked courses in English communication skills second only to mathematics in college courses considered "Most Valuable to Career." The engineering courses of their discipline ranked third. Nontechnical employees ranked English as the most valuable course.[1]

A 1977 survey of persons listed in *Engineers of Distinction* demonstrated once again the need for good communication in general and good writing skills in particular. The researcher summarized his results in this way:

- The respondents spent an average of 24.35 percent of their time writing.

- The respondents spent 31 percent of their time working with other people's written materials.
- Most of the respondents felt that the ability to write effectively is either very important or of critical importance to them.
- Almost all report that as their responsibility increased, so did their need to write.
- Almost all felt that the ability to write well had contributed to their advancement.
- In advancing subordinates, almost all considered their writing ability.[2]

A 1980 study of young professionals one to five years after their graduation from colleges of agriculture, home economics, and forestry revealed that 72 percent ranked writing competent letters and reports as important or very important to their careers.[3] In other words, over time and in a variety of occupations, few educated people escape without producing a share of the writing done at their place of work.

Your previous writing courses may have dealt with personal or literary writing. You'll find transactional writing considerably different. Read a few lines of John Donne's "The Bait":

> Come live with me, and be my love,
> And we will some new pleasures prove,
> Of golden sands, and crystal brooks,
> With silken lines, and silver hooks.

Donne is making a personal artistic statement with skill and beauty that are quite beyond most of us.

Look now at a piece of transactional writing:

> In a novel scheme for transporting coal from the mine to distant power-generating stations, powdered coal and coal-derived oil move through a pipeline as a nonaqueous slurry. During the journey through the pipeline (at temperatures between 300° and 400°C), solvation of the coal takes place, increasing the quantity of liquid and decreasing the amount of solid. A portion of the oil is removed for recycling at an intermediate station, and the remaining slurry is processed to remove sulfur, ash, and nitrogen. At the end of the line, the slurry is separated into its liquid and solid components, which are burned in separate facilities.[4]

The writer who wrote this paragraph was making an impersonal statement to convey a specific piece of information. The style is not particularly artistic, but it is competent. The paragraph is easily understood by its intended audience. To make sure it would be understood, the writer also included a graphic, which we have reproduced in Figure 1–1 on page 11. The paragraph represents a style and a method of writing within the grasp of most of us.

Transactional writing is a craft, not an art form. As a craft, transactional writing should be a rational process that can be learned and, in fact, it is. The process grows out of the underlying theme of this book— that transactional writing presents specific information to a specific audience for a specific purpose. The process involves analyzing your audience, setting objectives, checking and gathering information, planning organization, planning graphics, and writing and revising. We will take you through all six steps, but, first, by way of a metaphor, we suggest the levels of difficulty you may find in the process.

Both of your authors have the good fortune to be able to walk to work. For both of us, it is a journey of about a mile down several streets with several turnings. For these frequently traveled trips we need no maps other than the ones in our heads. We know the way. For most other trips we take regularly, we can also depend upon the maps in our heads. As we stray further afield, to confirm the route, we may have to glance at a map before we start. For a totally strange trip, we will obtain a map and prepare an itinerary from it. We will keep the itinerary and map close to hand as we travel.

But suppose we are traveling into strange territory for which we have no map. All of us have done that on occasion, perhaps in a city new to us or in rough back country. Here we find that we may make many false starts and turns. We start in one direction and walk or drive on bravely until we realize that we are not moving any closer to our goal. We back up and start over again. Along the way we may meet someone who gives us better directions for at least part of the way. So we proceed by trial and error and by gathering additional information until we reach our goal.

We hope the moral of the map metaphor is clear. Sometimes writing is easy. Writing about familiar subjects and in familiar ways—perhaps writing a letter to a friend or filling in a frequently used laboratory report—resembles our walks and drives to familiar places.

Sometimes the writing can be classified as medium difficult, but maps in the form of organizational and format patterns are available. For example, in doing a resume, you have the information about your education and work experience readily available, and you can find an acceptable pattern for the resume on pages 82 and 87 of this book. Throughout the book we present many such patterns to help you find your way. But sometimes, in writing as in traveling, you will be entering unexplored territory without a map. This last situation presents the highest level of difficulty.

The process we describe should help you at every level of difficulty. Depending on the level of difficulty, you may need to follow all of the steps only some of the time, but you will need to follow some of the steps all of the time.

ANALYZING YOUR AUDIENCE

Because transactional writing deals with audience, purpose, and information, you should start with one of the three. We suggest that you start with your audience. Having a reader in mind helps to keep a writer grounded in reality. In transactional writing, you can usually define your reader or readers rather narrowly: an executive with a college degree, a group of technicians with good knowledge of the field, a homeowner installing a lock, a farmer with an associate degree in animal technology, or your boss. You can define your audiences by experience, occupation, education, and relationship to you. You know to some degree their general knowledge and the special knowledge they already possess about your subject. You may also know their attitude about your subject: friendly, neutral, hostile, or apathetic. Jot down everything you can think of about your audience.

Audience analysis continues throughout the entire writing process. Keep your real or imagined reader in the forefront of your mind. As you plan and write, imagine yourself carrying on a dialogue with your reader. What are some of the questions your reader might ask you? We suggest a few here and some of the ways you might respond to them.

- So what? (A key question. Always be sure your reader knows the significance and implications of the information you present.)
- How do you know what you are saying is true? (Do you have either experience or research to back up what you are saying? Provide the needed evidence.)
- How does it work, exactly? (Perhaps an example or a comparison will help.)
- How is the task accomplished? (Provide clear instructions for the work to be done.)
- Why should I do the task your way and not mine? (Frequently, your methods and techniques have to be justified to others.)
- Why is this important to me? (Show where the reader's self-interest is involved.)
- How come? (Tell your reader why you're asking that something be done.)
- What does this word mean? (Provide a definition.)
- How does this idea tie to that one? (Provide a transition, a bridge of some sort, to link your ideas together.)
- Now that I understand you, what do you want me to do? (Make sure all conclusions and recommendations are firmly stated.)

And in any dialogue, don't overlook the journalist's always useful questions: Who? What? When? Where? Why?

SETTING OBJECTIVES

In the beginning of the process, when you have your reader firmly in mind, turn to purpose, both yours and your reader's; that is, set your objectives. What do you hope to accomplish with this piece of writing? What does your reader hope to accomplish by reading it? Usually these questions are two sides of the same coin. You may be trying to sell a certain brand of feed to a farmer. The farmer's purpose is to see if your feed is worth buying. You may be explaining to someone how to assemble a mail-order toy. The reader needs to assemble it.

Write your objectives down. Nothing clarifies thought as much as forcing yourself to set the thought down on paper. The writing process is more than a means of reporting thought. Often it is thought itself. Your objectives as stated should be measurable. That is, they should be stated in a way that allows you to know if they have been accomplished.

An objective such as *the reader will understand how to assemble the toy* is not measurable as stated. How do you plan to test the understanding? The objective stated as *the reader will be able to assemble the toy in half an hour* is measurable. You could give the reader the unassembled toy and the instructions. If the reader, using your instructions, assembles the toy in a half hour, your objective is met. Much transactional writing lends itself to such measurable goals. For example, the objective for the resume and letter of application used in a job campaign could be that at least 10 percent of the people receiving them grant the writer an interview.

Of course, some pieces of writing do have understanding rather than action as their objective. However, even when understanding is your objective, you can still set actions that the reader should be able to do after reading your work. Think of yourself as a teacher who wants to check students' comprehension and understanding. The teacher would devise a test of some sort. You can do the same. If you could go with your report, what questions would you ask the reader? In essence, you are continuing the dialogue described earlier, only now you are asking the questions. For example, a writer whose objective was for readers to understand how prejudice develops and operates in society could ask the reader to

- Define prejudice from a behavioral perspective.
- Cite examples of how our culture often teaches prejudice toward old people, children, women, men, and minorities.
- Illustrate behavior that acts to include people in groups or to exclude them.

Obviously, the writer as teacher must write the paper in such a way that the reader as student could answer the questions.

Writing down, first, your analysis of your audience, and, second, your objectives, fixes them in your mind. You have started the process that partly through cold rational thought and partly through intuitive insights will lead you to a complete piece of writing.

CHECKING AND GATHERING INFORMATION

The first step in checking and gathering information is to inventory the information you already have available in your head to satisfy your objectives. If your subject is one with which you are thoroughly familiar, you may already know much or all that you need to know to do the task. For instance, in planning our chapter on oral reports we found when we jotted down the information we already possessed on the subject that we needed little research to write the chapter. Except for some missing information on special uses of graphics in oral reports, we were in good shape.

On the other hand, were we planning a book on the railroad in nineteenth-century America, we would find our information rather sparse. It would consist mainly of knowing that there had been a tremendous expansion in railroad building in the second half of the century. We also have vague memories of movies like *Union Pacific,* in which favorite actors of our youth helped the railroads build east and west until the tracks met in Utah. In a situation with such thin information, we would have to start gathering information with some general source, such as an encyclopedia, to discover the basic information available.

In any event, write down what you do know about the subject. In your writing, use a method known as *brainstorming.* In brainstorming, without thought of organization or critical evaluation, you write down everything that comes to mind pertinent to the subject. Only by doing so can you truly tell what resources you have available to you.

If your information is thin, the next stage of the process is research. We have a good deal to say about one kind of research—library research—in Chapter 10. Library research is almost always the first step when you don't know enough to discuss a subject thoroughly and intelligently. You have to find out what is already known about the subject. You may also have to follow your library research with empirical research, such as experimentation or polling, using techniques taught in your own disciplines.

As you gather information, keep checking it against your knowledge of your audience and objectives. Question the relevance of your information to your audience and its needs. Does the information advance your objectives? Or, conversely, does your information change your notions about what your objectives should be?

As you gather information, your thoughts may leap ahead to organizing your paper. You may suddenly see in clear outline how your information can best be presented. You may even find yourself writing out drafts of paragraphs that you'll later include in your letter or report. Your mind will be making connections among all the parts of the writing process. Such connections are part of the intuitive creative process of the mind that no one thoroughly understands as yet. But what is clear is that the writing process, like any other creative process, is not an uninterrupted straight path from beginning to end. Rather, it is a pathway with many loops in it. We leap ahead on the path, and then we double back on our previous tracks. That is how it is.

Use the process; don't fight it. When such connections do occur, write them down; otherwise you will lose them. Many will later prove to be worthless, but one or two of them may be the keys to your report.

PLANNING YOUR ORGANIZATION

When your research is done, you have the planning chore before you. Now is the time to evaluate your material and to find the coherent organization that will satisfy you and your reader. Sit down with your notes and once again review your audience and objective statements. Revise them if necessary. Check to see if any of the organizational patterns that you know or that are presented in this book would be useful to you. Just a partial list of such patterns includes such general ones as the time, or chronological, approach; cause and effect; and scientific argument with its use of induction, deduction, and comparison. In addition, there are more specific patterns, such as application letters, sales letters, mechanism description, process description, and proposals.

If a pattern fits, use it, but recognize that patterns, even at their best, are still rather incomplete maps. In writing all but the most obvious kinds of correspondence and reports, you are usually entering unexplored territory to some extent. And you have to relate the map to the audience as well as to the territory. For example, the general outline for most sets of instructions is fairly clear: (1) an introduction that provides an overview of the process to be done, (2) a list of tools and equipment to be used in the process, and (3) a step-by-step account of the process.

But you must relate this general outline to what you know about your audience. Do the members of your audience already know all about the tools to be used—what they are and how to use them? If so, you need only give your audience a list of the tools. But what if some of the tools are not familiar to your audience? Then you would have to explain them and instruct your audience in their use. Does your audience know where to obtain the needed equipment? If not, you must supply that information. In the process itself, does the audience know the significance of all the steps? If so, you can run through the steps with little explanation. If not, you'll need to take time for some explanation. In effect, you are carrying on the dialogue with your audience that we recommended on pages 8–9.

Sometimes, no ready-made pattern, complete or otherwise, is readily available. At such times, you may organize best by returning to your objectives and breaking them up into subobjectives. As you do so, you should once again keep your audience and its needs in mind. For instance, a psychologist was planning a one-day workshop in which his objective was to teach his audience how to cope with stress and keep it from turning into harmful distress. His audience was to be composed of lay people, with, on the average, a high school education. They would probably know rather vaguely what stress and distress are, but possess little real knowledge of how to deal with them. Also, they were rural people who, for the most part, would ordinarily have little contact with psychologists unless a problem became serious. They would be, the psychologist reasoned, most interested in practical self-help advice and not much interested in theory. Building on that analysis, the psychologist organized his workshop around a series of subobjectives as follows:

- To identify stress in daily life.
- To identify symptoms of distress and causes of distress.
- To recognize a stressful situation and to know at what point to take action to prevent stress from becoming distress.
- To learn and apply tension-releasing techniques.
- To learn problem-solving techniques for decision making.
- To identify sources of expert help if needed.

Frequently, as they did in this case, the subobjectives become the topics that make up the organizational plan.

Just how complete you make your organizational plan depends to some extent on how well you know the territory. If you know the territory well, a sketchy plan of the major headings of the report may be all you need to begin. Sometimes, you may want to go a step further and break the topics down into subtopics. For example, for his rural audience, the psychologist divided his first topic, "To identify stress in daily life," into two subtopics: (1) problems and pressures of farming and (2) problems and pressures of basic human needs.

When the territory is really unfamiliar, you may want even more of a map. One useful technique is to write summaries of all the major parts of the report. Another is to construct a rough outline. In any event, do plan, and do evaluate your plan critically. Now is the time to catch flaws in your plan. It's easy to throw away an outline and start over again. On the other hand, it is painful when a fatal organizational flaw, discovered when you are well into the writing stage, forces you to scrap hours of work.

At times the occasion may call for a formal outline. For information on how to construct one, see pages 421–422.

PLANNING GRAPHICS

While you are still in the planning stage, consider what graphics, such as drawings, tables, and graphs, may be available to you or that you can construct yourself. In the world of work, writers rely on graphics of all sorts to help them deliver their message. They see no particular virtue in saying something in words if an illustration or graph will make the concept clear. Also, tables displaying needed statistical information will usually save the writer words and the reader time.

The illustration reproduced in Figure 1–1 makes the route of the slurry through the pipeline and its ultimate disposition abundantly clear.

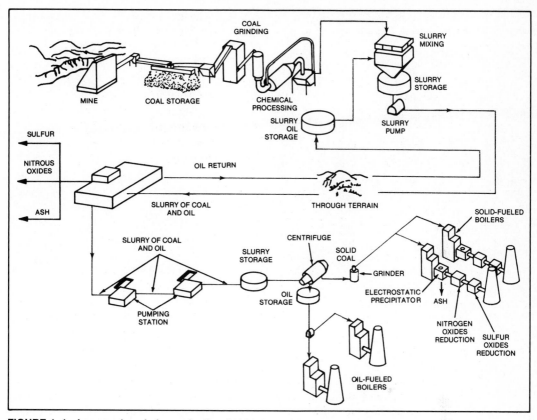

FIGURE 1–1 Improved coal-slurry pipeline *(NASA Tech Briefs,* Spring 1979, p. 47)

And even the proverbial thousand words would not describe your authors as well as the photographs in Figure 1–2 do.

Figure 1–3 shows the steady increase in the number of students of all races completing high school and the shrinking spread in the rate of completion between blacks and whites in a way that would be difficult to do in prose.

The table in Figure 1–4 makes the information it displays far more accessible than would a prose passage giving the same information. And putting your information in tables frees you to interpret the material important to your purpose. For example, in Figure 1–4 you might point out that federal deficits have been increasing at an alarming rate since 1975.

Because we consider graphics to be so important to transactional writing, we have not segregated a discussion of them in a single chapter. Instead, we have discussed and illustrated them wherever they are important to the kind of writing being considered. We urge you always to be alert to the possibility of using a graphic to carry part of your message.

FIGURE 1–2 Your authors (That's Cunningham with the beard. The photo of Pearsall was taken by Don Brady.)

Percent of adults who have completed four years of high school or more: 1950 to 1982

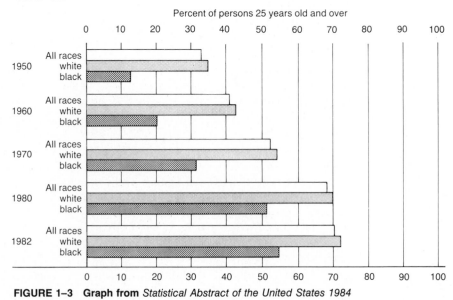

FIGURE 1–3 Graph from *Statistical Abstract of the United States 1984*

FEDERAL BUDGET: 1970–1982

Federal Government	Unit	1970	1975	1980	1981	1982
Budget receipts	$Bil.	192.8	279.1	517.1	599.3	617.8
Individual income taxes	Pct.	46.9	43.9	47.2	47.7	48.2
Income tax per capita	Dol.	413	584	1,102	1,239	(na)
Corporation income taxes	Pct.	17.0	14.6	12.5	10.2	8.0
Budget outlays	$Bil.	195.7	324.2	576.7	657.2	728.4
In constant (1972) dollars	$Bil.	220.2	260.2	316.7	327.5	338.7
Defense	Pct.	40.1	26.4	23.6	24.3	25.7
Nondefense	$Bil.	117.1	238.7	440.8	497.4	541.0
Deficit	$Bil.	−2.8	−45.2	−59.6	−57.9	−110.6
Gross debt outstanding	$Bil.	383	544	914	1,004	1,147

Source: U.S. Department of Commerce

FIGURE 1–4   Statistical table

WRITING AND REVISING

For some experienced writers the organizational stage merges almost without their realizing it into the writing stage. For less experienced writers, the two stages may be quite separate. In either case, you must write. Find a quiet place where you won't be disturbed. If possible use a large desk or table where you can lay your notes, graphics, and plans around you. Plant your feet firmly under the table and begin. (Sometimes *chain your feet* might be the more appropriate metaphor.) Write as rapidly as you can. Pay no particular attention to such things as style and spelling. Get something on paper. Follow your organizational plan, but don't be a slave to it. If in writing and thinking about your writing, a clearer, less obstructed path to your objectives opens before you, follow it. Also, if one segment of your report seems easier to you than another one, begin with it. You can always put things in proper order later. If you are using research material, indicate in your draft in rough parenthetical form its source.

Write for about two hours at a time. In two hours you can produce about a thousand words. After resting and getting your mind off your writing, write for another two hours if need be. Four hours of writing in a day is a lot of writing, usually enough for most people. If your writing is going to carry over to another time, quit when you are in full rush and know exactly what you are going to say next. It makes beginning again much easier. When you have finished, leave your work for at least a day. When you come back to it, revision will begin.

First, check your paper for purpose. Is it clearly stated early in your paper, either explicitly or implicitly? If your paper requires a full-scale introduction, have you clearly defined and limited your subject? Perhaps you are answering a letter of complaint. Is your opening sufficiently friendly? Would it calm a tense situation or make more trouble?

Next, get into the body of your paper. Have you followed through on your purpose? Does everything in your paper speak to your purpose? Are there any gaps or digressions in your paper where you lose sight of your subject as you have defined and limited it? Are the purpose and subject of your paragraphs clear? Are you sure of all your facts? Are your sentences well structured? Is your diction appropriate to the occasion? For most transactional writing, diction should be straightforward and unembellished—well mannered, neither heavy nor slangy. Good writing has a good sound to it. Read your work aloud. Does it sound right? Could you replace or supplement some of your writing with graphs or tables?

Put yourself in the readers's place and carry on a dialogue with the writing before you. Ask the questions we suggest on page 6. Are all the *so-whats* answered? Is your work believable? Have you provided evidence where it is needed? Are needed conclusions and recommendations furnished? Be hard on yourself. Everything is for the reader's convenience, not yours. Where you find fault, reorganize and rewrite. If you are working with a paper you have typed or written with pen or pencil, cut it up. Literally, cut it up. Take a pair of scissors to it and rearrange it for better organization. Insert better transitions or better-written sentences. For help with some of these revisions, see the entries on Diction, Paragraphs, and Sentences in Unit Four, "Writer's Guide."

If you are fortunate enough to be working with a word processor, revision is no less demanding, but the process can be a great deal easier. Words, sentences, and paragraphs can be quickly moved and rearranged. Text can be easily opened up to allow you to insert headings or new items of information. A faulty sentence can be deleted and a better one substituted with the press of a few keys. Revision is never thoughtless work, but with the word processor, revision has become increasingly less painful.

When you have the big things controlled to your satisfaction, look at some of the smaller things. Get your dictionary off the shelf and check out all the words you are doubtful about. If your paper is a typical piece of transactional writing, it probably contains numbers, abbreviations, and quotations. Have you handled them correctly and consistently? Do you have a consistent system for capitalization? Are there grammatical problems you know you have—faulty comma placement or dangling modifiers, for instance? Again see the "Writer's Guide" for help in such matters.

When you are completely satisfied with your paper, put it into the necessary format required by the situation. In Chapter 4, we describe letter and memorandum formats for you. In Chapter 9, we describe the formal elements of reports, such as title pages and tables of contents. Before sending your letter or report on its way, look at it one more time.

Proofread it for those little errors that may have slipped through despite all your care. Make whatever corrections are necessary. Then, and only then, send your work to your readers. And good luck.

SUGGESTIONS FOR APPLYING YOUR KNOWLEDGE

Any textbook can supply only a limited number of examples to illustrate its subject matter. Yet, for most of us, an ounce of example is worth a pound of theory. Therefore, we urge you to begin gathering examples of transactional writing that will help you to grasp the concepts in this book. Examples will bring the use of patterns and graphics to life. Examine them to see how they have been written to meet a specific purpose for a specific audience. Not all the examples you find will be equally good, so they'll provide you with ample material for discussion as well as instruction. There are many potential sources of examples.

Government Publications

Thousands of publications pour out from the federal government every year on a vast number of subjects. *U.S. Government Books,* probably available in your library, lists many of the more useful ones. Many are quite reasonably priced. For example, $3.00 buys *Heating with Wood,* which tells how to buy wood and wood stoves and gives the theory of stove operation. For $2.50, *Find and Fix the Leaks* shows how to reduce air leaks in a home without reducing air quality. Your library probably has a collection of government publications you can use at no cost at all.

Your state university almost certainly has an extension service. This service prints fact sheets, pamphlets, and booklets on a wide variety of subjects, such as choosing insecticides, detecting oak wilt, choosing a television set, and planning a meeting. Other state agencies, such as the department of transportation, also publish informational pamphlets of many kinds.

Magazines and Professional Journals

Your library should have a good collection of magazines and professional journals. These publications represent an enormous reservoir of examples. The advertisements in professional and trade journals, for instance, are often fine examples of high-level persuasion and also process and mechanism description. A magazine like *Consumer Reports* contains numerous examples of analytical essays written to compare various kinds of consumer goods.

Company Sources

Companies of any significant size must publish a good deal of material. They can often provide examples of handbooks, sales literature, proposals, and so forth. They have printed forms for such things as accident and trip reports. Business and government agencies depend for their very existence on the kinds of correspondence we describe in this book. If you have legitimate access to such correspondence, it will provide both good and, unfortunately, bad examples for evaluation and discussion.

A Note about the Suggestions

We have not supplied the traditional exercises at the ends of chapters. We believe that only the classroom instructor, perhaps in collaboration with the students, can design the exact exercises needed to fit the needs of any particular class. This belief stems directly from our basic principle that successful communication presents specific information to a specific audience for a specific purpose. Therefore, we have provided not exercises but "Suggestions for Applying Your Knowledge," addressed to both student and instructor. In these sections we suggest a wide range of possible methods and sources that can be used to construct the out-of-class and in-class exercises needed.

C H A P T E R

2

I n persuasion, you are trying to sell somebody something—from a piece of merchandise to an idea. In scientific argument, the notion of selling is gone or at least greatly subdued. Rather, you are trying in an emotion-free way to convey to the reader the accuracy of your information and the reasonableness of your interpretation of it. In truth, of course, there is a continuous line running from the emotionally persuasive to the completely scientific. In the world of work you will operate most of the time toward the middle of the continuum rather than at the extremes. Figure 2–1 illustrates the continuum and places a few typical pieces of transactional writing on it. You need to be aware of this continuum and position your piece of writing on it in accordance with your audience and purpose.

PERSUASION

We make daily use of persuasion, and we are daily exposed to it from others. We engage in persuasion when we try to convince someone to

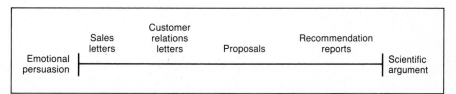

FIGURE 2–1 The emotional persuasion/scientific argument continuum

lend us money, to vote for our political candidate, to hire us, or to accept bad news gracefully. We can't pick up a magazine or turn on the television without being exposed to hundreds of persuasive advertisements. One could make a good case that persuasion is the most frequent use we make of language.

Despite being so all-pervading, or, perhaps, because of it, persuasion sometimes has a bad name. Perhaps we are merely nervous in the presence of so powerful a force. In truth, persuasion is a tool that can be used for good or evil. Winston Churchill's powers of persuasion helped the world to survive an evil time in World War II. But, unfortunately, Adolf Hitler's powers of persuasion had helped to bring on that evil time. Somewhat like the parent who teaches a child how to use a hammer and then hopes the child will use the hammer to hit nails and not people, teachers of persuasion hope for a moral use of persuasion from their students. In any event, because we use and are exposed to so much persuasion, it is well that we understand it.

To be persuasive, we must be credible, we may use emotional appeals, and we should use facts and logical analysis.[1]

Credibility

You have credibility if your readers perceive you, the writer, as someone reliable in whom they can trust and believe. Many factors can make your credibility rise or fall in the minds of your readers. Cheap stationery, sloppy typing, and poor spelling can bring you down. Conversely, good stationery, neat typing, and correct spelling can bring you up. Evidence of impracticality brings you down—for example, a letter of application for a position that your experience doesn't justify. Being seen as open and honest will bring you up, as will having a good grasp of your subject matter. Be careful of extremes. Excessive humility or arrogance brings you down; confidence in your knowledge, ability, or authority brings you up. In some instances, employment letters and proposals, for example, your credibility may be a major component of your persuasive strategy. You may have to spend a good deal of time detailing your education and experience to convince the reader that you are suited for some position or task.

Perhaps most important of all, your readers must see you as a person of goodwill who has their interests at heart. You must have a "you attitude"; that is, you must consider your readers' needs and viewpoints at all times. This is easier said than done. All of us view the world through our own eyes, shaded by our own concerns. The writer of the successful letter must be sensitive in the extreme. If you know the people you are writing to, try to anticipate their reactions. Think about what pleases them and what annoys them. If you don't know them, you probably won't go too far wrong by asking yourself how you would react in a similar situation. Statements that would make you feel abused or annoyed are likely to do the same to someone else.

Remember that all of us respond most favorably when we are convinced our own interests are being served. Every company is in business to turn a profit, yet to stay in business it must provide a service or product that people need or desire. In correspondence, you should emphasize the service, the product, the need, or the desire, and not the profit. You don't say things like

> Pay your bill because we need the money.

Rather you say,

> Prompt payment of bills protects your good credit rating.

Less obviously, we are often misled by our own skill and hard work into making statements of no concern to our readers. Consider this approach:

> We have created with considerable expense and time a new fire detector for use in private homes.

All wrong. The readers don't care about your time and expense. Also, although the readers may live in "private homes," they won't relate to such a nonspecific term. Compare this approach:

> You'll sleep more easily tonight and every night when you and your family are protected from smoke and flame by our new battery-operated fire detector.

In the second example you are dealing directly with your readers' concerns, not yours. In correspondence always ask yourself what your readers' needs and problems are. Use that knowledge to give your message from the readers' point of view, not yours.

We have discussed here some of the tactics used to achieve credibility, and, indeed, good tactics will help and bad ones will hurt. But you will also do well to remember the three major characteristics that Aristotle felt underlay true credibility: good sense, good moral character, and goodwill.

Emotional Appeals

The use of emotion may be the aspect of persuasion we distrust the most. Partially, this distrust comes from our fear that the use of emotional appeals can distort the truth. For this reason, we take emotion out of scientific argument and insist instead upon a logically organized array of facts and well-reasoned opinions. And, in truth, the use of emotion in many situations in which the readers expect logic and factual evidence would probably fail as a persuasive device. Also, our distrust of emotion likely stems from our belief that emotion may persuade us to act against our "better judgment." All of us can point to times in our lives when we have used our intellect to rationalize a choice that had actually been dictated by our emotions—sometimes to our later sorrow.

Nonetheless, the very power of emotion makes it a force that we are not likely to avoid using when it can be helpful.

An example used earlier shows the use of an emotional appeal, in this case, fear:

> You'll sleep more easily tonight and every night when you and your family are protected from smoke and flame by our new battery-operated fire detector.

It may or may not amuse you to know that advertising copywriters know this kind of appeal as "backing the hearse up to the door."

Notice the use of emotion-laden words in this ad for a man's leather vest:

> Team this vest with a turtleneck sweater or an Eddie Bauer chamois shirt and you have the ultimate in handsome defiance of winter chill.

The word *handsome* appeals to our vanity, *defiance* adds a macho touch, and *chill* suggests the discomfort we wish to avoid while being handsome and macho.

Emotional appeals are not restricted to advertising, of course. They also have their place in serious writing, as demonstrated in this passage from *Research,* "a magazine of scholarship for the lay reader published quarterly by the University of Minnesota":

> The national heroes who populate our collective idea of history have always been two-fisted, hardheaded white men. But in recent years we have come to doubt that these gentlemen have borne the burden of civilization all by themselves. We are discovering some images that have been missing.
>
> We now find it hard to believe, for instance, that a standard text such as Morison and Commager's *The Growth of the American Republic* could distort the black experience of slavery this way: "As for Sambo, whose wrongs moved the abolitionists to wrath and tears, there is some reason to believe that he suffered less than any other class in the South from the 'peculiar institution.' "
>
> Equally incredible has been the historians' treatment of women. Commager, in the course of a long-distance description of the typical American, made this claim; "Sundays he was troubled by a sense of sin—his womenfolk more often."
>
> Sambo suffered less? The American and his womenfolk? Apart from their quaintness, such statements suggest that historians have not always been in the vanguard of social change. Indeed, as we have come to understand, history tells us nearly as much about the period of its writing as the period of its subject.[2]

The quoted passage comes early in an article that demonstrates that after a period of long neglect, American historians are, at last, beginning to recognize the contributions of women to our history. The passage warms our interest by using examples and ironic comment to produce in us a sense of, at the least, incredulity, and, perhaps, even anger.

Winston Churchill mobilized a nation with such emotional words as *blood, sweat,* and *tears.* Unless you are engaging in a strict and rigorous scientific argument, you should consider the use of emotional appeals as a persuasive device, but for most readers you must use them with subtlety and discretion.

Facts and Analysis

When we are being persuasive, our audience can often be categorized into three groups: those who are already persuaded, those who can be persuaded, and those who will never be persuaded. For the last group, nothing you can do or say will have any effect. For the first group, perhaps establishing your credibility and making an emotional appeal may be enough to keep them persuaded. For the middle group you are likely to need facts and analysis. In a political race, for instance, a candidate may mount a negative attack to persuade the voters that his or her opponent should not be elected. The attack might go something like this:

- My opponent is incompetent (examples of incompetence).
- My opponent would ruin the economy (examples of past economic blunders).
- My opponent would lead us into war (examples of warlike statements and actions).

A positive argument is similarly constructed, only now the statements are positive and in support of the candidate:

- I am competent (examples of competence).
- (And so forth).

Such an organization was at work in the previous example about the failings of past history books. In the second paragraph, for instance, we are told that past history books distorted the black experience; we are then given a quote as an example of such distortion.

Much of your analysis will consist of making clear the implications and meanings of your facts. That is, as your readers absorb your facts, they will want to know what our students and we have come to call the *so-whats.* The *so-what* principle is amply illustrated in descriptions of merchandise in catalogs. Read the following description of a bicycle helmet taken from a Recreational Equipment, Inc., catalog:

> BELL BICYCLE HELMET High strength *Lexan*® shell with polystyrene lining for greater shock absorption. Wide air scoops for ventilation, foam pads for comfort. Adjustable sizing by means of *Velcro*® pads assures a perfect fit.

The following two columns list the facts and *so-whats* of the description:

FACTS	SO-WHATS
High strength *Lexan*® shell with polystyrene lining	Greater shock absorption
Wide air scoops	Ventilation
Foam pads	Comfort
Adjustable sizing by means of *Velcro*® pads	A perfect fit

Read the description with the *so-whats* removed:

> High strength *Lexan*® shell with polystyrene lining. Wide air scoops. Foam pads. Adjustable sizing by means of *Velcro*® pads.

People who know about bicycle helmets could no doubt provide their own *so-whats*. Those less knowledgeable may miss the true meaning of the facts presented. Even those who know may need to be reminded, and the *so-whats* will help to persuade even them.

The need for *so-whats* is not restricted to merchandise descriptions or advertising or even persuasion. It is a necessary part of many letters, memorandums, and reports. Providing the *so-whats*, in fact, is where your professionalism comes into play. Only you may be able to see the implications and conclusions that should be drawn from the facts. Suppose, for example, an accountant, after an organizational audit, reports to high company authority that the district office in Auburn, Alabama, is not following Company Accounting Procedure (CAP) 112 to the letter. Higher authority may or may not know the significance of being sloppy about CAP 112. The accountant might add the following:

> Despite the small irregularities in the observance of CAP 112, the records are in good order, and no significant problems are evident.

Higher authority relaxes. But suppose the accountant draws this *so-what* instead:

> Although the irregularities in the observance of CAP 112 are small, they are significant because they are in an area to which the Internal Revenue Service pays a great deal of attention.

Higher authority is now alerted and, indeed, now probably expects a recommendation to solve the problem, perhaps something like the following:

> I recommend that the district manager at Auburn be brought to the home office for training in CAP 112 and related procedures.

Read over the drafts of every letter and memorandum you write to see if you have clearly stated the necessary implications and conclusions—the *so-whats*. Without them, you may not have done the job you intended to do. In stating conclusions and recommendations, you have a clear choice in whether you state them before or after your supporting evidence. The placement of your implications and conclusions can often be of major importance. When the implications are important enough to be considered warnings, they should be stated early, perhaps as early as the introduction. When the reader is likely to consider the implications to be good news, you should again state them early. But when the reader is likely to consider the implications to be bad news, you might be wise to put them later.

In much business and technical writing, factual analysis leading to conclusions and recommendations becomes your major mode of presentation. When such is the case, you are moving toward the scientific end of the continuum—toward scientific argument.

SCIENTIFIC ARGUMENT

When is scientific argument your appropriate choice? An example may make the matter clear. Let's imagine for a moment that you are an employee of a small eyewear chain that is considering expanding from its present three-office operation in one city to a six-office operation in two cities. Your management gives you the job of gathering and analyzing the information about costs, available credit, markets, profits, and so forth. You analyze the data with no preconceived bias and reach the conclusion that, yes, to expand in the current economy would be profitable, although some risks are involved. When you make your report, you carefully and without emotion present your data and the analysis of that data that underlies your conclusions. You make sure that both the potential and the risks are clearly stated. In other words, you are not trying to sell management on the idea of expanding, but rather you are showing them what is involved in the decision. Because you are not trying to sell, you hide nothing from your audience. Any emotional bias or pressure at such a time might confuse the issue and lead to a bad decision.

In this section we show you how to present such a scientific argument. We talk first about the form of argument itself and then about induction and deduction, comparison, and causal analysis.

The Form of Argument

In argument we present the facts and the chain of reasoning about the facts that lead us to certain opinions, which we present as conclusions and sometimes as recommendations. (See also pages 152–157.) In its most basic form, an argument looks like this:

> The 55-mph speed limit should be maintained because, compared to higher speeds, it accomplishes three things:
> It conserves energy.
>> (factual support for this opinion)
>
> It causes less damage to highways.
>> (factual support for this opinion)

It is safer.
        (factual support for this opinion)

This example also illustrates why it is an argument and not merely a setting down of facts. We are, even in this simple example, interpreting facts and reaching conclusions. Other interpretations or additional facts may bring about different conclusions. Take the conclusion that the 55-mph speed limit is safer than higher speeds. As support for that conclusion we can offer the following data from the *Statistical Abstract of the United States 1984.*[3] In 1972, state monitoring of highways showed the average speed for all vehicles to be 64.9 mph. In 1981, similar monitoring showed the average highway speed to be 57.9 mph. In 1972, 56,300 people in the United States died in motor vehicle accidents. In 1981, only 51,500 people died in such accidents. The facts would seem to support the conclusion that the 55-mph speed limit is working and fewer people are dying as a result. The facts are accurate enough, but not everyone would agree with the interpretation of the facts. We have assumed that the lower speed has caused the lower number of deaths. Others may want to look for other causal agents, such as safer cars, safer highways, better driver education, and so forth.

What does this disagreement mean for you other than that human affairs are complex and difficult to interpret? Most importantly, perhaps, it means that you cannot assume that a few supporting facts will make your case. Your facts must be relevant, of course, but you must also attempt to cover as many of the variables as seem to apply. You cannot, for various good reasons, always think of all the variables or find all the information needed. Therefore, you will find that modesty, open-mindedness, and caution are necessary virtues in most scientific arguments. The scientist who wrote the following paragraph summarizing a scientific argument well illustrates these virtues:

> Hydrocarbon sampling of plant and animal tissues in Lower Cook Inlet has been rather limited. In one instance, two samples from the same area gave somewhat different results for the presence of petroleum hydrocarbons. Variations in hydrocarbon content within animal tissues can be inherently large due to environmental conditions. Sampling and extraction procedures also provide some error. Therefore, the small number of samples analyzed may not be conclusive evidence for the absence of petroleum carbons. However, the results obtained to date are consistent with results obtained from sediment and water samples.[4]

Induction and Deduction

In scientific argument, the basic methods of reasoning and presenting that reasoning are induction and deduction. In induction you analyze your data by generalizing from particular facts to reach your conclusion. In deduction you analyze your data by applying a known principle to your data to reach your conclusion.

INDUCTION The following paragraph written with data from the *Statistical Abstract of the United States 1984*[5] illustrates induction:

> In 1960, infant deaths among whites in the United States per 1,000 live births were 22.9. In 1970, 17.8 white infant deaths occurred; in 1980, 11. For the same years, infant deaths per 1,000 live births among blacks in the United States were as follows: 1960, 44.3; 1970, 32.6; 1980, 21.4. Therefore, from 1960 to 1980, infant mortality at birth was almost halved for both blacks and whites, but the death rate for black infants has remained about twice as high as for whites.

Notice two things about this inductive presentation. First, the conclusion, although interpretive, does not exceed the data presented. Nothing in the data tells why the difference exists between white and black infants. Therefore, the conclusion makes no attempt to generalize about causal factors. For causality to be explained, more information on such relevant factors as income, geography, medical assistance available, births at home, births in hospitals, and so forth would have to be gathered and analyzed.

Second, notice that in the presentation the data are presented first, followed by the conclusion. You can reverse the presentation and still present the material inductively:

> From 1960 to 1980 in the United States, infant mortality at birth for both blacks and whites was almost halved, but the death rate for black infants was still almost twice as high as for whites. In 1960, infant deaths among whites in the United States per 1,000 live births were 22.9. . . .

Both methods are perfectly acceptable, and you should choose the one that presents your material most effectively. Presenting the conclusion first may help the readers' understanding by putting the facts in a better context for them. But by putting your conclusion last, you leave your readers with your main point in mind.

DEDUCTION When reasoning deductively, you apply a known or generally accepted principle to your data and draw a conclusion based on the application. For example, you may establish a characteristic of some class and then, after determining something is in that class, conclude that the thing has the same characteristic, as in this famous syllogism:

> All men are mortal.
> Socrates is a man.
> Therefore, Socrates is mortal.

Often, in a presentation, you will not give all the terms of a syllogism; and for a really well-established principle, you may assume the reader knows the principle without being told. Therefore, you might rewrite the syllogism this way: "Because Socrates is a man, he will die someday."

Whether you are using a fully stated principle or an implied one, be sure not to commit the error of applying the second and third terms in reverse, as in this statement:

> All men are mortal.
> Socrates is mortal.
> Therefore, Socrates is a man.

From this statement of the syllogism, we really do not know deductively that Socrates is a man. He could be, for instance, a dog or a goldfish, both of which are also mortal.

Deductive reasoning and presentation can be very useful as long as you begin with established principles, or at least principles that your readers accept, as in this example:

> Generally speaking, lower-income groups in the United States do not obtain medical care as good as that obtained by groups with higher incomes. According to the *Statistical Abstract of the United States 1984,* in 1982 the median yearly income of black families in the United States was $11,968 as compared to a median income of $21,117 for white families. We would expect, therefore, that blacks in general do not obtain as good medical care as do whites.

For the people who accept your principle about the positive correlation between money and medical care, this deductive argument would be acceptable. If need be, you could strengthen your argument by combining your deductive argument with an inductive one—in this manner:

> Possible evidence that blacks in general do not receive medical care as good as that received by whites can be seen in the comparative figures for the races in infant mortality. From 1960 through 1980, the infant mortality rate for blacks was approximately double that of whites. In 1980, among whites, the infant mortality rate per 1,000 live births was 11. The comparable figure for blacks was 21.4.

Note that the infant mortality rate is given only as "possible" evidence. As noted before, there may be other variables. Nevertheless, if you use induction and deduction carefully and in combination, you can present your data logically and reasonably.

Some pitfalls lie in wait for the user of induction and deduction. Probably the most common and perhaps the most dangerous is to generalize from insufficient information. We are all guilty of this mistake from time to time. Perhaps we read in the newspapers about the scandalous conduct of a few members of Congress. We shake our heads and imagine Washington, D.C., as a hotbed of skulduggery. This would be generalizing from insufficient evidence. As Aristotle long ago pointed out, one swallow does not make a summer. Neither do a scandalous few indicate that all our representatives behave badly.

Walk carefully when you make conclusions, and make only those conclusions justified by your evidence. Don't attempt to fool others (or yourself) by building assumptions into the questions you ask about your material. Everyone is familiar with the old joke in the question "When did you stop beating your wife?" which illustrates this pitfall well. The question "Why do men make better business executives than women?" assumes a proposition that might produce considerable disagreement.

Comparison

As we have seen, induction and deduction are the chief modes of logical thought and of presenting scientific argument. Comparison is a specialized form of induction and deduction. (Comparison as we use it here is the comparing of things to see both their differences and similarities; therefore, contrast is also implied.) You can use comparison as a piece of a longer argument or in some instances as the organizational plan for an entire argument. You have already seen it used as a piece of an argument in the example on page 25 that compared black infant mortality rates with white rates.

In comparison we frequently look for correlation. For example, suppose we wished further evidence to support the concept that, in general, lower-income groups in the United States do not obtain medical care as good as that obtained by upper-income groups. One test of that concept would be to see if a positive correlation exists between per capita income in certain states and the numbers of doctors in the same states. After checking the data in the *Statistical Abstract of the United States 1984*, we could express what we find in this comparison:

> Evidence that good medical care correlates positively with income can be found by comparing the numbers of physicians in states with the per capita incomes in the same states. We do not find a perfect positive correlation; for example, North Dakota with a per capita income of $10,872 has fewer physicians per 100,000 population than does New Mexico with a per capita income of $9,190. However, we do find, in general, a positive correlation between numbers of physicians and per capita income as shown in this table, which compares the states ranked top, median, and bottom in per capita income:

STATES RANKED BY PER CAPITA INCOME	AVERAGE PER CAPITA INCOME[a]	AVERAGE NUMBER OF PHYSICIANS PER 100,000 POPULATION[b]
States ranked 1–5 (Alaska, Conn., N.J., Calif., Wyo.)	$13,607	183
States ranked 23–27 (N. Dak., Iowa, Wis., N.H., R.I.)	$10,778	159
States ranked 46–50 (W. Va., Ala., S.C., Ark., Miss.)	$8,435	126

[a]From *Statistical Abstract of the United States 1984*, Table 752.
[b]Ibid., Table 162.

In constructing this example, we paid attention to the principle of scrupulous honesty in scientific argument when we pointed out that the positive correlation was not perfect. Also, because we had fairly extensive statistical data to present, we used a table. Tables are great word savers, and also, the layout of a table will often make the comparison more obvious to the reader. (See also pages 188–189.)

In addition to using comparison as a piece of a larger argument, you will find it useful as the organizational plan for an entire argument. For example, an analytical report frequently used in the world of work is an evaluation that compares things with each other to see which is superior. The things compared may be almost anything, from machinery to methods for approaching a task.

In comparing things to each other, you need a set of standards—a way of measuring how one thing stacks up against another. The success or failure of your comparison will depend on how well you choose these standards and on how well you define them. Once the standards are chosen and well defined, you know what you are looking for in your comparison. And when it comes time to report your comparison, you must explain your standards carefully to your audience. In fact, explaining the standards, in some cases, could be the major part of the report. Once that is done, the actual results can often be presented very simply, perhaps in a summary table.

To illustrate how this is done, we use excerpts from an article in *Consumer Reports* that compares the merits of several electric drills.[6] The purpose of the report is to provide consumers with enough information to make a wise choice of a drill that would be suitable for their purposes. The audience is considered intelligent but not particularly informed about test equipment or even drills. The introduction to the report comes immediately to the point. It explains why electric drills are important and what types of drills were tested. It also distinguishes between single-speed and variable-speed drills and states some of the advantages of each. Then it gets into the heart of the evaluation, the standards. As is often the case, some standards take priority over others. In this case, three standards are labeled the important ones, and each is carefully explained. When necessary, technical terms such as *dynamometer* and *torque* are defined.

THE THREE IMPORTANT QUALITIES

Nearly any drill will do the easy jobs. What you need for the more difficult ones is plenty of raw power, the ability to resist stalling, and little tendency to overheat. To test for these qualities, we used a dynamometer, a device that put each drill under load while it measured the drill speed in rpm. Our Ratings were based primarily on the results we found in these three tests:

MAXIMUM POWER OUTPUT   This is the measure of how much power— torque (twisting strength) multiplied by rpm—a tool can deliver. For hard jobs, such as drilling tough wood with an outsize bit or sanding with a disk-sanding attachment, you should have a drill judged as a medium or better (see Ratings). The tougher the jobs you plan, the higher power rating you should reach for in one of these drills.

STALLED TORQUE   Increasing the load on a drill slows down its speed. Stalled torque is the measure of the twisting effort a drill exerts when loaded to a point where the chuck quits turning. That's important in such jobs as drilling sheet metal, since the bit may stick and stall if it takes too big a bite just before breaking through. With very high torque at low rpm a drill can usually meet a short, severe ordeal and follow through without stalling. Models noted as having very high stalled torque (see Ratings) should be able to continue drilling under those circumstances.

OVERHEATING   We put each drill under a load that slowed its rpm by 25 percent, then measured its temperature. The top-rated Black & Decker 7154 showed very little tendency to overheat. That, in combination with its high maximum power output, would let you run it steadily at peak power with little risk of overheating. When a drill overheats, its motor can burn out or be damaged. Drills with plastic housings are particularly susceptible to damage since their relatively cool handles mask the overheating of the motor.

Following the explanation of the high-priority standards, eight lower-priority standards, such as maximum no-load speed and clearance, are explained. The concept of clearance, which is difficult to explain in prose alone, is easily explained in a combination of pictures and prose (see Figure 2–2).

When the explanation of the standards is completed, the actual comparison is presented in a table that brings together the standards with

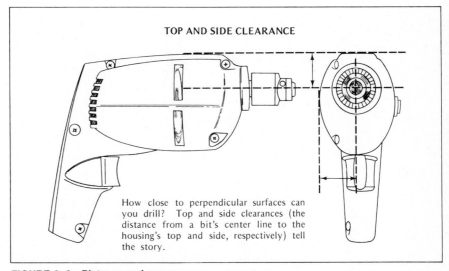

TOP AND SIDE CLEARANCE

How close to perpendicular surfaces can you drill? Top and side clearances (the distance from a bit's center line to the housing's top and side, respectively) tell the story.

FIGURE 2–2   Pictures and prose

ELECTRIC DRILLS

Listed in order of estimated overall quality, based primarily on power output, stalled torque, and tendency to overheat. All have a pistol grip, a trigger switch that can be locked at maximum speed, and a ³⁄₈-in. Jacobs-type chuck, and come with chuck key. Except as noted, all have power cord at least 5-ft. long, are double insulated, variable-speed models

KEY: E, Excellent; VG, Very Good; G, Good; F, Fair; P, Poor.

	Maximum power output	Stalled torque	Tendency to overheat	Maximum no-load speed	Speed under typical load	Decibels of noise
BLACK & DECKER 7154 (Black & Decker Mfg. Co., Towson, Md.) $40. 3 lb. 8 oz.	High	Very high	Low	1130 rpm	730 rpm	100 dBA
SKIL 917C (Skil Canada, Ltd., Toronto) $57. 3 lb. 11 oz.	High	Very high	Medium	740	620	99
SHOPMATE 2151 (McGraw-Edison Portable Electrical Tool Div., Geneva, Ill.) $45. 3 lb. 4 oz.	High	Very high	Medium	890	710	97
SHOPMATE 2151 (McGraw-Edison of Canada, Ltd., Toronto) $47. Identical to U.S. Shopmate 2151, preceding.	High	Very high	Medium	890	710	97
WIZARD 2H5208 (Western Auto) $45. 4 lb. 5 oz.	High	Very high	Medium	970	730	102
WARDS Cat. No. 9215 (Montgomery Ward) $32 plus shipping. 3 lb. 2 oz.	High	Very high	Very high	1190	900	96
MILLERS FALLS SP3139 (Millers Falls Co., Greenfield, Mass.) $41. 2 lb. 15 oz.	High	Medium	Medium	1260	940	95
STANLEY 91048 (Stanley Power Tools, New Bern, N.C.) $45. 3 lb. 12 oz.	Fairly high	Very high	Medium	1100	770	94

FIGURE 2–2 Part of the table used with the *Consumer Reports* article "Electric Drills." Once the rating standards have been explained, little needs to be done except to show the comparative results in some easy-to-follow way. Here, as is often the case, a table is used—both for ease of comparison and for cutting down on the wordage.

the drills being compared (see Figure 2–3). From the table we can learn, for instance, that the Black and Decker 7154 has high maximum power output, very high stalled torque, and a low tendency to overheat. From the standards, we know these to be desirable characteristics. By contrast, the Stanley 91048 has a medium tendency to overheat, a less desirable characteristic. Given this information, most readers should be able to make a wise choice. Nevertheless, to be on the safe side, the writer presents some conclusions and recommendations:

Drills are often sold at discount—and most of the high-rated models would be good values if available at prices lower than list. If you have plenty of uses for an electric drill and take your do-it-yourself jobs seriously, the high-powered, variable-speed reversible models are certainly your best bet. At $40, the top-rated Black & Decker 7154 is hard to beat. If you can't find that model (or want to spend less), consider the Wards 9215; it lists at $32 plus shipping. A good choice for Canadians would be the Skil 917C, at $57.

People who want this size drill mainly for small jobs around the house should probably buy a single-speed model with double insulation. The

with a reverse feature, and can be adjusted to lock at any intermediate speed. Prices are list, rounded to the nearest dollar; discounts are generally available. A maple leaf designates Canadian models; their prices are in Canadian dollars. All were judged Acceptable.

Non-pinching trigger	Handle position	Handle comfort	Auxiliary handle position	Clearance		Comments
				Top	Side	
No	Rear	F to G	None	1 in.	1¼ in.	Exposed metal on housing. Roller bearings on chuck shaft, an advantage. Locking button under trigger judged slightly inconvenient. Line cord can be unplugged when storing drill. Self-limiting brushes (see story).
Yes	Rear	P to F	Left	1	1¼	Exposed metal on housing. Ball bearing at rear of motor shaft and roller bearing on chuck shaft, advantages. Very heavy-duty chuck. Visible brushes (see story).
No	Middle	F	Either side	1⅛	1⅜	No comfortable resting place for thumb; thumb hits either reverse lever or locking button.
No	Middle	F	Either side	1⅛	1⅜	No comfortable resting place for thumb; thumb hits either reverse lever or locking button.
Yes	Rear	G	Left	1¼	1½	Not double-insulated. Judged rather unbalanced. Visible brushes (see story).
No	Middle	G	Either side	1	1¼	
No	Rear	F to G	None	1	1¼	
Yes	Rear	F to G	None	⅞	1¼	Not double-insulated. 1 speed. Nonreversible. Visible brushes (see story).

Rockwell 4100 is certainly the first choice in that category: Low price—just $13—in tandem with good quality made it a Best Buy.

The key to writing good comparison reports lies in bringing together the things compared with the standards or other factors by which they are compared. In the electric drill article, the standards are explained and the comparative results are presented in a table. Such a plan, perhaps presented in a formal report (see Chapter 9) or a memorandum report (see pages 67–68), would be quite suitable in a business setting. We look at the comparison organization in more detail in Chapter 16, "Recommendation Reports."

Causal Analysis

Causal analysis is yet another specialized form of induction and deduction. In causal analysis, you try to establish certain causal relationships through the use of inductive and deductive reasoning. The organizational plans for causal analysis are easy enough to outline, but you must exercise great care when drawing inferences from the evidence presented. The basic plan is that X caused Y. Variations for the basic plan exist, such as,

- If X continues, Y will result.
- Y exists; its probable causes are U, W, X.
- In itself, X is not undesirable, but its probable effect, Y, will be.

Here is a fairly straightforward cause-and-effect statement. Notice that it operates on two levels: Earthquakes cause certain effects, which in turn become the causal agents for other effects.

Earthquakes produce a variety of effects that must be considered in any hazard analysis for a region. A generalized list of effects for Lower Cook Inlet includes the following:

EFFECT	RESULTING DAMAGE
1. Ground shaking	Collapse of structures, weakening and future collapse, failure of unstable terrain (landslides), failure of dams (flash floods)
2. Ground rupture	Water and sewer line failure (contamination of water supplies), gas and oil line failures (fires), electrical line failure (fires, power outages), disruption of transportation lines[7]

Here an expert is speaking; his causal analysis is really an induction drawn from quite direct evidence of many observations of earthquakes. Because earthquakes and their effects are fairly well known to us through news stories, if not through direct experience, we have no trouble accepting the causal analysis.

Other causal analyses are more troublesome for us. The troublesome ones are based upon circumstantial evidence rather than direct evidence. Circumstantial evidence is indirect evidence from which we can sometimes, with great care, infer causality. We all know this in a common-sense way. Recently, we read two stories in a newspaper that illustrate the care needed when inferring causality from circumstantial evidence. One story was the report that two children living near a hazardous waste dump had lost all their hair. Two cases would indeed make us suspicious that a causal connection existed between some substance or substances in the dump and the loss of the hair. But lacking any direct medical evidence of the link, we probably would not be sure enough to claim any real certainty for the link.

However, in the face of more substantial relevant evidence, we can be more certain of our inferences. The other story reported that teenaged licensed drivers are involved in five times as many fatal motor vehicle accidents as are all licensed drivers aged 35 to 64. Furthermore, 16-year-old drivers had three times the death rate of 18-year-olds. Even lacking a direct causal link showing that youth was related to dangerous driving, such evidence makes the inference of such a causal link highly probable.

At the scientific level, people use even more care than we do in everyday life. Here is one group of medical experts expressing some reservations about a causal link perceived by other medical experts:

THE BRAN HYPOTHESIS   Nearly ten years ago. Drs. Painter and Burkitt noted the very low incidence of diverticulosis of the colon (see February 1979, *The HMS Health Letter*) in rural Africa, where high fiber diets are the rule. They suggested that the near epidemic of diverticular disease in Western society observed since 1900 is a consequence of refining flour and sugar, which removes much of the fiber from these products. It was thus proposed that colon diverticula—outpouchings of the wall of the large bowel that may become inflamed—are actually a disease of "dietary fiber deficiency." Other medical problems common in Western society and rare in Africa were also attributed to fiber deficiency—including colon cancer, appendicitis, ulcerative colitis, duodenal ulcers, gallstones, hernias, atherosclerosis, diabetes mellitus, varicose veins, and hemorrhoids. As might be expected many have criticized the highlighting of a single factor as an explanation for a difference in disease rates when numerous other differences (e.g., genetic, chemical and infectious exposures, other dietary components) also exist between such populations. Moreover, the cause of many of these diseases is complex, poorly understood, and certainly not apt to be due to any single factor. Given these many uncertainties, a perspective on dietary fiber is needed—and the following represents our current understanding in respect to specific medical problems:

(1) *Constipation:* Whether in the form of natural foods (unprocessed cereal, raw, unskinned fruits and berries, or root vegetables) or more expensive extracts (such as Metamucil prepared from seed husks), dietary fiber helps routine constipation and, unlike many other bowel "therapies," carries no danger when taken on a long-term basis.

(2) *Diverticular Disease:* Though the original concept that the advent of food processing produced the explosion of diverticular disease in Western society has been challenged (on the basis of contrary evidence from other population studies as well as a reassessment of total fiber content now deriving from fruits and vegetables), there is much to suggest that dietary fiber is useful in preventing the formation of diverticula. These outpouchings of the colon are believed to be caused by increased pressure within the bowel; it is known that a high fiber diet will protect from such a buildup of pressure. Moreover, there is excellent evidence that symptoms of diverticular disease improve when high fiber diets are begun—though it may take as much as two months (and enduring a brief period of increased bloating and flatulence) before such benefits are realized.

(6) *Other Diseases:* Whether high fiber diets really do reduce the occurrence of atherosclerosis, gallstones, diabetes, dental caries, hernias, hemorrhoids, ulcers, etc. is still a matter of conjecture. In some instances, theories can be advanced for a causal link (e.g., decreased straining on defecation may be beneficial for those prone to hernias or hemorrhoids). The arguments are more tenuous for such problems as diabetes or atherosclerosis, where other factors such as heredity and excessive caloric intake are more likely culprits than insufficient fiber. In other words, the lower incidence of many of these diseases in rural

Africa is probably due to a host of genetic and environmental differences and not just dietary fiber.

IN SUMMARY   Bran is not the magic for all that ails or might ail you. It is
not even unique as a source of dietary fiber; fruits and vegetables are a
more nutritious alternative. There is good evidence that dietary fiber will
help constipation and the symptoms of diverticular disease. The preven-
tive role of fiber in regard to the many diseases cited above is largely
speculative. Fortunately, there is no real hazard to eating more fiber and
it is a relatively simple way to "have an edge" on any possible risk factors
for those who are willing to accept a recommendation that does not make
any promises. How do you know how much is enough? Fortunately, each
of us has a direct "bottom line" signal—the frequency, comfort, and bulk
of bowel movements—that can serve as a guide in answering that question. Some will suffer from gas and bloating while increasing their dietary
fiber, but most of us can do so with little or no discomfort.[8]

Notice that where the evidence is purely circumstantial, as it is for
the reduction of such diseases as atherosclerosis, gallstones, diabetes, and
so forth, the experts are skeptical, mainly because of the possibility of
other variables such as genetic and environmental differences. Where the
evidence is more direct, as it is for constipation and diverticular disease,
the experts are more willing to accept the probability of the causal connection.

Although they exercise great caution, experts will accept circumstantial evidence if it passes strict tests of substantiality and relevance. For
example, most of the evidence connecting cigarette smoking to ill health
and early death is circumstantial, a long series of statistical associations.
Despite this absence of direct evidence—the "smoking gun," so to speak—
the overwhelming nature of the evidence makes virtually all medical experts outside of the tobacco industry willing to accept the causal link.
Here is one example of such acceptance, itself a good example of causal
analysis.

When experiments on animals turn up carcinogens in our favorite foods
and everyday consumer items, some critics invariably dismiss the data as
coming only from animals. The tobacco industry has, of necessity, taken
the opposite tack; for years it has argued that the evidence incriminating
cigarettes shows merely a "statistical association" because it comes from
studies of human deaths, not animal experiments. By now, though, the
evidence that cigarettes shorten life is overwhelming; the causal connection is as firmly established as any in medicine. "Indeed," writes John
Cairns, a molecular biologist and expert on cancer, "in retrospect, it is
almost as if Western societies had set out to conduct a vast and fairly well
controlled experiment in carcinogenesis, bringing about several million
deaths and using their own people as the experimental animals."
But the cancer connection, which was the most obvious and easiest to
establish, is not the major cause of death in smokers. Rather, it is coronary
heart disease. Second comes lung cancer. General deterioration of the

lung tissue is third. After these three major causes, a variety of other diseases and cancers make a further contribution to the high death rate of smokers. Cancers of the larynx, mouth, esophagus, bladder, kidney, and pancreas are all more common in smokers than nonsmokers. So are ulcers of the stomach and intestine, which are more likely to be fatal in smokers.

Women who smoke during pregnancy run a significant risk that their babies will die before or at birth. The newborns are likely to weigh less, to arrive prematurely, and to be more susceptible to "sudden infant death."

The risk of smoking is, in general, a 70 percent increase in the probability of dying at any age—100 percent for a two-pack smoker. As a rule of thumb, each cigarette knocks about five minutes off the smoker's life. For an average habit, that adds up to six or seven years (more for some, less for others). In the meantime, smokers lose more work days to illness than nonsmokers and spend more time in the hospital.[9]

USES OF PERSUASION AND SCIENTIFIC ARGUMENT

You will find that much of your transactional writing, whether in correspondence or reports, will be devoted to persuasion and scientific argument. Among the correspondence types we cover in this book, employment letters, customer relation letters, and sales letters, although using facts and analysis, are frequently closer to the persuasion end of the continuum than to scientific argument. In reports, proposals are often somewhere in the middle of the continuum. Recommendation reports are usually further along the continuum toward scientific argument. As in all transactional writing, your purpose and your audience will guide you to the appropriate place on the continuum.

SUGGESTIONS FOR APPLYING YOUR KNOWLEDGE

1. Examine several pieces of writing to determine where they belong on the persuasion–scientific argument continuum. See what efforts the writer has made to establish credibility. What emotional appeals, if any, are made? At what level does the writer use factual analysis? You can report your findings orally or in writing. You can find your examples in many places: advertisements; direct mail solicitations; business and college correspondence and reports; articles in magazines such as *Newsweek, Consumer Reports, Pop-* *ular Science, Scientific American,* and *Business Week;* stories and editorials from newspapers; and technical and scientific articles from journals in your field.

2. Take one of the pieces of writing from Exercise 1 and examine it more closely to see how well the writer has accomplished his or her purpose. How successful are the persuasive strategies? If you were the intended audience, would you be persuaded or satisfied with the scientific argument presented? How well has the writer handled credibility, emotional appeals, and factual analysis? Look for the organizational patterns used. See if you can find any errors of logic, such as generalizing from insufficient evidence.

3. Write two advertisements for a technical product such as an automobile, a camera, or a calculator. The first ad will be placed in a daily newspaper; the second in *Scientific American*.

4. Browse through a collection of statistics, such as the *Statistical Abstract of the United States* or the *Canada Yearbook,* looking for significant trends that interest you. For example, what is happening to the family farm? Are farms growing in size? Does this growth correlate with a drop in farm workers and a rise in crop yields? Do these two trends correlate in some way with increases in the use of machinery and commercial fertilizer on the farm, with a consequent rise in energy consumption? Could there be a causal relationship among all these trends?

For another example, are the number of women in the work force increasing? Are more women marrying later in life? Is the birthrate dropping? Is there a correlation among all these trends? Is there evidence of causality?

Interesting, fact-filled interpretive papers can be written on such subjects. Be careful not to press your conclusions beyond the supporting evidence. Also, in all such papers be sure to establish a purpose and an audience before you begin.

3

STYLE AND TONE

uite frankly, this chapter is meant to be persuasive as well as instructional. We wish to persuade you that the writing style represented by this example[1] is bad writing:

> Benefits are paid if an insured employee or eligible dependent incurs covered charges because of pregnancy. Reimbursement for hospital and out-of-hospital maternity charges will be made on the same basis as for any non-maternity condition covered under the plan.

We wish to persuade you that the writing style represented by this example is good:

> If you or one of your insured family members becomes pregnant, the Plan will pay for medical care in the same way that it pays for any other medical condition.

The style in the first example is difficult, too formal, and bureaucratic. The style in the second is clear, concise, and plain.

If you were trying to figure out your medical coverage, which of the two styles would you prefer? We prefer the second and suspect that you do, too. Most people do.

Businesses such as Citibank, J. C. Penney, Aetna Life and Casualty, and Shell Oil have all realized that plain language is good business and have gone to great lengths to get it.[2] Seven states have passed plain-language laws—Connecticut, Hawaii, Maine, Minnesota, New Jersey, New York, and West Virginia. These laws require that consumer contracts be written in an understandable style. Clearly, the person who enters the world of work today with the ability to produce plainly written correspondence and reports has a definite advantage over those who do not.

In this chapter we tell you how you can achieve an understandable style by writing with clarity, conciseness, and proper tone.

ACHIEVING CLARITY AND CONCISENESS

Much research has been done in the last 50 years to find out what makes writing more readable. Much of this research has been concerned with clarity and conciseness. Conclusions from this research boil down to two simple principles: Don't reach for long words, and keep an eye on general sentence length.

In telling you how to make your writing more readable, we'll follow these four principles:

- Keep sentences at a reasonable length.
- Use familiar words when possible.
- Eliminate unneeded words.
- Put action into your sentences.

Keep Sentences at a Reasonable Length

One measure of whether a sentence is of reasonable length is its efficiency. Does it express the intended thought without a lot of extra words? Using this criterion prevents you from assuming that, for example, a sentence of 11 words is of reasonable length and one of 35 words is too long. Look at this 11-word sentence:

> There is a direct line connecting us with the Seattle office.

If we count only the number of words in the sentence, we might call this a short sentence. But if we count the number of words needed to express the thought, we would have to call this a long sentence. Why? Because the 11 words communicate a 9-word thought:

> A direct line connects us with the Seattle office.

Compare the following two sentences. Both contain 10 words:

> The high-quality type soldering job was done by Glaser.
> Because Glaser did good soldering, he was promoted to supervisor.

The first sentence is too long. It uses 10 words to communicate a 6-word thought: *Glaser did the high-quality soldering.* Maybe even a 3-word idea: *Glaser soldered well.* These two versions would not always be the best possible sentences for the situation, but they are certainly better than the original 10-word sentence. The second sentence, about Glaser's promotion, is short. It contains 10 words, too, but it says twice as much in those 10 words as does the first sentence.

Although efficiency is perhaps the best criterion of whether a sentence is of reasonable length, word count itself is a second criterion. The answer to when a sentence can be considered to have too high a word count is somewhat subjective. The complete answer depends on how well the sentence is constructed and on the reading ability of the audience.

But perhaps the sentences of professional writers provide a useful clue to proper word count. Professional writers' sentences average about 21 words.[3] Note that this is an average. In good professional writing the sentences may range from several words to as many as 30 or 35. We do not give you these numbers as ironclad standards never to be violated, but the numbers do indicate what is a reasonable length in a sentence.

Most of us would agree, we suspect, that the following sentence fails both criteria—efficiency and word count:

> We were required to change back to the Effective Price as machines that were ordered after the announcement date of the price change and installed prior to the effective date were being priced at the new price before the effective date.[4]

Use Familiar Words When Possible

Occasionally you will have to use words that are unfamiliar to your readers. Every professional and interest group has its own accepted and necessary language. Physicians, for example, need technical language such as *coronary thrombosis* and *coronary sclerosis* to distinguish between these two kinds of heart problems. In the first case a heart artery is blocked by a clot. In the second case a heart artery is blocked by a thickening and hardening of the artery walls.

The paradox of technical language is that while it provides an economical way to convey specialized information to those who understand the language, at the same time it blocks information to those who don't understand it. The problem lies not in the technical words themselves but with technical people who use such words for a nontechnical audience without definition. In talking to a lay person, for example, the physician should either use familiar language, such as *heart attack,* or define the needed terms in familiar language as we have done here.

The hardest part of all is recognizing what words in our vocabulary are specialized and professional words known only to people who share our profession and interests. Customarily, we use such words so easily and frequently that we forget that most other people do not share our knowledge of them. As always in any writing, audience analysis is a prime factor here.

A far worse problem than the use of true technical language is the use of pseudotechnical language. Pseudotechnical language occurs when the writer or speaker needlessly substitutes unfamiliar multisyllable words for good, everyday, familiar words, for example, calling a garden a "personalized recreational eco-unit." Another bureaucratic example we have seen refers to a person without a car as "transportation disadvantaged."

Many people become addicted to such language, perhaps in the belief that they thus indicate their high educational attainments. For the most part, when you have a choice between words such as those in the left column and their simpler synonyms in the right column, choose the simpler words in the right.

HEAVY, FORMAL WORDS	FAMILIAR WORDS
abate, abatement	drop, decrease, cut down
behest	request
cognizant	aware
delineate	draw, describe
facilitate	ease, help
germane	relevant
hiatus	gap, interval
impair	weaken, damage, hurt
lethal	deadly, fatal
multitudinous	many
nadir	low point
obviate	prevent, do away with
palpable	obvious, visible, clear
remuneration	pay
salient	important
terminate	end
utilize	use
wherewithal	means

The list can be extended, but you have the idea. Every word, left and right, is an excellent word, but your steady use of words similar to those in the left column would convince readers not of your high intelligence but of your insensitivity—both to your readers and to the proper use of language.

Users of big words and unfamiliar words seldom stop at single words. Combinations of words to make meaningless phrases seem to have a special place in their hearts. But the impression made by such language is like that of pseudotechnical vocabulary—it's so much static. In fact, that is what is wrong with it. It's all noise and no meaning. Such phrase building is demonstrated ironically by Gerald Cohen's humorous Dial-A-Buzzword, a pseudotechnical vocabulary wheel that makes it easy to string words together until they register on the Richter Earthquake Scale.

The three dials rotate independently. From Figure 3–1 you might select combinations like "functional input compatibility," "operational systems environment," or "sequential output approach." A turn of the dials might result in the alignment shown in Figure 3–2, from which you could choose "overall communications implementation," "integrated performance analysis," or "conceptual interactive criteria." By adding a few necessary structural words to the selected phrases, we can easily build prefabricated sentences that say nothing:

> The *functional input compatibility* of the *operational systems environment* features a *sequential output approach.*

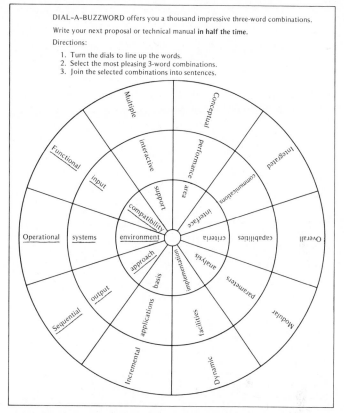

FIGURE 3–1   Cohen's Dial-A-Buzzword (Courtesy Gerald Cohen)

Overall communications implementation follows *integrated performance analysis* of the *conceptual interactive criteria.*

Try a couple of these sentences yourself:

If you didn't know how these sentences were generated, you might think they meant something to somebody.

When unfamiliar language crowds out more familiar language, writing becomes especially difficult to read. The solution is to avoid technical vocabulary when your readers don't understand it (unless you define

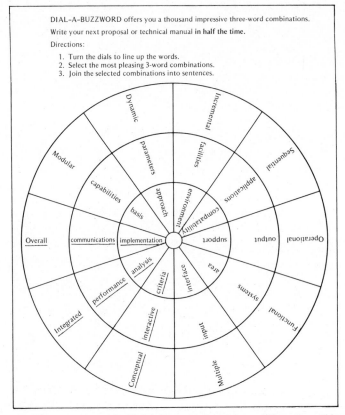

DIAL-A-BUZZWORD offers you a thousand impressive three-word combinations.

Write your next proposal or technical manual **in half the time.**

Directions:

1. Turn the dials to line up the words.
2. Select the most pleasing 3-word combinations.
3. Join the selected combinations into sentences.

FIGURE 3–2   Cohen's Dial-A-Buzzword, set for a different combination.

it) and to avoid pseudotechnical vocabulary at all times. Learn to live without it. You'll avoid a lot of foolishness.

Eliminate Unneeded Words

Unneeded words create static in your writing. To help limit your writing to necessary words, follow these three principles:

- Remove unneeded prepositional phrases.
- Remove fillers.
- Cut out unnecessarily repetitious words.

Remove unneeded prepositional phrases. Overuse of prepositional phrases bogs down sentences. The following are typical heavy phrases that should be replaced by lighter ones:

in accordance with   with
in the event of   if

due to the fact that	because
for the purpose of training	for training, to train
pursuant to	under
subsequent to	after
with regard to, in regard to	on, about
in order to	to
in view of the fact that	since, because
with reference to	about
at the present time	now
at this point in time	now
at that point in time	then
by means of	by
during the time that	that, while

Remove fillers. It and *there* are often used as fillers, words that fill out a sentence until you think of what you are going to say. When a filler is the subject of a sentence, it is followed by a linking verb, such as *appear, seem,* or *be,* and a word that is actually the logical subject of the sentence:

> *There are* three trusses the beam rests on.
> *There is* a suitable airplane available at Newark.
> *It appears* six workers were absent from the night shift.
> *It is* our plan to be in Chicago next Friday.
> *It seems* obvious that we must meet the deadline.

Such constructions as *there are, there is, there were, it is,* and *it seems . . . that* anticipate the logical subject and verb and distract from the natural emphasis they should have. Since fillers take up space and delay the logical subject and verb, removing them replaces emphasis on the logical subject and verb and shortens the sentence:

> The *beam rests* on three trusses.
> A suitable *airplane is* available at Newark.
> Six *workers were* apparently absent from the night shift.
> *We plan* to be in Chicago next Friday.
> Obviously, *we must meet* the deadline.

In some instances a *there is, there are* opening is acceptable, such as when the *there is* can be readily replaced only by a verb like *exist.* An example would be "There is really no sure-fire rule to follow about using the active or passive voice." To get rid of this *there is* construction, we would have to substitute "No sure-fire rule to follow about using the active or passive voice really exists"—not necessarily an improvement.

In any case, go over your sentences carefully to be sure the *there* constructions are needed.

Cut out unnecessarily repetitious words. A word or phrase that repeats itself or says the same thing twice is a redundancy. A redundant system in engineering is a backup system that provides alternative action if the primary system should fail. Redundant systems in space vehicles are desirable. Certain principles of redundance in writing are useful, too, such as an overview that gives the reader a good mental picture of the content and arrangement of a report, a heading system that identifies key topics that are restated and developed in detail in the report text, or a graphic that repeats what is described in words. But many expressions are so unnecessarily redundant as to be pointless. Examples are *red in color, rectangular in shape, large in size, return back, combine together,* and *25 in number.* Only the first word in each case should be kept. Other redundancies come early in phrases: *the month of July, the city of Woodstock, the field of biology,* and *a total of 30.* Only the last word should be kept.

Doublets are another source of unnecessarily repetitious words: *any and all, each and every, revered and respected, unless and until, if and when, cease and desist,* and *give and convey.* Many such doublets and even triplets are carryovers from "lawyer talk." Lawyers are very fond of such redundancies. Lawyers don't write contracts that merely sell property. Rather they "sell, transfer, and convey" not the property but the "right, title, and interest" to the property. Lawyers drawing up wills don't merely leave an estate to someone. Rather the will "wills, devises, and bequeaths" the estate plus the "rest, residue, and remainder" to the lucky heir.

Lawyers, some of them anyway, will argue that in law, as in a space vehicle, redundancy is necessary. The point is debatable, but the success of plain-language laws seems to be evidence that legal redundancy has been overdone. The problem lies not only with lawyers, however, but with those, often government bureaucrats, who imitate lawyers when there is no justification at all for redundancy. If you write a sentence like "Each and every one of our employees and workers is ready and willing to work and toil long and hard," you should be eager to cut out one of each of the doublets. Such a paring will result in a 50 percent loss in static.

Put Action in Your Verbs

Nouns used for verbs and the passive voice create unnecessary sentence length and sluggishness. In using nouns for verbs we substitute the noun form of a word for the verb itself. The process and the noun form are referred to as *nominalization.* Nominalization results always in unnecessary words and often in rather vague sentences as well. The following sentence[5] uses three nominalizations:

> *Failure* to affix a *signature* to the form will result in a *disallowance* of the claim.

The three italicized nouns stand for the verbs *to fail, to sign,* and *to disallow.* Not only has nominalization resulted in a longer sentence, as used here it has also resulted in a vague one. For example, whose signature should be affixed? Who will disallow the claim? Converting the nouns back into verbs and furnishing the actors the verbs need results in this better, clearer sentence:

> If you fail to sign the form, we will disallow the claim.

Even more simply:

> If you do not sign the form, we will disallow the claim.

Certain general verbs create nominalization by smothering the true verb. Verbs like *have, give, take, be, do, get,* and *make* are innocent enough by themselves, but when connected with nouns ending in *-ance, -ence, -ion, -ity,* and *-ment,* they create phrases loaded with static. Here are five such phrases that can be streamlined to single words.

to be in agreement	agree
to give assistance to	assist, help, aid
to have a preference for	prefer
to be desirous of	desire, want
to make application	apply

When you write a sentence like "It is our intention to submit the proposal by the deadline," think about it a bit. Is there a smothered verb hiding away in there somewhere? How about *intend* for *intention?* With that change we improve the sentence greatly:

> We intend to submit the proposal by the deadline.

A third way to put action into your verbs is to use the active voice. You frequently have the choice of making a particular noun either the subject or object in a sentence, with a resulting difference in verb form.

Active voice   The company *gave* each employee a bonus.
Passive voice   Each employee *was given* a bonus by the company.

In the active voice the subject acts *(The company gave).* In the passive voice the subject is acted upon *(Each employee was given).* The passive consists of some form of *be* plus the past participle *(is given, was given, has been given, will be given).* Verb tense has nothing to do with whether the verb is active or passive. Nor does the subject in an active-voice sentence have to be a person:

Active   Mr. Brady gave the book to John.
Passive   John was given the book by Mr. Brady.

Active   The pump pushes the fluid into the third receptacle.
Passive   The fluid is pushed into the third receptacle by the pump.

Active   The mirror reflects the light.
Passive   The light is reflected by the mirror.

An advantage of the active voice is that the actor is always identified because it's the subject:

> The *company* gave. . . .

In the passive voice the actor, no longer the subject, may or may not be identified:

> Each employee was given a bonus *by the company.*
> Each employee was given a bonus.

Most sentences use the active voice for a good reason: The logic of the active-voice sentence matches the grammar of the sentence. Whoever or whatever does the action is the subject of the sentence; whoever or whatever receives the action is the object.

At times, however, the passive voice is effective. When the doer of an action is obvious, it may often be more efficient to write a passive-voice sentence that refers only to the action and not to the doer. For example, in conducting an experiment, the experimenter may have performed all the procedures. To use the active voice while reporting the experiment, he or she would frequently have to say things like "I tested the solution for titanic acid." In the passive voice, the experimenter can avoid the obvious and repetitive "I" and write "The solution was tested for titanic acid."

Sometimes the receiver of the action is more important than the doer. When this is the case, you can use the passive to emphasize the importance:

> The bricks were then moved to the cooling chamber.
> The letter has been filed.

And, of course, there will be times when you don't know the actor:

> The office was robbed at 3:00 A.M.

There is really no sure-fire rule to follow about using the active or passive voice. In general, put what you want emphasized in the subject slot. If the passive buries your main idea the way nominalization and general verbs do, use the active voice.

Often, the biggest obstacle in the way of readable writing is a misplaced zeal to appear well educated, which causes people to feel uncomfortable about making clear, direct statements that are easy to understand. Remember, flesh-and-blood readers are out there; if you want to impress them, do so by writing clearly and precisely. (For more on sentences, see pages 433–436.)

To end this section on style, we thought you might enjoy this brief article that appeared a few years ago in the St. Louis *Globe-Democrat* and other newspapers. We offer it without comment.

GHOST EDITOR TRIMS MEMO ON HEW MESSAGE BREVITY
Eve Edstrom

WASHINGTON—There's a person at the Department of Health, Education and Welfare who should be writing all government memos. He or she just polished the newest "HEW gem"—a memorandum attempting to say that

HEW Secretary Robert H. Finch wants his top staff to send him shorter briefing memoranda.

Finch's executive assistant, L. Patrick Gray III, who has a considerable Pentagon background, tried to get the message across in a memorandum that was officially circulated. An unknown recipient translated Gray's memo for personal distribution, and showed that the word count could have been reduced by about two-thirds.

For example, Gray's opener was "As a general rule, and certainly not applicable in all situations, the briefing memoranda forwarded to the secretary have been loaded with an excessive amount of verbiage."

The translation read: "Most of the briefing memoranda forwarded to the secretary have been too wordy."

Gray's memorandum continued: "In the future, the briefing memoranda should highlight the issue, set forward alternative courses of action or approaches to resolve the issue, and finally, a recommendation regarding the action to be taken by the secretary should be made with reasons therefor."

Translation: "Briefing memoranda should highlight the issue, state alternatives to resolve the issue, and [recommend] the action to be taken by the secretary."

Gray said: "It is envisioned that this sort of writing will not require more than a page and a half to two pages at the most."

Translation: "No more than two pages should be required."

An equally terse translation—"Supporting data may be appended"—was substituted for Gray's statement that "Additional supporting data, information, comments, and supporting documentation may be included beneath the writing referred to above, as deemed necessary."

Gray concluded with "The secretary does not, in any way, intend that the free flow of information to him be restricted or limited; however, he does desire that the central issue be highlighted and acted upon in the manner set forth in this memorandum."

Translation: "The secretary does not want the flow of information to him restricted. He does insist that the central issue be highlighted and presented as described above."[6]

ACHIEVING PROPER TONE

Understanding tone is perhaps best approached first through analogy. We all know, for example, that the way we dress sets a certain tone. If we wake up on a Saturday morning and put on jeans and a sweatshirt, we are saying this is a casual kind of day. Things are going to be laid back. If we put on a dark suit with formal accessories, we are saying this is a serious day. We have important things to do.

We also know that certain clothes have the proper tone for certain occasions and not for others. A well-cut business suit is appropriate in most offices but would look pretty silly at a picnic. A party dress suitable for an evening social event would look out of place in church or at a football game.

To move to an analogy closer to writing, we all know that the words we use in conversation and the tone in which we speak them set the tone for the conversation as serious, friendly, funny, angry, or whatever. Again, we also know that we might use one tone at a football game, another on a fishing trip, and yet another when talking to an authority figure such as a bank's lending officer.

So it is in writing. You set the tone by the way you write—the words and the sentence structures you choose. For most transactional writing, you want to set a tone that's efficient and yet friendly, crisp but not rude, serious but not too formal. Tone is clearly related to style. For the most part, if you follow our advice about achieving clarity and conciseness you will be on your way to a good businesslike tone.

Our experience in consulting with people at work shows us that faulty tone, in correspondence particularly, results from one of two errors by the writer: trying to be too formal or being so brusque as to appear rude.

The too formal we have already looked at extensively while talking about clarity and conciseness. The pseudotechnical language we discuss on pages 39–41 usually shows up in the writing of people who feel that to sound educated and professional they have to talk and write as though they have swallowed a dictionary plus a thesaurus. As a result they sound pretentious and pompous and usually irritate their readers. Here is the body of a letter received by one of us that, although not extreme, illustrates how the writer fell into the pitfall of the too formal:

> I noted with interest your speech on computer-assisted instruction given recently in Los Angeles.
> It is requested that you send a copy to me at the above address.

Take a moment to read that letter aloud. Actually *listen* to it. What is the tone of "I noted with interest"? Would you *speak* such a phrase? The tone is faintly patronizing, and we doubt that you would speak that way.

Try speaking the second sentence: "It is requested that you send a copy to me at the above address." Does it sound pompous and impersonal to you? Would you speak such a sentence? How would you react to someone who came up to you at work or in school and said, "It is requested that you send a copy to me at the above address"?

The answer is clear. We speak a great many things we shouldn't write. But when we write we should not get too far from the tone of common, courteous, educated speech. Put the "It is requested" sentence into plain talk. It will come out something like "I'd appreciate your sending me a copy of your talk," or, perhaps, "Please send me a copy of your talk."

Notice that in speaking you rather naturally use the active voice and personal pronouns such as *I, we, you,* and *me.* Don't be afraid to use personal pronouns in transactional writing such as correspondence and instructions. They give *your* writing a personal, friendly tone—which is why *we* have used a *we-you* approach in this book.

Notice how cold and impersonal the following is:

> The top portion of this statement will be used to mechanically process the payment to the user's account and its enclosure in the envelope supplied with the bill will aid in the accurate crediting of the user's account.[7]

The passage contains no personal pronouns. It is also in the passive voice and uses two nominalizations: *enclosure* and *crediting*. For a better tone you would need to make the following changes:

- Change the passive voice to active.
- Drop the impersonal *user* for the more personal *you*.
- Transform the nominalizations into verbal forms.

Here is the result:

> We will use the top portion of your statement to mechanically process your payment to your account. If you enclose it in the envelope that we supplied with the bill, we will be better able to credit your account accurately.

The difference in tone is, we hope, obvious. There is an added bonus. Research shows that people read material written in this personal, narrative style faster and remember it longer than they do material written in a more impersonal, less narrative style.[8]

The second problem that businesspeople have is sounding rude. We are not talking here about being deliberately stern—as a business might be in telling a customer that an overdue debt is about to be turned over to a collection agency. Rather, we refer to an inadvertent rudeness that results from carelessness by the writer.

In conversation we get immediate feedback from our listener. If we say something friendly, the listener smiles. If we say something rude, our listener frowns. We always know where we are. In writing, we lack this immediate feedback. We may write something that we think is crisp, efficient, and businesslike without realizing that we have fallen into a tone that is brusque to the point of rudeness. The following letter is a case in point:

> Dear Ms. Cortez:
>
> Enclosed find UPS Express Invoice #4-653-98246. Please let it be understood that it is not the policy of ITC Corporation to accept for payment any shipping charges for packages mailed to our attention.
> We request that you look into this matter at once.
>
> Sincerely,

Again, read this letter aloud. Imagine it being spoken to you or your speaking it to someone. There is no way you can read it aloud without sounding rude and unfriendly. The writer, we can assure you, had no intention of being either. He simply wanted to be businesslike.

In writing such a letter, imagine you are in conversation with the recipient. In your mind's eye, place her in front of you. Hear what you are saying and imagine her response. Is she angry when what you are hoping for is a nod of understanding? If so, rewrite your letter. You have been inadvertently rude. The previous letter rewritten for proper tone might read as follows:

Dear Ms. Cortez:

With this letter we are returning UPS Express Invoice #4-653-98246 to you. It came with your April shipment of loan packages to us.

Our policy is that the sender pays the cost of such shipments. Therefore, we are returning the invoice to you and ask that you pay it.

Thank you for the shipment. If you have any questions regarding shipping costs, please write or call.

Sincerely,

The rewritten letter is clear about who pays the cost, but the tone, although businesslike, is friendly. Notice also that it contains more useful information than does the first letter.

Reports, when compared to letters and memos, are likely to be less personal in tone. Their tone, nonetheless, should still be courteous and should not be too formal or pseudotechnical. As in most writing, audience analysis helps decide the proper tone. The following excerpt is taken from a report aimed at a lay audience. The report describes the sound and lighting systems used in a musical show, in this case, one by Barbara Mandrell:

A road production as professional as this one is entirely self-sufficient; it has to be, for this tour will encompass 40 performances in 11 weeks. The theater provides the stage and the electrical power. Pope and his pocket-size army arrive in the crew bus, accompanied by the two tractor-trailer rigs packed with a bewildering array of lighting grids and sound equipment. The entire shipment is packaged in custom-built cases, all of them made to roll easily on swiveling casters, and designed to absorb the continual cycle of travel, assembly, and disassembly.

"Without electronics, there would be no live performing on this kind of road," says Irby Mandrell. "Take away electronic instruments and amplification, and the maximum audience size would be 250 people. With it, you can perform before 250,000."[9]

The tone in this selection is relaxed and easygoing, a bit informal but not sloppy. Some of the information is given in a quotation, which gives it a personal tone. We can identify a little with the people involved.

The next excerpt, concerning readability formulas, is from a report aimed at experts in the field. More formal that the first example, it nevertheless is plainly written. The sentences are in the active voice. The vocabulary, although professional, is not chosen to impress anyone. The sentence lengths, somewhat on the long side, are still reasonable given the intended audience. There is no attempt to personalize the material:

> Readability formulas can make gross distinctions between relatively simple or sophisticated text. They may be useful in making finer distinctions among instructional prose for elementary school students, because the formulas were developed on the basis of materials, readers, and reading tasks at that level. They are not fine-tuned enough to indicate reliably and validly the difference between eighth and ninth or ninth and tenth grade material for adult readers. A computer program that gives a new reading score with each editorial change of sentence length or word substitution may be doing the document designer and the reader a great disservice.[10]

CONCLUSION

In transactional writing, work for a plain style and a courteous tone. In certain situations, such as correspondence and instructions, you may also use a personal tone. Certain kinds of reports may be more impersonal in tone but should still be plainly written and avoid the trap of overformal and pseudotechnical language. In any kind of writing avoid the blown-up, bureaucratic style typified by the Gray memo on pages 146–147. *Listen* to your writing. It should sound good to your ear and should never be inadvertently rude.

SUGGESTIONS FOR APPLYING YOUR KNOWLEDGE

1. For each of the following words and phrases substitute a more familiar word or phrase that means the same thing.

assuage	inchoate
delectable	nadir
demeanor	neophyte
domicile	palpable
eschew	promulgate
geotome	remuneration
germane	substantiate
impecunious	vitiate

a natural geologic protuberance
a geriatose female of the Homo sapiens species
totipalmated feet
observed in a state of rapid locomotion
a sampling of fluid hydride of oxygen
a member of the team precipitately descended

2. Remove the noise from the following sentences by substituting verbs where appropriate for the nominalizations. Keep the same verb tense.

a. We are in agreement that new circuit breakers should be installed.

b. These payments are in excess of those specified by the contract.

c. Mr. Donleavy was present when we conducted an inventory of unassembled equipment.

d. Our staff has done a survey of health needs of the five surrounding counties.

e. The night clerk is supposed to make a record of the daily activities.

f. The committee will give consideration to alternatives.

g. Figure 3 is a list of the centrifugal pump replacement parts.

3. Fillers weaken verb power and distract from the logical subjects of the following sentences. Strengthen these sentences by removing the fillers *it* and *there*, rewriting to emphasize the logical subjects and verbs.

a. There are many mechanics who own their own tools.

b. It was noticed by the pilot that the ground-speed indicator was malfunctioning.

c. There are two screws that fasten the cover to the wall box.

d. There is a house at 212 Normal Avenue that is being converted into a day-care center.

e. It is evident that the time needed to repair the hoses is still too long.

f. There are two grooves that run the length of the handle.

g. There are several different types of needles that can be used.

4. Eliminate the unnecessary words in these sentences.

a. This morning at 8:00 A.M. the prisoners were transferred away to the prison facility by means of a bus.

b. In view of the fact that the two companies are not in agreement with each other about the important essentials, it is the consensus of opinion of the board that advance planning is of great importance.

c. It is absolutely essential that the scalpels be sharp-edged in order to bisect the specimens in two.

d. Prior to the conductance of these tests, we made a decision to make use of disposable culture plates in lieu of glass ones because of the cost factor involved.

e. I am of the opinion that the city and county agencies are at this point in time cooperating together.

f. A total of ten (10) registered nurses will be needed to staff the proposed new intensive-care unit.

g. The locking device that suffered breakage is triangular in shape and red in color.

h. Remove any and all foreign objects from the sensor mechanism.

i. Either one or the other of the timetables is totally acceptable.

j. The received message is decoded into two separate and distinct signals for correct and positive identification purposes.

5. Rewrite verbs in these sentences to make them active voice. Be sure to keep the same verb tense.

a. A review of the case by the appeals board was requested by the representative.

b. For the final test five dyes were used.

c. At our Newark plant semiconductors are manufactured.

d. The causes of wood warping are discussed in Part 4.

e. A 1 percent earnings tax is imposed by the new ordinance.

f. The necessary equipment for constructing a battery eliminator is listed in Part 1 of this manual.

6. Rewrite the following letter using plain, courteous, personalized language. Tell Mr. Sarver what he must do to get his loan:

Dear Mr. Sarver:

Your request for a policy loan has been rejected. Although the policy has a loan value in excess of the amount requested, the owner may obtain an advance only if the policy has been assigned as security. It was not specified in the letter requesting the loan that the policy could be used as security.

Sincerely,

UNIT II

CORRESPONDENCE

C H A P T E R

4

BASIC PRINCIPLES OF CORRESPONDENCE

The professionalism we wish to illustrate in this book is demonstrated well in correspondence. There is a difference between school and the world of work; school is more forgiving. A teacher may pass a letter that is good except for a sloppy format. In business the letter may be considered totally unsatisfactory. It may lose you the job you seek or the order you want, or it may convince someone you are irresponsible. The letters that get you the order or the job are successful professional efforts. Letters that do not accomplish your goals are unsuccessful, no matter how close they come.

In Chapters 5 through 8, we tell you how to compose common business letters dealing with inquiry and response, employment, customer relations, and sales. Because these and most other business letters are persuasive or analytical to some degree, we discuss persuasive strategies and scientific argument in Chapter 2. In this chapter we give you some basic principles for preparing letters and memorandums.

FORMATS

Business letters must be neat and follow consistent formats. They must be typed. Sloppiness and inconsistency will be taken as indicators of carelessness and lack of professionalism on your part. In Figures 4–1 to 4–4, we show acceptable formats for nonletterhead stationery and indicate the conventional spacing and punctuation. Choose a format you like and follow it. We comment in the text about a few major points concerning the letter and its parts.

1260 Hazel Avenue
Gallatin, IL 60404
April 8, 1986

[2 spaces]
Mrs. Mary Bolt
Customer Service
Sunset Van Lines
2224 Wake Boulevard
Contra Costa, CA 90233
[2 spaces]
Subject: Your letter of March 29, 1986
[2 spaces]
Dear Mrs. Bolt:
[2 spaces]

_____
_____
_____

[2 spaces]

_____
_____

[2 spaces]

_____

[2 spaces]

Sincerely,

Mary H. Palmer

[4 spaces]

Mary H. Palmer

[2 spaces]
MHP:eis
[2 spaces]
Enclosure: Furniture inventory
[2 spaces]
cc: United Services Automobile Association

FIGURE 4-1   Block format

```
                                               1492 Columbus Avenue
                                               Biloxi, MS 39530
                                               October 4, 1986
[2 spaces]
Mr. Richard Ferguson, Head
Public Documents
Distribution Center
Pueblo, CO 81009
[2 spaces]
Dear Mr. Ferguson:
[2 spaces]
Re: Shipment of Index of National Park System
[2 spaces]
```

[2 spaces]

[2 spaces]

[2 spaces]

```
                                    Sincerely,

[4 spaces]                          Maria G. Cortez

                                    (Mrs.) Maria G. Cortez
[2 spaces]
Enclosures
[2 spaces]
cc: Superintendent of Documents
```

FIGURE 4–2 Modified block format

5200 Gatlin Road
Fayetteville, VA 22212
26 February 1986
[2 spaces]
Mr. James W. Whittaker
General Manager
Recreational Equipment, Inc.
1225-11th Avenue
Seattle, WA 98122
[2 spaces]
Dear Mr. Whittaker:
[2 spaces]

_____

[2 spaces]

_____
_____

[2 spaces]

_____

[2 spaces]
Sincerely,

Gerard B. Hewlett   **[4 spaces]**

Gerard B. Hewlett
[2 spaces]
cc: Anne K. Chimato

FIGURE 4–3   Full block format

```
2098 Colfax Avenue
Denver, CO 80279
29 January 1986
```
[2 spaces]
```
The Harvard Medical School Health Letter
79 Garden Street
Cambridge, MA 02138
```

[3 spaces]

```
SUBSCRIPTION RATES
```

[3 spaces]

_____
_____
_____

[2 spaces]

_____
_____

[2 spaces]

_____
_____
_____

Penny Hutchinson   **[5 spaces]**

```
PENNY HUTCHINSON, M.D.
```
[2 spaces]
```
Enclosures (2)
```

FIGURE 4–4   Simplified letter

Stationery

Go to the campus bookstore or a stationery store and choose a good-quality white bond paper of about 20-lb. weight—a paper that looks good and feels good in your hand. Don't buy cheap, lightweight paper. It's a false economy.

Typewriter or Word Processor

Work with a clean typewriter in good repair. Dirty type produces fuzzy, broken letters. Choose a standard typeface such as pica or elite. For business correspondence, don't choose a face such as italic. It will be considered unprofessional. If you can't type well enough to produce a clean, evenly printed letter, hire someone to type important letters, such as letters of application, for you. Better still, learn to type well. It will be a skill that will be useful all your life.

The comments we have made for a typewriter hold true for the word processor as well. In addition, be sure, for important work, to use a letter-quality printer. Many of the dot matrix printers produce a poor-quality print that will mark you as unprofessional in the eyes of your readers.

Margins

Letters should never look crowded or off-balance on the page. Leave generous margins, at least one inch on either side and one and one-half inches on top and bottom. For a short letter, come down farther on the page so that your letter doesn't hang at the top like a balloon on a string.

Heading

The heading includes your complete address but not your name. Do not abbreviate words like *street* or *avenue*. You may abbreviate the state, using the postal services's two-letter abbreviations. (See the list of abbreviations in Figure 4–5.) The date is part of the heading. It may be written *August 18, 19xx,* or *18 August 19xx*. Do not write numbers as *9th* or *3rd*. Use the number by itself.

Inside Address

Set up the inside address as you do your own address in the heading. Do include your correspondent's name, however, and any titles. The titles *Mr., Mrs.,* and *Dr.* are abbreviated. Most other titles are written out in full, such as *Professor* and *Sergeant*. Do not use a title after a name that has the same meaning as the title before the name. Write *Dr. Penny Hutchinson* or *Penny Hutchinson, M.D.,* but not *Dr. Penny Hutchinson, M.D.*

Alabama	AL	Montana	MT
Alaska	AK	Nebraska	NE
Arizona	AZ	Nevada	NV
Arkansas	AR	New Hampshire	NH
California	CA	New Jersey	NJ
Colorado	CO	New Mexico	NM
Connecticut	CT	New York	NY
Delaware	DE	North Carolina	NC
District of Columbia	DC	North Dakota	ND
Florida	FL	Ohio	OH
Georgia	GA	Oklahoma	OK
Guam	GU	Oregon	OR
Hawaii	HI	Pennsylvania	PA
Idaho	ID	Puerto Rico	PR
Illinois	IL	Rhode Island	RI
Indiana	IN	South Carolina	SC
Iowa	IA	South Dakota	SD
Kansas	KS	Tennessee	TN
Kentucky	KY	Texas	TX
Louisiana	LA	Utah	UT
Maine	ME	Vermont	VT
Maryland	MD	Virginia	VA
Massachusetts	MA	Virgin Islands	VI
Michigan	MI	Washington	WA
Minnesota	MN	West Virginia	WV
Mississippi	MS	Wisconsin	WI
Missouri	MO	Wyoming	WY

FIGURE 4–5   State abbreviations

Subject Line

A subject or reference line is frequently used in business correspondence. Placed above or below the salutation—see Figures 4–1 and 4–2—it is preceded by either the term *Subject* or *Re* followed by a colon. Using a subject line allows your correspondents or their secretaries to locate previous correspondence on the same subject. It also saves your readers from trite, trivial openers like "With reference to your letter of July 7, 19xx."

Salutation

Most of us are still slaves to convention in the salutation and use *Dear* _____ when we are writing to someone whose name we know. Most people accept the *Dear* as a convention and don't take it seriously. Yet they would probably notice and even resent its absence. Therefore, you should probably continue to use salutations such as *Dear Ms. Andrews, Dear Dr. White, and Dear Professor Souther.* Use a first name if you and the letter's recipient are on a first-name basis. Use a colon after the salutation.

What should be done when you don't have a name of an individual to address has been complicated by the fact that many people now feel that exclusively male salutations such as *Dear Sir* and *Gentlemen* are no longer appropriate. No universally accepted substitute has been found as yet. Some people have begun to address a department directly, as in *Dear Credit Department* or *Dear Consumer Complaints.* Perhaps the best approach is to use the simplified letter shown in Figure 4–4, in which no salutation is required. In routine correspondence it may not matter very much which of these alternatives you use, but in important correspondence do everything you reasonably can to get a name to address.

Body

In the body, single-space the paragraphs and double-space between them. In very short letters of several lines, you may double-space everything. In the modified block format, indent the paragraphs five spaces; in the other formats, do not. Keep sentences and paragraphs short. Average 14 to 17 words a sentence and don't let paragraphs run more than six or seven lines. Generous use of white space in a letter invites readers in. Cramped, crowded spacing shuts them out.

Complimentary Close

Use a conventional close such as *Sincerely* or *Sincerely yours* for people you don't particularly know. For people with whom you have some friendship, you may close with *Warm regards, With best wishes,* and so forth. Capitalize only the first word in the close. Follow the close with a comma.

Signature Block

Type your name four spaces below the complimentary close. A woman without an honorific title, such as *Colonel* or *Professor,* will usually be considered a *Ms.* these days, just as a man without a title will be considered a *Mr.* If a woman prefers the title *Miss* or *Mrs.,* she should indicate the title preferred in parentheses to the left of her typed name. A married woman should use her own first name, not her husband's. Below the typed name, put your business title if you have one. Sign your name legibly above your typed name.

Special Notations

Three special notations—identification, enclosure, and carbon copy—are frequently made below the signature block. Their order and spacing are indicated in Figures 4–1 to 4–4.

IDENTIFICATION   When a typist rather than the writer types a letter, an identification line is used. Usually the writer's initials are uppercase letters, and the typist's are lowercase, as in

AJB:whm

ENCLOSURE   The enclosure line tells the reader that something is enclosed with the letter. The format of the line and the amount of information given vary. Typical lines might be

Enclosure
Enclosures (3)
Encl Medical examination form

COPY LINE   In most circumstances, you will use a copy line to inform your primary reader of others who have been sent copies of the letter. The notification requires a simple notation such as the following:

cc: Ms. Janet Kimberly

Continuation Page

The format for one or more continuation pages is shown in Figure 4–6. Use plain white bond for page 2 and beyond; do not use letterhead stationery. Plan your spacing so that at least two or three lines of the body are carried over to the continuation page.

Envelope

The envelope format is shown in Figure 4–7. Letters sent to business people will sometimes quite legitimately be opened by their co-workers, for example, when the person addressed is ill or on vacation. The assumption is that the letter concerns company business, and business goes on regardless of who is present to conduct it. Therefore, if you are writing a personal or confidential letter to a person at a business address, mark it with the words PERSONAL or CONFIDENTIAL, directly under the address on the envelope.

MEMORANDUMS

Letters are external business correspondence that carries messages outside of an organization. Memorandums—usually called *memos*—are internal business correspondence that carries messages inside an organization. Memos go from office to office, branch to branch, supervisor to subordinate, and so forth. Like letters, memos have many uses. For example, you may use them to confirm a conversation, clarify a previous message, re-

[person receiving letter]
Miss Janice C. Huer   –2–   April 8, 1985

[4 spaces]

_____
_____
_____

[2 spaces]

_____
_____
_____

[2 spaces]
Sincerely,

John R. Gilmore   **[4 spaces]**

John R. Gilmore
Highway Department Technician
[2 spaces]
JRG:hrw

FIGURE 4–6   Continuation page

Mary H. Palmer
1260 Hazel Avenue
Gallatin, IL 60304

                              Mrs. Mary Bolt
                              Customer Service
                              Sunset Van Lines
                              2224 Wake Boulevard
                              Contra Costa, CA 90233

FIGURE 4–7   Envelope

PROPERTY CONSULTANTS INC.

TO *Dave Carson*   FROM *Anne Huntrods*

SUBJECT *Horberg Computer's employment figures*

DATE *8 Mar.* 19 *86*

   Before my meeting with Art Walzer on 11 March, I need the projected employment figures for the proposed Horberg Computer plant in Oakdale. Would you please get them for me?

FIGURE 4–8   Handwritten memo of inquiry

quest information, supply information, congratulate someone, announce changes in policy, report meetings, or transmit documents.

Most organizations have preprinted memo forms that differ from the forms used for letters. Generally, these forms contain the organization's name, but not address, and guide words for *To, From, Subject, and Date.* See Figures 4–8 and 4–9. Because of the preprinted format, memos don't require a salutation or signature. Frequently, though, people write their initials next to their names on the *From* line. To speed correspondence and avoid taking a secretary's time, many organizations allow short memos to be handwritten—a good reason for developing a legible handwriting.

Few fundamental differences exist between writing the body of a memo and any other piece of correspondence. You must be as clear and well organized as you would be in a letter. Maintain the "you attitude." Use persuasive strategies and scientific argument as appropriate to audience and purpose.

Because of the frequent contacts that people in the same organization often have, however, memos can be somewhat different from let-

---

PROPERTY CONSULTANTS INC.

TO Anne Huntrods   FROM Dave Carson

SUBJECT Horberg Computer employment figures

DATE 10 Mar 1986

    With staged development beginning
in 1987 or 1988, Horberg Computer
Company estimates employment at the
Oakdale site will be approximately
600 in 1989, 8,500 in 1994, and
20,000 by 2002.
    My source for this info is the
Horberg Computer Company Site Environmental Assessment submitted to
the state Environmental Quality
Board, 20 April 1984.

FIGURE 4–9 Typed memo of reply

ters. Often, the person receiving the memo knows all about a situation except for the point being raised in the memo. Consequently, no long explanations are necessary. The memo's writer can come immediately to the point. Often, too, friendships that exist within an organization allow for more informality than you might use in external correspondence. Do not allow either of these points, however, to mislead you into thinking memos need not be both complete and courteous. Missing information or a tone too brisk and abrupt can be as annoying in a memo as in a letter. Figures 4–8 and 4–9 show two typical memos.

MEMORANDUM AND LETTER REPORTS

Memos are often longer than the two short samples shown in Figures 4–8 and 4–9. Frequently, longer memos and certain letters are actually memo or letter reports. Many of the reports we describe in Unit III, such as instructions, recommendations, and proposals, may actually be written as one- to five-page memos or letters. These memo and letter reports will not need such formal apparatus as a title page and table of contents, but they will need good introductions and conclusions and, frequently, headings. See pages 132–137 and 148–157 for information on these matters. For an example of such a short report, see the memo report in Figure 4–10.

SUGGESTIONS FOR APPLYING YOUR KNOWLEDGE

For each kind of correspondence discussed in Chapters 5 through 8 we suggest specific applications at the ends of those chapters. For the moment, we suggest that you prepare for your study of correspondence by gathering examples of business letters and memos. Most members of the class have probably received various kinds of selling letters. Many students generate correspondence with department stores, book clubs, and similar institutions. Some students already work and have legitimate access to business correspondence.

The staff members of your school send and receive an enormous amount of correspondence. People such as the dean, bursar, placement officer, maintenance superintendent, and admissions officer do much of their business by mail, so much so that they often use form letters. Some members of the class can go to these school officials and ask permission to reproduce some samples of their correspondence for classroom use. The names of people involved should be removed, of course, when letters are reproduced.

Look around you and gather as many examples of real letters and memos as you can. They will be invaluable in your study of correspondence.

When you have the letters and memos in class, you can use them as the basis for discussion. What is your honest opinion of

MEMORANDUM

Date: 15 November 1985

To: Richard Sauer, Director

From: R. Vance Morey and Harold A. Cloud

Subject: Economic analysis of alternatives to high-speed corn drying

We hope the following will answer your questions about how to make economic comparisons of the alternatives to high-speed corn drying. As you know, energy costs will be reduced by using any of the alternatives. However, energy is only one part of the total cost of the drying and storage system. For instance, investment or fixed costs are always significant. We recommend that your economic analysis include both costs and returns.

Costs

--Investment costs associated with additions to, and changes in, material-handling equipment and storage bins. (For storage bins, cost factors may include drying floors, fans, shallower bins for natural-air drying, and less storage space because of level-fill requirements and space lost for drying air plenums.)

--Larger electrical service required in some cases to meet increased peak-power demands.

Returns

--Energy cost savings.

--Increased dryer capacity, which may allow more timely harvesting or eliminate the need to increase high-speed drying capacity.

--Improved grain quality, which may result in less dockage.

--Reduced reliance on propane fuel.

Some of these factors will affect a specific economic analysis; some will not. Therefore, you will need to analyze each situation separately. If we can help further, call us at 373-1321.

FIGURE 4-10 Memorandum report

them? Do they work? Is their information complete? Is their tone right? Have their writers sufficiently considered audience and purpose as well as the information they intended to convey? How successful are their persuasive strategies? How have the writers handled credibility, emotional appeals, and facts and analysis? Do any of the formats differ markedly from the norm? If so, do the differences help or distract?

C H A P T E R

5

INQUIRY
AND RESPONSE
LETTERS

Much of the routine correspondence you'll write will ask someone to do something for you: provide information, perform a
service, send materials and equipment. These are inquiry, request, and order letters. In addition, you are likely to write
letters that respond to such letters. Although these letters are routine,
you'll need to know how to write them well, because the quality of these
letters reflects your and your organization's ability to communicate
clearly.

INQUIRY AND REQUEST LETTERS

Even though inquiry and request letters arise from almost any situation
and deal with almost any subject, their function is always the same—they
begin a correspondence cycle by asking one or more questions or making
one or more requests. If successful, they obtain a favorable response from
the persons to whom you send them.

Writing inquiry and request letters may at first appear to be easy.
But many things can go wrong. Your question might be worded so
vaguely that your readers will have to guess at what you want. You might
ask so bluntly for something that requires a special favor that your readers will be offended. You might even forget to include your complete
return address.

There are two keys to writing a successful inquiry or request letter.

First is the ability to ask questions and to phrase requests so clearly (yet politely) that you receive the exact information or services you want; second is the ability to determine whether your question or request is reasonably routine or involves a special favor from your reader.

Make Your Inquiry or Request Clear

If questions or requests are vague or general, readers will have little way of knowing exactly what is wanted. The result is likely to be an incomplete or unnecessary response, causing extra letters to be sent back and forth. Look how vague this request is:

> Would you please send me information about your new fuel pump.

What kind of information? Assuming that the recipient can figure out which new fuel pump the inquirer would like to know about, he or she might state the price, assure that it will fit any engine, and explain how soon it can be delivered. But what if the inquirer already knows those things but needs to know where and how the fuel pump can be mounted? Result: a second exchange of letters.

Making the inquiry or request specific reduces the risk of the recipient's arriving at the wrong idea of what is needed:

> Can your new adjustable pressure electric fuel pump type AK306J be used with the Continental O-470R engine, and can it be mounted in any position?

This illustrates another way to clarify: by using questions rather than statements to make inquiries. The question mark underscores the question and implies that an answer is expected.

A third way to clarify more complicated inquiries is to tabulate the information needed. Such a series of questions might read like this:

> Please send me the following information about your new adjustable pressure electric fuel pump type AK306J:
>
> 1. Can it be mounted anywhere and in any position?
>
> 2. Does it come with a mounting bracket?
>
> 3. Does it operate independently of the engine?
>
> 4. How many pounds of pressure does it adjust to?
>
> 5. Is the flow adequate for a Continental O-470R engine?

Tabulating questions or requests encourages specific phrasing that will provide easy reference for the recipient.

Decide Whether Your Inquiry or Request Is Routine or Special

Inquiry and request letters are of two kinds, and you need to know which kind you're writing. If your inquiry or request will benefit the reader as much as it will you, your letter will be easy to write, because the reader will be predisposed to respond favorably to it. An example of such a letter is a request for a catalog or other information that was evoked by a sales-person or a sales document—a sales letter, an advertisement, or a news release. If your inquiry or request has been solicited, your letter can be brief and to the point. You won't need to persuade your readers to re-spond; they'll be ready to reply. A routine request that will benefit the receiver is good news. A special request that will cause the receiver work and perhaps be of no benefit to him or her is bad news.

MAKING A ROUTINE REQUEST   Your major objective in making a solicited inquiry or request is to state it so that you get exactly what you want. Don't forget to be courteous as well—even with the most routine inquiry or request. Politeness should be so natural that you practice it almost un-consciously. It's as easy as saying *please*. The easiest way to show appreci-ation is to use *Thank you* as your complimentary close. We can't urge you enough to be courteous. A warm note is always pleasant to receive—and rewarding to send.

The writer who asked about the fuel pump was clear and polite. Because the inquiry was routine and might benefit the reader as much as the inquirer (the writer is interested in the product, and the information might lead to a sale), the questions started the letter. Here is another routine inquiry letter, written in response to an invitation to write for information:

Dear Ms. Parker:

Please send me the technical information package for product RD2-1160.

Since my company is considering applying for an exclusive license to develop your glass repair procedure, I would also appreciate the following information if the package does not provide it:

- What is the patent status of your procedure?
- Can the license be awarded for five years?
- What royalties would be required on sales?

Thank you,

Is the second paragraph necessary? Yes. Any information that might help the reader give the information or material needed should be included. In this case, the writer cannot be sure that the technical infor-mation package contains the information about patent status, license, and royalties.

MAKING A SPECIAL REQUEST Just because you want something is no guarantee that your readers will feel obliged to give it to you. If you initiate the inquiry or request, or if you will primarily benefit from its fulfillment, you're asking a special favor of your readers. Such a situation calls for you not only to state your inquiry or request clearly and politely but also to persuade your readers to comply with it. The best ways to encourage your readers to respond favorably are to help them understand your need and your rationale for sending the letter to them. Going beyond the inquiry or request itself lets readers know you're aware that you're asking a favor. Here's a sample:

Dear Mr. Bradley:

I am an industrial technology student at Northern Polytechnic Institute and am writing a paper for one of my courses on the hiring and recruiting practices of large industrial firms like yours.

I have done considerable library work on the subject, but I want to augment my reading with information collected from the six largest industrial firms in the tri-state area. The results of my study will be shared with the other members of my class. I would also be very happy to send a copy of my completed report to you, should you desire one.

Would you spend a few minutes to answer the following questions about the way your firm recruits employees?

1. What priorities are placed on candidates' academic performance, experience, and on-campus or in-plant interviews?

2. What is expected of candidates' behavior and dress when they report for an interview?

3. How much importance is placed on recommendations from faculty, school officials, and previous employers?

4. Do you give any standard or in-house tests to candidates? If so, how much weight is given to their scores?

My paper is due April 10, so I would like very much to receive your response by early March. I certainly appreciate your taking the time to read my letter, and am very hopeful of receiving a reply from you.

Sincerely,

Jack Kenney

Jack Kenney

Because the letter is asking a special favor of the reader, the writer holds up the questions until he identifies himself, establishes his need, and explains why he's written. He also offers some potential benefit to the reader by offering to share the results with him. He then itemizes the questions for easy reference and closes by explaining when he'd like to have the information. The writer prepares the reader for the inquiry because he realizes he is asking questions that are normally not asked and that might even be for information not normally given.

We think this letter is structured appropriately. By introducing himself and explaining why he is writing, the writer buffers the request. But he doesn't bury the question or request so deep in the letter that it comes at the very end. Even a bothersome question or request should not be delayed until the end of the letter. There needs to be room at the end of the letter to build goodwill of some kind.

The strategy when making an unsolicited inquiry or request is as follows:

1. Introduce yourself and explain why you are addressing your inquiry or request to that particular reader.
2. State your inquiry or request.
3. If appropriate, explain when you need the information or service.
4. Close by expressing your appreciation, but do not use a trite expression like "Thanking you in advance."

ORDER LETTERS

You'll write order letters when you wish to place written purchase orders but don't have your own forms or those of companies you're ordering from. As with inquiry letters, order letters range from the simple to the complicated. First, you won't need to persuade readers to respond. Order letters are good-news letters. Readers are prepared to respond to all orders. Just start by making your orders as clear and exact as possible. Then supply the necessary details of payment and shipment.

The things to remember about an order letter are these:

- Tell exactly what you want: article name, catalog or stock number, price, color, style, size, and so forth.
- If you're ordering more than one item, list them in tabular form and double-space after each item.
- Tell how you intend to pay: by check, money order, credit card, or a charge to your account if you have one established with the seller; in advance or after delivery; all at once or in installments; and so on.
- If you wish to have the order delivered a certain way by a certain time, tell how and when you want it sent.
- Be courteous. Your order will probably be filled, regardless of how im-

politely it's placed, but saying "please send" is a more polite and businesslike than "I want" or "I need."

Orders can be placed like this:

Please ship by truck express the following items, totaling $1,274.60:

10	Rear Tire Carriers (15″, 4-lug wheel)	Stock #193–6Y @ 149.98
10	Cab Step for Trucks (Deluxe Step, 19″ wide to fit 1982 Chevrolet)	Stock #154–3B @ $24.50
10	Pick-up Camper Stabilizers	Stock #752–1T @52.98

Make no substitutions and cancel the order if not deliverable within a month.

Bill my account (No. 335G1982).

Sincerely,

Before you mail the order, check a second time to ensure that you have included all necessary information. Incomplete or incorrect information means another letter or the wrong product. And that's a bother to both you and your reader.

RESPONSE LETTERS

"Every inquiry is an opportunity to make a friend," according to an old business adage. So it goes with receiving inquiries, requests, and orders. If you show a sincere interest in your readers and their needs, your response builds goodwill. Your courteous and prompt response demonstrates your willingness to help.

To write a good response letter, you must know exactly what the reader wants, what you can and should say in response, and how to organize what you say. Since your letter is always at least the second letter in a correspondence cycle, your response must be shaped by the letter it is answering. Let's look at the circumstances in which you might write a response letter and what the characteristics of your response should be.

The "Yes" Answer

When you can fill an order or send requested items routinely, it's fine to use a standardized acknowledgment that thanks readers for their orders and requests and indicates what's being sent to them. It can be enclosed with an invoice and shipped with the order, attached to the requested items, or it can be sent separately. Such acknowledgment forms are illustrated in the following examples:

THANK YOU FOR YOUR ORDER

The green sheet enclosed is an invoice showing the items shipped along with the date and method of shipment.

If the shipment is not correct, please return your order with your request for adjustment.

We appreciate your order. We hope you will let us be of service to you again in the future.

PERRY'S ELECTRONICS
1010 Hill Avenue
Cincinnati, OH 45223

It is a pleasure to send you the enclosed material in response to your recent request.

TRS Homes, Inc.
400 West Aldeah Street
Sharkeytown, IL 62001

Such standardized acknowledgments are a good way to respond to many routine orders and requests. Nobody will feel that his or her order or request has been handled indifferently; after all, the items are on their way. But it might appear brusque simply to send something without some accompanying message.

Of course, you must be able to determine when more than a standardized acknowledgment is required. If, for instance, you have information your readers want and you can give, you should take a different course of action—you should write a letter that explains amply what they want to know. Because you're providing the information the reader wants, your letter carries good news. Here's the way Mr. Bradley answered the letter on page 73 asking him about the way his firm recruits employees:

Dear Mr. Kenney:

Because our drivers operate $100,000 vehicles carrying highly flammable cargo and are our company's most visible representatives, we take great care in hiring them. A specific job description helps us greatly in judging whether an applicant will make a good driver. It also gives applicants a clear idea of what their job will be. If the applicant is hired, it also guides our supervisors in providing the new driver with adequate training.

We obtain as much pertinent information as we can about applicants. Our application form (which I have enclosed) and personal interview allow us to gain a fairly comprehensive picture of the applicant. Personal appearance, physical characteristics, ability to write routine reports, friendliness, education, and experience are the aspects we evaluate. A physical examination is important because of the strength and endurance required for loading and driving operations.

We have found that it costs about $2,500 to find and train a new driver. But we have also found that the money is well spent, for good drivers keep our operating costs down and our business up.

I'm sure you've conducted a thorough search of the subject in your library, but just in case you have overlooked a source, may I recommend that you look through The Fleet Owner, which frequently publishes information about hiring and training good truck drivers.

Sincerely,

R P Bradley

R. P. Bradley
Vice President of Personnel
Acme Trucking Company

Enclosure (1)

In this letter the writer has done a good job. He gives the information requested and indicates where the reader can get additional information. He doesn't restate the original request or acknowledge receipt of the original letter. The reader will remember his request; the response makes it obvious the request was received. Because the writer complies with the reader's request, the response is good news. Therefore, the writer doesn't delay giving the reader what he wants to know.

The "No" Answer

If you aren't able to provide readers with what they have asked for, your answer is essentially "no"—for your letter carries bad news. And bad news should be communicated indirectly so your readers can sense it before they see it. Such strategy helps them prepare for it. Actually, most bad news isn't all that shattering, but if there's any good news at all, it should come first. Let's see how the writer of the following letter handles a request she can't comply with:

Dear Ms. Matthews:

I have referred your letter to Ms. Jayne Miles, Director of Nursing Services at Appleby Memorial Hospital, because Appleby Memorial is the hospital in this area that specializes in long-range geriatric nursing.

You might also write to Dr. Priscilla Cox, University of Missouri School of Medicine, Columbia, Missouri 60521, who has done much research on the subject of hospital staff stereotypes of elderly patients. In addition, you might look into the series of annotated bibliographies published by the Gerontology Branch of the Public Health Service, Department of Health and Human Resources, Washington, D. C. 20201.

I wish I could provide you with the information you request, but our hospital does not receive many elderly patients. I'm sure that Ms. Miles and Dr. Cox will be most happy to respond to your requests.

Sincerely,

Patsy Dickson

Patsy Dickson
Assistant Director,
Nursing Services

The writer softens her "no" answer by explaining that she has passed the inquiry on to someone who might be able to help and by suggesting other likely sources. Then she explains why she can't comply with the request. Although the reader may have hoped for the information immediately, she should appreciate the efforts of the writer.

SUGGESTIONS FOR APPLYING YOUR KNOWLEDGE

Several situations call for writing inquiry, request, and order letters and writing responses to such letters. Here are some things you might try:

1. Select an advertisement that invites you to send away for a free catalog, brochure, booklet, or sample. Write the letter requesting the material. Include with your letter a photocopy of the advertisement so your instructor can better evaluate your letter.

2. Select an advertisement in a nationally circulated magazine and write a letter asking for more information about the product or service advertised. Include a photocopy of the advertisement so your instructor can better evaluate your letter.

3. If you are writing a research paper for one of your courses, supplement material you've found locally by writing to several companies for additional information. Get your instructor's opinion of your letters before you mail them.

4. Exchange inquiry and request letters you have written with other students and write responses to their letters. Include a photocopy of the letter you are answering so your instructor can better evaluate your letter.

5. Collect several order forms and write a brief report explaining what features they have in common and what special features they have that help customers prepare their orders. Include the order forms as appendixes to your report.

6. Working with the printed order form of a catalog or advertisement, make out an order. Then, disregarding the printed order form, write an order letter.

7. Collect a number of acknowledgment forms that serve as letters of transmittal for orders and requests that can be routinely filled. Write a brief report explaining what features they have in common and what special features they have that attempt to personalize the acknowledgment. Include the acknowledgment forms as appendixes to your report.

C H A P T E R

6

EMPLOYMENT LETTERS AND INTERVIEWS

Every step of seeking employment is highly competitive in matters both large and small. A letter from an ex-student to one of the authors illustrated this point rather painfully. He told us that in one instance he and his staff were choosing between two recent graduates who seemed equal in every professional way. The decision was finally made by taking the person who had prepared the neatest application. Seeking employment will thrust you into many such competitive communication situations, both written and oral. Your first contact with a potential employer may be by means of a letter of application and a resume of your education and experience. If your letter and resume succeed, you will probably be interviewed. You may also need to write requests for letters of recommendation and several follow-up letters, such as letters of acceptance and refusal. To help you successfully reach your goal of a job, we discuss all these communication situations in this chapter.

PREPARATION

Before the letter writing begins, you must prepare yourself. The first step should be to inventory your own interests, education, experience, and abilities. Many personnel directors recommend writing an autobiography—an account of the significant things in your life. What did you do in high school? What do you remember of your course work there? Which courses did you enjoy? Which courses could you barely tolerate? Where did you get your highest grades? Your lowest? Answer the same questions for your vocational or college education.

What were your extracurricular activities? Have you any long-standing hobbies such as photography or needlepoint? Have you been active in political, social, or religious groups? Do you enjoy athletics, singing, or dramatics?

What has been your work experience? What was your first job? Your last? What have been your duties and responsibilities? What sort of work have you really enjoyed? Have you been in the military? What training and jobs did you have there?

The autobiography, at least in its first draft, is for your own use. It can be roughly written as long as it is complete, and it should be as honest and private as you want it to be. However, some employers now ask for a brief autobiography as part of the application. You can draw on your rough autobiography for this, but now you must write as well as you can. The rewrite will be a public document; omit anything that is purely your private business.

The autobiography is a useful document for at least two reasons. First, it helps you get in touch with your own identity. Look at the things you have succeeded in and enjoyed. Which did you enjoy more, shop or English? Do you prefer math to social science or the other way around? Do you relate best to people or to things? Which would you rather do, read a book or go to a large, noisy party? Never mind which you think you *should* like. Which do you *really* like? Have you ever sold merchandise in a store? Did you enjoy it? Is money extremely important to you or not? Do you stick to jobs? Do you see new ways to get an old job done? Are you willing to take a chance on people or jobs? Do you find the most satisfaction in stability or change? Do you work well independently?

Be honest in your answers and analysis. It's your life. You would not want to spend it doing something you don't enjoy. And it's likely you'll be more successful at work you truly enjoy and have the capabilities for. The good sales representative might make a terrible horticulturist and vice versa.

A second use of the autobiography is to remind yourself of all the education and experience you have had that will make you attractive to a potential employer. While you're analyzing yourself, be alert for evidence of those qualities employers value: loyalty, willingness to shoulder responsibility, ability to stick to a task until it is done, initiative, enough sense of proportion to realize that things don't always go perfectly. You can use this information during job interviews, occasions when you are expected to be able to talk about your abilities and goals.

You'll be able to draw upon the autobiography for information used in writing letters of application and your resume and for filling in employers' application blanks—the written communication of the job hunt.

WRITTEN COMMUNICATION

Look for a moment at Figures 6–1 and 6–2. Figure 6–1 is a company application blank. Many employers will ask you to complete such a form before they consider hiring you. If you do have to complete such a form, print your answers as neatly as possible in ink. Better, type in your answers. Figure 6–1 is doubly useful, because from it you can learn what employers want to know about you. So study it with some care. Notice that for the most part it covers the same areas we have urged you to cover in your autobiography. Sometimes you must complete the application at the employer's office. So be sure to have all the needed information with you—from your Social Security number to specific details of education and experience.

Resume

Figure 6–2 is a sample resume (pronounced *rez-uh-may* and sometimes given its original French accent marks—résumé). Many formats are acceptable for resumes. We recommend a fairly simple one-page format as being most suitable for young people without extensive experience. If you need samples of longer forms, check your library's card catalog under *business correspondence* for books on the subject.

You can use the resume in combination with a letter of application to attract the attention of potential employers. You can mail them a copy of your resume and a personal letter of application or simply bring the resume to an interview that has been arranged in some other way.

Whatever form you choose for your resume, keep it as brief as is consistent with good coverage of your education and experience. Use phrases and dependent clauses rather than complete sentences. Don't give merely a static list of your courses and job titles. Rather, describe what you have actually learned, done, and accomplished in school and on the job. Both Figures 6–1 and 6–2 suggest the full range of possibilities for appropriate headings you can use. Don't crowd things on the page. Leave lots of white space. If you have to, don't be afraid to go to a second page. However, employers will be attracted more by a well-organized brief summary than they will be by a long, detailed discussion of everything you have ever done. They are busy people.

Have your resume professionally typed and then reproduced in as many copies as you anticipate needed. Use a process such as photocopying or lithography, neither of which is too expensive. Check the yellow pages of your telephone directory under *photocopying* or *printing* for shops that can do the work for you.

Letters of Application

The letter of application is your way of introducing yourself to an employer. When accompanied by your resume, it should present a picture

FMC

FMC Corporation An equal opportunity employer

Application for employment | salaried personnel

It is the policy of FMC Corporation to provide equal opportunity for all qualified persons and not to discriminate against any employee or applicant for employment because of race, creed, color, sex or national origin and to insure that employees are treated during employment without regard to their race, creed, color, sex or national origin. In any state whose laws prohibit discrimination on account of age, do not answer any question regarding your age.

Date

Return completed application to

NORTHERN ORDNANCE DIVISION
4800 Marshall Street Northeast
Minneapolis, Minnesota 55421

Telephone 560-9201
Area Code (612)

Identification

(print) First name	Middle name	Last name	Social security number

Local address Street and number	City	State	Zip	Telephone

Permanent address Street and number	City	State	Zip	Telephone

Name of person to be notified in case of emergency		Telephone

Address Street and number	City	State	Zip

Are you a U S citizen? If no, what type visa do you hold?
☐ Yes   ☐ No

U S military service

Branch of U S service	Date entered		Date discharged		Rank at discharge	Type of discharge
	Month	Year	Month	Year		

Nature of duties and any special training and honors received

Have you ever received a military disability pension?   If so, give nature of disability

Present draft, reserve or military status

References

If applying for professional or technical position, include at least one professional reference familiar with your work performance

Name (not a relative or employer)	Complete mailing address	Occupation

FIGURE 6–1   Application blank (Reprinted by permission of FMC Corporation)

Education and training

Education

Name of school	Location	Dates attended From	Dates attended To	Years credit	Year grad.	Degree	Course or major subject
High school							
Business or trade school							
College or university							
Graduate study							
Other							

Note: A copy of your college transcript should accompany this application if you graduated from college within last 5 years

High school and undergraduate record

	High school	College (undergraduate)
Scholastic standing (estimate if not known)	Average grade, standing in class, etc.	Average grade, gradepoint, standing, etc.
Scholastic honors		Significant courses in major subject if attended within last 5 years
Significant extracurricular activities if attended within last 5 years		
		Expenses earned (percent and how earned)

Graduate study

Field of graduate study	Scholarships, fellowships, assistantships, etc.	Name of major professor
Courses in specialized fields	Research problems	

Special training or qualifications

Languages spoken fluently	Languages read fluently	Factory or shop machines operated
Office machines operated		
Typing speed _____wpm	Shorthand speed _____wpm	

Describe any other special training or skills which are in any way related to the kind of work you want to do

FIGURE 6–1 **Application blank** *(cont.)*

Work experience If additional space is needed, attach separate sheets

Present or last employment

Name of present or last employer			Type of business		Address		
Starting date		Leaving date		Starting pay	Final pay	Reason for leaving	May we contact?
Month	Year	Month	Year				

Job title (present or last)	Name of supervisor	Supervisor's job title

Description of work and responsibilities

Previous employment

Name of next previous employer			Type of business		Address		
Starting date		Leaving date		Starting pay	Final pay	Reason for leaving	May we contact?
Month	Year	Month	Year				

Job title (last)	Name of supervisor	Supervisor's job title

Description of work and responsibilities

Name of next previous employer			Type of business		Address		
Starting date		Leaving date		Starting pay	Final pay	Reason for leaving	May we contact?
Month	Year	Month	Year				

Job title (last)	Name of supervisor	Supervisor's job title

Description of work and responsibilities

Additional experience

State what you did in any periods not already covered, including part time or self employment

Dates	

Unless otherwise indicated, state any prior work experience with FMC Corporation, its divisions or subsidiaries

FIGURE 6–1 Application blank *(cont.)*

Activities

Professional organizations, including offices (Omit union organizations and organizations which would indicate race, creed, color or national origin)	Hobbies and leisure interests

Publications

Title (include patents)	Journal reference or patent number

Work preferences

Kind of work most wanted

Other kinds of work in which interested

Location preferences or limitations	Approx. salary range expected	Date available to start work

Previous address

List home address in U.S for last 5 years

Dates	Street and number	City	State	Zip

Remarks

Have you ever been convicted of, or entered a plea of guilty to, a felony or misdemeanor other than parking or minor traffic violation?

☐ Yes   ☐ No   If yes, explain fully

List serious operations, accidents, illnesses, disabilities, and limitations (if none, so state)

Have you ever received workman's compensation for an industrial illness/injury?   ☐ Yes   ☐ No   If yes, explain

Signature

Are you aware of any reason why you might not be able to obtain a fiduciary bond or government security clearance, if required?
☐ Yes   ☐ No
It is understood and agreed that any misstatement made by me in this application will be sufficient cause for discharge from the company's service if I have been employed. It is also understood that this employment is subject to satisfactory physical examination by the company physician at the time of employment and thereafter at any time required by the company.

Date _____

Signature of applicant _____

FIGURE 6-1   Application blank *(cont.)*

RESUME OF MARK G. PATTERSON
956 Roberts Street
Rochester, New York 14622
Phone: (716) 554-6231

Education

1983-1985   FOREST PARK COLLEGE, ROCHESTER, NEW YORK

Candidate for Associate in Applied Science   **[Use clauses and**
degree in June 1985. Concentrating in   **phrases, not**
Electronic Technology with emphasis on   **complete**
reading schematic drawings and sketches,   **sentences]**
building and testing prototype circuits,
and modifying electronic apparatus. Have
FCC license: second-class radiotelephone.
Member of Drama Club. College expenses 100%
self-financed.

1975-1979   ALEXANDER HAMILTON HIGH SCHOOL, ROCHESTER,
NEW YORK

Graduated 1979 in upper 50% of class.
Played varsity soccer. Member of Drama Club
and Radio Club. Treasurer of senior class

Work
Experience

1983-1985   RADIO SHACK, ROCHESTER, NEW YORK

Work 20 hours a week as salesperson. Sell   **[Note reverse**
all types of radio and electronic   **chronologi-**
equipment, which involves explaining the   **cal order for**
equipment, showing people how to operate   **education and**
it, and demonstrating tuning and minor   **experience]**
repair procedures.

1975-1979   MISCELLANEOUS

Newspaper delivery boy, record announcer at
roller skating rink, request line operator
at radio station.

Military
Service

1979-1983   U.S. NAVY

After recruit camp and a 6-months
electronics course, assigned to seaplane
tender U.S.S. San Pablo. Duties included
repairing, testing, calibrating, and
maintaining electronic devices including
airborne radio and radar equipment. Highest
rank: Aviation Electronics Technician 2/c.

Personal
Background   Grew up in Rochester, New York. Have
traveled in Spain, Italy, and Greece.
Interests include singing, amateur
dramatics, ham radio operation, and cross-
country skiing.

References   Furnished upon request

                                    February 1985

FIGURE 6-2   Resume

that is complete enough so that prospective employers can decide whether or not they want to find out even more about you. Your desire, of course, is for the letter to result in an interview. In a very real sense, therefore, the letter of application is a selling letter.

Letters of application should be neat, correct, and well written. Type them, or have them typed, on good bond paper of about 20-lb. weight. You may be short of cash when you're job hunting, but letters and resumes are not the places to be cheap. They represent you, and they should represent you well. Ill-typed, fuzzy letters littered with blotches or misspelled words will lower your credibility.

Read the letter in Figure 6–3. Notice that the salutation uses a name and not "Dear Sir." If necessary, you can get such names through phone calls and letters of inquiry. The introduction of this letter straight-forwardly tells the employer how the writer learned about the job. It names the job and makes it clear that the writer seeks it. Avoid tricky openers. One of us recently received a letter that began, "If you don't want to hire a well-educated, fine, industrious instructor, stop right here." Unfortunately for the writer, his reader took him at his word and stopped. Courtesy, tact, and solid information will take you further than trickery.

In the middle of the letter in Figure 6–3, the writer does several things. First, he makes it clear that he knows something about the company, thus letting the personnel director know that he has been doing his homework. Where can you get such information? For large companies and government agencies your best source is the *College Placement Annual,* a directory of employers that also includes the names of personnel directors and good advice on how to conduct a job hunt. Other sources are *Standard Statistics, Reference Book of Manufacturers,* and *Standard Corporation Reports.* You may want to write a letter of inquiry asking for company brochures and other promotional literature. Often your school placement office will have information. Don't overlook newspaper ads. For federal jobs, see the *Federal Career Directory.* Check with your state employment office or personnel department about state employment. Your librarian can help you find many other sources. Finding such information should be part of your preparation for the job hunt. Having it shows your professionalism.

In the late-middle part of the illustrated letter, the writer digs into his autobiography and comes up with facts that should interest the employer. Normally, these will concern past work and educational experience. But don't overlook the value of referring to extracurricular activities if they tie in to the job you seek. This portion of the letter may repeat information that is also in the resume, but try to include additional information as well. Knowing something about the employer helps you choose appropriate facts. Stick to the facts. Don't express opinions about yourself. Let employers form their own opinions. If you have the right facts and choose them well, the opinions will be favorable.

956 Roberts Street
Rochester, NY 14622
24 March 1985

Ms. Joan B. Mills
Employment Manager
Warren Radio Company
252 Foss Avenue
Bedford, MA 01730

Dear Ms. Mills:

The placement director at Forest Park College has drawn
my attention to your need for an FCC licensed
Communication Technician. I have a second-class
radiotelephone license and will be available for work
in June of this year.

**[Identify position
sought and the
way you heard of
it]**

I have had considerable theoretical training and
practical experience in your company's field of
designing, manufacturing, and selling electronic
instruments and testing and measuring systems. As a
Navy Aviation Electronics Technician 2/c, I had over
three years of practical experience doing first- and
second-echelon maintenance of radio and radar equipment.
My experience includes working with most of the
sophisticated electronic testing equipment that the Navy
furnishes its electronic maintenance units.

**[Show knowledge
of employer and
give details of
education and
experience]**

At Forest Park, I have majored in Electronic Technology.
with courses in electronic circuit theory, tests and
measurement, and microwaves.

Please see my enclosed resume that gives the details of
my education and experience.

[Refer to resume]

May I drive over to Bedford to talk with you? I can
arrange my schedule to be available for an interview on
any weekday afternoon.

**[Request
interview]**

Sincerely,

Mark G. Patterson

Mark G. Patterson

Enclosure: Resume

FIGURE 6-3   Letter of application

In the closing part of the letter, the writer refers the reader to his resume for additional information. Finally, he attempts to set up an interview—almost always the object of a letter of application. Make the interview as easy and convenient for the employer as possible.

Never send out duplicated letters of application. You may have one standard letter that you modify only slightly from employer to employer, but each letter must be freshly typed.

If you have access to a word processor for your letters you may be in luck. The word processor makes it easy to have one basic letter that you can vary in its particulars to suit employers' needs. However, a word of caution is in order here. Do not, *under any circumstances,* send out letters of application (or resumes) printed on a dot matrix printer. Dot matrix print is grainy and badly textured. The print seldom resembles any of the standard typewriter styles. The poor print quality and peculiar print style will make it obvious to the reader that the letter has been computerized. Use a word processor only in combination with a letter-quality printer. If you don't have access to such, stick to the typewriter.

Other Letters

Several other letters are either necessary or desirable during the job hunt: requests for recommendation, interview follow-up letters, acknowledgments, job offers, status inquiries, job refusals, and job acceptances. The sample letters in Figures 6–4 to 6–9 illustrate how to proceed in each of these matters. Only a few additional points are necessary here.

Always be as courteous as possible in business correspondence and especially in employment letters. Don't overlook the value of the letter following up an interview, even if all you do is thank the interviewers for their time and courtesy. The letter will be appreciated, and your name will become that much more familiar to the employer. Other excellent letters to write express appreciation to people who have provided references for you or helped in other ways. (See pages 103–105.) Such people deserve your thanks, and they'll be more inclined to help you another time if their first experience with you has been a pleasant one.

INTERVIEWS

If your letters of application succeed, the next stage of the job hunt is usually the interview. Interviews frighten a great many job hunters, probably more than they should. Interviewers really aren't out to trap people. Their job is to evaluate people, to find people that their employers need, and also to help people find out what they are best suited for. Experienced interviewers know how to assess your qualities. They ask questions to determine if you are a responsible person. They

956 Roberts Street
Rochester, NY 14622
20 February 1985

Lieutenant David L. Gomez
Box 4822
Headquarters USNE
FPO New York 09555

Dear Lieutenant Gomez:

During 1981 and 1982, I worked as an electronics   **[Recall the**
technician in your maintenance unit aboard the U.S.S.   **association]**
San Pablo. I remember the assignment as a happy one and
know that I learned a good deal about electronics in
those two years.

In June of this year, I'll graduate from Forest Park   **[Explain need for**
College with an A.A.S. degree in Electronic Technology.   **recommendation**
I'll be seeking employment soon. Would you be kind   **and request it]**
enough to allow me to give your name as a reference?

I intend to start sending out my resumes on 15 March and   **[Set a date and**
hope that I'll hear from you before that time. I enclose   **send a resume]**
a copy of my resume to bring you up to date on my
activities.

Thank you for all your past kindnesses to me.

Best regards,

Mark G. Patterson

Mark G. Patterson

Enclosure: Resume

FIGURE 6–4   Request for recommendation

956 Roberts Street
Rochester, NY 14622
16 April 1985

Ms. Joan B. Mills
Employment Manager
Warren Radio Company
252 Foss Avenue
Bedford, MA 01730

Dear Ms. Mills:

Thank you for the opportunity to interview with your
company. I particularly enjoyed the chance to tour your
Bedford plant and to talk to your chief technical
representative, Mr. Brunson.

[Thank for interview]

Mr. Brunson's suggestion that I might qualify for a job
as a field technical representative of Warren Radio
surprised me. I had thought I was interviewing for a job
in your plant. I didn't realize the importance of my
sales and instructional work with Radio Shack.

[Give or request additional information]

After thinking over whether or not I would like to
travel regularly, I have decided that I would like such
an opportunity. Therefore, please tell Mr. Brunson that
I am definitely interested.

Sincerely,

Mark G. Patterson

Mark G. Patterson

FIGURE 6–5   Interview follow-up

956 Roberts Street
Rochester, NY 14622
20 April 1985

Mr. Robert B. Small
Employment Manager
Power Electronics
5643 Parker Avenue
Rochester, NY 14608

Dear Mr. Small:

Thank you for offering me a position as communication
technician with Power Electronics.

[Acknowledge offer]

I am considering several other possibilities as well. I
will, however, decide by 5 May and send you a definite
answer at that time.

[Give reason for delay and request or give a deadline]

Thank you for your consideration.

Sincerely,

Mark G. Patterson

Mark G. Patterson

FIGURE 6–6 Acknowledgment of job offer

956 Roberts Street
Rochester, NY 14622
27 April 1985

Ms. Joan B. Mills
Employment Manager
Warren Radio Company
252 Foss Avenue
Bedford, MA 01730

Dear Ms. Mills:

I enjoyed my pleasant interview with you and Mr. Brunson   **[Recall the**
on 13 April. At that time you indicated that I would   **association]**
have some word about my employment with you in a week
or two.

At the present time I have been offered another   **[State reason for**
position, and the company expects an answer from me   **need]**
by 5 May.

I am still nevertheless interested in the position you   **[Request**
outlined for me. Would it be possible for you to give me   **information]**
a definite answer before 5 May? I will appreciate your
help in this matter.

Sincerely,

Mark G. Patterson

Mark G. Patterson

FIGURE 6–7   Status inquiry

956 Roberts Street
Rochester, NY 14622
5 May 1985

Mr. Robert B. Small
Employment Manager
Power Electronics
5643 Parker Avenue
Rochester, NY 14608

Dear Mr. Small:

Thank you for your offer of a position with Power   **[Acknowledge and**
Electronics. However, I have decided to accept another   **decline offer]**
offer.

Thank you very much for your time and patience with me.   **[State your**
I enjoyed talking to you and the other employees at   **appreciation]**
Power, particularly Mr. Walker.

Sincerely,

Mark G. Patterson

Mark G. Patterson

FIGURE 6–8   Job refusal

956 Roberts Street
Rochester, NY 14622
5 May 1985

Ms. Joan B. Mills
Employment Manager
Warren Radio Company
252 Foss Avenue
Bedford, MA 01730

Dear Ms. Mills:

I was happy to hear that Warren Radio wants me as a tech rep for the company. I see it as a splendid opportunity and accept your offer.

[Acknowledge and accept offer]

I will be in Bedford as requested by 20 June to start my six weeks of training.

[Confirm reporting date]

Thank you again.

Sincerely,

Mark G. Patterson

Mark G. Patterson

FIGURE 6–9   Job acceptance

want to see if you are friendly and good humored, someone who will work well with other people. They examine your vocational and professional skills. You will find most professionally trained interviewers helpful and friendly.

You have certain responsibilities for the interview as well. You have to prepare for the interview beforehand. Here again your autobiography is good preparation. Look through it and select those items from your background that demonstrate those characteristics employers value, such as loyalty and initiative. Also, look through your autobiography for jobs, education, and extracurricular activities that relate to the job sought. If you did your homework for the letter of application, you'll already know something about the employer. If you haven't, find out what you can before the interview.

How should you dress for the interview? Like it or not, first impressions are important. Studies show interviewers are more favorably inclined toward suitably dressed people. For men this means shined shoes, sport coat, slacks, shirt, and tie. For some positions, particularly office work, a suit is probably even better. It doesn't matter that you may wear informal clothes on the job sought. Dress well for the interview. For women, a dress or suit appropriate for business use is the best attire. Avoid extremes of all sorts: For men, hair too long and beard too bushy are extremes. Excessive makeup or perfume, many jangling bracelets, or flashy, dressy clothes are extremes for women.

Naturally, you should be well groomed. Dirty fingernails have lost as many jobs for people as low grades. Don't chew gum during the interview. Don't smoke even if invited to.

Now you're suitably dressed. You arrive at the place of the interview at least ten minutes early. You meet the interviewer and shake his or her hand firmly but comfortably—avoid bone crunchers or limp-as-a-fish shakes. You get the interviewer's name straight and sit down erectly but comfortably. How will the interview go from that point forward?

Interviews usually last about thirty minutes. After introductions are over, interviewers usually spend a few minutes setting you at ease. They do not want you to be tense. The best interviews are relaxed and friendly, even a bit casual. Neither party should dominate. After some casual talk, perhaps about sports or current events, the interviewer may then shift into telling you something about the employer. If so, listen closely and be prepared to come in at natural pauses with intelligent questions. But don't interrupt the interviewer when he or she is going full steam. If your question can demonstrate previous knowledge about the employer, so much the better.

Sometimes this talk about the employer comes later in the interview. In any event, questions and answers about you are the heart of the interview. Sometimes, even testing may be part of the interview. The questions may be deliberately rather vague to see if you can develop ideas on your own, or they may be quite specific and penetrating. Here are some samples:

- Why do you want to work for us?
- Tell me something about yourself.
- What sort of summer work have you had?
- What were your responsibilities?
- Why did you leave your last job?
- Do you enjoy sales (office), (experimental), (manual), (troubleshooting), (etc.) work? Why?
- Can you take criticism?
- Why have you chosen your vocation?
- What subjects did you enjoy most in school? Why?
- How have you paid for your education?
- What are your strong (weak) points?
- What do you want to be doing ten years from now?
- If you were rich enough not to have to work, how would you spend your life?

Be aware that various state and federal laws prohibit interviewers from asking you for information that is not job related or that could be discriminatory—for example, "Are you married?" or "Do you have children?" In general, all questions about race, color, creed, national origin, religion, sex, age, ethnic background, marital status, family relationships, and political beliefs are off-limits to interviewers. Neither do you have to provide such information on resumes or in letters of application.

Like athletic events, no two interviews are exactly alike. But certain situations and questions do repeat. Good answers prepared for the questions listed here would go a long way to get you ready for any interview. And you can practice. Get together with friends and interview each other. Learn how to talk about yourself and your accomplishments and how to articulate your desires. Learn how to be assertive about yourself, but stop short of being aggressive.

At some point in the interview the interviewer will discuss with you the job or jobs the employer has to offer. Here you should be able to display your professional knowledge about jobs for which you are suited. You should be fairly firm about your goals but flexible enough to discuss a related job if it looks good. But avoid the appearance of being willing to take any job at all.

When the interviewer discusses salary and job benefits, such as hospitalization insurance, pensions, and vacations, you are free to ask questions about these items. But don't ask about them until the interviewer brings them up.

You will rarely be offered a job at a first interview. Sometimes this may be done at a second interview. Normally, however, the job offer will come at some later time. Don't try to extend interviews. When the interviewer closes up your folder and indicates that the interview is over, for better or for worse it is. Stand up, shake hands once again, thank the interviewer, and leave.

What characteristics should you display to have a successful interview? According to many interviewers, the following rank high on the list:

- Be neat and well groomed.
- Be natural, friendly, and relaxed, but not sloppy or overly casual.
- Be more interested in the work involved on the job and in its potential than in salary and benefits.
- And these last may be most important: Have definite goals. Know your abilities and what you want to do. Be ready to articulate these goals.

SUGGESTIONS FOR APPLYING YOUR KNOWLEDGE

The employment situation, with its correspondence and interviews, is one place where your practice can approach or even be the real thing. The facts you have to work with are the real facts of your own life along with information you can gather about real employers you might want to work for.

Begin by writing a rough-draft autobiography of your life. Keep it as reference material for the other assignments you may write, such as letters of application and resumes.

With the help of your school placement officer make up a list of potential employers for people with your skills. Look up companies and organizations in places like the *College Placement Annual, Standard Statistics, Standard Corporation Reports,* and the *Federal Career Directory.* Most states have an agency that keeps track of employment opportunities for state citizens. Check the *Readers' Guide to Periodical Literature* for articles about large companies and agencies. Work up some letters of inquiry to potential employers asking for promotional literature and application blanks. And don't overlook friends who work in places where you might want to

work. They can tell you a good deal about working conditions, chances for advancement, company policies, needed skills, and so forth. In other words, you can obtain a good deal of information from many sources about employers. Gather as much as you can.

All the communications of the job-hunting situation are potential assignments: letters of application, autobiographies, resumes, interview follow-up letters, and so forth. All should be typed and thoroughly professional looking.

Go into the interviewing aspects of job hunting as well. For a start, divide the class into pairs. Have each person interview the other, developing the information about the interviewee mentioned in this chapter as being important—favorite courses, job experience, hobbies, and so forth. This interview relaxes people and gets them talking freely about themselves. A good follow-up to this interview is to have the interviewer write a letter of application for the interviewee. Some people have difficulty drawing attention to their own strong points but can do it easily for others.

Conduct mock interviews before the entire class. Students can even role-play in these interviews. One person can play an ill-prepared, unsuccessful interviewee, another a well-prepared, successful one. If your school has the proper equipment, videotape interviews for later study.

People who have participated in real interviews should tell the class about their experiences. Outside of class you can practice interviews with friends. Get so familiar with the process that you are totally at ease with it.

C H A P T E R

7

CUSTOMER
RELATIONS
LETTERS

Chapter 7 discusses basic strategies for building goodwill through persuasive writing that reflects the writer's honesty and sincerity and concern for readers. Every letter you write should build goodwill for you and your organization. Nowhere is goodwill more important than in the letters you write to customers. One way of viewing letters is as good-news and bad-news letters. Good-news letters—thank-you letters and adjustment letters that say "yes"—are automatic goodwill carriers. As such, they are fairly easy to write. However, bad-news letters—complaint letters, adjustment letters that say "no," and collection letters—are potential destroyers of goodwill. But the long-range goal of bad-news letters should be to build or reestablish goodwill.

The strategies we outline for good-news letters and bad-news letters are followed closely in all the letters discussed in this chapter.

GOOD-NEWS LETTERS AND BAD-NEWS LETTERS

Most letters, we're happy to say, are good-news letters, even those you would not ordinarily think of in this light. Every letter that moves business forward, even if it's only a routine notice that a shipment is on the way, is a good-news letter. Any letter that slows business—for example, a letter denying a request or postponing an expected shipment—is bad news.

Good News

When you get good news, what do you want first—the good news or the details behind it? If someone writes to say that you have landed a job you were after, the first thing you really want to know is "You have the job." You'll be delighted to read in the rest of the letter why you got the job and on what date you report to work. So point number one in a good-news letter is *announce the big news first:*

> We're delighted to tell you that we want you to come to work for us.

> Your bicycle is repaired and is ready for pickup.

> Congratulations on your promotion to head of merchandising.

And we really do mean that the big news should come first. Don't delay it with trivialities.

After the reader has been pleasantly moved by the big news, provide the details. Dates, prices, explanations, analyses—whatever is needed—become the second part of your letter.

For the third part of your letter, do something that salespeople call "reselling the customer." Recently, we bought an appliance to seal plastic bags air- and watertight. As the salesperson was wrapping our package, she said, "You are really going to be delighted by this. It's so easy to use. And the money you save by freezing leftovers in these bags will pay for the appliance in a couple of months." She had already made her sale. What she was doing was reselling the customer. She wanted us to go away happy, convinced that we hadn't thrown away our money on a useless gadget. You end your good-news letter in a similar manner:

> We know you'll be happy working for Julia Alm. She's a fine person.

> For your one-stop convenience, we carry a full line of bicycle supplies.

> You'll make a great supervisor.

The letter writers and the appliance salesperson have identical goals—*to achieve goodwill.* We have numerous short-term goals in our correspondence—to order, to request, to sell, to move to action. But our long-range goal must always be to create and maintain goodwill. The good-news strategy helps to do precisely that. So remember:

1. Report the good news first.
2. Supply the necessary details.
3. Resell the customer.

Bad News

A small number of letters bring bad news. Examples are the letter denying a request for an adjustment or the collection letter for an overdue bill.

For these letters a different strategy makes sense. Rather than announcing your big news first, delay it a bit and open with a buffer statement of some sort. Buffer statements should not be self-serving soft soap but genuine attempts to express regret or to seek common ground. If you write, "We share your concern for the problem you have raised," you should mean it.

After your buffer statement, provide details and analysis that support the bad news that is coming. After the analysis is complete, announce the bad news:

A complete refund of your money does not seem justified.

Then, you present an alternative if you possibly can:

We will be happy, however, to discuss a partial refund with you.

Finally, you close in a friendly way:

Thank you for drawing this problem to our attention.

You hope to persuade your reader that your bad news is unavoidable. At the same time you want to retain goodwill. Obviously, to do this your analysis has to be detailed and persuasive, and it must precede the bad news. So remember the order:

1. Buffer statement
2. Explanation and analysis
3. Bad news
4. Alternative
5. Friendly close

THANK-YOU LETTERS

Goodwill is a two-way street, especially with customers. A thank-you letter to loyal customers is an especially effective way to let them know how important they are to your organization and that you do not take their business for granted.

Since readers enjoy receiving thank-you letters, you should use the good-news strategy. Start the letter with an expression of your appreciation. Here, for example, is a letter of appreciation written to a person who has been a steady customer for 10 years. After thanking the reader for being a model customer, the writer mentions her specific virtues as a customer and makes the customer feel good about her purchasing record with the company.

Dear Mrs. Gertzman:

Rockford's has a policy of keeping track of loyal customers, and our records show that you have had a Rockford's account for ten years. Your loyalty deserves recognition.

Your credit has always remained good, with bills paid promptly, and more than once you have encouraged a friend to try Rockford's by showing enthusiasm over a particular product or service of ours. These are just two of the qualities we have appreciated in you over the years you have permitted us to serve you.

So thank you, Mrs. Gertzman, for being a reliable customer. Your business is important to us, and we are appreciative of your continued relationship with us. We look forward to the opportunity of serving you for another pleasant ten years.

Sincerely yours,

In addition to thanking customers, you may also want to show your appreciation to other people who have done something for you. Not every act of kindness and thoughtfulness requires a letter, of course. But when people have gone out of their way to do something special for you, you should write them a cordial letter of appreciation. It doesn't matter if you've already thanked them in person, you should still write a thank-you letter. Write the letter within a day or so after you realize their help or consideration.

The following is a letter written to R. P. Bradley, whose letter on pages 76–77 answered Jack Kenney's unsolicited request letter. Mr. Kenney just naturally felt like telling Mr. Bradley how grateful he was for the letter.

Dear Mr. Bradley:

Thank you for explaining your company's procedures in hiring new employees. It was kind of you to get the information to me so soon.

You gave me new insight into the importance of selecting employees. I had no idea how carefully new drivers had to be considered. Your information helps make a big point about careful recruiting.

And thanks for the lead on The Fleet Owner. Our library doesn't subscribe to it, but a trucking firm in my home town receives it, and I've been able to read the last few issues.

You'll be receiving a copy of my report in about two weeks.

Thanks again,

Jack Kenney
Jack Kenney

Notice how Mr. Kenney develops the letter briefly to point out exactly what was helpful. This kind of specific detail is effective in two ways. First, it prevents the thank-you letter from being an extremely short—almost embarrassingly brief—one-line thank you. Second, it provides "feedback" to Mr. Bradley that Mr. Kenney understands the significance of what he received.

Congratulatory letters that you receive are also occasions for thank-you letters. After all, when people have been thoughtful enough to write and congratulate you, you owe them a note of thanks in acknowledgment.

> Dear Frank,
>
> Thanks much for your good wishes. I know now what you meant last year when you told our management association that managers "manage" information as much as they do people.
>
> I'm planning to attend the Western Management Association Convention in Springfield March 5 and 6. How about lunch on me at The Purple Mousetrap?
>
> Cordially,

And, of course, those who provided references for you or were in some way helpful in your successful application for a job should also receive your written appreciations.

COMPLAINT LETTERS

> The best-laid plans of mice and men . . . .

How often have you heard this modern rephrasing of the famous line from Robert Burns's "To a Mouse"? Occasionally things don't go the way they are supposed to: the shipment of new fall shirts contains several sewing flaws . . . all those new terminals for which you paid $600 apiece are going on the blink more and more frequently . . . 2,500 sheets of letterhead stationery come with a misprint in the address. When such things happen, we tend to be disappointed at best—irritated, perhaps even extremely angry, at worst.

But it does little good to moan about the inconvenience we've suffered or to allow our blood pressure to rise. What we must do is register our complaint with those we feel can straighten the matter out.

Once you remind yourself that a letter of complaint—like all letters you write—should present facts clearly, completely, concisely, and courteously, you are well on your way to being able to write a successful one. The more objective and businesslike your complaint is, the easier it is for your reader to answer. No matter how irritated you are, don't be sarcastic or make idle threats.

The best way to get results with your complaint letter is to try to put yourself in the position of the person who must read your letter. She or he will be helped if you do the following:

- Identify the transaction, with references to contracts, invoices, dates, account numbers, and so on. Provide photocopies of relevant material.
- Describe fully any product or service you mention, especially the model or serial number or access code.

- Explain clearly and simply what is wrong.
- Explain what you want the reader to do to satisfy you, and explain why you believe your complaint is justified.
- Give your name and address, and a telephone number where you can be reached during the day.

These features are shown in Figure 7–1, which is a letter written by the architect of a building project to the general contractor. The letter is brief and the situation is clearly stated: four points, four paragraphs. The opening paragraph refers to the pertinent project and the involved parties. The second paragraph explains clearly what is wrong. Serial numbers of the ovens are given so there will be no misunderstanding about which ovens are malfunctioning. The third paragraph explains what two actions will satisfy the writer. The fourth paragraph tells where the writer can be reached during business hours. Reviewing the problem, providing relevant information (perhaps even documentation), and requesting specific action give the reader the information needed to judge the validity of the complaint.

ADJUSTMENT LETTERS

Some of the worst letters we have ever seen were adjustment letters—those written in answer to complaint letters. When they are bad, they are really bad—with ready-made phrases that might apply to almost any situation, but work well for none . . . with decisions based on vague, unexplained "policy" . . . with buck-passing and red-tape entanglements . . . with countercharges that the complaint is unreasonable. Bad adjustment letters lose customers forever. It's as simple as that.

So what do you do when you're faced with a complaint about some work or merchandise that you or your company has provided? Here are some guidelines.

1. *Take every complaint seriously.* Regardless of whether or not you can allow the adjustments the complainants want, you must make them feel their complaints are important to you. This means you do four things: (1) handle complaints quickly, (2) have as liberal an adjustment policy as sound business practices will allow, (3) shape your response to match the specific complaint, and (4) state exactly what you intend to do about the complaint.

When people make complaints, they feel they are justified in doing so. You must study the situation carefully, make your decision with "all deliberate speed," and work toward maintaining goodwill regardless of your decision.

Many large companies try to give customers what they want. James Cash Penney, that enterprising businessman with the prophetic name, built a national chain of department stores on one simple rule—"The customer is always right." We're not suggesting that you give in to obviously unreasonable complaints, because there will be times when you have to say no.

Offutt's Architectural Services

100 Walnut Street
Derby, CT 06418

September 22, 1985

Haldeman Mechanical Contracting
9 McCabe Avenue
Orange, CT 06477

Dear Mr. Roberts:

Three convection ovens furnished by Cookcraft Metals Company for the McKenzie Cafeteria project are not giving satisfactory service. The ovens were installed July 19, and it has been necessary for the supplier to make a number of service calls in the two months that the ovens have been in operation.

Two of the ovens (#5336190 and #5336187) do not heat properly, apparently because of malfunctioning thermostats. The other oven (#5336188) is not operating as of this date. It appears to have been used at some time before this installation.

Would you please have your subcontractor either replace these ovens or take some measure to ensure that the cause for underheating is eliminated. And would you please investigate whether oven number 5336188 has been used before this installation.

I can be reached at 842-7600 from 8 to noon and 2 to 6 Monday through Friday.

Sincerely,

Christopher J. Offutt

Christopher J. Offutt, FAIA

CJO/bu

cc: Cookcraft Metals Company

FIGURE 7-1 Complaint letter

When people make a complaint, they expect some specific word that tells them that *their* complaint has been read and investigated and that the decision has been based on the merits of their specific circumstances. Therefore, address the letter to the complainant and be specific. If the complaint is about seat cushions your company installed in a theater or about several warped doors you shipped to a retailer, mention the seat cushions or the warped doors. Form letters are out.

2. *When you can grant full adjustment, do so—and announce it early in your letter.* When circumstances call for full adjustment, grant it and explain why the mistake occurred. Granting full adjustment is good news to the reader, so begin your letter by explaining what adjustment you're making. After all, it's the most important news you can give. And do it cordially. A gruff adjustment letter might as well be a negative reply, for the reader will feel the begrudging tone.

Follow up your opening paragraph by a second one that explains what caused the foul-up and what you intend to do to reduce the chances that it will happen again. Your explanation will lengthen your letter, but it is length well invested. Your readers will feel that you really care about the mistake and that you looked into the matter to see what happened and why.

An experience one of us had a few years ago will illustrate the difference a cordial adjustment letter can make. The difficulty was over the payment of our subscription to a magazine. We had paid the bill for a three-year subscription by check, but we kept receiving collection letters. After the second collection letter, we sent the company a brief note explaining that we had paid our bill and enclosed a copy of the canceled check. For the next three months we continued to get requests for payment. Finally, after we received the *seventh* monthly plea for payment, a rather nasty note, we were mad. We wrote a moderately restrained letter to the manager of the company's customer service department explaining the situation to him, again enclosing a copy of our canceled check. Here's the letter we received:

> We are sorry to learn of the problem you've had with your subscription.
>
> We're happy to inform you that we have taken action to stop the bills which were sent after your payment was received. It may be that one more bill which we were unable to prevent will reach you; please disregard it.
>
> We hope you will enjoy the coming issues of the magazine.
>
> Cordially,
>
> *Henry Dysart*
>
> Henry Dysart
> Manager Customer Service

HD/pl
cc: Ms. Jean Binkley
    Mr. Chris Harrell

We were relieved that we at least got the billing stopped. But other than that, we weren't very satisfied. After all, the company had threatened to sue us over the alleged nonpayment. Their response that they were "sorry to learn of the problem" didn't put us in much of a mood to "enjoy the coming issues of the magazine."

A letter that arrived three days later made us a lot happier:

> You are right. You paid your subscription bill exactly when you said you did. We are wrong and we apologize.
>
> Please let me explain what happened. The reason that a bill was sent repeatedly to you is that the payment got caught in the new data processing machine recently installed to give customers faster and more accurate service, and it kept getting marked unpaid. Yours was one of several payments recycled this way. We now have the system straightened out, and you should not be receiving any more bills.
>
> At least no bill until three years from now, when your three-year subscription is up. We want you to have the past seven monthly issues at no cost to you. I hope this will help compensate for the trouble we've caused you.
>
> Sincerely,
>
> *Jean Binkley*
>
> Jean Binkley
> Vice President of Sales
>
> JB/fr
> cc: Mr. Henry Dysart
>   Mr. Chris Harrell

What do you think of that? Can you figure out why we received that second letter? Look at the signatures of the two letters and the names in the distribution lists. Jean Binkley was undoubtedly Henry Dysart's boss, and she didn't like the answer Mr. Dysart gave us. Notice how she disarmed us by admitting the mistake and apologizing for it. It's difficult not to forgive in a situation like that. The second paragraph was especially welcome in that we now knew what had caused the problem and what the company was doing to prevent its happening again. And check that sweetener at the end. It melted us. Talk about reestablishing goodwill! We still subscribe.

Such concern can earn you a special place in the heart of complaining customers who are right.

3. *When you must refuse adjustment, prepare the reader for the bad news and work toward reestablishing goodwill.* When circumstances do not allow an adjustment to be granted, your letter carries bad news. You need to buffer the negative decision by at least a sentence or two and to end by attempting to reestablish goodwill.

Never open with the bad news. Such a beginning is like a slap in the face. Delay your negative decision at least to the second paragraph to give your reader a chance to sense the refusal before actually seeing it in writing. But don't put the refusal at the very end of the letter, where there's no room left to work toward reestablishing goodwill.

The opening buffer is important. Try to begin by making a statement your reader can agree with. This establishes a common ground from which you can move into your refusal.

After the opening buffer, give your analysis of the facts to indicate why you cannot grant the adjustment; then state your refusal. Give your answer so the reader cannot misunderstand your decision or the reasoning behind it.

After your refusal, try to reestablish goodwill by offering to help the reader solve the problem. This ending will swing your letter away from the psychological low point of the refusal and tell the reader you're anxious to help in some other way.

The following letter shows how to explain a refusal:

Dear Mrs. Rhodes:

Our service representative has examined your dryer and discovered that the motor was clogged with lint, which caused it to overheat and cut off. The cutoff is a protective feature of your dryer to keep the motor from burning out.

However, he also found that the motor has been overheated so much that it is damaged to the point that it should be replaced. In his investigation he discovered that the lint filter was so clogged with lint that it was not functioning properly. Instead of being trapped in the filter, the lint packed into the motor, causing it to overheat. He also reported that on a previous service call to your home he had found the lint filter full. At that time he showed you the instruction in your operating manual where it says to clean the filter after each drying load to prevent lint from getting into the motor.

Since the replacement guarantee for the motor includes only defects by the manufacturer and improper installation by us, we feel that in this circumstance we cannot replace the motor free, as you request.

However, we are anxious to help you get your dryer working again. Should you want our service representative to install a new motor, please let us know. Because the installation would be a continuation service call, your cost would be only $125 for the motor and $20 for the installation, instead of the normal installation fee of $95.

Sincerely,

Willoughby Johnson

Willoughby Johnson
Service Manager

4. *When you grant partial adjustment, prepare the reader for the mixed good news and bad news and work toward reestablishing goodwill.* A liberal adjustment policy sometimes allows you to make a goodwill gesture of partial adjustment rather than a flat refusal. Because you are not granting full adjustment, your letter carries bad news. It is thus a variation of the basic refusal letter. You must review the situation that caused the complaint so your reader understands why you cannot grant full adjustment and, at the same time, is satisfied with the partial adjustment.

Granting partial adjustment is a lot like walking a tightrope. If you sound the least bit unsure about your reasons for not granting full adjustment, or if you sound unduly charitable, you may fail to achieve the goodwill your partial adjustment intends. You have to know your reader. Explaining that you're allowing partial adjustment to a "preferred customer" satisfies some and irritates others. If preferred-customer status is the main grounds for partial adjustment, it's probably best not to say so. The reader knows this and would probably not like to be reminded that it is the preferred-customer status rather than the legitimacy of the complaint that has caused the settlement.

So the partial adjustment letter can be tricky to write. Let's go back to the previous letter, in which Willoughby Johnson had to refuse Mrs. Rhodes' request to replace her dryer motor free. Assume that because of the family's long and steady patronage, Mr. Johnson believes that a goodwill partial adjustment is in order. How might he write the letter?

The letter would probably be much the same as the refusal letter until the third paragraph, where the decision is announced. After the second paragraph the letter might go like this:

> Since the motor damage was caused by excessive lint, not by a manufacturing defect or improper installation, we feel that we cannot replace the motor under the terms of the replacement guarantee.
>
> However, we can install a new motor at less than retail price. You may have a new motor for the wholesale price of $85. And since we would also consider the installation a continuation service call, you would pay only the wholesale price and $20 for installation. Under normal pricing, the cost would be $170.
>
> If you would drop us a card or call us within the next few days, we can send our service representative within 24 hours to replace the motor.
>
> Sincerely,
>
> *Willoughby Johnson*
>
> Willoughby Johnson
> Service Manager

COLLECTION LETTERS

Writing collection letters is an unpleasant but necessary task. Fortunately, of the many customers to whom credit is extended, perhaps less than 10 percent ever need reminding of their indebtedness. But for those few who do not pay promptly, you should design a series of letters that ask for payment with increasing insistence. Once the bill is overdue, probably four letters will do: an initial friendly reminder; a second friendly reminder; a tactful, insistent reminder; and a final demand. These letters can be spaced about three or four weeks apart.

The first letter should be regarded as a standardized (but friendly) reminder of debt. A "please remember us" note will do. Simply state the debt, tactfully remind the customer, and ask for payment:

> Have you forgotten something?
>
> On February 8 you bought a 36-inch Carthage Cooktop Unit for $375.50. Perhaps you've overlooked this bill, so we'd like to bring it to your attention.
>
> Will you please help us clear the charge?

If your reminder is ignored, send a second letter that tactfully, but clearly, asks for the money. Here are the ideas you wish to convey in whatever letters are necessary after the initial reminder:

- that you want your money;
- that you want it as quickly as possible;
- that you're willing to listen to extenuating circumstances, but you need to know what they are;
- that you wish to accomplish this with as little hassle as possible to yourself and your customer;
- that you expect to be paid;
- that it is in the reader's interest to pay the bill.

Setting up this series of expectations is important.

In your second letter be polite, assume your readers intend to pay, and give them a chance to explain their predicament if they can't pay immediately—maybe even offer a partial payment plan. But in this second letter be more forceful:

> We have a problem.
>
> Your charge of $375.50 for a 36-inch Carthage Cooktop Unit on February 8 has not been paid.
>
> If there is some reason why you are unable to pay the bill, won't you come in and talk it over with us?
>
> If not, please send us your check so we can clear our books and bring your account up to date.

This second letter reminds readers once again of the amount and date of their debt. The invitation to discuss the nonpayment is of utmost importance. Readers may have some temporary problem that prevents their meeting the bill, they may be dissatisfied with their purchase, or they may be waiting for a correction to be made in what they believe is an erroneous billing. Perhaps they have not received the merchandise if it's something you shipped them. Of course, they should have told you why they are not paying but for some reason have not done so. This second letter is a good time to ask them about it. Assure your readers that you are reasonable and willing to cooperate if they will only tell you what the problem is. Like the first reminder, the second one closes by stating the action you want your readers to take.

Persistence is important. If your second reminder is also ignored, send a third letter that is still polite and tactful but that shows readers the seriousness of their failure to pay. This third letter can express surprise that they haven't paid you or contacted you:

> Because you have paid your bills promptly in the past, we are surprised that you have not paid your February 8 charge of $375.50 for the 36-inch Carthage Cooktop Unit.
>
> The bill is now more than three months overdue.
>
> Good credit is an asset that is very important to you. Good customers are a very important asset to us, too, and we would like very much to have you continue doing business with us.
>
> So won't you please send us a check at once?

If your third reminder is also ignored, send a last letter that is still polite and tactful but that shows readers the urgent need to settle the claim. Don't worry about being too forceful. The only conciliatory note is to ask once again for payment to avoid possible legal action by you. But don't rant and rave. It will do no good:

> Your bill of $375.50 due us for purchase of a 36-inch Carthage Cooking Unit on February 8 is now more than four months overdue.
>
> Since you have not responded to our three earlier notices to settle your account and to our invitation to explain to us your reason for not paying the bill, we must assume that you do not intend to pay it.
>
> Therefore, if we do not hear from you by June 15, we will turn this claim over to our attorney.
>
> Won't you act now and save yourself the additional expense and annoyance of a lawyer's fee and court costs?

A word of caution is necessary, though, about writing letters that threaten legal suit. Customers have a legal right not to be plagued for bills they don't owe. If your billing is inaccurate, whether caused by machine or human error, they can take legal action against you. Although no federal law specifically covers this kind of action, some states do have such laws. Besides, persons who feel they are being harassed for an unowed bill can legally charge you with harassment. So make sure that the debt you're attempting to collect really exists.

SUGGESTIONS FOR APPLYING YOUR KNOWLEDGE

1. Write a thank-you letter to someone who has done something helpful for you.

2. Write a complaint letter that would be appropriate for one of the following situations: receipt of damaged merchandise, receipt of wrong merchandise, receipt of merchandise or service of unsatisfactory quality, or receipt of incorrect billing.

3. Exchange the complaint letters you have written with your fellow students and write three different adjustment letters in response: one that grants full adjustment, one that refuses adjustment, and one that grants partial adjustment. Include a photocopy of the letter you are responding to so your instructor can better evaluate your letters.

4. Collect several examples of collection letters and write a brief report explaining what phrases and approaches they have in common. Make note of any that attempt a humorous or casual approach to the collection and analyze their effectiveness or lack of effectiveness. Include the sample letters as appendixes to your report.

5. Study a series of collection letters and write a report explaining under what circumstances each letter is to be mailed and what approaches each letter takes. Include the sample letters as appendixes to your report.

6. Assume someone owes you $500 and the debt is overdue. Write a series of four collection letters designed to be mailed out at 30-day intervals.

C H A P T E R

8

When you think of sales letters, you perhaps think in terms of selling people merchandise. They are used for that, naturally. But there are many other things to sell besides material goods. You may be selling ideas or services or asking for political or charitable contributions. You may be selling yourself. The letter of application for a job is a specialized form of sales letter. (See pages 182–190.) The proposal, which we take up in Chapter 17, sells someone on your organization's or your capability to do a task. Sales letters can be used to keep you in touch with customers. In November, regular customers of a department store may receive a letter like this one:

> The holidays aren't too far away, and we'd like to help you select some gifts for your family. Right now our selections are at their peak. You'll see a great variety of things in almost every price range you desire.
> Please come by. It will be good to see you again.

Gentle and understated, this letter reminds the reader that the holidays are coming. It does not sell anything directly, but it is likely to draw the reader into the store in the future.

You receive many such sales messages in the mail, perhaps almost daily. You see ads in newspapers and magazines day after day. Some you read thoroughly; some you start to read and stop; others you ignore comletely. In part your attention is attracted by those letters and ads that speak to your particular interests—tools, cars, computers, education, travel, clothes, whatever. In part your attention is attracted and held by the power of the message. And behind the power is the skill of the writer.

In this chapter we let you in on a few secrets of the direct-mail writer's trade—the art of writing persuasive sales letters.

Basically, the writers of sales letters apply the persuasive strategies we describe for you in Chapter 2: credibility, emotional appeal, facts and analysis. In addition, the writers of sales letters use a specific organizational plan known as AIDA, an acronym for *attention, interest, desire, action*. That is, they get the reader's attention, they awaken interest and desire in the reader, and they ask for action. Here's how you can do the same thing.

ATTENTION

Remember that your letter is uninvited. Most people will open your letter and at least glance at it. But your opening sentence has to give them a good reason to continue reading. If not, they're likely to throw your letter away immediately.

What reasons do people have to continue reading? Most ad and direct-mail writers recognize at least three—promoting self-interest, gaining new information, and satisfying curiosity. To put it another way, there must be some reward for readers if they are to continue reading.

Self-Interest

Self-interest is perhaps the strongest of the three appeals. People respond strongly to openings that promise them such things as health, comfort, leisure, popularity, good looks, status, money, education, love, social success, admiration, or sensory pleasure. People respond to appeals that promise them ways to avoid work, worry, discomfort, and embarrassment.

Ads are quite instructive in how to begin a sales letter. The headline in an ad and the opening sentence of a letter serve the same attention-getting purpose. One of the most successful ads in history began with the question "Do you make these mistakes in English?" This is primarily a self-interest opening, although it also arouses curiosity. The appeal to the readers is the avoidance of embarrassment through the avoidance of mistakes in English. The readers are promised a reward. By reading on, they will learn about some *specific* mistakes. The key word in promising such a reward is *these*. The headline would not be nearly as powerful if phrased, "Do you make mistakes in English?" No specific information or reward is implied in this statement. The reader, not given a clear reason to continue, is likely to stop.

Another successful opener has been "To people who want to write—but can't get started." Here the appeal is to a selected audience. A specific, common writing problem—getting started—is pinpointed. A way of solving the problem is implied. Readers who are interested in writing but who don't know how to begin are hooked.

New Information

In other openers the reward is new information: "Now, General Electric refrigerators have a roll-out freezer." Other examples:

- Announcing a new broiler-toaster.
- New from NRI! 25″ color TV that tunes by computer, programs an entire evening's entertainment.
- Now you can shift to 4WD without shifting.

The appeal in such openers is similar to that of a newspaper head-line. It gives readers a little piece of the story and whets their appetites for more.

Curiosity

Openers that arouse curiosity are the third most used, and often curiosity is wedded to self-interest. The classic "Do you make these mistakes in English?" combines both curiosity and self-interest, as does the following:

- Do you really need an operation?
- What are your chances of survival?
- What are the alternatives, if any?

Key Words and Questions

Certain key words show up in openers again and again—words such as *how, who, what, when, which, where,* and *why. Announcing, new,* and *now* are common. When you're stuck for an opener, write one of these words and see what you can build onto it to hook your reader's interest in your subject.

Questions are another frequently used approach. An ad for a weight-reducing diet drink asked, "Is this the day you do something about your weight?" Millions of Americans are slightly overweight. This opener appeals to most of them. It assumes that they want to do something about their weight—they just need a little push in the right direction.

Be as specific as you can in your questions. Which of these openers would be the best for a Navy recruiting message?

- Do you want a job in the Navy?
- Which of these 45 jobs do you want?

Right: the second, much more specific question is the best, and, in fact, it was the opener used.

GAINING INTEREST AND DESIRE

How do you keep people reading after you have gained their attention? How do you build a desire in them for what you are selling? First of all, you must get your readers into the picture. If your opener doesn't do it, you must do it immediately thereafter. If you don't, you'll lose your readers to a so-what attitude.

Place your readers in the picture by showing how the product or service relates to them. The ad that began, "Do you make these mistakes in English?" continued as follows:

> Sherwin Cody's remarkable invention has enabled more than 100,000 people to correct their mistakes in English. Only 15 minutes a day is required to improve your speech and writing.

If you think you make mistakes in English, you are now interested. You are in the picture. It takes only 15 minutes a day.

Involve your reader. The weight-reducing ad that begins, "Is this the day you do something about your weight?" includes charts that show desirable weights for different heights. Few people can resist checking such charts to see how close their weight is to the desired level. If their weight is more than desirable—as is likely—they are immediately interested.

To build desire you take advantage of the reader's attention and interest by making specific claims for your product or service. You must be quite specific here. If you are vague, you will lose credibility and lose the interest you have already gained. If physical facts, such as size, weight, color, or ingredients, are needed, you must supply them. Don't forget the *so-whats* of your facts. What does your product or service do? How well does it do it? What is its use? What problems does it solve? Most important, how will it benefit the reader? Mail order catalog writers are masters at compressing a good deal of specific detail into a small space. Notice in this ad from a Gokey's sporting goods catalog how AIDA can be compressed into just a few lines if need be:

> SHEEPSKIN BOOT SOCKS
> When you're wearing rubber boots, waders or rubberized footwear, here's the best way to keep your feet warm and snug. Cut 6″ high from the long wool sheepskin, these boot socks will take up extra moisture in rubber boots. For men only in sizes 6 through 13. No half sizes. Indicate shoe size when ordering.*

The first sentence combines facts and an emotional appeal. The writer speaks knowingly about rubber boots, waders, and rubberized footware and appeals to a basic desire—the wish to be comfortable. In the second sentence, the writer furnishes a fact and a *so-what:* Because of the nature of their construction, these boot socks will take up extra moisture.

In a sales message like this one, you are seeing a specific application

*All excerpts from Gokey's are reprinted by permission.

of the you-attitude. Successful ad and direct-mail writers always have a specific reader in mind. They visualize this person before them as they begin their sales message. What sort of person would buy sheepskin boot socks? We visualize a middle-aged man, ruddy of complexion from being outdoors, hair touched with gray. As he reads the message, he is sitting comfortably in an easy chair, a favorite hunting dog nearby. He likes natural materials next to his skin. He prefers soft wool to polyester. He is a fisherman who has often had cold and damp feet. When he was young that was okay, but now he'd like a bit more comfort. This message will speak to him. A romanticized image? Probably so. But that image would put us in the proper frame of mind to write a sales message to a fisherman who probably romanticizes his image of himself.

Look at another successful sales message; like the first one, this is from *Gokey's Fall Catalog.*

> WOMEN'S HIKING SLACKS AND SHORTS
> For the lady hiker, camper or vacationer in a choice of 2 fabrics: 50% Polyester-50% Cotton Twill or 100% Cotton Pin Wale Corduroy. Machine washable. Specially cut and tailored to give a trim fit. Four front pockets give all the room you need for carrying necessities—no back pockets. Slacks come in ample inseam length so that you may set them to any desired length. Shorts have 4½" inseams and are hemmed and cuffed. Twill colors: Light Blue or Beige. Corduroy color: Slacks, Beige only. Sizes 8 to 18. Give fabric, color, and size when ordering.

Facts such as those in these two Gokey's ads provide credibility. Remember, in most cases you are appealing to both emotion and intellect—heart and brain. The heart may want something—like sheepskin boot socks—but the brain may overrule the desire unless it gets sufficient factual evidence. Notice, for example, how the ads for Mercedes-Benz automobiles emphasize the engineering marvels of the car. Truthfully, the people who can afford $30,000 for a car are more likely to be seeking status—a desire of the heart. But the brain needs to be told that the engineering features are worth the extra money, that the car has a high resale value, and so forth. We all rationalize our desires, and supporting facts make it easier for us to do so.

What kinds of facts can be used in sales persuasion? As we have already seen, physical descriptions and functional characteristics are appropriate. You can mention the reputation of your company or product. You can point to long years of experience. You can offer test and performance data. You can give testimonials from satisfied customers. You can show the product or service in action. The famous Charles Atlas ads used action. For years these ads promised skinny weaklings a way to build their bodies. The ad, in the form of a comic strip, always ended by showing the skinny weakling, now grown into a man rippling with muscle, knocking down the bully who had picked on him at the beginning of the ad—the service in action.

A more subtle use of the same in-action principle is at work in this coat ad from *Norm Thompson Outfitters Fall and Winter Catalog:*

> The Imperial possesses a unique elegance you'll wear with pride. It was designed primarily for town and travel, but it's so adaptable, you can team it up with casual and country clothes for a look that's bound to turn heads your way.*

Before writing a sales message, research your audience and your product or service as thoroughly as possible. Dig out as much information as you can. Then try to choose those facts that give you an edge over the competition. Just be sure your claims are credible—that what you are selling will live up to your description.

GETTING ACTION

If you want action from your reader, you must ask for it. In most sales letters it's desirable to ask your reader to do something—if not a major action, such as buying your product, at least an intermediate step, such as sending for a brochure or filling in a questionnaire. Make the action as easy to do as possible. Provide specific details on how to order, for example. Or provide specific information on how to reach your place of business, even using a map if necessary. Notice how even the small Gokey's catalog ads call for action through statements like "Indicate shoe size when ordering." Sometimes the calls for action can be extensive. The end of a sales letter from *Writer's Digest* concludes with no fewer than five calls for action. Count them:

> Return the Half-Price Savings Certificate enclosed and try Writer's Digest *without risk.* If after sixty days you don't feel it can help you become a better writer, just let me know and I'll see you receive a *full refund* of your subscription payment.
> Rejoin us as a subscriber now and we'll send you the next year of Writer's Digest for *just half the regular subscription price.*
> You get the next twelve issues of Writer's Digest for only $6. And you have my personal guarantee of *satisfaction or your money back.* I challenge you to become a better writer this year. And through Writer's Digest, I can help you do it.
> So please check the "YES" box on the enclosed Savings Certificate and return it to me today. I've enclosed a postage-paid envelope for your convenience.
> I will look forward to your reply.
>
> Sincerely,
>
> *John Brady*
> Editor

*Reprinted by permission.

P. S. I'd be very much interested to learn of your experiences as a writer and of your reactions to the changes we're making in Writer's Digest. So please take this opportunity to rejoin us at the special half price rate, and let me hear from you soon.

P.P.S. If, for some reason, you are no longer interested in writing, I'd like to know that too. If you aren't interested in seeing how the new Writer's Digest can help you, please check the "NO" box on your Savings Certificate and return it to me at my expense. Thanks.

PUTTING IT ALL TOGETHER

Figure 8–1 is a sales letter sent to its members by the National Geographic Society. Read it over before you read the discussion that follows.

The National Geographic letter solicits attention by the question printed in the box above the salutation. The use of an actual headline is a fairly common practice in sales letters. The same question would work well as the opening sentence after the salutation. The attention-getting approach in the letter is curiosity. Our immediate reward for reading on is to find out what a pack rat, a campfire, a hornet's nest, and a dolphin trainer have in common.

Once into the letter, the reader is put into the picture with the phrase "The 4-through-8-year-old children in your life." The audience is now selected, and it's a wide audience when you consider that parents, grandparents, uncles and aunts, even older brothers and sisters, could have 4-through-8-year-old children in their lives. There is an emotional appeal as well. Most of us have a good deal of love and affection for the children in our lives.

The writer quickly begins to give specific information to hold the readers' interest and to build desire for the adventure books. Reading the letter, you learn about the books' contents and that the books were pre-tested on children. The fact of pretesting lends credibility. The books contain "big, bright photographs." The *so-what* is that even "little folks" (emotional appeal in this phrase) who can't read will find the books a "learning adventure." Near the end of the letter the writer tells us that "nearly 5 million copies have been purchased!"—a striking testimonial to the books' worth that enhances their credibility considerably. Our emotions are appealed to once again when we are urged to think of our children on Christmas, birthdays, and rainy days.

The letter closes with a request for action: "Simply complete the enclosed postage-paid order form and drop it in the mail." Note how easy it is for the reader to act. No money needs to be sent. The Society will bill later.

The letter is simply written, but it does not talk down to the reader. The average sentence length is just short of 15 words. Frequent ellipsis points (. . .) make the longer sentences seem even shorter. Paragraphs run three or four lines long; the longest is only six lines. Indented material is

NATIONAL GEOGRAPHIC SOCIETY
17th and M Streets, N.W. Washington, D.C., U.S.A. 20036

Office of The Secretary

> What do a desert pack rat -- a
>
> campfire ... a hornet's nest ... and
>
> a dolphin trainer have in common?

Dear Member,

The answer is -- they're all featured in National Geographic's new Books for Young Explorers. Those wonderful, color-splashed books that we publish especially for the 4-through-8-year-old children in your life.

The titles of this year's four-volume Set V are WONDERS OF THE DESERT WORLD ... CAMPING ADVENTURE ... ANIMALS THAT BUILD THEIR HOMES ... and THE PLAYFUL DOLPHINS. These books are sure to become your children's favorite reading fun. And here's why....

The books' subjects were actually chosen by children in a special survey of preschool and elementary students. So they are books that children really want to read.

The text is fresh and friendly. It is printed in big, easy-to-read type. And it is written in the vocabulary and at the comprehension level of beginning readers. Yet -- unlike many books written for the younger reader -- these talk to your children, and never "down to" them.

The big, bright photographs that illustrate the text make these books a learning adventure -- even for the little folks who haven't yet begun to read.

Best of all, Books for Young Explorers Set V has the answers to the kinds of questions that kids ask -- the "gee whiz" facts that kids love to learn....

> A dolphin can find things underwater -- even if it's
>
> blindfolded! A badger can dig faster than a man
>
> with a shovel! Cactuses as tall as trees live in
>
> the desert! There are tiny plants (without leaves)
>
> that grow on rocks!

Each book has 32 pages brimming with this kind of wonder. And -- each has

FIGURE 8–1   Advertising letter (Courtesy Marian Reeser, National Geographic Society; reprinted by permission of the Society.)

heavy, child-tested paper ... durable, hardbound covers ... easy-to-handle 8 3/4"-by-11 1/4" size ... and full color on every page.

And there's an additional bonus: Each four-volume set of Books for Young Explorers comes with a fascinating booklet for adults entitled More About....

This 24-page illustrated guide contains additional information about each book's subject ... more colorful photographs ... a look at how the books were created ... and a suggested reading list. A useful supplement that encourages discussion and further study.

And all this - four wonderful books plus More About... - is only $6.95! A National Geographic book bargain that we are very proud to be able to offer our members.

One of the reasons we can bring you this value is that Books for Young Explorers are sold only by direct order from your Society. Another is the enormous volume of sales these books generate. Since 1972, when the first set was published, nearly 5 million copies have been purchased! This kind of success allows us to offer them to you at a much lower price than books of similar quality available in bookstores.

And just wait until you and your children get a look at this year's Books for Young Explorers Set V. It's a winning combination of fun, learning ... and value.

The enclosed brochure will give you a small sample of the color, excitement, and child appeal in these books. Look it over ...

... then think of your children (nieces, nephews, grandchildren, neighbors) ... the occasions (Christmas, birthday, rainy days) ... and order the number of sets you'd like to give your young friends.

Simply complete the enclosed postage-paid order form and drop it in the mail. Send no money now. We will bill you for your order when it is delivered in October.

We know you'll be delighted with Books for Young Explorers Set V. And what's even better -- we know your children will love them ... and learn from them. And that's the best gift of all!

Sincerely,

Owen R. Anderson

Secretary

ORA/ab

P.S. For those of you who missed it, we are also making available the current Set IV of Books for Young Explorers. See the enclosed folder for details -- and, if you choose, check the Set IV box on your order form.

FIGURE 8-1 Advertising letter *(cont.)*

used, both to emphasize certain facts and to break up the page. The shorter paragraphs and the indentations make the page inviting to the eye.

With few exceptions, simple subject-verb, active-voice sentences are used. (See pages 43–45, 433–436.) The language is mature but not jargon or overly difficult.

All in all, it's a well-done, persuasive sales letter that brings together credibility, emotional appeal, and facts and analysis. At the same time, it is done with a taste and dignity that befit the National Geographic Society.

Not all sales letters are selling a product or even a service. Sometimes you are trying to sell an idea or convince someone to take some action. When such is the case, your persuasive strategy of credibility, emotional appeal, and facts and analysis may be best presented in the AIDA format. Our next example attempts to persuade faculty members at a university to contribute to the university YMCA. Although not as obvious as a letter selling merchandise might be, it clearly follows AIDA:

NO GYM, NO POOL, JUST DYNAMIC PEOPLE PROGRAMS

Dear Colleague:

Indeed, it's true. The University YMCA has no gym and no pool, and, what's more, it doesn't want either one. What it does want is to help our students have experiences that will broaden their perspectives and perhaps help them see their futures more clearly.

If you're the way I was a few years ago, you may not even know that a Y is associated with the University, let alone what it does. In 1980, my daughter, a junior at the University, participated in the Y's Metro Internship program. Through the program she received leadership training and spent a term as a business intern with a local firm.

Before her participation in the program, she had no clear idea of what her post-university career might be. During the internship she discovered that she had an aptitude and a liking for business. An MBA seemed a natural next step for her after graduation. Today, she's embarked on a satisfying career she might never have considered without the Y.

What other programs does the Y substitute for a pool and a gym? Here are a few:

- 20/70 Vision—bringing young people together with older people so that they may share their experiences
- Eight Weeks to Live—learning, by role-playing only eight weeks to live, to understand our mortality and the meaning of death
- Global Perspectives—learning the reality that the nations of the world are increasingly interdependent
- Project Motivation—pairing University students with grade school children so that each can learn from the other

Dollars for the Y touch many lives every year, the young and the old as well as our students. Dedicated staff members and volunteers see to it that your money does as much good as possible. We hope you will want to help.

Won't you please fill out the enclosed postpaid pledge card and mail it back today. You'll be glad you did.

Sincerely,

The writer gains attention by a curiosity-catching headline pointing out an apparent inconsistency. Most Y's are associated with gyms and pools. This one is not; it concentrates on "people programs." The writer gains credibility by pointing out that, until a few years ago, he did not know of the Y's existence, most likely the current state of the letter's reader. Facts, some with definite emotional appeal, are presented to bolster the claim that the Y should have the faculty member's support.

The writer does not ask for money immediately. Rather the action asked for is the return of a postpaid card pledging money. Everything is made as easy for the reader as possible.

Most of the sentences are under 20 words. The paragraphs are of moderate length. Sentence structures and vocabulary, while mature, are not elaborate.

You will have many occasions in your life to write persuasive letters, sales or otherwise. When you do, remember AIDA—attention, interest, desire, action. Much persuasion is built around this pattern.

SUGGESTIONS FOR APPLYING YOUR KNOWLEDGE

Real examples of the material discussed in this chapter are all around us in newspapers and magazines and probably in our mailboxes. Ads and sales letters provide a rich field for short assignments. Here are some things you might try, in class and out:

1. Write a sales letter for some product or service you are connected with in an off-campus job.

2. Analyze a sales message you have recently received. What is its persuasive strategy? Pay attention to its vocabulary and sentence and paragraph structure. See how closely it follows AIDA.

3. Write a sales letter for some campus activity such as the cafeteria, student center, library, or audio-visual center. Remember, you must research an activity and its potential users before you can sell it successfully.

4. Analyze the distinctions between ads that appear in technical and professional journals and those found in popular magazines. Be particularly alert for differences in emotional and factual content. Which appeal mostly to the head, which to the heart?

5. Elsewhere in the book (Chapters 12 and 13) we discuss process and mechanism descriptions. Analyze a sales message that contains such a description. See where it follows the techniques we have described and where it does not.

6. Write a letter persuading someone to take on a tough job or to make a contribution. Use AIDA.

7. Think of some of the many situations in which persuasive techniques are needed. Can AIDA help you in any of them?

U N I T

III

C H A P T E R

9

BASIC
PRINCIPLES
OF REPORTS

S uccessful business and industrial organizations get their jobs done. To do them, they gather information and move it to those who need it or to those whom they want to have it—employees, suppliers, customers. They transfer all kinds of information in all forms of letters and reports. Unsuccessful organizations don't keep records or transfer information efficiently. Productivity decreases. Ignorance and guesswork replace knowledge and information. The idea is simple: The effectiveness of an organization is tied to its reporting.

Because good reporting is so important to an organization's functioning, all organizations are in the business of communication. Whether your job is in accounting, engineering, production, sales, or service, as an employee you can expect report writing to be an important part of your work. You won't work in a vacuum: You'll work with and through other people, and you'll have to communicate with them. Without the ability to inform, you will not be successful.

The basic principles that apply to all your writing and speaking are discussed in Unit I. The major types of correspondence that you might be expected to write are covered in Unit II. We cover in this unit the more complex task of reporting and show you the different choices you have to make while planning and preparing reports.

But before we take up those tasks and choices as they relate to different types of reports in Chapters 11 through 18, we present helpful ways for you to look at specific types of reports and at your obligation to make information in your reports easy to read, understand, and find.

TYPES OF REPORTS

Reports carry information to those who want it or need it. The information is usually expected or requested by those receiving the report.

When you prepare a report—regardless of its length, content, and form and whether it's written or oral—you'll be presenting specific information to a specific audience for a specific purpose. What information you include and what relationship you establish with your audience will depend largely on your reason for reporting. Exactly what information does your audience need or expect? Of what use will the information be? The answers to these questions will give you a good idea of what your purpose is.

Most reports either inform; inform and analyze; or inform, analyze, and persuade. The informational report informs your audience what you have found out, and it includes little or no commentary and interpretation. The analytical report presents the facts together with an analysis of them. The persuasive report seeks to influence the reader's belief or action. Learn to think in terms of the purpose or function the information in your report serves, and you'll know what to put in your report. You'll be able to decide better what information to include, what information to emphasize, and how to organize your report.

How beneficial your report is to your audiences depends on how well you meet their interests and needs and estimate their ability to understand what you're trying to tell them. So get to know your audiences and their needs and keep them in mind while you're planning and preparing your report. If you really know your audience, you've got a leg up on the job. If you don't, there's no way you're going to prepare a good report—no matter how much you hack away at it.

Two important things to remember when considering your audiences are that they are real persons like yourself and that probably they'll be eager to gain the information you have for them.

But don't assume that just because your audiences may be eagerly waiting for your report that they are captive. Don't let your knowledge of the subject and your convenience totally govern how you prepare the report.

In the heat of on-the-job reporting don't overlook the courtesy that you naturally owe your audiences. You must get your report to them in plenty of time—when they need it or want it. By all means, if you have doubts about any aspect of the report, ask your audiences if they have any special requests concerning the report. They may give you information that will help you cut down on their reading or listening time and increase their comprehension. There may be times when they make the conditions for the report and establish specific requirements concerning the content, organization, format, and publication procedure or delivery.

In such situations your anticipation of your audiences' desires is relatively easy. You've got their point of view from the start. Sometimes, though, in the case of written reports, your readers may not be available for references. In the absence of such clear identification of your readers' needs, there still exist several principles you can follow to make your reports easy to read and to make your information easy to understand and find. The rest of this chapter discusses five such principles:

- The report should be legible.
- The report should be formatted to reveal its organization.
- If necessary, the report should contain formal elements, such as a title page, a letter of transmittal or preface, a table of contents, a list of graphics, appendixes, and so on.
- If necessary, the report should be documented.
- The report should be illustrated to clarify certain types of information.

MAKING THE REPORT LEGIBLE

Legibility relates to how easy or difficult your report is to read once it's on the printed page. Keep these points in mind:

- Use good-quality paper, heavy enough to make the typing stand out. Type your report on white bond paper, 20-lb. weight, 8½ by 11 inches.
- If copies are required, make them by the best reproduction process you have available. Carbon copies are generally undesirable.
- Maintain 1-inch margins all around.
- If you're going to put your report in a binder, leave 2 inches of margin on the left-hand side.
- If your report is typed single space, allow a double space between paragraphs and above and below headings, lists, long quotations, and graphics.
- If it is typed double space, allow no extra space between paragraphs, but allow a triple space above headings and above and below lists, long quotations, and graphics.
- Use legible, nondistracting type. Avoid script and types with fancy lines and flourishes.
- Use typographical elements to make words, phrases, and sentences stand out. Catch your readers' attention by using italics (underlining), all-capital letters, and different colors. But don't overdo such devices.
- Enclose graphics in boxes.
- If the sequence of a list is random (as this list's is) or arbitrary, use bullets (•) or dashes (—). If the order is important, use Arabic numerals (1, 2, 3 . . .).
- Keep paragraphs fairly short (under 100 words) to break the page vertically.

Don't let your report fail because of physical obstacles.

REVEALING THE ORGANIZATION OF THE REPORT

In addition to being legible, your report should be organized and arranged in a format so that its organization is obvious to the reader.

Because we can express only one idea at a time, we always must choose what to say first, second, third, or last. In doing so, we of necessity organize our reports in some way. We discuss a great many organizational plans in this book. We've already talked about good-news and bad-news approaches, and we will later discuss process and mechanism description, instructions, and proposals.

But knowing how to organize a report is not enough. If you don't *reveal* the organization of a report, your readers may think you are like the rattle-brained George Nupkins, Esq., the talkative mayor of Ipswich in Charles Dickens' *The Pickwick Papers*, whose "ideas come out so fast they knock each other's head off and you can't tell what he's driving at."

You, of course, know what you're driving at and have a map to follow—your inner picture of the organization of your report. However, your readers may not share that same picture. Commenting on the difference between the writer's view and the reader's view of the same material, James W. Souther and Myron L. White describe the problem this way:

> Readers get their information line by line, sentence by sentence. Information comes to them one idea at a time, one behind the other. They receive ideas in *sequence,* but the writer's view contains more than sequence. It has coordination and subordination as well.[1]

Souther and White illustrate this difference in Figure 9–1.

You need to transfer your inner picture to your readers. Format—the physical arrangement of a message on the page—is used to transfer this picture.

Almost all features of modern writing may be regarded as format. Capital letters and small letters are format, punctuation is format, and the space between words is format. Anything to do with the arrangement and appearance of the page is format. If we did not have these format devices, our writing would look like an unbroken string of letters of the same size with no space between them and with no punctuation. Without format, our writing might look like this:

WITHOUTFORMATOURWRITINGWOULDLOOKLIKETHISANDITWOULDBEV

GNOLSECNETNESRUOFYLNOSIEGASSAPSIHTDAEROTTLUCIFFIDYRE

THINKOFHOWDIFFICULTITWOULDBETOREADSEVERALPAGESLIKETHIS

Capitalization, spacing, punctuation, and paragraphing have become useful format for you—and your reader. But as important as these are, they do not reveal the organization of your ideas beyond the paragraph level. Your inner picture of organization is still not revealed fully to your readers.

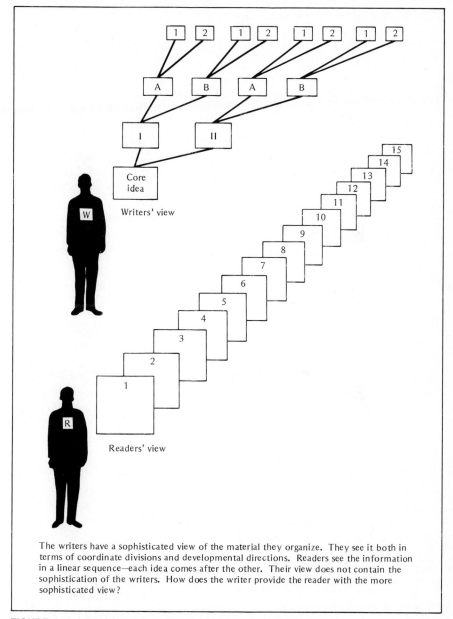

The writers have a sophisticated view of the material they organize. They see it both in terms of coordinate divisions and developmental directions. Readers see the information in a linear sequence—each idea comes after the other. Their view does not contain the sophistication of the writers. How does the writer provide the reader with the more sophisticated view?

FIGURE 9–1   Writer's view versus readers' view of same material (James W. Souther and Myron L. White, *Technical Report Writing,* 2nd ed. [New York: John Wiley & Sons, 1977], p. 41. Copyright © John Wiley & Sons, 1977. Used by permission.)

To reveal the organization of large blocks of information, other format devices are worth knowing about—devices you have seen on many pages of this book: headings and enumeration.

The value of headings and enumeration should be self-evident. Posters, brochures, illustrated magazines and books, and television and movies have responded to—and in turn shaped—an audience that would rather look than read. People want their information highlighted. If your reports are going to succeed, they must have the willing participation of these visual-minded readers. It's not so much a question of whether readers will understand your report as it is a question of whether they will be willing to read it. When readers are put off by pages of information unbroken by headings or enumeration, they probably will not read the report or at best read it begrudgingly. If they become discouraged and stop trying to wade through pages of solid text, all the interest and firmness of purpose you had in writing your report will do you no good, for it is the reader, not you, who measures how successfully you've communicated your ideas.

Headings and enumeration help fulfill the readers' assumptions that your information is shaped into an organized and meaningful whole. In *Memory and Attention: An Introduction to Human Information Processing,* Donald A. Norman views "the human as a complex system, struggling to impose organization on the information received through the sense organs" trying "to detect, recognize, attend to, and retain incoming information."[2] As a way of visually packaging information, format helps readers discover your plan of organization. If headings and enumeration are not used to reveal your plan of organization, the reading becomes tedious. Without headings and enumeration to emphasize them, the main ideas remain buried and lost from view in the mass of words that make up the report.

The reader should be able to pick out the major ideas of your report well enough to set them down in writing. But a report without headings or enumeration—even in a short excerpt like the following—does little to make the work of the reader easier.

RECOMMENDATION OF REPLACEMENT OF FIRE SUPPRESSION TRACTOR IN AREA I

The purchase of a new caterpillar D4D dozer will give Area I the dependable equipment needed for fire suppression, fire protection, and routine management activities. This purchase will result in the continued maximization of fiber yield and minimum loss to wild fire.

The potential loss of Area I plantations, due to fire, because of the downtime is critical with the present unit. The area has 58,191 acres of timberland; 22,629 acres are in plantations one to twenty years old. To assure development of these plantations fire suppression is essential.

A new fire suppression tractor is also essential in developing a road system in these plantations to give better fire protection and aid in suppression.

Our commitment to maximum yield from our timberlands and the future dependency of the DePhalant Mill to this commitment makes dependable equipment a must. The fire suppression tractor is also used in minor road construction projects and tree planting, which are also essential in the commitment to maximum yield.

The present tractor had maintenance costs of $10,101 and $9,600 for the past two years. In contrast, during this same period the two-year-old tractor in Area II had maintenance costs of $1,500 and $3,000. These tractors are for the same purposes and the hours of operation were essentially the same. The cost of operating the present tractor in Area I is prohibitive.

The unit to be replaced is a D4D diesel crawler, purchased in May 1970, Asset No. M548, which is totally depreciated. This crawler has no book value and will be traded in or sold.

The alternatives to purchasing a new tractor would be to lease a tractor or continued use of the present tractor. Experience indicates that this type of equipment is more costly to lease than to own. Continuing to operate our present tractor would be impractical due to extensive downtime, high maintenance costs, and its potential unreliability.

To grasp the major ideas in this passage you probably had to read it and note the major ideas, separating them from subordinate ideas and details, by underlining them or by reconstructing the outline of the material by brief notes in the margin.

Now look at another version of this passage. Notice how the enumerated list and the headings make it easier to read and understand what the writer has written. In a single brief exposure, the reader sees immediately the writer's inner picture of organization—what Souther and White call the coordination and subordination of information. The more visible the content and arrangement, the greater the impact on the reader.

RECOMMENDATION FOR REPLACEMENT OF FIRE SUPPRESSION TRACTOR IN AREA I

I recommend the replacement of the fire suppression tractor in Area I, for the following reasons:

1. Loss of production to downtime of the tractor is critical.

2. The maintenance cost of the tractor is excessively high.

3. The tractor is completely depreciated.

Loss of Production to Downtime

The potential loss of Area I plantations, due to fire, because of downtime is critical with the present unit. The area has 58,191 acres of timberland; 22,629 acres are in plantations one to twenty years old. To assure development of these plantations fire suppression is essential.

A new fire suppression tractor is also essential in developing a road system in these plantations to give better fire protection and aid in suppression.

Our commitment to maximum yield from our timberlands and the future dependency of the DePhalant Mill to this commitment make dependable equipment a must. The fire suppression tractor is also used in minor road construction projects and tree planting, which are also essential in the commitment to maximum yield.

High Maintenance Cost

The present tractor had maintenance costs of $10,101 and $9,600 for the past two years. In contrast, during this same period the two-year-old tractor in Area II had maintenance costs of $1,500 and $3,000. These tractors are for the same purposes and the hours of operation were essentially the same. The cost of operating the present tractor in Area I is prohibitive.

Depreciation

The unit to be replaced is a D4D diesel crawler, purchased in May 1970, Asset No. M548, which is totally depreciated. This crawler has no book value and will be traded in or sold.

<u>Alternatives</u> <u>to</u> <u>Purchase</u> <u>of</u> <u>New</u> <u>Tractor</u>

The alternatives to purchasing a new tractor would be to lease a tractor or continued use of the present tractor. Experience indicates that this type of equipment is more costly to lease than to own. Continuing to operate our present tractor would be impractical because of extensive downtime, high maintenance cost, and its potential unreliability.

This version is slightly longer than the first because the format conventions of enumeration and headings take up space. However, the trade-off of additional length for easier reading is worth it. This second version, although slightly longer, is much quicker to read and easier to remember—because readers can quickly identify the points of discussion and the order in which the points are made. It's almost as if the writer were saying "I won't keep you long and I'm going to stick closely to the major points."

FORMAL ELEMENTS

We discussed format, or the layout of material, as the major way to suggest organization to the reader's eye. Here, we turn to the formal elements of reports that help the reader find information.

Reports can be anything from four or five sentences scribbled on a notepad to a dozen paragraphs reporting the results of a laboratory experiment to a 22-volume feasibility study on the development of a supersonic transport. No clear-cut distinction exists between informal and formal reports; simple problems and situations require only simple reports, perhaps resembling letters and memorandums more than anything else. (See Chapter 4) But the more complex and lengthy the report, the further removed your audience is from the project you're reporting on, and the more valuable the report is as a long-term reference, the greater the need to formalize certain elements of the presentation to save readers time and effort and to prevent confusion. The formal elements help readers recognize the various units of a report, consequently speeding up the retrieval process by highlighting important information. In short, formalizing certain elements of a report fights against the loss of meaning, however slight, that inevitably takes place when a message is transmitted. But it would be an academic exercise of little importance to decide when a report is "formal" and when it is "informal."

Some companies and agencies use a rigid, standardized plan for long reports; others are more flexible. Our advice is that you learn whatever plan you are expected to follow. Our discussion of the formal elements of long reports is purposely general and flexible, so that you can design each report to fit its own subject matter, purpose, and audience.

You may have to arrange for your report to be typed or produced on a word processor or do it yourself. Typing a report isn't hard, but it does take time and patience. Whether you type 80 words a minute or "hunt and peck" 80 words an hour doesn't really matter once you have the report typed. What matters then is how it looks—if it's neat and easy to read and if it follows the principles of good format. Those principles are important. Editors and readers can be quite picky about things like margins and documentation form. They tend to frown on typing that breaks the rules and smile on papers that look good.[3]

Here is a list of formal elements:

I. Prefatory elements
   A. Title page
   B. Letter of transmittal or preface
   C. Table of contents (needed for all except short reports)
   D. List of figures and tables (needed when your report contains five or more formal graphics)
   E. Abstract
II. Main elements
   A. Introduction
   B. Body (with headings and subheadings)
   C. Ending (which may include a summary, conclusions, recommendations, end notes, list of references, and so on)
III. Supplemental elements (which may include a glossary, appendixes, and so forth)

Prefatory Elements

The prefatory elements initially present your report to a reader before he or she comes to the main elements. Their function is to identify the report—its author, audience, date, subject, coverage, and organization. Prefatory pages are numbered in small Roman numerals—iii, iv, v, and so on.

TITLE PAGE   The title page (Figure 9–2) gives identifying information about the report. It shows the title of the report, the name and position of the person or group for whom you prepared the report, the distribution list (if anybody besides your primary reader receives a copy), your name and position, and the date you submitted the report. This information is important because it introduces the subject, identifies the primary audience and author, establishes the currency of the information, helps in filing and retrieving the report, and makes it easy to refer to.

Here are some suggestions on providing the necessary information for the title page:

1. *Title.* Think of your title as a one-phrase summary of your report. It should indicate the subject as briefly and specifically as possible. Make

<u>NUCLEAR ATTACK AND</u>
<u>THE NATION'S WATER SUPPLY</u>

Submitted to
Dr. Robert A. Phelps
Professor of Environmental Science
Patterson Technical Institute
Acallah, FL 33110

by
Elizabeth Griffey
Biology Major

November 30, 1985

FIGURE 9–2   Title page

your title concise and emphatic; avoid unhelpful expressions like *A Report on . . .* , *A Study of . . .* , *An Investigation of. . . .* Four to eight words are usually enough. One or two words are often vague; more than ten words work against easy comprehension. Here are some satisfactory titles that describe succinctly the purpose and subject of reports:

> Proposed Changes in Traffic Pattern of Lockwood Shopping Center
>
> Nuclear Attack and the Nation's Water Supply
>
> Comparative Merits of Copy Machines on the Market
>
> Tooth Transplantation in Pediatric Dentistry
>
> Battery Eliminators Save Money in the Shop

Such key terms as "Proposed Changes," "Traffic Pattern," "Lockwood Shopping Center," "Nuclear Attack," "Nation's Water Supply," "Copy Machines," "Tooth Transplantation," "Pediatric Dentistry," and "Battery Eliminators" facilitate indexing and cross-referencing reports in files and data bases.

2. *Name and Position of Primary Reader.* Identify the audience of your report by name, position, and organization.
3. *Distribution List.* Identify by name, and, if appropriate, by title and organization, others who receive the report. It is courteous to indicate to the primary reader who else will be receiving the report.
4. *Name and Position of Author.* Identify yourself by name, position, and organization. If the report has been written by a team, the authors' names should be in alphabetical order or in some other customary order, such as listing the principal investigator, team leader, or senior author first.
5. *Date of Report.* Date your report according to when you submit it to your reader. Never abbreviate the date; give the month, day, and year: November 16, 1985, or 16 November 1985.

The finished title page should look balanced, as in Figure 9–2. Center and underscore the title of the report, beginning about ten single spaces from the top of the page. Single-space and divide the title into two lines if it looks too long for one line. The dateline is about two inches from the page bottom. The title page is understood to be page i of the prefatory elements, although it is not numbered.

LETTER OF TRANSMITTAL   The letter of transmittal (Figure 9–3) officially transmits or presents the report to your readers. It may be in memorandum or letter form. Addressed to your readers, it provides sufficient background by

- explaining the authorization or occasion for the report;
- restating the title of the report (in case the letter is mailed separately from the report);
- explaining the features of the report that may be of special interest;

2302 17th Street
Acallah, FL 33110
November 30, 1985

Dr. Robert A. Phelps
Professor of Environmental Science
Patterson Technical Institute
Acallah, FL 33110

Dear Dr. Phelps:

The accompanying report titled <u>Nuclear Attack and
the Nation's Water Supply</u>, is submitted as my major report
for Biology 1339: Environmental Biology.

The primary purpose of the report is to explain
how fallout from a nuclear war would affect the nation's
water supply. The major findings are that fallout will
affect the nation's water supply, that the greatest immediate danger would come from suspended radioactivity,
that the long-range danger would come from dissolved
radioactivity, and that treatment plants would not remove
much, if any, dissolved radioactivity.

Dr. Rachel Cohen, Coordinator of the Waste Management
Center, and Mr. James W. North, Director of the Environmental
Studies Center, have been very helpful in explaining certain
technical procedures of waste water management to me.

I sincerely hope that this report will meet with your
approval. I will be most happy to provide you with additional
information should you desire it.

Sincerely,

Elizabeth Griffey

Elizabeth Griffey
Sophomore
Biology Major

FIGURE 9–3 Letter of transmittal

- acknowledging special assistance in performing the study or preparing the report, especially from those who funded the project or provided materials, equipment, or information and advice.

Close the letter politely by stating your willingness to provide similar services in the future or to provide further information if the readers desire it, whichever seems appropriate.

Like any good business letter or memorandum, the letter of transmittal should be in a format that makes it easy to read (see pages 56–68 for formats of letters and memorandums). If the letter is bound with the report, it is understood to be page ii of the prefatory elements, though it is not numbered. If the letter is placed in front of the title page, it is not regarded as part of the report and is not counted as a page of the prefatory elements.

PREFACE The preface (Figure 9–4) is almost identical to the letter of transmittal. It should contain statements about the purpose, scope, and content of the report and acknowledgment of assistance received. If you include a letter of transmittal, there's no point in including a preface, too.

Whether you use the letter of transmittal or the preface depends on your audience. Use the letter of transmittal when your audience is a single person or a well-defined group. Use the preface when your audience is more general and you don't know specifically who will be reading your report. The tone of the preface is often less personal than that of the letter of transmittal.

Center and underscore the word *Preface* at the top of the page. When the preface takes the place of the letter of transmittal, number it as page ii of the prefatory elements. Center the number ii at the bottom of the page, three-quarters of an inch up.

TABLE OF CONTENTS The table of contents (Figure 9–5) is a list of the major headings and subheadings in the report. These provide a handy outline of the report that helps readers locate any major section quickly. Preparing the table of contents involves two major steps: (1) making a rough copy, gathering headings and subheadings from the finished report, and (2) putting it in correct form on the page.

1. *Making a rough copy.* First, make a rough draft of the table of contents by listing every part of the report that comes after it. After each item, put the page number on which it appears.

Second, make the wording, capitalization, and order of entries exactly as in the report.

Third, indent the subheadings under each main heading to show their subordination, and indent progressively subordinate subheadings under their headings. If you numbered the chapters or major sections of the report, those numbers should be placed before the main headings in the table of contents.

2. *Putting it in correct form on the page.* Center and underscore the words *Contents* or *Table of Contents* at the top of the page. Arrange the

PREFACE

This report presents the results of a study of the
effects on the nation's water supply of fallout from a
nuclear war. The major findings are that fallout will
affect the nation's water supply. The greatest immediate
danger would come from suspended radioactivity. The
long-range danger would come from dissolved radioactivity,
and that treatment plants would not remove much, if any,
dissolved radioactivity.

Dr. Rachel Cohen, Coordinator of the Waste Management
Center, and Mr. James W. North, Director of the Environmental Studies Center, both at Patterson Technical Institute, Acallah, Florida, have been very helpful in explaining
certain technical procedures of waste water management to
me.

This report was written for Dr. Robert A. Phelps as
the final project in Biology 1339: Environmental Biology.

ii

FIGURE 9–4 Preface

TABLE OF CONTENTS

iii

FIGURE 9–5 Table of contents

information into three columns. The left column contains capital Roman numerals as major divisions or chapter numbers. The center column contains the main headings and subheadings of the report. Remember to indent to show subordination of subheadings. The right column contains the page numbers on which the headings appear. The right side of the numbers should be even. Use double-spaced dots, called leaders, to connect the headings with their page numbers.

Double-space between entries and single-space any heading that is too long for one line.

Number the table of contents page as page iii at the bottom of the page, three-quarters of an inch up. From here on, number all pages of the prefatory elements in sequence with lowercase Roman numerals.

LIST OF FIGURES AND TABLES   The page that lists figures and tables (Figure 9–6) shows your readers the location of graphics and tables. You should include it only if your report contains more than five figures or tables. If there are many figures and tables, you may group them into separate categories: "List of Figures," "List of Tables," and so on.

The list of figures and tables is set up just like the table of contents. Center and underscore the words *Figures and Tables* or *List of Figures and Tables* or whatever is appropriate, one inch down from the top of the page.

Arrange the information in three columns, similar to the table of contents: The left column contains the figure or table number (normally, tables are given capital Roman numerals and figures are given Arabic numbers); the center column contains the title of the figure or table; the right column contains the number of the page it is on or is facing. Use double-spaced dots to connect titles of figures and tables with their page numbers.

ABSTRACT   The abstract (Figure 9–7) is a brief, condensed statement of the most important ideas of your report. It provides your readers with a compressed overview of the report by mirroring both its content and organization. It must be informative; that is, it should not simply describe the coverage of the report but also actually present what's in it.

The length of the abstract depends on the length of the report. The typical abstract is a paragraph of 150 to 200 words. But longer reports—say 20 or more pages—probably would require additional paragraphs. We can't tell you exactly what the length of an abstract should be for longer reports, but a working estimate is that it should not be more than 5 percent of the whole report. Thus, a 40-page report would have an abstract of approximately two pages at most. The abstract for a longer report might consist of a series of brief paragraphs that summarize each major section of the report. (See Chapter 11, "Bibliographic and Literature Reviews," for examples of other abstracts and summaries.)

Although the abstract is a compressed version of the report, you should not write it in a telegraphic style. Its words and sentences must be in good prose style.

<u>LIST</u> <u>OF</u> <u>FIGURES</u> <u>AND</u> <u>TABLES</u>

FIGURE 9–6 List of figures and tables

ABSTRACT

Fallout from a nuclear war will affect the nation's water supply. The two types of radioactivity that will be a hazard to the supply of water are suspended and dissolved radioactivity. Suspended activity directly causes immediate problems and indirectly causes long-range problems. Dissolved activity, which presents long-range problems, cannot be removed by treatment plants. How water becomes radioactive and how fallout affects streams and rivers, reservoirs, and treatment plants present the nation with problems as acute as civil defense shelter problems.

v

FIGURE 9–7   Abstract

Center and underscore the word *Abstract* at the top of the page, triple-space, and begin the abstract.

Main Elements

The main elements of your report follow the prefatory elements and consist of three main parts—the introduction, the body, and the ending.

THE INTRODUCTION   The introduction attracts attention and presents a general idea of the topic of the report.

When readers turn to your report, they are likely to have a lot of things on their minds. What you have to do is get your report on their minds—quickly. No matter how much or how little they are expecting your report, no matter how much or how little they are motivated to read it, your readers are going to start looking for answers to several questions as they try to settle into your report. They'll want to know or be reminded why you are writing to them, why you are writing to them now, what you have to say, and how you are going to say it. And they'll want the answers to these questions before they read very far.

If you don't deliver the answers, your readers will start getting restless and will soon find something to do besides read your report.

The English author C. S. Lewis put it another way:

> I sometimes think that writing is like driving sheep down a road. If there is any gate to the left or right, the reader will certainly go into it.

To hold your readers' attention and prevent mental wandering, you must pave a road that's easy to follow, build an entrance that's unavoidable, and close the gates to the sides. These are the jobs of your introduction, the first main portion of your report.

The introduction may consist of a few paragraphs or perhaps several pages. When it's lengthy, you should use subheadings to indicate its subparts. Whether the introduction is short or long, it should perform the following functions:

1. *Explain the subject.* Your readers need to know what they are going to read about. The title, letter of transmittal or preface, and abstract give them some information, but they might not provide adequate orientation. Often it is necessary to define the subject, explain some of the key terms used in your discussion, or give historical and other background information about the subject. Finally, you need to comment on the significance of the information. Work a bit on arousing your readers' interest. Why is your subject important? Why should your readers want to know about it? The more your readers want or need your report, the less you need do to arouse interest.

2. *Explain the purpose.* Although the purpose of your report should be self-evident to you, make sure it's also evident to your readers. Your purpose might be to report on a study requested by your readers. If so,

review the facts of the request or authorization: When did they make the request? How did they make it? Did somebody else make it? Such a review is especially important if there's no letter of transmittal. If the report is unsolicited, explain thoroughly the situation that led to your writing the report. The value of the report and the objectives and purposes of your reporting should be clear to your readers.

Sometimes there's only a thin line between the purpose of a study that a report is about and the report itself. But what is meant by *purpose* here is the purpose of the report, not the study. For example, the purpose of a study may be to pinpoint weaknesses in a machine's design. But the purpose of the report is to explain the amount of deflection and the source of the stress causing a machine to vibrate too much, and to recommend what rate of speed and what kind of mounting brackets would solve the problem. That is, the purpose of the report is to present the results of the study.

3. *Explain the scope.* Always let your readers know the extent of your presentation or the limits of your study. In other words, explain just how much ground the report is covering. The statement of scope tells your readers what you see yourself responsible for reporting.

4. *Explain the plan and order of presentation.* Always preview the report for your readers. Tell them what the order of topics will be. This statement usually is the last function of the introduction and serves as a transition to the body of the report.

Almost every important or long report will need a formal introduction that fulfills these four requirements. For special circumstances you may need to discuss in detail the problem your report is designed to solve; you may need to state a hypothesis; you may need to review the literature relevant to the problem or hypothesis; you may need to explain the nature of the investigation—the sources and methods of collecting data; you may need to define important terms used in the report that you feel your readers will be unfamiliar with; and if the purpose of your report is to communicate your position on a set of issues, you may need to summarize your significant findings or recommendations.

In short, your introduction should include whatever is needed to prepare your readers for the information they are about to receive. Don't be hasty in an introduction, but neither should you be long-winded. Get on with the main event as soon as possible. See Figure 9–8 for an example of an introduction to the student report entitled "Nuclear Attack and the Nation's Water Supply."

THE BODY The body, the longest section of your report, presents your detailed message. It has no set organization, but its contents should be arranged in some logical, unified order. Regardless of the content and arrangement of your report, you must help readers to skim your report, to read it thoroughly, or to refer to specific parts of it by using headings and subheadings, which separate the text into major divisions

INTRODUCTION

Two days after a nuclear attack, 46 percent of the United States would be covered with fallout.[1] The exact amount of fallout the United States would receive as the result of a nuclear war could not be predicted. However, an attacking enemy would not take the precautions used in testing in order to minimize fallout. Thus there would be extensive fallout after a war, and it would affect almost everything and everyone in this country in some way.

Although many people would be killed in blast areas, in much of this country the greatest threat to life would come from radioactive fallout. Radiation can damage body tissue and even cause death. Certain substances, such as radioactive strontium and iodine, settle in bones and glands and cause concentrations of radioactivity in these areas. Since radioactivity can accumulate in the human body, the total of all radioactivity entering the body through the various sources, such as food, air, and water, must be limited.

Since water is used for drinking, cooking, bathing, and for many industrial processes that require the presence of human beings, the effects of a fallout on our nation's water supply ought to be considered. Most of the water used in this country comes from lakes, streams, and rivers, rather than from wells, so consideration will be given only

1

FIGURE 9–8   Sample introduction

2

to the effects of fallout on surface water. The increase
or decrease of radioactivity in water after it has passed
through a treatment plant will be considered primarily
in conjunction with contamination of the treatment plant.
Processes for removal of radioactivity from water will
not be considered.[2]

This report discusses these effects on the nation's
water supply in three major sections:

    I. Effects on Rivers and Streams

   II. Effects on Reservoirs

  III. Effects on Water Plants and Distribution Systems

FIGURE 9–8 Sample introduction *(cont.)*

(similar to chapters in books) and divide each major division into sections. The outline of your report is a good source for headings and subheadings.

Probably no other scanning aid will help readers more than the liberal use of headings. To test this claim take any report, article, or manual more than two or three pages long, remove the headings, and see how suddenly the text appears to be tediously uninterrupted and how the major topics disappear into the text. (See also pp. 134–135.)

For those who read your entire report, the headings will be a comforting reminder of the readers' progress. For those who read only certain parts, the headings provide easy reference to those parts the readers are looking for by indicating key topic, at a glance. The headings and subheadings should agree with the entries in the table of contents; in fact, the headings are an "exploded" table of contents inserted at appropriate places throughout the text.

Although slight variations exist in the use of headings, their format is usually handled as shown and explained in Figure 9–9. You'll probably use the complete three-level heading system shown only in longer, more formal reports. Short, informal reports use only certain of these headings. For instance, for brief two- or three-page passages you may use only the sideheadings.

In addition to making sure the levels of importance of your headings are clear from their positions, you should make sure they

- point to the text that follows and relate to each other grammatically;
- are not followed immediately by a pronoun that refers to a word or phrase in them;
- have written text between them, even if it's only an explanation of subdivisions to come;
- have at least two lines of text between the last head on a page and the bottom of a page.

Remember that headings serve as excellent clues to the content and arrangement of material. Think three times before you submit a report that doesn't have them.

THE ENDING   The last major part of the main elements of your report is the ending. Like your introductory section, the ending should emphasize the most important ideas in your report, so make it as strong as your introduction. Some typical functions of formal end sections are (1) to summarize the major points of your report, (2) to state your conclusions, and (3) to state your recommendations. Depending on the type of report and the needs of your readers, the ending may contain any one or a combination of these functions. There may also be times when you may want to provide up-front visibility for your conclusions and recommendations—for instance, when your readers are primarily interested in results and conclusions and recommendations and regard the body of the

CENTER HEADING

The center heading introduces a major division of your report. Center it horizontally about one and a half inches below the top of the page. Capitalize all letters or capitize the first letter of the first word and of all other important words. Underscore the heading. If the center heading is too long for one line, divide it into two or more lines, single-spaced, with the longest line at the top and each succeeding line shorter than the one preceding it. Unless the center heading ends with a question mark or exclamation point, do not punctuate.

Sideheading

The first subheading is the sideheading, which introduces a subdivision of a major division of your report. Begin at the left margin on a separate line, with double or triple space above and double space below. Capitalize the first letter of the first word and of all other important words. Underscore the heading. Unless the sideheading ends with a question mark or exclamation point, do not punctuate.

Paragraph heading. The second subheading is the paragraph heading, which introduces a further subdivision of the major division of your report. Begin at the usual indentation point for new paragraphs. Capitalize the first letter of the first word and of all other important words. Underscore the heading. Put a period after the heading and start the first line of the paragraph two spaces after the period.

FIGURE 9–9 Headings and subheadings

report secondarily. In such instances, you should move them to the front of the report.

1. *Summarizing the major points.* Reports that are primarily informative usually end with a summary that helps readers make sense of the mass of details presented in the body by recalling the essential ideas covered. Just as the introduction offers readers a preview of the body, the summary offers readers a postview. Such a summary is shown in Figure 9–10.

2. *Stating your conclusions.* Reports that are primarily analytical usually end with a conclusion, which lists the logical implications of your findings—the *so-whats.* Sometimes the formal end section combines a summary of the major points and the conclusions reached. Such an ending is shown in Figure 9–11.

3. *Stating your recommendations.* Reports that are primarily analytical and persuasive usually end with recommendations, which fulfill the advisory function of the report. That is, the recommendations tell the reader what to do or not to do. The recommendations should be laid out in a series of parallel statements, each separately paragraphed. Such a list of recommendations is shown in Figure 9–12.

In addition to a summary, conclusion, and recommendations, the ending of your report lists sources that you have cited by either notes or author-year parenthetical entries. Such a list can be end notes, end notes and references, or a reference list that is used with author-year citations. We discuss these matters of documentation in the section Documenting the Report, which begins on page 159.

Supplemental Elements

After the main elements of your report come the supplemental elements, which contain information related to your report that may be of interest to readers but is not essential enough to interrupt your main line of discussion. You must decide what information can be placed in the supplemental elements to help reduce the length and complexity of the main body of the report.

Appendixes contain information or documents that, although useful, might hamper easy reading of the text. Although it is not always easy to decide what material to put in appendixes, we suggest material that has direct—but secondary rather than primary—importance to your reader. Glossaries, copies of questionnaires, related correspondence, reports, and the texts of speeches or interviews, along with samples, exhibits, and all kinds of supplemental tables, figures, and case histories, are the kinds of material we have in mind. A glossary or list of symbols that may be too lengthy to place in the introduction of the report could be placed in an appendix. The first part of a typical glossary is shown in Figure 9–13.

A bibliography that lists readings related to a particular topic—but does not serve as a list of the sources you have cited in your report—

SUMMARY

This report has described problems of ground control of floor heaving encountered in underground coal mines. The history of floor heave problems in the coal seams, the floor and roof analysis techniques used to determine rock stress values, and the recommended mine design solutions to problems of ground control have been presented.

There are probably as many types and causes of floor heave as there are types of roof falls. The investigation and analysis described in this report may not apply to mines experiencing floor heave in which the floor contains significant amounts of clay. However, since the apparent cause of floor heaving in this area is the existence of a high, biaxial, horizontal stress field running through the thrust fault system of eastern Kentucky, southwest West Virginia, and western Virginia, the techniques may have wide applicability to the area's mining industry. Although the recommendations for mining are directed at floor problems, the suggested orientations and geometries should also improve roof stability.

FIGURE 9–10 Summary

SUMMARY AND CONCLUSIONS

An attempt has been made in this report to inform the reader about the nature of radioactive fallout and how it is currently being handled by conventional measurement and removal methods with regard to surface water supplies.

1. Fallout will affect the nation's water supply. Although the quantities of radioactivity cannot be predicted, the nature of radioactivity can be predicted.

2. The greatest immediate danger would come from suspended activity. After an atomic attack radioactive material would tend to settle. Streams and rivers would scour sediment from their beds at times of flooding and high water. Later the sediment would be deposited downstream.

3. Dissolved radioactivity presents a long-range danger to water supply. Radioactive sediments would be leached from the bottoms of streams, rivers, and reservoirs.

4. Treatment plants would not remove much, if any, dissolved radioactivity. Radioactive filter sand can increase the radioactivity of treated water.

FIGURE 9–11   Summary and conclusions

VII. RECOMMENDATIONS

Based upon the conclusions reached, we recommend the following:

1. That the State launch a program for the restoration and preservation of the land grant records and other aged documents which are lodged in the office of the Secretary of State. A physical plant for this purpose could be equipped for no more than $25,000 and manned by two persons.

2. That, since the primary function of the Historical Society is the collection and preservation of information, documents, and relics pertaining to Kentucky history and since the society's personnel has been engaged in a substantial microfilming of historical data and is now annually accumulating approximately one million pages of records on film, the restoration shop should be the responsibility of, and located in, the Historical Society. Judgments must necessarily be made, and priorities set, on the historical worth of certain documents nominated for preservation.

3. That the Historical Society, in cooperation with the Secretary of State and the Finance Department, produce, in bound volumes, microfilmed copies of the land grant records for public use and that the original be stored in a safe place.

FIGURE 9–12 Recommendations

APPENDIX A: GLOSSARY

acre-foot – The amount of water required to cover one acre to a depth of
        one foot; equal to 43,560 cubic feet of water, or 326,000 gallons.

adsorption – Retention of an ion or molecule of variable size onto the
        surface of a molecule or molecular complex due to attractive
        physical chemical forces.

aeration – The bringing about of intimate contact between air and a
        liquid by spraying the liquid in the air or by agitation of the
        liquid to promote surface absorption of air.

   step aeration – A procedure for adding increments of sewage along
        the line of flow in the aeration tanks of an activated sludge
        plant. (C. F. Gould, U.S. Patent 2,337,384.)

algae – Primitive plants, one- or many-celled, usually aquatic and
        capable of elaborating their foodstuffs by photosynthesis.

algicide – Any substance that kills algae.

average daily flow – Average of all daily flow during at least one
        entire year (includes storm drainage).

average dry weather flow – Average daily flow comprised of domestic
        sewage, industrial waste, and ground water infiltration (no storm
        drainage).

biochemical oxygen demand (BOD) – The quantity of oxygen used in the
        biochemical oxidation of organic matter for five days at 20°C,
        usually expressed in parts per million.

calcination/recalcination – The process of regenerating lime from lime
        sludge after lime coagulation. Up to 70 percent of the lime can be
        recovered for reuse.

chloramines – Compounds of organic amines or inorganic ammonia with
        chlorine that are highly toxic to fish; their effect on man is
        unknown.

chlorination – The application of chlorine to disinfect the sewage.

clarifier – A tank or basin in which water, sewage, or other liquid
        containing settleable solids is retained for a sufficient time, and
        in which the velocity of flow is sufficiently low, to remove by
        gravity a part of the suspended matter. Usually, in sewage
        treatment, the retention period is short enough to avoid anaerobic
        decomposition. Also termed Settling or Subsidence Tank or
        Sedimentation.

FIGURE 9–13 Glossary (Adapted from The Conservation Foundation, *Water Quality, Training Institute,*
Washington, D.C.: The Foundation, n.d. [c. 1974])

could also be placed in an appendix. It may be arranged alphabetically, chronologically, or by type of publication. It may be done in either the humanities or science style. We discuss these matters in the next section of this chapter and in Chapter 11, "Bibliographic Reports and Literature Reviews."

DOCUMENTING THE REPORT

In writing your report, you may draw on information already made available by others in published or unpublished sources. When you refer to the work of others, document the source you are quoting or paraphrasing by citing the source, either with notes or with parenthetical author-year entries keyed to a reference list. In this section we explain how to handle quotations and paraphrases, how to write notes and parenthetical author-year entries, and how to write bibliographies and reference lists.

Quotations

An important tactic that helps readers follow *your* writing is the skillful handling of quoted material in your reports. If you use quotations ineptly, you lose control of your report. It is important, therefore, to know when to quote and how to quote. Here are some conventions of quoting that will help you stay on top of quoted material and let you use it to support your views.

1. Ordinarily avoid beginning or ending a report or a paragraph with quotations for two reasons. First, quotations in these positions produce a weak effect by drawing the focus away from your own writing. Because the beginning and end are the two most emphatic positions, you should use them for your own ideas and conclusions. Second, quotations at the beginning of a report or paragraph make it appear as though you're too indebted to the ideas of others and that *your* writing serves only to explain the quotation. An important exception to these suggestions occurs when you want to use a quotation as an attention-getting device. Just remember to select quotations for the added authority they can give to *your* ideas.

2. Introduce quotations by acknowledging them with a general comment such as "As one recent research study has found . . ." or with a specific reference, such as "Dr. Hiram Walton states. . . ."

3. All quotations must correspond exactly with the original wording, spelling, and interior punctuation. If you choose to omit words from a quoted passage, you must indicate the omitted words by using ellipsis points (three or four spaced periods). See Writer's Guide, page 412. If you add a word or short phrase within a quotation, enclose the added words in brackets. Don't use parentheses because readers will assume that the parenthetical statement exists in the original passage. See Writer's Guide, page 404.

4. All quotations within text are enclosed inside quotation marks. A quotation within a quotation is enclosed in single quotation marks (typed by using the apostrophe). See Writer's Guide, page 429–431.

5. Single-space quotations longer than three typewritten lines, indenting and centering the quotations. Don't place quotation marks around single-spaced, indented quotations—they are unnecessary additional punctuation. See Writer's Guide, pages 429–431, and Figure 9–14.

6. Document every quotation and paraphrase with a note or with a parenthetical author-year entry keyed to a reference list. When you cite information from another source, include enough information about the source to enable your readers to locate the cited item. In notes (pages 160–169), this information is given in the first note to a source, so it is usually not necessary to include a reference list at the end of the report unless your reader expects one or the report specifications require one. In parenthetical author-year entries, only the last name of the author or editor, the year of publication, and the specific part of the source cited are normally given, so you must provide a reference list at the end of the report that gives readers complete publication information. (See pages 182–185.)

Notes are used mostly in reports and papers in the humanities; author-year entries are used primarily in reports and papers in the natural and physical sciences and are being used more and more in the social sciences and the humanities.

Notes and Author-Year Citations

You must identify the sources that you have quoted or paraphrased. This identification comes in many varieties, but most provide the same information. However, these different forms shouldn't bother you. Just learn the form you are expected to use and stay consistent. If you are not required to use a particular form, we suggest that you learn the following forms based on the standardized and widely used forms in *The Chicago Manual of Style,* 13th edition (1982).

NOTES Making notes involves citing a source in two places:

- Making a reference to the note by placing a superscript note number (like this[1]) in the text, as shown in Figure 9–15.
- Displaying the note at the bottom of the page on which the note number appears (footnotes), as shown in Figure 9–15, or at the end of the report (end notes) in a section headed "Notes," as illustrated in Figure 9–16.

The first note to a source contains the name of the author or editor of the work, the title of the work, and the facts of publication. The punctuation between the author's or editor's name, the title of the work, and the facts of publication consists of commas and parentheses. The author's or editor's name is given in normal order—first name or initial, middle name

11

Researchers seem to agree that the questionnaire
should be as simple as possible. McKinney and Oglesby
suggest testing the questionnaire for readability level
"to insure that the content is pitched neither too high
nor too low for the intellectual capabilities of the
respondents" (1982, 322).

Recent studies (Griffey 1983; Peavler and McBride
1984) show that the questionnaire should be personalized,
as well as simple. Every attempt must be made to get
responses from all the subjects. According to Griffey
(1983, 41), who returns the questionnaires can affect
results:

> In a Wisconsin study with a 46.9 percent response,
> it was discovered that 78 percent of the former
> students in the top percentile of their class re-
> turned the questionnaire, while only 28 percent
> from the bottom percentile returned the questionnaire.

The tendency for successful students to return more questionnaires than their less successful counterparts can invalidate
findings and conclusions.

Snelling (1979) suggests that a high response rate is
possible from all segments of the population if the questionnaire is highly personalized. Snelling hypothesized that
"if every possible effort were made so that the material
received by the graduate appeared to be prepared for him or

FIGURE 9–14 Author-year citations in parentheses. In the center of the page is a "long" quotation—a direct quotation longer than three lines. Such quotations are set off single-spaced and indented. Quotation marks are unnecessary when long quotations are in this format.

Generic foods have been marketed for a long time. According to the Grocery Manufacturers of America, Inc., many years before brand name manufacturers guaranteed the quality, safety, and cleanliness of their products, people bought their groceries out of jugs, barrels, sacks, and bins.[1] So generic foods are not new. What is new is the way they are being marketed. Stephanie Azzarone, a field editor for Supermarket Magazine, reports that the Jewell Food stores in Chicago began marketing low-priced, plainly packaged products in its stores in February 1977.[2] What

1. Grocery Manufacturers of America, Inc., The Label Tells the Story (Grocery Manufacturers of America, Inc., n.d.), 9.

2. Stephanie Azzarone, "Generic Foods: No Frills, Lower Bills," Consumers Digest, November–December 1979, 24.

FIGURE 9–15 Notes on a page

NOTES

1.　Arthur T. Turnbull and Russell N. Baird, The
Graphics of Communication, 4th ed. (New York: Holt,
Rinehart and Winston, 1980), 116.

2.　James B. Rule, "Goodbye Gutenberg: The Newspaper
Revolution of the 1980s," Datamation 27 (December 1981):
188.

3.　Ibid.

4.　E. J. Kyle, "Which Is the Image?" Screen Printing
72 (February 1982): 36.

5.　Turnbull and Baird, 154.

6.　William J. Denk and W. Scott Grover, "Retaining
Color Originals: Concerns and Assurances," Gravure Technical
Association Bulletin 32 (January 1982): 94.

7.　"Bindery Speeds not Keeping up with Other Areas of
Production," Folio 12 (January 1982): 22.

8.　E. J. Kyle, "Special Mesh Fabrics, Part 2," Screen
Printing 72 (January 1982): 40.

9.　Bruno J. Vieri, Charlotte K. Beyers, and Bob Gilmore,
"Optics and the Office of the Future," Optical Spectra 15
(November 1981): 48.

10.　E. J. Kyle, "Special Mesh Fabrics, Part 2," 38.

11.　Ibid.

12.　Ibid., 40.

FIGURE 9–16　List of notes

or initial, and last name. The specific page number or numbers are cited. The first line is indented five spaces and the note number is placed on the line. These features can be seen in Figure 9–17 and Figure 9–18 and in the following examples. Afterward are examples of subsequent notes to sources.

- Book by one author:

> 1. Shirley Biagi, <u>A Writer's Guide to Word Processors</u> (Englewood Cliffs, N.J.: Prentice-Hall, Inc., 1984), 114.

List the author's name as it appears on the title page of the book.

- Book by two authors:

> 2. Robert J. Baron and Linda G. Shapiro, <u>Data Structures and Their Implementation</u> (New York: Van Nostrand Reinhold Company, 1980), 108–12.

List both authors as they appear on the title page—not necessarily in alphabetical order.

- Book by three authors:

> 3. Ralph D. Nyland, Charles C. Larson, and Hardy L. Shirley, <u>Forestry and Its Career Opportunities</u>, 4th ed. (New York: McGraw-Hill Book Company, 1983), 115.

- Book by more than three authors:

> 4. Tim O'Sullivan et al., <u>Key Concepts in Communication</u> (London: Methuen & Company, Ltd., 1983), 188.

List the first author and designate the other authors by "et al., " from the Latin *et alii,* "and others."

- Book by corporate or organizational author:

> 5. American Concrete Institute, ACI Committee 547, <u>Refactory Concrete</u> (Detroit: American Concrete Institute, 1979), 200.

When a book issued by an organization does not carry an author's name on the title page, list the organization or responsible group as the author.

> 6. National Air Transportation Association, <u>Refueling and Quality Control Procedures for Airport Service and Support Operations</u> (Austin, Texas: Texas Aeronautics Commission, 1983), 28–29.
>
> 7. Deere and Company, <u>Welding</u> (Moline, Ill.: J. Deere, 1971), 3.

- Book with editor:

> 8. J. A. Ross, ed., <u>The National Electric Code Handbook</u> (Quincy, Mass.: National Fire Protection Association, 1981), 16.

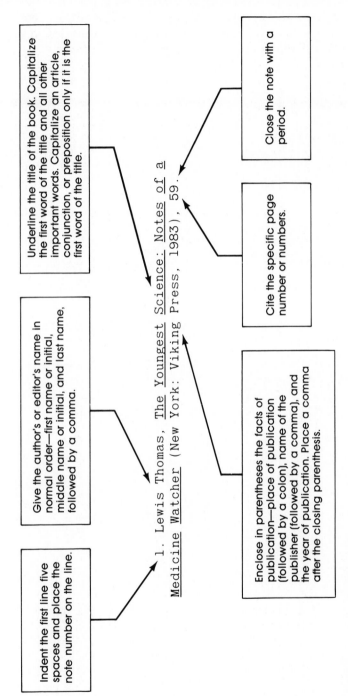

Indent the first line five spaces and place the note number on the line.

Give the author's or editor's name in normal order—first name or initial, middle name or initial, and last name, followed by a comma.

Underline the title of the book. Capitalize the first word of the title and all other important words. Capitalize an article, conjunction, or preposition only if it is the first word of the title.

Close the note with a period.

Cite the specific page number or numbers.

Enclose in parentheses the facts of publication—place of publication (followed by a colon), name of the publisher (followed by a comma), and the year of publication. Place a comma after the closing parenthesis.

    1. Lewis Thomas, The Youngest Science: Notes of a
Medicine Watcher (New York: Viking Press, 1983), 59.

FIGURE 9–17 Note for a book

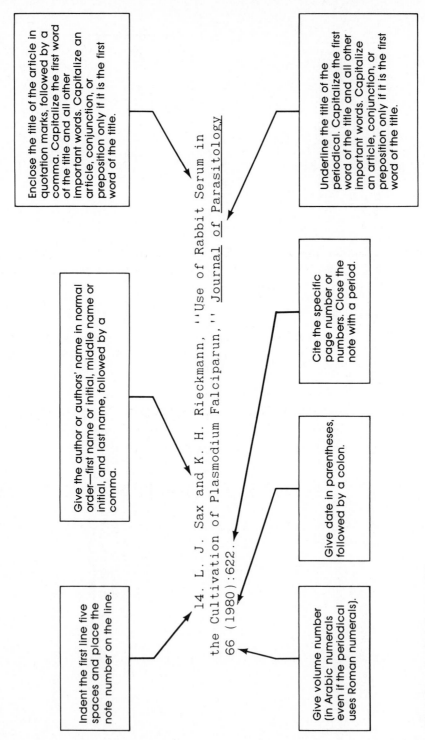

Enclose the title of the article in quotation marks, followed by a comma. Capitalize the first word of the title and all other important words. Capitalize an article, conjunction, or preposition only if it is the first word of the title.

Underline the title of the periodical. Capitalize the first word of the title and all other important words. Capitalize an article, conjunction, or preposition only if it is the first word of the title.

Give the author or authors' name in normal order—first name or initial, middle name or initial, and last name, followed by a comma.

Cite the specific page number or numbers. Close the note with a period.

Give date in parentheses, followed by a colon.

Indent the first line five spaces and place the note number on the line.

Give volume number (in Arabic numerals even if the periodical uses Roman numerals).

14. L. J. Sax and K. H. Rieckmann, ''Use of Rabbit Serum in the Cultivation of Plasmodium Falciparun,'' Journal of Parasitology 66 (1980):622.

FIGURE 9–18 Note for an article

9. D. R. C. Kempe and Anthony P. Harvey, eds., The Petrology of Archeological Artifacts (New York: Oxford University Press, 1983), 219–21.

• Multivolume books:

10. Elaine Noffze et al., Multiple Learning Strategies: Dietetic Assistant, vol. 1 (Mason, Mich.: Capital Area Career Center, Ingham Intermediate School District, 1971), 16.

When a book is published in more than one volume, give the volume number after the title.

11. David Dery, Computers in Welfare: The MIS-Match, vol. 3 of Managing Information (Beverly Hills, Calif.: SAGE Publications, 1981), 114.

When a multivolume work has a general title as well as individual volume titles, list the title of the individual volume first, followed by its volume number and the general title.

• Part of a book:

12. Emily Slopes, "Alternative Work Patterns and the Double Life," in Women, Power, and Policy, ed. Ellen Boneparth (New York: Pergamon Press, 1982), 88.

• Book in other than the first edition:

13. Eva Medved, The World of Food, 3rd ed. (Lexington, Mass.: Ginn and Company, 1981), 392–93.

• Journal article:

14. L. J. Sax and K. H. Rieckman, "Use of Rabbit Serum in the Cultivation of Plasmodium Falciparun," Journal of Parasitology 66 (1980): 622.

Use Arabic numerals for the volume number even when a journal itself uses Roman numerals.

• Popular magazine article:

15. Jamie Murphy, "Dodging Celestial Garbage," Time, 21 May 1984, 92.

16. Lois Wingerson, "Robot Junkies," Science 84, June 1984, 58.

If desirable, you may include the volume number, so the entry would read: . . . Science 84 5 (June 1984): 58. But be consistent.

• Newspaper article:

17. Jerry Knight and Caroline Atkinson, "Does Anybody Out There Have Any Good Answers? Washington Post, 26 October 1983, Sec. F, p. 3.

18. "University Prepares to Grow Oil," <u>New York Times,</u> 3 January 1980, p. 3.

When the newspaper article is unsigned, begin with the title of the article.

● Article in a reference book:

19. <u>Encyclopaedia Britannica: Macropaedia,</u> 15th ed., s.v. "Technology of Photography."

Place "s.v." (*sub verbo,* "under the word") before the item.

20. <u>McGraw-Hill Encyclopedia of Environmental Science,</u> 2nd ed., s.v. "Coal Gasification."

● Unpublished documents:

21. D. L. Begley et al., "Lightning: Hazard to Wind Turbines" (paper read at the Second Annual Wind Technology Conference, Plainfield, Texas, 18 March 1984), 10.
22. J. L. Lolly, "Use of Instructional Resources by Community Junior College Occupational Instructors" (Ph.D. dissertation, North Texas State University, 1978), 28–33.

● Interview and personal communications:

23. Mary Kiser, interview with author, Morehead, Kentucky, 4 August 1985.
24. Ida Martinez, telephone conversation with author, 10 January 1985.
25. John T. Barker, letter to author, 29 April 1984.

The first citation of a source contains the complete information described in the preceding examples. For subsequent citations to the same reference, a variety of shorter entries are used.

When you cite a source already identified fully in a previous note, with no intervening notes, the note must contain only "Ibid." (from the Latin *ibidem,* "in the same place"). When you are referring to the same entry but to a different page or pages, the footnote must contain the new page numbers—"Ibid., 78–80."

1. Lewis Thomas, The Youngest Science: <u>Notes of a Medicine Watcher</u> (New York: Viking Press, 1983), 59.
2. Ibid.
3. Ibid., 79–80.

When other documents come between a first reference and subsequent references to the same work, give the author's last name and the appropriate page number or numbers.

1. June Goodfield, "Vaccine on Trial," <u>Science 84,</u> June 1984, 79.
2. Lewis Thomas, The Youngest Science: <u>Notes of a Medicine Watcher</u> (New York: Viking Press, 1983), 59.
3. Goodfield, 79.
4. Thomas, 63–66.

However, if you have cited two or more publications by the same author, you'll have to include a short version of the title in the subsequent note to avoid confusion. In the following example, if the fourth note stated only "Thomas, 77" and the seventh note stated only "Parrish, 94," the reader would not know which of Thomas' or Parrish's works the author was referring to.

1. Lewis Thomas, The Youngest Science: Notes of a Medicine Watcher (New York: Viking Press, 1983), 100.

2. Lewis Thomas, The Medusa and the Snail: More Notes of a Biology Watcher (New York: Viking Press, 1979), 116.

3. H. M. Parrish, "Early Excision and Suction of Snakebite Wounds in Dogs," North Carolina Medical Journal 16 (1955): 93.

4. Thomas, The Youngest Science, 77.

5. H. M. Parrish, "Hospital Management of Pit Viper Envenomations," Clinical Toxicology 3 (1970): 501.

6. S. A. Minton, Jr., Venom Diseases (Springfield, Ill.: Charles C Thomas, 1974), 169–75.

7. Parrish, "Early Excision and Suction of Snakebite Wounds in Dogs," 94.

AUTHOR-YEAR CITATIONS Citing sources with parenthetical author-year entries in the text involves two steps:

1. Identifying parenthetically in the text the author's or editor's name and year of publication (and when specific pages or other parts are cited, those too), as shown in Figure 9–14.
2. Listing alphabetically the cited documents at the end of the report in a section headed "Works Cited," "List of References," or some other appropriate title, as shown in Figure 9–19 (humanities style) and Figure 9–20 (science style).

Here's how the system works. The reader reads a passage like the following and sees the author and year cited in parentheses:

Several nonmetallic materials have been considered for large wind turbine blades. Both fiberglass and wood composite appear to be alternatives to steel and aluminum, but because fiberglass and wood are both poor conductors, a direct lightning strike could cause severe damage. Fiberglass radomes have been shattered when no protection was provided (Fisher and Plumer 1977). Other research has shown that epoxy-wood blades can be severely damaged if they are not protected (Bankaitis 1982).

Should the reader wish to know more about the article by Fisher or Plumer or the report by Bankaitis, the works cited or reference list section at the end of the report would provide complete publication information.

The following examples demonstrate the various ways to handle parenthetical author-year citations in the text. Afterward, we illustrate the format for entries in the references.

WORKS CITED

"Bindery Speeds not Keeping up with Other Areas of
Production." _Folio_ 12 (January 1982): 22.

Denk, William J., and W. Scott Grover. "Retaining Color
Originals: Concerns and Assurances." _Gravure Technical
Association Bulletin_ 32 (Fall 1981): 94-97.

Kyle, E. J. Special Mesh Fabrics, Part 2." _Screen Printing_
72 (January 1982): 36, 38, 40.

_____. "Which Is the Image?" _Screen Printing_ 72 (February
1982): 34, 36, 113.

Rule, James B. "Goodbye Gutenberg: The Newspaper Revolution
of the 1980s." _Datamation_ 27 (December 1981): 187-8.

Turnbull, Arthur T. and Russell N. Baird. _The Graphics of
Communication_. 4th ed. New York: Holt, Rinehart and
Winston, 1980.

Vieri, Bruno J., Charlotte K. Beyers, and Bob Gilmore,
"Optics and the Office of the Future." _Optica Spectra_
15 (November 1981): 47-49, 50-51.

FIGURE 9–19 Works cited (using humanities-style entries)

REFERENCES

Bindery speeds not keeping up with other areas of production.
1982. <u>Folio</u> 12 (January): 22.

Denk, W. J., and W. S. Grover. 1981. Retaining color originals:
Concerns and assurances. <u>Gravure Technical Association
Bulletin</u> 32 (Fall): 94-97.

Kyle, E. J. 1982a. Special mesh fabrics, part 2. <u>Screen
Printing</u> 72 (January): 36, 38, 40.

_____. 1982b. Which is the image? <u>Screen Printing</u> 72
(February): 34, 36, 113.

Rule, J. B. 1981. Goodbye Gutenberg: The newspaper revolution
of the 1980s. <u>Datamation</u> 27 (December): 187-8.

Turnbull, A. T., and R. N. Baird. 1980. <u>The graphics of
communication</u>. 4th ed. New York: Holt, Rinehart and
Winston.

Vieri, B. J., C. K. Beyers, and B. Gilmore. 1981. Optics and
the office of the future. <u>Optica Spectra</u> 15 (November):
47-49, 50-51.

FIGURE 9–20 List of references (using science-style entries)

- Place the year in parentheses immediately after the author's or editor's name:

    > Primeau (1983) disagrees with earlier interpretations of the event.

The designation of "editor" is not given in the parenthetical reference.

- If you don't use the author's or editor's name in the sentence, include both the name and the year in parentheses:

    > At least one author (Primeau 1983) disagrees with earlier interpretations of the event.

- When citing a specific page or part of the work, separate it from the year by a comma:

    > Primeau considered the event to be "a natural phenomenon" (1983, 414).

    > The event has been considered "a natural phenomenon" (Primeau 1983, 414).

    > Cotton growers in semi-arid counties are increasing their use of surge irrigation (Bailey 1984, Figure 2).

- When citing works of multiple authorship, include the names of two or three authors and "et al." or "others" for more than three authors:

    > In 1975 researchers succeeded in fusing a myeloma tumor cell, capable of producing antibodies, with a spleen cell from an animal which previously had been primed with a known antigen (Kohler and Milstein 1975).

    > During the past decade several projects have used surge irrigation (Johnson, Martin, and Nordeen 1985).

    > Recent tests (Kleinmann et al. 1984) show that whereas the grenade is effectively spin-stabilized in flight, it tends to drift to the right as it descends from its maximum ordinate.

- When citing a work that has a corporation or organizational author, use the name of the organization or group as the author:

    > According to a recent study (Northeastern Commission on Higher Education 1985) more and more adults are returning to college.

- When citing a work that has no ascertainable author, use the title of the article or book as the author:

    > Soil resistivity can be decreased by adding moisture or chemicals to the soil ("Recommended Practice for Grounding of Industrial Power Systems" 1980).

    > There are three important sources of data-entry operators: (1) graduates from schools and colleges, (2) data-entry operators currently in the work force, and (3) secretarial and clerical

personnel currently in the work force (The Phosphorus on the Screen 1986).

- When referring to a volume of a multivolume work, use the abbreviation "vol." to distinguish the volume number from a page number:

    A relatively new specialization in management, as described by several practitioners, is hotel and motel management (Kreck and McCracken 1975, vol. 1).

- When citing a specific page or pages of a multivolume work, separate the volume number from the page number with a colon:

    Magnetic cards are replacing keys in electronic security systems (Kreck and McCracken 1975, 1:416–17).

- Use lowercase letters (a, b, c) to identify two or more works published in the same year by the same author:

    Brazing alloys that contain phosphorus should never be used with any nickel alloy (Weinsheimer 1985a).

- Use a semicolon to separate two or more references in the same parenthesis:

    A slightly etched surface has better capillary action for the flow of copper (Uhlig 1984; DeLong and Shinoda 1985).

- Since telephone conversations, interviews, and personal correspondence normally are not included in the reference list, include full information in the parenthetical citation:

    Rose McClure of the University of Guelph, Ontario, Canada, believes that "contrary to popular opinion, electronic communication will generate more paperwork, not less" (telephone interview, April 1, 1985).

    In a recent research project on the social dynamics of Barnacle geese, investigators tested the relationship between "facial expression" of the geese and dominance patterns (Jakob Probst, letter to author, July 16, 1985).

When you cite publications with author-year parenthetical entries, you must key them to a reference list at the end of the report.

Bibliographies and Reference Lists

There are two kinds of bibliographies. For reports and papers in the humanities, notes are ordinarily the basic form of documentation. However, on those occasions when you want to group all the sources cited with notes into a single list for the convenience of the reader, you can provide a list at the end of the main elements of the report. Such a bibliography would come after the last page of a report using footnotes or after the notes section of a report using end notes. In addition, a bibliography can be a list of sources that serves as a guide for reading on a particular subject. Such a bibliography, if included in a report, would be an appendix in the supplemental elements of the report. Also, such a bibliography as a guide to reading can be a report in itself. We discuss the bibliography as a report in itself in Chapter 11, "Bibliographic Reports and Literature Reviews."

For reports using parenthetical author-year citations, a reference list must be used that includes full publication information of all sources that have been cited in the report. Such a reference list is included as the last item in the main elements of the report.

The Chicago Manual of Style recommends different styles for entries in bibliographies and reference lists in the humanities and sciences. The humanities style for book and article entries is shown in Figure 9–21 and Figure 9–22; a humanities-style reference list is shown in Figure 9–19.

The science style for book and article entries in a reference list is shown in Figure 9–23 and Figure 9–24. A science-style reference list is shown in Figure 9–20.

HUMANITIES-STYLE ENTRIES   Humanities-style entries for bibliographies and reference lists provide basically the same information as note entries—the name of the author or editor, the title of the work, and the facts of publication. But there are these differences:

NOTE ENTRIES	HUMANITIES-STYLE ENTRIES
The punctuation between the author's or editor's name, the title of the work, and the facts of publication consists of commas and parentheses.	The punctuation between the author's or editor's name, the title of the work, and the facts of publication consists of periods.
The author's or editor's name is given in normal order—first name or initial, middle name or initial, and last name.	The author's or editor's name is reversed (last name first) for alphabetizing the entry in the list.
The specific page number or numbers are cited.	Inclusive page numbers of articles and parts of books are included.
The first line is indented five spaces, and the note number is placed on the line.	The first line begins flush with the left margin and subsequent lines begin five spaces to the right of the left margin.

These differences can be seen by comparing the format of notes on pages 160–169 and the format of humanities-style entries for bibliography or reference lists that follow. The examples correspond to the items used to illustrate note form.

• Book by one author:

> Biagi, Shirley. <u>A Writer's Guide to Word Processors.</u> Englewood Cliffs, N.J.: Prentice-Hall, 1984.

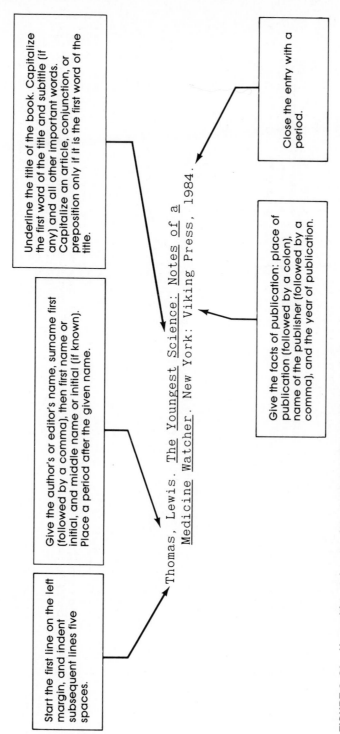

Start the first line on the left margin, and indent subsequent lines five spaces.

Give the author's or editor's name, surname first (followed by a comma), then first name or initial, and middle name or initial (if known). Place a period after the given name.

Underline the title of the book. Capitalize the first word of the title and subtitle (if any) and all other important words. Capitalize an article, conjunction, or preposition only if it is the first word of the title.

Close the entry with a period.

Give the facts of publication: place of publication (followed by a colon), name of the publisher (followed by a comma), and the year of publication.

Thomas, Lewis. <u>The Youngest Science: Notes of a Medicine Watcher.</u> New York: Viking Press, 1984.

FIGURE 9-21. Humanities-style entry for a book in bibliography or reference list

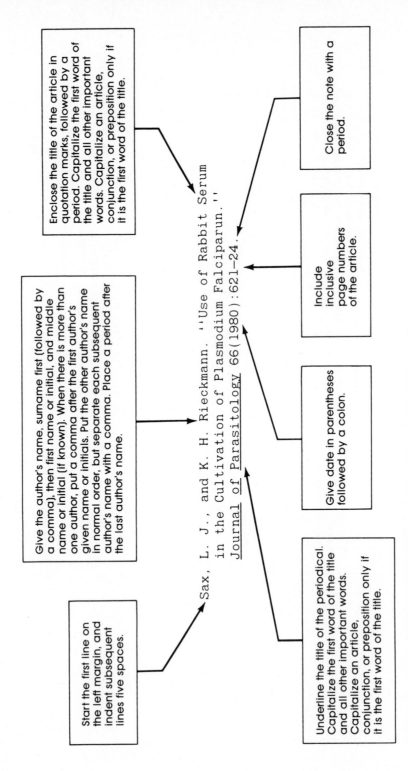

Give the author's name, surname first (followed by a comma), then first name or initial, and middle name or initial (if known). When there is more than one author, put a comma after the first author's given name or initials. Put the other author's name in normal order, but separate each subsequent author's name with a comma. Place a period after the last author's name.

Enclose the title of the article in quotation marks, followed by a period. Capitalize the first word of the title and all other important words. Capitalize an article, conjunction, or preposition only if it is the first word of the title.

Close the note with a period.

Include inclusive page numbers of the article.

Start the first line on the left margin, and indent subsequent lines five spaces.

Give date in parentheses followed by a colon.

Underline the title of the periodical. Capitalize the first word of the title and all other important words. Capitalize an article, conjunction, or preposition only if it is the first word of the title.

Sax, L. J., and K. H. Rieckmann. ''Use of Rabbit Serum in the Cultivation of Plasmodium Falciparun.'' Journal of Parasitology 66(1980):621–24.

FIGURE 9–22 Humanities-style entry for an article in bibliography or reference list

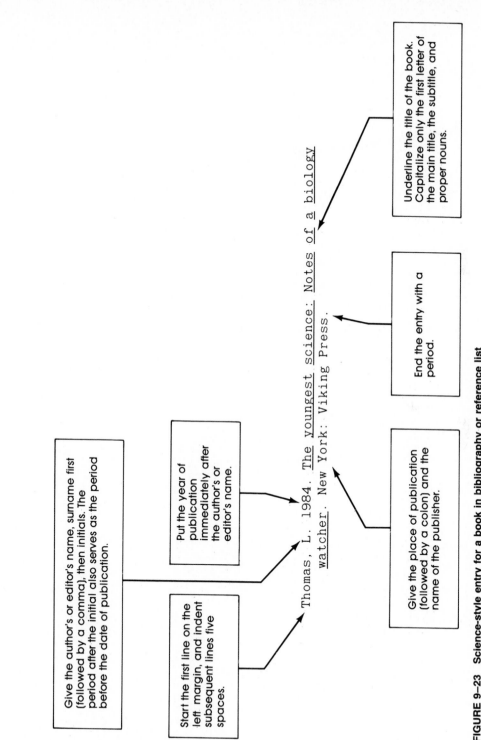

Give the author's or editor's name, surname first (followed by a comma), then initials. The period after the initial also serves as the period before the date of publication.

Put the year of publication immediately after the author's or editor's name.

Start the first line on the left margin, and indent subsequent lines five spaces.

Thomas, L. 1984. <u>The youngest science: Notes of a biology watcher.</u> New York: Viking Press.

Underline the title of the book. Capitalize only the first letter of the main title, the subtitle, and proper nouns.

End the entry with a period.

Give the place of publication (followed by a colon) and the name of the publisher.

FIGURE 9–23 Science-style entry for a book in bibliography or reference list

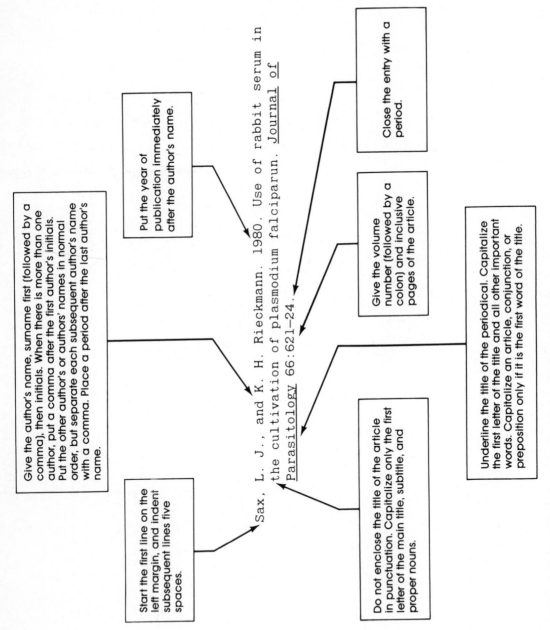

Give the author's name, surname first (followed by a comma), then initials. When there is more than one author, put a comma after the first author's initials. Put the other author's or authors' names in normal order, but separate each subsequent author's name with a comma. Place a period after the last author's name.

Put the year of publication immediately after the author's name.

Close the entry with a period.

Give the volume number (followed by a colon) and inclusive pages of the article.

Start the first line on the left margin, and indent subsequent lines five spaces.

Sax, L. J., and K. H. Rieckmann. 1980. Use of rabbit serum in the cultivation of plasmodium falciparun. *Journal of Parasitology* 66:621-24.

Do not enclose the title of the article in punctuation. Capitalize only the first letter of the main title, subtitle, and proper nouns.

Underline the title of the periodical. Capitalize the first letter of the title and all other important words. Capitalize an article, conjunction, or preposition only if it is the first word of the title.

FIGURE 9–24   Science-style entry for an article in bibliography or reference list

- Book by two authors:

  Baron, Robert J., and Linda G. Shapiro. Data Structures and Their Implementation. New York: Van Nostrand Reinhold Company, 1980.

- Book by three authors:

  Nyland, Ralph D., Charles C. Larson, and Hardy L. Shirley. Forestry and Its Career Opportunities. 4th ed. New York: McGraw-Hill Book Company 1983.

- Book by more than three authors:

  O'Sullivan, Tim et al. Key Concepts in Communication. London: Methuen & Company, Ltd., 1983.

- Book by corporate or organizational author:

  American Concrete Institute. ACI Committee 547. Refactory Concrete. Detroit: American Concrete Institute, 1979.

  National Air Transportation Association. Refueling and Quality Control Procedures for Airport Service and Support Operations. Austin: Texas Aeronautics Commission, 1983.

  Deere and Company. Welding. Moline, Ill.: J. Deere, 1971.

- Book with editor:

  Ross, J. A., ed. The National Electric Code Handbook. Quincy, Mass.: National Fire Protection Association, 1981.

  Kempe, D. R. C., and Anthony P. Harvey, eds. The Petrology of Archeological Artifacts. New York: Oxford University Press, 1983.

- Multivolume books:

  Noffze, Elaine et al. Multiple Learning Strategies Project: Dietetic Assistant. Vol. 1. Mason, Mich.: Capital Area Career Center, Ingham Intermediate School District, 1977.

  Dery, David. Computers in Welfare: The MIS-Match. Vol. 3 of Managing Information. Beverly Hills, Calif.: SAGE Publications, Inc., 1981.

- Parts of a book:

  Slopes, Emily. "Alternative Work Patterns and the Double Life." In Women, Power, and Policy, edited by Ellen Boneparth, 90–108. New York: Pergamon Press, 1982.

Note that "edited by" is used in the bibliographic entry. If desired, you may give the inclusive page numbers of the part of the book; they should follow the book's title and its editor.

- Book in other than first edition:

  Medved, Eva. The World of Food. 3rd ed. Lexington, Mass.: Ginn and Company, 1981.

- Journal article:

  Sax, L. J., and K. H. Rieckmann. "Use of Rabbit Serum in the Cultivation of Plasmodium Falciparun." Journal of Parasitology 66 (1980): 621–24.

In the bibliography entry, give the inclusive page numbers of the article.

- Popular magazine article:

  Murphy, Jamie. "Dodging Celestial Garbage." Time, 21 May 1984, 92.

  Wingerson, Lois. "Robot Junkies." Science 84, June 1984, 56–63.

  . . . Science 84 5 (June 1984): 56–63.

- Newspaper article:

  Knight, Jerry, and Caroline Atkinson. "Does Anybody Out There Have Any Good Answers?" Washington Post, 26 October 1980, Sec. F, p. 3.

  "University Prepared to Grow Oil." New York Times, 3 January 1981, p. 3.

- Article in a reference book:

  Encyclopaedia Britannica: Macropaedia, 15th ed. S.v. "Technology of Photography."

  McGraw-Hill Encyclopedia of Environmental Science. 2nd ed. S.v. "Coal Gasification."

- Unpublished documents:

  Begley, D. L., et al. "Lightning: Hazard to Wind Turbines." Paper read at the Second Annual Wind Technology Conference, Plainfield, Texas, 18 March 1984.

  Lolly, J. L. "Use of Instructional Resources by Community Junior College Occupational Instructors." Ph.D. dissertation. North Texas State University, 1978.

- Interviews and personal communications:

  Kiser, Mary. Interview with author. Morehead, Kentucky. 4 August 1984.

  Martinez, Ida. Telephone conversation with author. 10 January 1985.

  Barker, John T. Letter to author. 29 April 1985.

Entries in a humanities-style bibliography may be arranged in alphabetical or chronological order or by type of publication. However, almost all reference lists are arranged alphabetically by the last name of the author or the editor. A work that has a corporate or organizational author is alphabetized by the first word of the corporation or association (excluding *A, An, The*). A work that has no identifiable author is alphabetized by its title (excluding *A, An,* and *The*). Here's a sample alphabetized listing:

Azzarone, Stephanie. "Generic Foods: No Frills, Lower Bills." Consumers Digest, November-December 1979, 24–25.

Baker, Gordon. Interview with the author. West Palm Beach, Florida, 21 December 1984.

"Generics 'Eroding' Market, Book Reveals." Advertising Age, 22 June 1981, 42.

Grocery Manufacturers of America. The Label Tells the Story. New York: Grocery Manufacturers of America, Inc., n.d.

The *n.d.* in the last entry indicates that the document has no date of publication.

When several works by the same author are listed, arrange them either alphabetically by title or chronologically by date of publication. Use a seven-space underline in place of the author's name after the first appearance. Here is an alphabetical listing of several works by the same author:

Parrish, H. M. "Early Excision and Suction of Snakebite Wounds in Dogs." North Carolina Medical Journal 16 (1955): 93.

_____. "Hospital Management of Pit Viper Envenomations." Clinical Toxicology 3 (1970): 501–2.

_____. "Poisonous Snakebite." New England Journal of Medicine 269 (1963): 624.

_____. "Seven Pitfalls in Treating Pit Viper Bites." Resident Physician (1969): 108–12.

Here are the same works listed chronologically:

Parrish, H. M. "Early Excision and Suction of Snakebite Wounds in Dogs." North Carolina Medical Journal 16 (1955): 93.

_____. "Poisonous Snakebite." New England Journal of Medicine 269 (1963): 624.

_____. "Seven Pitfalls in Treating Pit Viper Bites." Resident Physician (1969): 108–12.

_____. "Hospital Management of Pit Viper Envenomations." Clinical Toxicology 3 (1970): 501–2.

List single-author entries before multi-author entries beginning with the same name. Do not use the seven-space underline with coauthors. Repeat the author's name.

Parrish, H. M. "Early Excision and Suction of Snakebite Wounds in Dogs." North Carolina Medical Journal 16 (1955): 93.

_____. "Hospital Management of Pit Viper Envenomations." Clinical Toxicology 3 (1970): 501–2.

_____. "Seven Pitfalls in Treating Pit Viper Bites." Resident Physician (1969): 108–12.

Parrish, H. M., and C. Carr. "Bites of Copperheads in the United States." Journal of the American Medical Association 201 (1967): 927.

SCIENCE-STYLE ENTRIES   The science style for bibliographies and reference lists provide basically the same information as the humanities style: authors's or editor's name, title of the work, and facts of publication—separated by periods. However, when parenthetical author-year citations are keyed to a reference list, the year of publication immediately follows the author's or editor's name and comes before the title of the work. Here are the similarities and differences between the two styles.

HUMANITIES-STYLE ENTRIES	SCIENCE-STYLE ENTRIES
The author's or editor's given name is usually spelled out.	The author's or editor's given name is usually in initials.
Date of publication is placed after the publisher of a book and after the volume number of a periodical article.	Date of publication is put immediately after the author's or editor's name.
For titles of books, articles, and periodicals, the first letter of words (except articles, conjunctions, and prepositions) are capitalized. If the title begins with an article, conjunction, or preposition, it is capitalized too.	For titles of books and articles, only the first letter of the main title, the subtitle, and proper nouns are capitalized. Titles of periodicals are capitalized as in the humanities style.
The titles of books and periodicals are underlined (to indicate italics).	The titles of books and periodicals are underlined (to indicate italics).
The title of an article is enclosed in quotation marks.	The title of an article is not enclosed in quotation marks.

The differences can be seen by comparing the format of humanities-style entries on pages 174–182 and the format of science-style entries that follow.

- Book by one author:

  Biagi, S. 1984. <u>A writer's guide to word processors.</u> Englewood Cliffs, N.J.: Prentice-Hall.

- Book by two authors:

  Baron, R. J., and L. G. Shapiro. 1980. <u>Data structures and their implementation.</u> New York: Van Nostrand Reinhold Company.

- Book by three authors:

  Nyland, R. D., C. C. Larson, and H. L. Shirley. 1983. <u>Forestry and its career opportunities.</u> 4th ed. New York: McGraw-Hill.

- Book by more than three authors:

  O'Sullivan, T. et al. 1983. <u>Key concepts in communication.</u> London: Methuen & Company.

- Book by corporate or organizational author:

  American Concrete Institute. ACI Committee 547. 1979. <u>Refactory concrete.</u> Detroit: American Concrete Institute.

  National Air Transportation Association. 1983. *Refueling and quality control procedures for airport service and support operations.* Austin: Texas Aeronautics Commission.

  Deere and Company. 1971. <u>Welding.</u> Moline, Ill.: J. Deere.

- Book with editor:

  Ross, J. A., ed. 1981. <u>The national electric code handbook.</u> Quincy, Mass.: National Fire Protection Association.

  Kempe, D. R. C., and A. P. Harvey, eds. 1983. <u>The petrology of archeological artifacts.</u> New York: Oxford University Press.

- Multivolume books:

  Noffze, E. et al. 1977. <u>Multiple learning strategies project: Dietetic assistant.</u> Vol. 1. Mason, Mich.: Capital Area Career Center, Ingham Intermediate School District.

  Dery, D. 1981. <u>Computers in welfare: The MIS-match.</u> Vol. 3 of <u>Managing information.</u> Beverly Hills, Calif.: SAGE Publications, Inc.

- Parts of a book:

  Slopes, E. 1982. Alternative work patterns and the double life. In <u>Women, power, and policy,</u> edited by E. Boneparth, 90–108. New York: Pergamon Press.

- Book in other than first edition:

> Medved, E. 1981. <u>The world of food.</u> 3rd ed. Lexington, Mass.: Ginn and Company.

- Journal article:

> Sax, L. J., and K. H. Rieckmann. 1980. Use of rabbit serum in the cultivation of plasmodium falciparun. <u>Journal of Parasitology</u> 66: 621–24.

- Popular magazine article:

> Murphy, J. 1984. Dodging celestial garbage. <u>Time,</u> May, 92.

> Wingerson, L. 1984. Robot junkies. <u>Science 84</u>, June, 56–63.

> . . . <u>Science 84</u> 5 (June): 56–63.

- Newspaper article:

> Knight, J., and C. Atkinson. 1980. Does anybody out there have any good answers? <u>Washington Post</u>, 26 October, sec. F, p. 3.

> University prepares to grow oil. 1981. *New York Times,* 3 January, p. 3.

- Article in a reference book:

> <u>Encyclopaedia Britannica: Macropaedia.</u> 15th ed. 1984. S.v. Technology of photography.

Normally the date of publication of an encyclopedia is not included in the facts of publication. However, to be consistent in the author-year style, you should include it immediately after the title and edition number (if the edition is other than the first edition). Place "S.v." (*Sub verbo,* "Under the word") before the item.

- Unpublished documents:

> Begley, D. L. et al. 1984. Lightning: Hazard to wind turbines. Paper read at the Second Annual Wind Technology Conference, Plainfield, Texas, 18 March.

> Lolly, J. L. 1978. Use of instructional resources by community college occupational instructors, Ph.D. dissertation. North Texas State University.

- Interviews and personal communications:
Normally such citations are given in complete form in the parenthetical citation. However, if you include the source in the reference list, the following forms are sufficient:

> Kiser, M. 1984. Interview with author. Morehead, Kentucky. 4 August.

> Martinez, I. 1985. Telephone conversation with author. 10 January.
> Barker, J. T. 1985. Letter to author. 29 April.

Science-style bibliographies that serve as a guide to reading on a particular topic may be arranged in alphabetical or chronological order or by type of publication. Science-style reference lists are arranged alphabetically by the last name of the author or editor. A work that has a corporate or organizational author is alphabetized by the first word of the corporation or organization (excluding *A, An, The*). A work that has no identifiable author is alphabetized by its title (excluding *A, An, The*).

When there are two or more works by the same author, they are arranged in chronological order, like this:

> Parrish, H. M. 1955. Early excision and suction of snakebite wounds in dogs. <u>North Carolina Medical Journal</u> 16: 93.

> Parrish, H. M. 1970. Hospital management of pit viper envenomations. <u>Clinical Toxicology</u> 3: 501–2.

You may also use the seven-space underscore instead of repeating the author or editor's name.

> Parrish, H. M. 1955. Early excision and suction of snakebite wounds in dogs. <u>North Carolina Medical Journal</u> 16: 93.

> _____. 1970. Hospital management of pit viper envenomations. <u>Clinical Toxicology</u> 3: 501–2.

When there are two or more works by the same author published in the same year, the entries are listed by date and alphabetically by title, as follows:

> Lukas, M. 1981a. Gould and Teilhard's "fatal error." <u>Teilhard Newsletter</u> 14: 4–6.

> Lukas, M. 1981b. Teilhard and the Piltdown hoax: A playful prank gone too far? Or a deliberate scientific forgery? Or, as it now appears: nothing at all? <u>America,</u> 23 May, 424–27.

Note that works published in the same year are distinguished by lower-case letters after the date.

ILLUSTRATING THE REPORT

We often think there is only one way to report information—through sentences and paragraphs. But tables (containing columns and rows of words, phrases, or commonly, numbers) and figures (photographs, drawings, and charts) are frequently the best way to display certain kinds of information prominently. And finding the right way to provide information is your goal every time you report.

Tables and figures should not be used unless they add to the understanding of your report. But if you've always relied solely on sentences and paragraphs to present your ideas in writing, you should stop to consider the use of tables and figures to present information. There is, of course, no substitute for prose in conveying most ideas. But there are times when you can depend too much on prose, when prose reaches its limits of effectiveness. It all depends on the nature of the information to be conveyed. Take, for instance, an idea that is primarily pictorial, such as the proper distribution of lawn fertilizer using a drop-type spreader. The reader can understand more easily and quickly how to distribute the fertilizer evenly by looking at the drawing in Figure 9–25 than by reading a statement such as "For even distribution, apply one lot of fertilizer lengthwise and the other crosswise over the lawn."

Tables and figures are sometimes really informal listings or pictorials or charts incorporated into the text. As such, they are part of the information within a paragraph and are not set apart or identified by a number, a title, or a lined boundary. An informal table, for instance, might be presented as shown in Figure 9–26. More complicated tables and figures are often set apart from the text, either through the use of a lined boundary or by being placed on a separate page. When separated, tables and figures are usually given titles. If more than three or four formal tables and figures are used in a report, they are usually also given

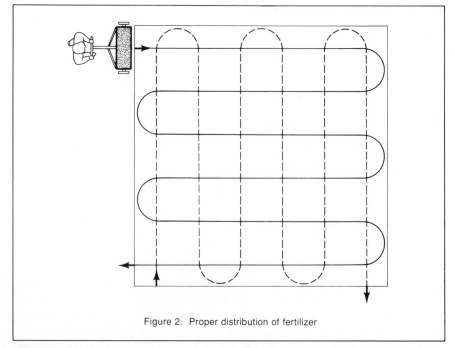

Figure 2. Proper distribution of fertilizer

FIGURE 9–25 Drawing to show the proper distribution of lawn fertilizer using a drop-type spreader. (Source: Texas Agriculture Extension Service, The Texas A&M University System)

Some fairly dramatic changes have occurred in harvesting and handling methods since 1950. In 1956, field shelling of corn was introduced, and the proportion harvested as ear corn has declined steadily since that time. In Illinois, for example, about 2 percent was harvested as shelled corn in 1956. In 1965, the proportion field-shelled had increased to 53 percent, mostly harvested using a combine with corn head. The proportion of Illinois corn harvested by various methods in 1980 was as follows:

Method of harvest	Percent
Combine with corn head	91.5
Mechanical picker	6.5
Field picker-sheller	2.0

The higher machinery cost associated with field shelling and larger acreages has encouraged early harvesting. Corn

FIGURE 9–26 Informal table (Source: Mack N. Leath, Lynn H. Meyer, and Lowell D. Hill, *U.S. Corn Industry,* Agricultural Economic Report No. 479 [Washington, D.C.: U.S. Department of Agriculture, 1982], 15)

numbers. The following information on using tables and figures will help you decide when to use them and how to set them up as formal graphics. (Also, various types of graphics used in mechanism description, process description, instructions, and analytical reports are discussed in Chapters 2, 12, 13, and 14.)

Tables

Tables are word savers. They present simply and clearly large blocks of information without all the connecting devices needed in prose. Data on five crops are arranged in a formal table in Figure 9–27. Notice that the column headings on the top of the table project *down* the table. Only the captions on the side project *across* the table.

Unless you take care in preparing tables, they can become the most confusing part of your report. The following general rules will help you set them up properly:

- Whenever possible, set up a table so it can be typed on the page in normal fashion. Center it between the left and right margins.
- Whenever possible, make each ruled column or row the same width.
- Label each column and row to identify the data. If a column shows amounts, state the units in which the amounts are given, using standard symbols and abbreviations to save space. Center a column heading above the column.

Table I.

District Crop Irrigation Requirements

10-year Average

Crop	District 1	District 2
Corn, gain	69%	57%
Corn, silage	13	12
Grain sorghum	11	18
Alfalfa	5	7
Winter wheat	2	6
Total	100%	100%

FIGURE 9–27 Table

Table VII. Projected Population, Employment, and Dwelling Unit Characteristics

		Study area		Washington County			7–County metro area		
	popula-tion	employ-ment	dwell-ing units	popula-tion	employ-ment	dwell-ing units	popula-tion	employ-ment	dwelling units
1960	27,960	5,209	7,385	52,431	8,640	13,716	1,523,956	607,032	451,974
1970	40,462	8,647	10,699	82,890	16,001	21,258	1,874,093	853,138	573,265
1980	60,600	15,700	18,558	118,800	29,200	34,765	2,230,100	1,106,600	702,629
1990	99,000	28,700	31,799	185,800	49,300	55,633	2,687,000	1,330,800	871,601
2000	144,100	54,400	48,263	267,500	90,300	83,981	3,176,300	1,610,250	1,029,985

Source: Metropolitan Council.

FIGURE 9–28   Table using vertical lines to separate columns

- If the space between columns is wide, use spaced dots or dashes as leaders (as in a table of contents).
- If columns are long, double-space after every fifth entry.
- If column entries are of unequal length, center the longest one and align the rest by using the expressed or implied decimal points as a guide. If the table is a word- or phrase-table, align entries on an imaginary left margin in each column.
- If a particular column or row lacks data, use three periods or dashes in each space lacking data.
- If they improve legibility, use vertical lines to separate columns. See Figure 9–28 for an example.

Figures

Like tables, figures are word savers. They also have high visual impact and help break up what would otherwise be pages of solid type.

MULTIPLE-BAR CHARTS   (See Figure 9–29.) These compare relationships and show trends. Many lay persons find bar charts easier to understand than line charts. Each bar represents a quantity. The height or length of the bar indicates the amount of the quantity. It makes little difference whether the bars run horizontally or vertically, but horizontal bar charts are often used to report quantities of time, length, and distance; vertical bar charts to report heights, depths, and so on.

To make a multiple-bar chart:

- Determine whether horizontal or vertical orientation is appropriate for your data.
- Choose a scale for determining bar length (for instance, having 1 inch represent every 1,000 hours a machine has run).
- Measure off the lengths of each bar.

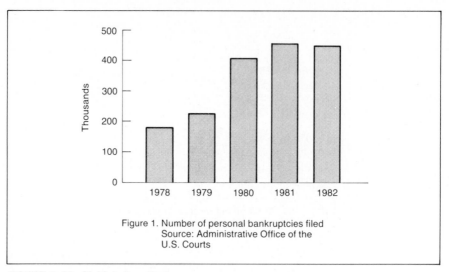

Figure 1. Number of personal bankruptcies filed
Source: Administrative Office of the
U.S. Courts

FIGURE 9–29   Multiple-bar chart

- Draw the lines to make each bar. Make all bars the same width. Separate each bar with an equal space.
- Shade the bars to make them show up.
- Label each bar (what it represents) and each scale (what the quantities and units of measure are). If desired, indicate the exact value at the end of each bar.
- If desired, rule a border around the chart.

DIVIDED-BAR CHARTS   (See Figure 9–30.) Consisting of one bar divided into segments, these show and compare percentages very well. The entire field of the bar represents 100 percent; each segment represents a portion of the 100 percent. They can be presented vertically or horizontally.

The attributes of a multiple-bar chart and a divided-bar chart can be combined, as shown in Figure 9–31. The bars represent the amount of wheat produced annually from 1978 to 1982 by the world's leading wheat-producing countries. Each year's bar is divided to indicate the amount that the wheat-growing countries produced that year, thus showing particular sums as well as the total.

To make a divided-bar chart:

- Choose a scale to determine percentages of overall length.
- Measure off segments of the bar and draw lines to mark each segment. Start at one end and arrange segments from smallest to largest.
- Label each segment to identify item and percentage.
- If desired, rule a border around the chart.

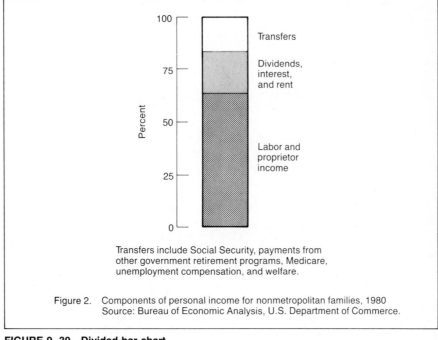

Transfers include Social Security, payments from other government retirement programs, Medicare, unemployment compensation, and welfare.

Figure 2.   Components of personal income for nonmetropolitan families, 1980
Source: Bureau of Economic Analysis, U.S. Department of Commerce.

FIGURE 9–30   Divided-bar chart

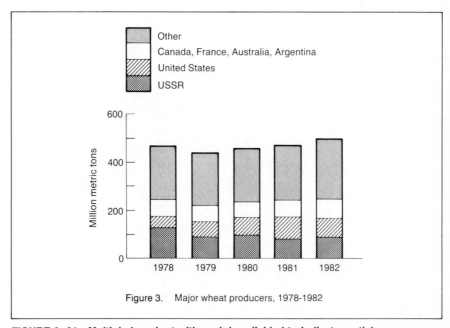

Figure 3.   Major wheat producers, 1978-1982

FIGURE 9–31   Multiple-bar chart with each bar divided to indicate partial sums

CIRCLE OR PIE CHARTS   (See Figure 9–32.) Like divided-bar charts, these show and compare percentages of a whole.

To make a circle chart:

- Draw the circle.
- Beginning at the 12 o'clock position and moving clockwise, slice the circle into appropriate-sized wedges.
- Make the slices in descending order.
- Group extremely small percentages (less than 2 percent) into one segment. The grouped segment may be labeled *miscellaneous* or *other,* with the individual groups and percentages given in parentheses or in a footnote.
- Label slices to identify items and percentages.

As just mentioned, you should arrange the wedges according to size, beginning the largest at the 12 o'clock position and continuing with progressively smaller wedges. However, when you are comparing two sets of data, both presented in circles or pie charts, as shown in Figure 9–33, the wedges of the second pie chart can be arranged in the order of those in the first pie chart for easy comparison. For instance, individual savings in the form of money market funds dropped from 23 percent in 1981 to 6 percent in 1982, and savings accounts doubled from 14 percent in 1981 to 28 percent in 1982. Even though those values have changed, the wedges are kept in the same order in both pie charts for easy comparison.

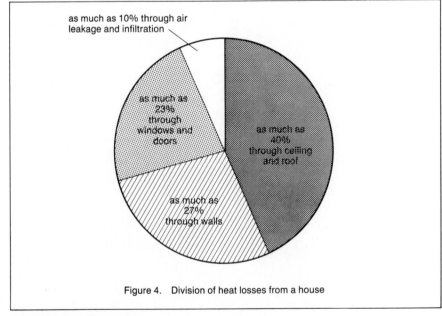

Figure 4.   Division of heat losses from a house

FIGURE 9–32   Pie graph

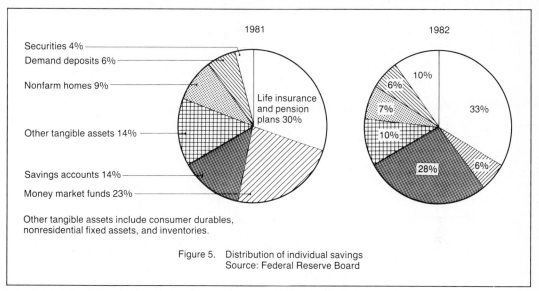

1981

1982

Securities 4%
Demand deposits 6%
Nonfarm homes 9%
Life insurance and pension plans 30%
Other tangible assets 14%
Savings accounts 14%
Money market funds 23%

10%
6%
7%
10%
33%
28%
6%

Other tangible assets include consumer durables, nonresidential fixed assets, and inventories.

Figure 5.   Distribution of individual savings
Source: Federal Reserve Board

FIGURE 9–33   Side-by-side pie charts for easy comparison of values

LINE CHARTS   (See Figure 9–34.) Like multiple-bar charts, these show comparisons betwen two or more quantities and trends. Their curves help readers quickly grasp the results of comparative data. Since line charts are usually derived from plotting on graph paper during an investigation, you should trace the chart on a regular sheet of report paper without the original chart lines. Keep line charts simple, particularly if you do not have an audience skilled in reading them.

To make a line chart:

- Determine the scale for variables.
- Rule horizontal and vertical scale lines.
- Mark off points for measurement, including interim "tic" marks.
- Label variables, units of measure, and so on.
- Plot data on the chart and connect them to make a continuous line.
- If desired, rule a border around the chart.

ORGANIZATIONAL CHARTS   (See Figure 9–35.) These resemble flow charts (see pages 288–295) but show static rather than moving relationships. They are used to show departmentalization, chains of command, and subordinate corporate levels by means of connected, labeled blocks. When completed, an organizational chart looks like a pyramid, with the top executive or office at the top.

To make an organizational chart:

- Determine the number of corporate levels you want to show.
- Draw geometrical figures large enough to hold names of units on each level.

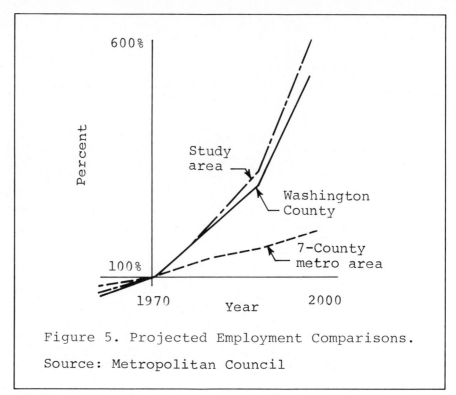

Figure 5. Projected Employment Comparisons.

Source: Metropolitan Council

FIGURE 9–34   Line chart

- Label each geometrical figure.
- Draw lines to show chain of command. Use different types of lines to show other relationships (for instance, relationships of special supervision or authority that differ from the formal hierarchical authority).
- If desired, rule a border around the chart.

Some report writers have problems using graphics. Here are six suggestions that will help you handle them. If you follow these suggestions, you will make your readers' task easier when they come to the graphics in your report.

1. Make your graphics large enough to be read easily. If possible, keep them of a size to fit sheets of paper with the same dimensions as your report. If you can fit them on a sheet with some text of your report, do so. Separate them from the text above and below them with adequate white space—triple space on a typed page should do it. Remember to maintain the one-inch margins.

When your graphics are too large to fit on a page with text, put them on a page by themselves immediately following or facing the page on which you analyze their contents. When they are too large to fit on a page, they may be folded or photographically reduced. The latter is preferable if the reduction doesn't make them too small to read without a magnifying glass.

2. Place your graphics where they will help readers most. Lists are part of the natural sequence of information in your reports, and their placement is no problem. But graphics require your readers to read both them and the text, sometimes jumping back and forth from text to graphic. Failure to place them near the text they illustrate can cause readers to do a lot of flipping around through your report, rereading text and reexamining the graphic. Place the graphic at or very near your discussion of it.

3. Label everything clearly and carefully so your readers know exactly what they are looking at. If possible, arrange all lettering to be read from left to right. Identify figures by Arabic numerals and descriptive titles, as in "Figure 1. The Ignition System." Identify tables by capital Roman numerals and descriptive titles, as in "Table I. Yield of Boneless Cooked Meat from Retail Pork Cuts." Number or letter graphics in the order in which you want them to appear in your report.

Label by name or symbol the parts of objects and components of diagrams that you want your readers to pay attention to. If you use letters to identify parts, identify the letters in any explanatory legend below the figure.

Label every column, row, axis, bar, and line in charts and tables.

If you borrow or adapt a graphic from other sources, give credit in parentheses following the figure number or table number or letter and descriptive title.

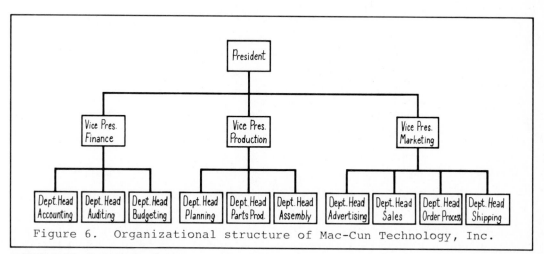

Figure 6. Organizational structure of Mac-Cun Technology, Inc.

FIGURE 9–35 Organizational chart

4. Introduce graphics before readers get to them. They are introduced or referred to by call-outs, which are references in the text of your report to your graphics. They are referred to like this:

Figure 1 shows . . .	Table I shows . . .
. . . as shown in Figure 1 . . .	. . . as shown in Table I . . .
. . . (see Figure 1) . . .	. . . (see Table I) . . .
. . . (Figure 1) . . .	. . . (Table I) . . .

If the graphic is not on the same page as the call-out, include its location in the call-out, as in this example:

> Recommended storage tanks (see Figure 2 on page 6) can be either buried or above ground.

Check to make sure that your graphics are numbered or lettered consecutively, that they appear in the order you want them to, and that they are referred to by call-outs.

5. Make sure that your graphics are clear and easy to understand. Always ask another person if he or she can interpret the graphic. Just as prose is always clear to the one who wrote it, graphics are always clear to the one who created them. If necessary, point out the significance of the data presented in the graphic. You cannot assume that your readers will see their significance unless you make it clear.

6. In most cases, you should use black and white artwork, because it is easy and quick to prepare and inexpensive to reproduce. Shading from black to various tones of gray or using different patterns of diagonal lines, crosshatching, or other simple designs are usually as effective as color.

SUGGESTIONS FOR APPLYING YOUR KNOWLEDGE

1. At the end of Chapter 1, "The Process of Transactional Writing," we suggested that you start gathering examples of transactional writing. Examine one of the examples you have collected and write a report for your teacher and classmates that explains the following:

- What type of report it is.
- Who its intended audience is.
- What features aid or hinder legibility.
- What features provide clues to its organization and hierarchical structure.

- What kind of documentation, if any, is used to cite sources.
- What kinds of graphics, if any, are used.

2. On pages 278–280 is a report entitled *Controlling the Fire in Bevo #3 Mine* and our analysis of the report. Assume that you have written the report. Provide the following prefatory elements:

- Letter of transmittal to Dennis Payne, Director of Mining Safety and Security, Nickeltown Coal Corporation, Warsaw, Pennsylvania 19455.

- Table of contents.
- List of figures and tables.
- Abstract.

Information that you will need from the original report but that is not included in the version on pages 278–280 follows:

- Figure 1. Vicinity Map of Sherman Township Showing Location of Fire Area, facing page 1
- Figure 2. Cross-Section Through Fire Area, facing page 1
- Figure 3. Photograph of Isolation Trench to Newcome Bed, Showing Evidence of Hot Area Over Courtney Bed, facing p. 1
- Figure 4. Surface Map of Fire Area, Showing Various Phases of Fire Control Work, facing p. 2
- Figure 5. Photograph of Wet-Sand Seal on Exposed Newcome and Courtney Beds, facing p. 2
- Figure 6. Aerial Photograph Showing Fire Project Area after Completion of Fire Control Work, facing p. 3
- Appendix A: Invoices, Contracts, and Work Orders Related to Stage 1, pp. A–1 through A–6
- Appendix B: Invoice, Contracts, and Work Orders Related to Stage 2, pp. B–1 through B–9
- Appendix C: Sales Receipts for Coal Shipments, pp. C–1 to C–3

3. The following sources are given in the order in which they are cited in a report. Arrange them in proper order and with proper format as they would appear in

A. The list of notes.
B. The reference list, using either humanities-style or science-style entries.

- New Robot Patent Category is the title of an article appearing in the January 1984 issue of Robotics Age (sixth volume) on pages 36 through 39. The author is S. B. Rifkin. Specific citation is to page 38.
- Industrial Robots: Application Experience is a collection of essays edited by J. J. Warnecke and R. D. Schraft and published by I.F.S. Publications of Kempston, England, in 1982.
- An article by A. M. Andrews appearing in Automotive Industries on pages 45 through 47, volume 164, dated January 1984. The title of the article is Is the Industry Overdoing on Automation? Specific citation is to pages 46 and 47.
- An article appearing in the fourth volume of Computers in Industry, the October 1983 issue, on pages 293 through 295. The article is titled Robot Network Analysis and written by A. Far and G. Messina. Specific citation is to page 293.
- A book published in Silver Spring, Maryland, in 1983 by IEEE Computer Society Press and written by C. S. G. Lee, R. C. Gonzalez, and K. S. Fu. The title of the book is Tutorial in Robots. Specific citation is to page 100.
- An article entitled Spot Welding by Robots in an Automated Assembly, written by John Mattox and appearing in a book entitled Designing Your Products for Robots, published by the Society for Automotive Engineers, Inc., in 1982 in Warrendale, Pennsylvania.
- An article entitled Robot in the sixth edition of Van Nostrand's Scientific Encyclopedia.
- An article entitled Robot to Derivet Navy's Aircraft, which appeared in the January 26, 1984, issue of Machine Design, page 2 of volume 56.

4. Present the following information, supplied by the United Supply Cooperative and Kentucky Association of Electric Cooperatives, in a formal table and in a pie chart:

Assuming that gas might soon cost $1.30 per gallon again, here is an approximate breakdown of where the money will go: (1) crude oil and other ingredients—0.73; refining and distribution costs—0.20; federal and state tax—0.17; dealer costs and margins—0.17; oil company profits—0.03. Projecting that gas might later cost $2.50 per gallon, here is an approximate breakdown: crude oil and other ingredients—1.80; refining and distribution costs—0.29; federal and state tax—0.175; dealer costs and margins—0.20; oil company profits—0.035.

5. Present the following information in a formal multiple-bar chart and in a formal line chart:

Minimum wage rates from 1974 through 1981 were as follows:

January 1974	$2.00
January 1975	2.10
January 1976	2.30
January 1978	2.65
January 1979	2.90
January 1980	3.10
January 1981	3.35

6. Present the following information in a formal table, a formal pie chart, a formal multiple-bar chart, and a formal multiple-bar chart with each bar segmented.

Voter turnout in the 1914 and 1918 senate elections in Missouri were as follows: Kansas City and Jackson County, 1914 (51,569) and 1918 (50,107); St. Louis City and County, 1914 (133,241) and 1918 (134,207); Outstate, 1914 (433,377) and 1918 (393,207). The total votes cast in senate elections were 618,187 in 1914 and 577,521 in 1918.

C H A P T E R

10

LIBRARY
RESEARCH

Good reports require good research. Writers should know how to gather information from many sources—from personal experiences, site inspections, questionnaires, interviews, letters of inquiry, experiments, and libraries. The information will help writers discover the facts and ideas of their reports.

Writers who don't know how to use a library properly suffer from two strangely different afflictions. Either they don't realize the phenomenal amount of information available at their fingertips or, if they do, they are overpowered by it because they don't know how to find this information. Regardless of the affliction, the result is the same—inadequate data or information for reports.

But something happens to writers who begin to learn their way around libraries. After finding the information they were seeking, they begin to regard libraries as a natural extension of their study or office.

The purpose of this chapter is to identify the basic reference sources available in most libraries and to give you some idea of the kind of information found in them. The more familiar you become with these sources, the easier it is for you to find the information you need. We have divided this chapter into five sections:

- The first describes reference books—almanacs, yearbooks, atlases, biographical dictionaries, and encyclopedias.
- The second describes periodical indexes, abstracting journals, and guides to books and government documents.
- The third discusses computerized data bases.
- The fourth shows you how to locate the materials you need.
- The fifth explains how to take notes on your reading.

REFERENCE BOOKS

All libraries have a special reference section. The books in this section are collections of facts and statistics that you'll never read through but will frequently consult. Eugene Sheehy's *Guide to Reference Books,* an annotated bibliography of about 7,500 reference books, is an excellent introduction to the whole field of reference books. It will be in your library's reference section or will be available from your reference librarian. In this section we cover almanacs, atlases, yearbooks, biographical dictionaries, and encyclopedias. You can find the ones in your library by looking under the words *almanacs, atlases,* and so on in the card catalog.

Almanacs

The word *almanac* comes from the Arabic word for *camp* or *settlement* and the weather associated with that place. It wasn't long until an almanac was a calendar to which astronomical and weather information had been added. But if you think almanacs are books that tell you when to plant potatoes or go fishing, you haven't looked in a modern almanac lately. Almanacs contain enormous amounts of miscellaneous information, usually in the form of lists, charts, and tables. Most almanacs are published annually, so much of the information is associated with the events of the previous year. But a few contain historical information of a broader scope.

  To give you an idea of the variety of information to be found in almanacs, we have listed some of the information that can be found on every hundredth page of a typical almanac—*The World Almanac and Book of Facts.* We'll start with page 100.

- 100—Names and addresses of the headquarters of U.S. corporations from Martin Marietta Corp. to Procter & Gamble Co.
- 200—Congressional seats by states, 1970 and 1980; area population of the United States, 1970–1980 (including census; gross area, land area, and sea area in square miles; percentage increase over the preceding census population); black and Hispanic populations by state.
- 300—U.S. cabinet officers; burial places of U.S. presidents.
- 400—Rulers of Scotland and of France.
- 500—Miscellaneous information about the Republic of Ghana and Greece.
- 600—Ranking of large rivers in Canada (including outflow and length); location and heights of famous waterfalls of the world.
- 700—Recent explosions and fires (dates, location, and number of deaths).
- 800—NBA team statistics for 1982–1983; NBA Most Valuable Player, 1956–1983; NBA Rookie of the Year, 1954–1983.
- 900—Major actions of the 98th Congress, 1983.

But even this sampling doesn't illustrate the variety of factual information in the almanac. Here's a taste of more that's available in *The World Almanac and Book of Facts:*

- Number of fatal accidents involving bicycles, per year.
- Tallest buildings in the United States (including the name of the building, height in feet, number of stories, and location).
- Nuclear power reactors in the United States (including site, name, capacity in kilowatts, ownership, and first year of operation).
- State estate tax rates and exemptions.
- Fuel economy in 1984 automobiles (comparative miles per gallon).
- Monthly pay scale of the U.S. uniformed services, fiscal year 1982.
- Average television viewing time for American adults, teenagers, and children.
- Raw steel production in the United States for 1980, 1981, and 1982.
- Disability and death rates in the United States from selected causes.
- Notable ocean and intercontinental flights (including type of craft, point of departure, destination, miles, time of flight, and date).

This listing may give you the impression that the information in almanacs is given in random order. Actually, most almanacs are arranged by topics and have extensive indexes. We urge you to read the introductory pages of almanacs to learn how to locate information there.

Here are some good general almanacs that are likely to be in your library:

- *CBS News Almanac*
- *Economic Almanac*—Covers information on business, labor, and government in United States and Canada.
- *Information Please Almanac, Atlas and Yearbook*
- *Reader's Digest Almanac and Yearbook*
- *World Almanac and Book of Facts*

Many other almanacs specializing in restricted subjects are also available. A good example is *Canadian Almanac and Directory.*

Yearbooks

Like almanacs, yearbooks are published annually and contain information about the previous year. They differ from almanacs in being restricted to selected topics indicated by their titles. Nearly every major professional organization publishes a yearbook. Following are some good yearbooks, with brief descriptions of the information they contain.

- *Commodity Year-Book*—Covers basic commodities from alcohol to hogs to zinc. Sample articles are titled "Commodity Futures as a Hedge Against Inflation," "Analyzing Hogs and Pork Belly Price Trends," and "New Factors in Forecasting Cattle Futures Prices."

- *The Canada Year Book: The Official Statistical Annual of the Resources, History, Institutions, and Social and Economic Conditions of the Dominion*—Published by the Canadian Bureau of Statistics, it reports current information on government, population, scientific and industrial research, fisheries, transportation, banking, and other aspects of Canadian life.
- *The County Yearbook: The Authoritative Source Book On County Governments*—Compiled by the National Association of County Governments since 1975, this book summarizes activities and statistical data and provides directories of officials of individual county governments.
- *Demographic Yearbook*—Published by the statistical office, Department of Economic and Social Affairs, United Nations Organization. Each annual issue treats a special topic. The 1973 issue, for instance, concerns population census statistics—the third consecutive issue to feature the results of world population lists compiled during 1965–1973. There is tabular information on rates of population increase, life expectancy, birthrates, infant mortality, marriage and divorce rates, and so on.
- *The International Year Book and Statesmen's Who's Who*—Provides information about world organizations; the government structures in the United Kingdom, the United States, France, the People's Republic of China, and the USSR; data on countries from Afghanistan to Zimbabwe; biographical sketches of prominent persons.
- *The Municipal Year Book: An Authoritative Resume of Activities and Statistical Data of American Cities*—Published by the International City Management Association since 1934, this book contains articles on such municipal concerns as taxes and fire and police protection and provides statistical tables on all major U.S. cities. It also contains a bibliography on municipal concerns.
- *Statesman's Year-Book: Statistical and Historical Annual of the States of the World*—Contains information about countries and their governing bodies and about world organizations like the United Nations and the World Council of Churches.
- *Statistical Abstract of the United States*—Prepared by the U.S. Bureau of the Census, this book gives statistics on various industrial, social, political, economic, and cultural activities in the United States. This book may be the most important data book of all for Americans. It includes data on every subject of public interest in the United States. In addition, it is a guide to other statistical publications.
- *Year Book of the United Nations*—Records the significant activities of the United Nations: disarmament; peaceful uses of ocean beds, outer space, and atomic energy; peace-keeping operations; strategies to encourage international trade and development; and activities related to international law.

Major encyclopedias also publish yearbooks as annual supplements to keep their material up to date.

Atlases

Atlases are compendiums of tables and maps that illustrate many of the same facts found in almanacs. Maps are the most valuable feature of an atlas. They present information on just about anything you'd ever need to look up—highway and railway routes, topography, climate, important places, population distribution, and so on.

To give you a sampling of the information you can find in an atlas, following are some of the data reported in maps at the front of the *Rand McNally Commercial Atlas and Marketing Guide,* an annual atlas that gives the latest information on the United States:

- zip codes
- telephone area codes
- college population
- major military installations
- retail sales distribution
- trading areas
- metropolitan areas
- manufacturing centers
- national forests

If you want to find out whether Brazil is larger than Australia, how many people live in China, what the longest island is, what the smallest ocean is, or what type of government Luxembourg has, you can get the information from a world atlas. Major world atlases that are likely to be in your library include:

- *Goode's World Atlas*—Contains maps showing distribution of rainfall, urban resources, topography, and population; world maps, distribution maps, and so on
- *National Geographic Atlas of the World*—On oversized pages, this atlas provides enormous amounts of detailed information about all countries on large-scale maps.

If you look under the subject *atlases* in your library's card catalog, you'll probably find three inches' worth of catalog cards on atlases of every description. You name it—continents, counties, diseases, hobbies—there's an atlas for it.

Biographical Dictionaries

Biographical dictionaries consist principally of brief, factual information about prominent persons. Some biographical dictionaries are arranged alphabetically by the subject's last name, some by field of achievement, and some by chronology. Some are general, and some are specific (there's even a book covering the great sinners of the past!). Some are restricted to persons who are dead at the time of publication; others include both living and dead persons. Some of the titles follow.

About people past:

- *Dictionary of American Biography*
- *Dictionary of National Biography* (British)
- *Dictionary of Scientific Biography*
- *Who Was Who in America*

About people living:

- *American Men and Women of Science*
- *Current Biography*
- *Who's Who in America*
- *Who's Who* (British)
- *Who's Who in Finance and Industry*
- *Who's Who in Science in Europe*

About people both living and dead:

- *Asimov's Biographical Encyclopedia of Science and Technology*
- *Baker's Biographical Dictionary of Musicians*
- *Chamber's Biographical Dictionary*
- *Webster's Biographical Dictionary*
- *McGraw-Hill Encyclopedia of World Biography*

Two helpful indexes to biographical material are *Biography Index,* which lists biographical information in both periodicals and books, and *Biographical Dictionaries Master Index,* which indexes entries to over 725,000 persons that appear in 59 biographical dictionaries.

Encyclopedias

Atlases, almanacs, yearbooks, and biographical dictionaries aren't the only quick sources of information. Encyclopedias are also indispensable, providing information on various subjects and personalities. Following are just a few of the more general encyclopedias. There are many others in almost all subject areas.

Multiple-volume encyclopedias:

- *Collier's Encyclopedia*—Strong in contemporary science and biography; excellent bibliographies and study guides in the index volume.
- *Encyclopaedia Britannica*—Strong in scholarly treatments of art, history, politics, and the biological sciences; atlases in the index volume.
- *Encyclopedia Americana*—Strong in science, technology, government, and business.
- *Encyclopedia of World Art*—Preface states that coverage includes "architecture, sculpture, and painting, and every other man-made object that,

regardless of its purpose or technique, enters the field of esthetic judgment because of its form or decoration."

- *The International Encyclopedia of Social Sciences*—Strong in anthropology, economics, history, political science, and sociology.
- *The Lincoln Library of Essential Information*—Covers vast array of subjects: literature, history, geography, mathematics, all departments of science, economics, government. Entries are arranged not alphabetically but by topics.
- *McGraw-Hill Encyclopedia of Science and Technology*—Strong in physical, natural, and applied sciences.
- *The Worldmark Encyclopedia of Nations*—According to its preface, a "practical guide to geographic, historical, political, social and economic status of nations."

Single-volume encyclopedias:

- *The Columbia Encyclopedia*—Covers a wide range of material found in general reference works: arts, literature, geography, life and physical sciences, and social science.
- *Van Nostrand's Scientific Encyclopedia*—According to its preface, covers "the physical sciences, the earth sciences, the biological sciences, the medical sciences, the various fields of engineering, and the pure and applied mathematics and statistics."

PERIODICAL INDEXES, ABSTRACTING JOURNALS, AND GUIDES TO BOOKS AND GOVERNMENT DOCUMENTS

A good way to start your search is to look through the basic reference documents we've already mentioned, especially encyclopedias. They often have a list of references at the end of articles or have study guides and bibliographies on particular subjects in the index volume.

Next go to the various periodical indexes. For now, let's put off the card catalog as a primary research tool for identifying material, since its function is mainly to identify and locate holdings in a particular library. The time will come, though, when you'll want to use it as an index, too. We will now explain how to use indexes and will describe several important indexes, abstracting journals, and guides to books.

Periodical Indexes

Magazines and journals are called *periodicals* because they are issued at regular intervals—weekly, monthly, quarterly, semiannually, or whatever. A periodical index is a reference that covers a given number of periodicals and gives the author, title, volume number, page numbers, and date of issue for items published in the periodicals covered by the index. The cover of the issues and the bound volumes of an index (see Figure 10–1) indicate the time period covered.

Since you should use indexes in every library research project, find out where they're kept in the library and spend some time reading their prefatory material. At the front of every index are pages that explain how to use that particular index.

To find what periodicals are covered by a specific index, check the list at the front of the index. Each index covers its chosen field of periodicals (coverage is usually determined every few years by a vote of index subscribers). Figure 10–2 is the first page of the list of periodicals covered by *Applied Science and Technology Index.*

To find out how an index abbreviates entries, check the explanations at the front of the index before the list of entries. The explanations from *Applied Science and Technology Index* show what such sections look like. The first page of the list of the abbreviated titles of periodicals indexed is shown in Figure 10–3. The abbreviations used in the highly abbreviated and condensed form of index entries are shown in Figure 10–4.

A portion of a sample page from *Applied Science and Technology Index,* showing entries under the general heading "Concrete, Reinforced" and the subheading "Testing," is shown below. The second entry tells us that the article "Early loading effects on bond strength," with bibliography, illustrations, and diagrams, written by C. R. Clark and D. W. Johnston, appears in the November/December 1983 issue of *Journal of the American Concrete Institute,* volume 80, on pages 532 through 539.

Concrete, Precast
  Point loads on precast concrete floors. J. F. Stanton. bibl diags *J Struct Eng* 109:2619-37 N '83
Concrete, Reinforced
  Finite element analysis of reinforced and prestressed concrete structures including thermal loading. D. R. J. Owen and others. bibl(p364-6) diags *Comput Methods Appl Mech Eng* 41:323-66 D '83
    Failure
  Deformation and failure in large-scale pullout tests. W. C. Stone and N. J. Carino. bibl il diags *J Am Concr Inst* 80:501-13 N/D '83
  Epoxy-coated reinforcing bars. D. P. Gustafson. bibl il diag *Concr Constr* 28:826+ N '83
  Force-displacement behavior of concrete bridge. G. E. Ramey. bibl il diags *J Struct Eng* 109:2600-18 N '83
    Mathematical models
  Modeling of R/C joints under cyclic excitations. F. C. Filippou and others. bibl diags *J Struct Eng* 109:2666-84 N '83

    Testing
  Deformation and failure in large-scale pullout tests. W. C. Stone and N. J. Carino. bibl il diags *J Am Concr Inst* 80:501-13 N/D '83
➤Early loading effects on bond strength. C. R. Clark and D. W. Johnston. bibl il diags *J Am Concr Inst* 80:532-9 N/D '83
  Radial tension strength of pipe and other curved flexural members [discussion of 80:33-9 Ja/F '83] F. J. Heger and T. J. McGrath. diags *J Am Concr Inst* 80:544-6 N/D '83
Concrete bridges *See* Bridges, Concrete

VOLUME 73   NUMBER 2   FEBRUARY 1985

Applied Science & Technology Index

A CUMULATIVE SUBJECT INDEX TO PERIODICALS IN THE FIELDS OF AERONAUTICS AND SPACE SCIENCE, CHEMISTRY, COMPUTER TECHNOLOGY AND APPLICATIONS, CONSTRUCTION INDUSTRY, ENERGY RESOURCES AND RESEARCH, ENGINEERING, FIRE AND FIRE PREVENTION, FOOD AND FOOD INDUSTRY, GEOLOGY, MACHINERY, MATHEMATICS, METALLURGY, MINERALOGY, OCEANOGRAPHY, PETROLEUM AND GAS, PHYSICS, PLASTICS, TEXTILE INDUSTRY AND FABRICS, TRANSPORTATION, AND OTHER INDUSTRIAL AND MECHANICAL ARTS.

The H. W. Wilson Company

FIGURE 10–1.   **Periodical index cover** *(Applied Science and Technology Index.* Copyright © 1985 by The H. W. Wilson Company and reproduced by permission of the publisher.)

PERIODICALS INDEXED

All data as of latest issue received

A

AAPG Bulletin. $70. m American Association of Petroleum Geologists, Inc., 1444 S. Boulder Ave., Tulsa, OK 74119
ACM Communications. See Communications of the ACM
ACM Computing Surveys. See Computing Surveys
ACM Transactions on Database Systems. $66. q Association for Computing Machinery, Inc., P.O. Box 12105, Church St. Sta., New York, NY 10249
ACM Transactions on Mathematical Software. $66. q Association for Computing Machinery, Inc., P.O. Box 12105, Church St. Sta., New York, NY 10249
Acoustical Society of America Journal. See The Journal of the Acoustical Society of America
Adhesives Age. $25. m (extra issue My) Communication Channels, Inc., 6255 Barfield Rd., Atlanta, GA 30328
Aerospace America. Price on request. m Aerospace America (AIAA EDP), 1633 Broadway, New York, NY 10019
  Formerly Astronautics & Aeronautics; name changed with January 1984
AIAA Journal. Price on request. m American Institute of Aeronautics and Astronautics, Inc., 1633 Broadway, New York, NY 10019
AIChE Journal. $100. bi-m American Institute of Chemical Engineers, 345 E. 47th St., New York, NY 10017
Air Pollution Control Association Journal. See Journal of the Air Pollution Control Association
Air Progress. $13.95. m Air Progress, 6725 Sunset Blvd., P.O. Box 3294, Los Angeles, CA 90028
Alternative Sources of Energy. $25. bi-m Circulation Dept., Alternative Sources of Energy, Inc., 107 S. Central Ave., Milaca, MN 56353
American Ceramic Society Bulletin. $12.50. m American Ceramic Society, 65 Ceramic Dr., Columbus, OH 43214
American Ceramic Society Journal. See Journal of the American Ceramic Society
American Chemical Society Journal. See Journal of the American Chemical Society
American City & County. $37. m Communication Channels, Inc., 6255 Barfield Rd., Atlanta, GA 30328
American Concrete Institute Journal. See Journal of the American Concrete Institute
American Dyestuff Reporter. $17. m SAF International, Inc., 50 W. 23rd St., New York, NY 10010
American Industrial Hygiene Association Journal. $60. m American Industrial Hygiene Association, 475 Wolf Ledges Pkwy., Akron, OH 44311-1087
American Institute of Chemical Engineers Journal. See AIChE Journal
American Journal of Physics. $91. m Subscription Fulfillment Div., American Association of Physics Teachers, Graduate Physics Bldg., SUNY at Stony Brook, Stony Brook, NY 11794
American Journal of Science. $80. m (except Jl & S) Kline Geology Laboratory, Yale University, New Haven, CT 06511
American Machinist. $35. m Fulfillment Manager, American Machinist, Box 430, Hightstown, NJ 08520
American Meteorological Society Bulletin. See Bulletin of the American Meteorological Society
American Metric Journal. bi-m AMJ Pub. Co., P.O. Box 3200, Camarillo, CA 93010
The American Mineralogist. $85. bi-m Mineralogical Society of America, 2000 Florida Ave., N.W., Washington, DC 20009
American Mining Congress Journal. $50. bi-w American Mining Congress Journal, 1920 N St., Washington, DC 20036
American Oil Chemists' Society Journal. See Journal of the American Oil Chemists' Society
American Scientist. $24. bi-m Scientific Research Society, 345 Whitney Ave., New Haven, CT 06511
American Society of Heating, Refrigerating and Air-Conditioning Engineers Journal. See ASHRAE Journal
American Water Works Association Journal. $50. m American Water Works Assn., Inc., 6666 W. Quincy Ave., Denver, CO 80235
AMJ-SI-Metricpac. See American Metric Journal

Analytical Chemistry. $30. m American Chemical Society, Subscription Services, P.O. Box 3337, Columbus, OH 43210
  Extra numbers: Review issue in April; Laboratory Guide in August
Applied Optics. $280. semi-m American Institute of Physics, 335 E. 45th St., New York, NY 10017
Applied Physics. See Journal of Physics. D, Applied Physics
Artificial Intelligence. fl558. 9 times a yr (in 3 vols) Elsevier Science Publishers B.V. (North Holland), P.O. Box 211, 1000 AE Amsterdam, Netherlands
ASHRAE Journal. $35. m American Society of Heating, Refrigerating and Air-Conditioning Engineers, Inc., 1791 Tullie Circle N.E., Atlanta, GA 30329
ASLE Transactions. $90. q American Society of Lubrication Engineers, 838 Busse Hwy., Park Ridge, IL 60068
Association for Computing Machinery Journal. See Journal of the Association for Computing Machinery
ASTM Journal of Testing and Evaluation. See Journal of Testing and Evaluation
ASTM Standardization News. $12.50. m American Society for Testing and Materials, 1916 Race St., Philadelphia, PA 19103
Astronautics & Aeronautics. Price on request. m (bi-m Jl-Ag) American Institute of Aeronautics and Astronautics, EDP, 1290 Ave. of the Americas, New York, NY 10104
  Name changed to Aerospace America with January 1984
AT&T Bell Laboratories Record. See Record (Bell Telephone Laboratories, Inc.)
AT&T Bell Laboratories Technical Journal. $35. 10 times a yr AT&T Bell Laboratories, Circulation Dept., Rm. 1E-335, 101 John F. Kennedy Pkwy., Short Hills, NJ 07078
  Computing Science and Systems section and special issues included as available
  Formerly The Bell System Technical Journal; name changed with January 1984
Atmospheric Environment. $450. m Pergamon Press Inc., Maxwell House, Fairview Park, Elmsford, NY 10523
Audio. $15.94. m CBS Publications, P.O. Box 5318, 1255 Portland Pl., Boulder, CO 80322
Audio Engineering Society Journal. See Journal of the Audio Engineering Society
Automobile Quarterly. $39.95. q Automobile Quarterly, Inc., P.O. Box 348, Route 222 and Sharadin Rd., Kutztown, PA 19530-0348
Automotive Engineering. Price on request. m Society of Automotive Engineers, 400 Commonwealth Dr., Warrendale, PA 15096
Automotive Industries. Price on request. m Chilton Co., Chilton Way, Radnor, PA 19089
Aviation Week & Space Technology. $60. w Aviation Week & Space Technology, P.O. Box 1505, Neptune, NJ 08736

B

Bell Laboratories Record. See Record (Bell Telephone Laboratories, Inc.)
The Bell System Technical Journal. $35. published in 3 parts: part 1 10 times a yr, parts 2 & 3 as available Bell Laboratories, Circulation Dept., Rm. 1E-335, 101 John F. Kennedy Pkwy., Short Hills, NJ 07078
  Name changed to AT&T Bell Laboratories Technical Journal with January 1984
Bulletin of the American Meteorological Society. Price on request. m American Meteorological Society, 45 Beacon St., Boston, MA 02108
Bulletin of the Seismological Society of America. $60. bi-m Seismological Society of America, Secretary, 2620 Telegraph Ave., Berkeley, CA 94704
Bulletin of the Society of Economic Geologists. See Economic Geology and the Bulletin of the Society of Economic Geologists
Business and Commercial Aviation. $30. m Ziff-Davis Pub. Co., B/CA, Box 5850, Cherry Hill, NJ 08034
Byte. $21. m (except 2 issues in Ag and O) Byte Publications, Inc., P.O. Box 590, Martinsville, NJ 08836

FIGURE 10–2 Periodical list (*Applied Science and Technology Index.* Copyright © 1985 by The H. W. Wilson Company and reproduced by permission of the publisher.)

ABBREVIATIONS OF PERIODICALS INDEXED

For full information consult the list of Periodicals Indexed

A

AAPG Bull — AAPG Bulletin
ACM Trans Database Syst — ACM Transactions on Database Systems
ACM Trans Math Softw — ACM Transactions on Mathematical Software
Adhes Age — Adhesives Age
Aerosp Am — Aerospace America
AIAA J — AIAA Journal
AIChE J — AIChE Journal
Air Prog — Air Progress
Altern Sources Energy — Alternative Sources of Energy
Am Ceram Soc Bull — American Ceramic Society Bulletin
Am City Cty — American City & County
Am Dyest Rep — American Dyestuff Reporter
Am Ind Hyg Assoc J — American Industrial Hygiene Association Journal
Am J Phys — American Journal of Physics
Am J Sci — American Journal of Science
Am Mach — American Machinist
Am Metr J — American Metric Journal
Am Min Congr J — American Mining Congress Journal
Am Miner — The American Mineralogist
Am Sci — American Scientist
Am Water Works Assoc J — American Water Works Association Journal
Anal Chem — Analytical Chemistry
Appl Opt — Applied Optics
Artif Intell — Artificial Intelligence
ASHRAE J — ASHRAE Journal
ASLE Trans — ASLE Transactions
ASTM Stand News — ASTM Standardization News
Astronaut Aeronaut — Astronautics & Aeronautics
AT&T Bell Lab Tech J — AT&T Bell Laboratories Technical Journal
Atmos Environ — Atmospheric Environment
Audio — Audio
Automob Q — Automobile Quarterly
Automot Eng — Automotive Engineering
Automot Ind — Automotive Industries
Aviat Week Space Technol — Aviation Week & Space Technology

B

Bell Syst Tech J — The Bell System Technical Journal
Bull Am Meteorol Soc — Bulletin of the American Meteorological Society
Bull Seismol Soc Am — Bulletin of the Seismological Society of America
Bus Commer Aviat — Business and Commercial Aviation
Byte — Byte

C

Can Chem Process — Canadian Chemical Processing
Can J Chem Eng — The Canadian Journal of Chemical Engineering
Ceram Ind — Ceramic Industry
Chem Eng (Engl) — The Chemical Engineer
Chem Eng News — Chemical & Engineering News
Chem Eng Prog — Chemical Engineering Progress
Chem Eng (U S) — Chemical Engineering
Chem Ind — Chemistry and Industry
Chem Rev — Chemical Reviews
Chemtech — Chemtech
CIM Bull — CIM Bulletin
Civ Eng (Am Soc Civ Eng) — Civil Engineering (American Society of Civil Engineers)
Civ Eng (Engl) — Civil Engineering (London, England)
Coal Age — Coal Age
Combust Sci Technol — Combustion Science and Technology
Commun ACM — Communications of the ACM
Comput Des — Computer Design
Comput Ind — Computers in Industry
Comput J — The Computer Journal

Comput Methods Appl Mech Eng — Computer Methods in Applied Mechanics and Engineering
Comput Surv — Computing Surveys
Computer — Computer
Concr Constr — Concrete Construction
Constr Contract — Construction Contracting
Consult Eng — Consulting Engineer (Barrington, Ill.)
Control Eng — Control Engineering
Corros Sci — Corrosion Science
Corrosion — Corrosion
Cosmet Toiletries — Cosmetics & Toiletries
Crit Rev Environ Control — Critical Reviews in Environmental Control
Cryogenics — Cryogenics

D

Data Process — Data Processing
Datamation — Datamation
Db — Db
Des News — Design News

E

Earthqu Eng Struct Dyn — Earthquake Engineering and Structural Dynamics
Econ Geol — Economic Geology and the Bulletin of the Society of Economic Geologists
EDN — EDN
EDP Anal — EDP Analyzer
Elastomerics — Elastomerics
Electr Commun — Electrical Communication
Electr Constr Maint — Electrical Construction and Maintenance
Electr World — Electrical World
Electron Des — Electronic Design
Electron Eng — Electronic Engineering
Electron Power — Electronics and Power
Electron Week — Electronics Week
Electronics — Electronics
Energy — Energy (Dublin, Ireland)
Energy Conv Manage — Energy Conversion and Management
Energy Eng — Energy Engineering
Energy Sources — Energy Sources
Eng Dig — Engineering Digest
Eng J (Can) — Engineering Journal (Montréal, Québec)
Eng J (U S) — Engineering Journal (Chicago, Ill.)
Eng Min J — Engineering and Mining Journal
Eng News-Rec — Engineering News-Record
Engineer — The Engineer (London, England)
Engineering — Engineering (London, England)
Environ Res — Environmental Research
Environ Sci Technol — Environmental Science & Technology
EPRI J — EPRI Journal
Exp Mech — Experimental Mechanics
Exp Tech — Experimental Techniques

F

Fire Command — Fire Command
Fire Eng — Fire Engineering
Fire J — Fire Journal
Fire Serv Today — Fire Service Today
Fire Technol — Fire Technology
Food Eng — Food Engineering
Food Technol — Food Technology
Fusion Technol — Fusion Technology

G

Geol Soc Am Bull — Geological Society of America Bulletin
Geology — Geology
Geophysics — Geophysics
Glass Ind — Glass Industry
Glass Technol — Glass Technology
Ground Water — Ground Water

FIGURE 10–3 List of periodical abbreviations (*Applied Science and Technology Index.* Copyright © 1985 by The H. W. Wilson Company and reproduced by permission of the publisher.)

ABBREVIATIONS

+	continued on later pages of same issue	Mr	March
		My	May
abr	abridged	N	November
Ag	August	n s	new series
Ap	April	no	number
Aut	Autumn		
bibl	bibliography	O	October
comp	compiled, compiler	p	page
cond	condensed	pl	plate
cont	continued	por	portrait
		pt	part
D	December	rev	revised
diag	diagram		
		S	September
		sec	section
ed	edited, edition, editor	Spr	Spring
		Summ	Summer
		supp	supplement
F	February	tr	translated, -ion, -or
il	illustrations	v	volume
inc	incorporated		
Ja	January	Wint	Winter
Je	June		
Jl	July	yrbk	yearbook

For those unfamiliar with the form of reference to magazines used in the entries, the following explanation is given :

Sample entry:
Computers
Print-out equipment
Typewriter to computer interface. B. Green. il diags
Radio-Electron   54:75-8+ D '83; 55:61-4 Ja '84;
55:75-8+ F '84

Explanation:
An illustrated article, including diagrams, on the subject of computer print-out equipment entitled "Typewriter to computer interface," by B. Green, will be found in volume 54 of *Radio-Electronics*, pages 75 to 78 (continued on later pages of the same issue) in the December 1983 number. The article is continued in volume 55, pages 61 to 64 of the January 1984 number and pages 75 to 78 (continued on later pages of the same issue) in the February 1984 number.

FIGURE 10–4   List of abbreviations *(Applied Science and Technology Index.* Copyright © 1985 by The H. W. Wilson Company and reproduced by permission of the publisher.)

There are two kinds of indexes—general indexes, which cover many periodicals in a wide general field, and restricted subject indexes, which cover periodicals in a narrow subject field.

General Periodical Indexes

- *Readers' Guide to Periodical Literature* (1900–present) is an author-subject index of about 160 American periodicals of general interest. It covers such magazines as *American Heritage, Better Homes and Gardens, Esquire, Farm Journal, Hot Rod, Reader's Digest, Scientific American,* and *Sports Illustrated.*
- *Applied Science and Technology Index* (1958–present) is a subject index to articles in over 225 science, engineering, and industrial periodicals. It's concerned with material on aeronautics, automotives, chemistry, construction, electricity, engineering, geology, metallurgy, machining, physics, and other related subjects. It covers such magazines as *Journal of American Water Works Association, Coal Age, Fire Technology, Machine Design,* and *Welding Journal.*
- *Art Index* (1929–present) is an author-subject index to domestic and foreign art periodicals and museum bulletins. It's concerned with material on archeology, ceramics, engraving, graphic arts, landscaping, painting, sculpture, photography, industrial design, city planning, landscape design, and related subjects. It covers such periodicals as *The Art Journal; Ceramics Monthly; Landscape Architecture;* and *Sight and Sound: The International Film Quarterly.*
- *Biological and Agricultural Index* (1964–present) is a subject index that covers magazines from the biological sciences and magazines, bulletins, and books on agricultural science. It's concerned with material on agricultural chemistry, agricultural economics, agricultural engineering, animal husbandry, biochemistry, botany, conservation, food science, ecology, dairying, and other related subjects. It indexes such periodicals as *Agronomy Journal, Biochemical Journal, Biological Reviews, Crops and Soils, Developmental Biology, Journal of Forestry,* and *Western Horseman.*
- *The Business Periodicals Index* (1958–present) is a subject index to articles in approximately 115 English-language periodicals dealing with business, trade, finance, public administration, accounting, advertising, banking, and taxation. It covers such magazines as *Advertising Age, The Banker, Dun's Review, Harvard Business Review, Management Review,* and *Textile World.*
- *Education Index* (1929–present) is an author-subject index to material in some 200 periodicals, proceedings, yearbooks, bulletins, and monographs. It's concerned with material on all aspects of education, counseling and guidance, and psychology. It indexes such periodicals as *Agricultural Education Magazine, Business Education Forum, The Quarterly Journal of Speech,* and *The Vocational Guidance Quarterly.*

- *Engineering Index* (1906–present) is a subject-author index to over 1,500 technical, engineering, and scientific periodicals in 20 languages. It also indexes papers, reports, and proceedings issued by government bureaus, research institutes, industrial organizations, and professional societies. An especially helpful feature is the annotations of entries. It covers such periodicals as *Assembly Engineering, Journal of Safety Engineering, Ocean Engineering,* and *Water Well Journal.*
- *General Science Index* (1979–present) is a subject index to English-language periodicals in astronomy, atmospheric science, biology, food and nutrition, genetics, microbiology, oceanography, and so on.
- *Humanities Index* (1974–present) is an author-subject index concerned with material on archeology, classical studies, folklore, history, languages and literature, political criticism, performing arts, philosophy, religion, and related subjects. It covers such periodicals as *American Literature, Dance Magazine, Film Journal,* and *Religious Studies.* A book review section follows the main body of the index.
- *Industrial Arts Index* (1913–1957) is a subject index to articles in some 240 technical, engineering, science, business, and trade periodicals.
- *Public Affairs Information Service, Bulletin* (1915–present) is a subject index to government documents, reports, and articles from social science periodicals. It's concerned with material on public administration, international affairs, economics, and related subjects. It indexes such periodicals as *Business Economics, Journal of Police Science and Administration, Journal of Consumer Research,* and *Soviet Union.*
- *Social Sciences Index* (1974–present) is an author-subject index of 262 periodicals from the fields of anthropology, economics, environmental science, law and criminology, psychology, sociology, and related subjects. It covers such periodicals as *American Journal of Nursing, Bulletin on Narcotics, Community Development Journal, American Psychologist, Social Work,* and *Technology and Culture.* A book review section follows the main body of the index.
- *Zoological Record* (1964–present) contains twenty sections of literature. The first is comprehensive zoology followed by sections on the literature relating to a phylum or class of the animal kingdom. The final section covers the new genera and subgenera indexed in that year's volume.

Restricted Subject Periodical Indexes

Restricted subject periodical indexes, which are usually sponsored by national professional organizations, attempt to complete the coverage of materials in special fields by indexing material from sources not covered by general periodical indexes. Most are quite new, but some have been around for over fifty years. Here are some typical ones.

- *Accountant's Index* (1920–present), published by the American Institute of Certified Public Accountants, is an author-subject-title index covering periodicals, pamphlets, and government documents relating to accounting, auditing, data processing, financial management, investments, taxation, and similar fields. It covers such magazines as *Abacus, Georgia CPA, Price Waterhouse Review,* and *Tax Counselor's Quarterly.*

- *Bibliography and Index of Geology* (1969–present), published by the American Geological Institute, indexes earth science literature of the world. It is photocomposed from the citations of GeoRef, a computer data base file of geological periodicals, reports, maps, theses, and books. It continues the coverage of its predecessor, *Bibliography and Index of Geology Exclusive of North America* (1933–1968).

- *Business Education Index* (1940–present), sponsored by Delta Pi Epsilon, National Honorary Graduate Fraternity in Business Education, is an author-subject index to 32 business education periodicals, including several state business education newsletters and bulletins. It also lists new books in the field. Among nationally circulated periodicals covered are *The Balance Sheet, Journal of Business Communication,* and *Today's Secretary.*

- *Cumulative Index to Nursing Literature* (1956–present), published by The Seventh Day Adventist Hospital Association, is an author-subject index to nursing and related health sciences periodicals, such as *American Journal of Nursing, Children Today, Hospital Medicine,* and *Patient Care.*

- *The Environment Index* (1971–present), published by the Environmental Information Center, Inc., indexes thousands of citations from several hundred periodicals and books searched for significant environmental information.

In addition to the periodical indexes described in this section and the guides to books in the following section, you should know about another basic reference—*Ulrich's Periodical Directory,* an annual guide to American and foreign periodicals that classifies alphabetically by subject and title about 20,000 periodicals. A particularly useful entry in *Ulrich's* is the notations of indexes and abstracts in which periodicals are listed.

Abstracting Journals

Abstracting journals are especially helpful because they contain summaries of each entry indexed. The following 11 abstracting journals are only a few of the many that are available in almost all subject areas.

- *Bibliography and Index to Geology* (1969–present) abstracts by broad subject areas world publications on all areas of geology, geophysics, and geochemistry.

- *Biological Abstracts* (1926–present) indexes by subject and author over 8,000 journals, as well as books, symposia, and technical reports.

- *Chemical Abstracts* (1907–present) gives access by general subject, chemical substance, chemical formula, ring system, patent, and author. It surveys over 12,000 journals, conferences, patents, and technical reports.

- *Computer Abstracts* (1956–present) abstracts articles, papers, conference proceedings, and books about computer theory, artificial intelligence, programming, and computer applications in a variety of fields from aerospace to transportation.
- *Entomology Abstracts* (1969–present), an author and combined taxonomic-subject index, monitors approximately 5,000 journals and other resources on entomology. Each issue contains approximately 750 abstracts on such topics as morphology, anatomy, histology, biology and ecology, and fossil forms and faunas.
- *Food Science and Technology Abstracts* (1969–present), an author-subject index covering over 1,200 journals from over 50 countries, is divided into 19 sections, including food microbiology, food additives, and food packaging.
- *Index Medicus, New Series* (1960–present) indexes by subject over 2,600 biomedical journals. Since 1976, it covers conference proceedings.
- *Oceanic Abstracts* (1964–present), an author-subject index, covers over 2,000 world publications in the areas of oceanography, fisheries, desalination, ships, buoys, and so on.
- *Petroleum Abstracts* (1960–present), an author-subject index, reviews technical publications in more than 500 U.S. and foreign journals, conference papers, and patent journals. About 10,000 to 12,000 abstracts and 4,000 to 5,000 patent abstracts are printed each year on topics such as petroleum geology, drilling, well logging, pipelining, ecology and pollution, alternative fuels and energy sources, and mineral commodities.
- *Pollution Abstracts* (1970–present) is an author-subject index that abstracts from over 2,500 journals, technical reports, patents, and conferences. It covers most topics related to pollution: air pollution, sewage and wastewater treatment, solid waste, pesticides, radiation, noise pollution, and so on.
- *Psychological Abstracts* (1927–present) summarizes the world's literature in psychology and such related disciplines as psychometrics, communication systems, educational psychology, and applied psychology.

Guides to Books and Government Documents

In addition to general and restricted subject indexes to periodicals, there are guides that serve the same purpose for books, pamphlets, and government documents.

- *Cumulative Book Index* (1928–present) lists English-language books published throughout the world. It does not cover government documents, most pamphlets, inexpensive paperbacks, editions limited to fewer than 500 copies, and other minor material. Entries are listed alphabetically by author, subject, and title. The main entry (author entry) gives the author, title, edition (if other than the first), pagination, price, publisher, and year of publication.

- *A Guide to Science Reading* (1963), edited by Hilary J. Deason, is an annotated guide to more than 900 paperbound science books arranged into 54 science and mathematical categories.
- *Scientific, Medical, and Technical Books,* 2nd ed., edited by R. R. Hawkins, is a subject index to important scientific, medical, and technical books published in the United States. Entries are arranged by fields of knowledge (chemistry, automotive engineering and repair, agriculture, and so on) and contain tables of contents and descriptive notes about the book. It describes about 8,000 books published from 1930 to 1956.
- *Vertical File Index* (1935–present) is a subject-title index to pamphlets, brochures, folders, leaflets, and some state and federal government documents. Often it provides short descriptive notes for entries.
- *Energy Research Abstracts* (formerly titled *ERDA Research Abstracts*), published by the Department of Energy, indexes and abstracts U.S. government–sponsored research reports, conferences, and patents.
- *Government Reports Announcements and Index,* issued semimonthly since 1946, abstracts available reports from the National Technical Information Services. Abstracts are arranged by subject; reports are indexed by author, subject, contract number, and accession report number.
- *Nuclear Science Abstracts* (1948–1976) abstracted the Atomic Energy Commission's reports and other government agencies and research centers' literature. *Atomindex* (1970–present), published by the International Nuclear Information System, replaces *Nuclear Science Abstracts* in part.
- *Scientific and Technical Aerospace Reports* (1963–present), issued semimonthly, abstracts international technical literature in the fields of aeronautics and space science and technology. It is published by the National Aeronautics and Space Administration.
- *United States Government Publications: Monthly Catalog* (1895–present) has been published monthly ever since the office of the U.S. Superintendent of Documents was established. It indexes the publications of U.S. government agencies. Arranged by issuing agency, entries give author, title, publication data, and price or availability. Separate annual indexes arrange entries by subject, author, and title.

Guides to Book Reviews

Should you want to learn more about a book before deciding to buy it or search for it, check the following guides to book reviews for evaluations of the book.

- *Book Review Digest* (1905–present) contains excerpts from reviews of books published or distributed in the United States. The reviews are restricted to those appearing within eighteen months following a book's publication, so it is therefore necessary to know the date of publication. Entries are arranged alphabetically by the name of the author of the book. The review excerpts are arranged alphabetically by title of the periodical in which the review appeared. A subject and title index follows the author entry.

- *Book Review Index* (1965–present) lists thousands of review citations of thousands of books. The 1974 annual cumulation gives an idea of the enormous coverage of *BRI:* approximately 76,400 reviews of approximately 35,400 books taken from 228 periodicals. The index is arranged alphabetically by author of the book reviewed.

- *Computing Reviews* (1960–present) contains signed reviews of current books, proceedings, and nonbook literature on all aspects of computer science.

- *Current Book Review Citations* (1976–present) indexes book reviews to more than 1,000 periodicals. Each entry consists of the author's name and book's title, and the title, volume, pagination, and month and year of the periodical in which the book was reviewed. The name of the reviewer, if known, is also given.

- *New Technical Books* (1915–present) lists noteworthy English-language books submitted for the monthly exhibits of new technical books in the Science and Technology Research Center, the Research Library, New York Public Library. Entries include publication information, table of contents, and a descriptive note about the book. The coverage is primarily of books in pure and applied sciences, mathematics, engineering, industrial technology, and related disciplines.

- *Science Books and Films* (1965–present) reviews books, 16mm films, and filmstrips. It is printed five times a year and is organized by broad subject areas.

- *Technical Book Review Index* (1917–present) is arranged alphabetically by author of the book reviewed. Entries include brief quotations from reviews.

COMPUTERIZED DATA BASES

In addition to the printed resources mentioned so far in this chapter, you should also become familiar with computerized data bases. You can use computer searching instead of manual searching of indexes and abstracting journals, especially if a topic is interdisciplinary. For example, let's assume that you are researching the recreational use of forest lands in national parks. If you look up "Recreational Use of Public Lands," you might get a hundred or so references. If you look up "Forest Lands," you might get nearly a thousand references. If you look up "National Parks," you might get another thousand references. You can either manually search nearly 2,100 references, or you can spend $30 to $40 on an online search.

Since libraries vary a great deal in what computerized literature searches they offer, you should ask the reference librarian at your library about what is available to you. Most libraries have librarians trained in computerized literature searches. If your library doesn't have access to such a system, perhaps a nearby public library or industry library does.

Most computerized systems work similarly to manual searching. After you have discussed your proposed search with a reference librarian and after you or the librarian have logged in to the computer, you can ask the computer such a question as "Is there any literature on underwater welding in submarine repair?" Or you might ask the computer to expand the key word of your general topic—*lubrication,* for instance. Within seconds the computer will list several closely related index terms and the number of published items under each term, such as

LUBRICATING OIL, 60 ITEMS

LUBRICATING OIL ADDITIVES, 5 ITEMS

LUBRICATING OIL, SOLID, 1 ITEM

LUBRICATING OIL STORAGE, 3 ITEMS

LUBRICATING OIL TESTING, 8 ITEMS

LUBRICATING OIL THICKENING, 6 ITEMS

and so on alphabetically. You then may ask the computer to see the citations under any of these headings. If you want the bibliographical facts, an abstract of the item, or a printout of the item, you give the computer the identification number of the citation.

The cost of computer literature searches varies according to how much time you spend on line, the number of off-line reprints you want, and the amount of time used on the communications system. Your reference librarian will explain all fees.

Here are just a few of the several hundred data bases available.

Social Sciences

AAVIM (vocational and technical education)

ASI (U.S. government statistical publications)

CHILD ABUSE AND NEGLECT (research projects, service programs)

ERIC (Educational Resources Information Center)

INTERNATIONAL STATISTICAL ABSTRACTS

PSYINFO (psychology)

Business and Economics

ABI/INFORM (business, finance, and related fields)

INTERNATIONAL STATISTICAL ABSTRACTS (foreign business and economic forecasts)

Technology and Engineering

APTIC (Air Pollution Technical Information Center)

COMPENDIX (engineering)

ENERGYLINE (papers and proceedings of environment-related conferences, research papers from private and government agencies, and transcripts of congressional hearings)

FSTA (food science and technology)

WAA (World Aluminum Abstracts)

Sciences

AGRICOLA (AGRICulture On-Line Access—agriculture economics, rural sociology, agricultural engineering, entomology, and so on)

ASFA (Aquatic Sciences and Fisheries Abstracts—aquatic and marine biology)

BIOSIS (life sciences, including agriculture, food technology, and microbiology)

CA Search (Chemical Abstracts covering chemistry and chemical engineering)

GEOARCHIVE (geosciences)

GEOREF (geosciences)

SCISEARCH (biological and applied sciences)

For more information on computerized data bases, consult Martha E. Williams, ed., *Computer-Readable Data Bases: A Directory and Data Sourcebook* (Washington, D.C.: American Society for Information Service, 1979), which describes 528 data bases available through major on-line vendors.

LOCATING THE MATERIAL

After you know what material you want, you'll need to locate it. Some of the material is going to be in your library, but some isn't.

To find out whether your library has a particular periodical, check the card catalog or periodical list (a locally compiled list is usually kept in your library's periodical or reference area). It will tell you what periodicals are in your library and exactly how extensive the holdings are—which volumes and issues are available.

If your library holds the periodical, find out where the recent unbound issues and the older bound issues are kept. Unbound issues are usually kept for a year; then the year's supply is bound and placed with the other bound volumes on the shelves. The recent unbound issues may be kept in the current periodicals reading room or some other place set aside especially for them, or they may be with the bound volumes on the shelves.

Many libraries have books, back issues of periodicals, and other material on microform instead of in their originally published form. If your library has microform material, find out where it is located and how it is arranged. Microform material is regarded as part of the library's holdings and will be included in the library's card catalog.

To find out whether your library has a particular book, check the card catalog. All cards in the catalog are filed alphabetically. A card will be alphabetized under three or more entries: (1) author (or editor), (2) title, and (3) subject(s). The card catalogs of some libraries are divided in two—the author-title catalog and the subject catalog. But in most small- and medium-sized libraries, the author, title, and subject cards are filed together in one alphabetical sequence.

On the front of each drawer of the card catalog are guide letters or words. All cards beginning with words between these guide letters or words will be found in that drawer. Here are two examples:

NUCLEAR–NURSERY   NURSES–NUTRITION

If you're working from a bibliography, you can simply look for the author's name. If you have only the title of the material, look it up. Even if you don't know the names of authors or titles of material on the subject you're investigating, you can use the card catalog as a subject index to see if the library has anything about that particular subject.

Although each library makes its own decisions on how to alphabetize its card catalog, the following principles are usually followed:

- *The, A, An* are ignored in alphabetizing. A book entitled *The Modern Technician* would be alphabetized in the *m's*. But articles within an entry are important. A book entitled *Work for the Beginner* would follow *Work for a Man.*
- Foreign prefixes such as *de, von,* and *van* in names are usually ignored in alphabetizing.
- Names beginning with *Mc* and *Mac* are usually filed as if they were *Mc* and placed at the front of the *m's.*
- Abbreviations like *Dr., Mr., and St.,* and numbers like *19th,* are filed as if they were spelled out. But *Mrs.* is usually filed as written.

Once you locate the catalog card, you'll find it contains much information. An author card is shown in Figure 10–5. Some cards, such as this example, consist of two or more cards to provide ample space for information.

1. The call number in the upper-left corner of the card is what you need to find where the book is shelved.
2. The author line gives the full name of the author. It may also give the author's year of birth, and if dead, the year of death. The authors of this book are Ralph D. Nyland, Charles C. Larson, and Hardy L. Shirley. Only Nyland's name appears at the top of this card. There are other author cards with Larson's and Shirley's names on them.
3. The complete title and publishing information of the book, including the coauthors' names, give you the bibliographical information you need to make a bibliography card or bibliography entry.
4. Notations on the special features of the book, including the number of pages, illustrations, and the height of the book (in centimeters), give you significant information about the physical aspects and contents of the book.

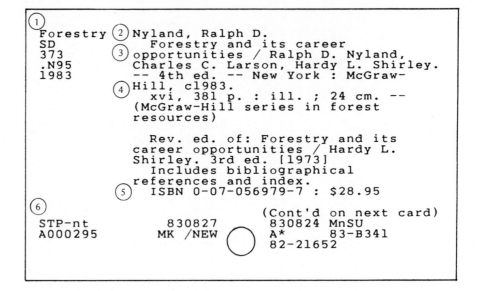

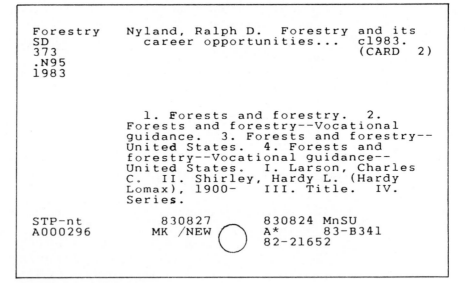

FIGURE 10–5 Author card

5. These letters and numbers give the International Standard Book Number (ISBN). This information will be of little interest to you, but it is important to librarians.

6. This information gives you other ways the book is cataloged in the library card catalog. But more important, these words also are related key words you can look under in the card catalog to see whether there are other books on the subject.

The title card (see Figure 10–6) is identical to the author card except that the title of the book is typed above the author's name as well as appearing in its regular position.

The subject card (see Figure 10–7) is identical to the author card except that the subject under which the card is filed is typed above the author's name as well as appearing in its regular position. (This book has other subject cards filed under "Forests and forestry," "Forests and forestry—vocational guidance—United States," and "Forests and forestry—United States"—related key words that might contain entries of other material related to the topic.)

In addition to author, title, and subject cards, you should know about two important cross-reference cards when using the library card catalog as a subject index. The "see" card (as shown in Figure 10–8) guides you from a subject heading not used in the system to those that are. For instance, if you're looking for subject cards on *Guns,* you'll find, as the "see" card in Figure 10–8 shows, that *Firearms* and *Ordnance* are the subject headings for material on guns.

The "see also" card (as shown in Figure 10–9) guides you from a subject heading that is used to other closely related subject headings that are used.

When, with the help of the card catalog, you find the book you want, copy the call number. Then find out where books with that call number are located, go to the shelf, and get the book. Be sure to copy the call number accurately and completely, because you won't be able to locate the book easily without the entire call number.

```
                    Forestry and its career opportunities.
    Forestry      Nyland, Ralph D.
    SD                  Forestry and its career
    373           opportunities / Ralph D. Nyland,
    .N95          Charles C. Larson, Hardy L. Shirley.
    1983          -- 4th ed. -- New York : McGraw-
                  Hill, c1983.
                      xvi, 381 p. : ill. ; 24 cm. --
                  (McGraw-Hill series in forest
                  resources)

                      Rev. ed. of: Forestry and its
                  career opportunities / Hardy L.
                  Shirley. 3rd ed. [1973]
                      Includes bibliographical
                  references and index.
                      ISBN 0-07-056979-7 : $28.95


    STP-nt            830827  (  )   830824 MnSU
    A000130           MK /NEW  \_/   A*       83-B341
                                     82-21652
```

FIGURE 10–6   Title card

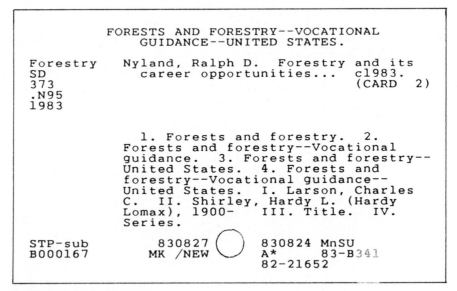

FIGURE 10–7   Subject card

TAKING NOTES

The final step in library research is extracting information from the articles and books you've found. Careful note-taking is essential. After all, notes are the products of your work. Our memories are simply too short to hold the information we've found. So get a couple of packs of 3-by-5 and 4-by-6 cards and a pen so you can take notes as you read. Take your

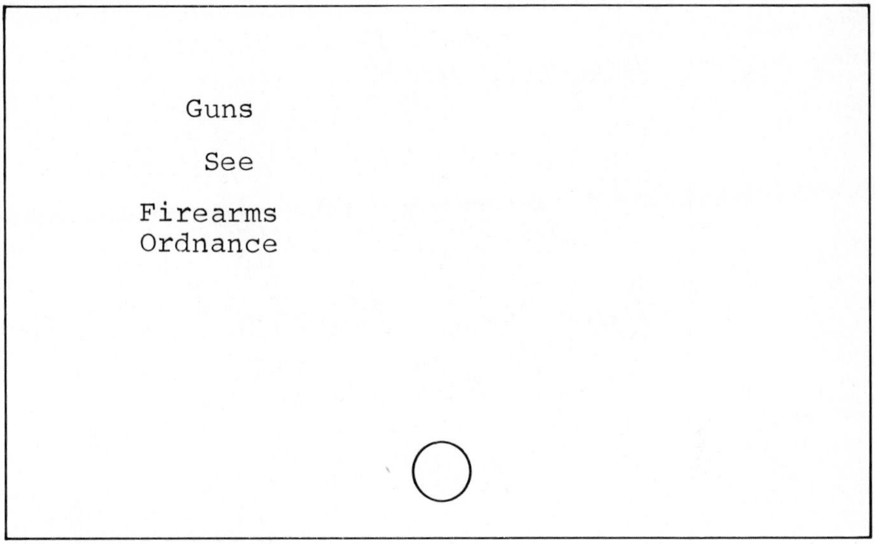

```
        Guns

         See

    Firearms
    Ordnance




                        ◯
```

FIGURE 10–8 "See" card

notes on these cards. They are easy to handle and rearrange and stand up better than pieces of paper.

When you compile a bibliography of potential source material, you'll make out bibliography cards. Fill out a separate card for each possible source. Usually 3-by-5 cards are adequate for this, and they'll be easy to tell from the 4-by-6 cards used to take notes on. As Figure 10–10

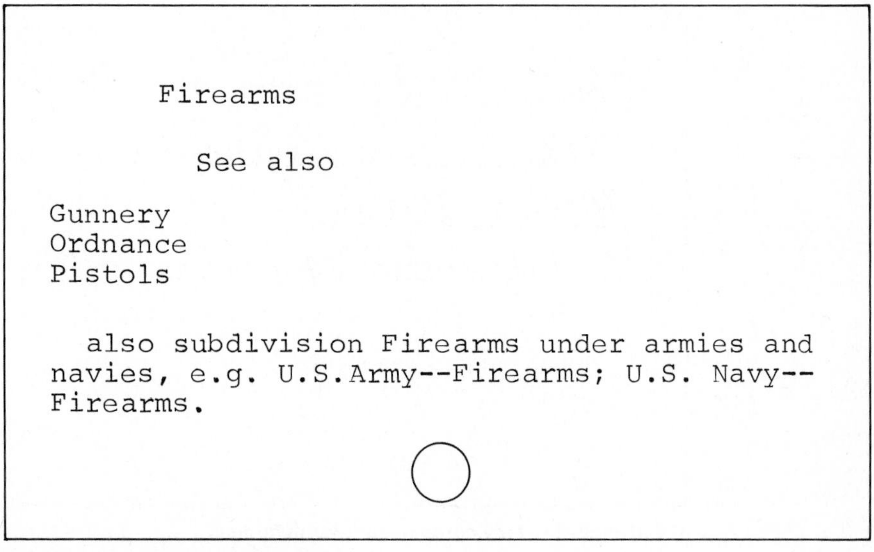

```
     Firearms

        See also

  Gunnery
  Ordnance
  Pistols


    also subdivision Firearms under armies and
  navies, e.g. U.S.Army--Firearms; U.S. Navy--
  Firearms.

                        ◯
```

FIGURE 10–9 "See also" card

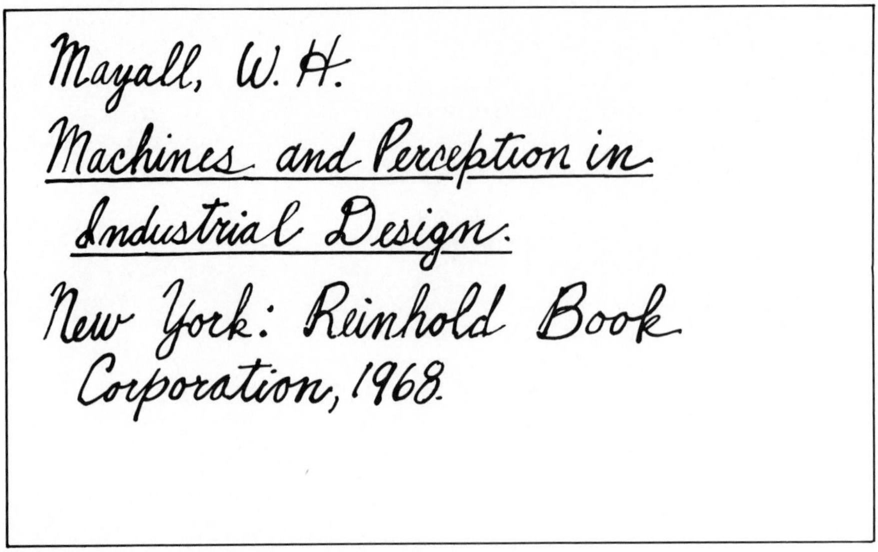

Mayall, W. H.
Machines and Perception in
Industrial Design.
New York: Reinhold Book
Corporation, 1968.

FIGURE 10–10 Bibliography card for book

shows, you can divide the bibliographical information for a book
into three parts: (1) author's or editor's name, (2) title of work, and
(3) publishing information.

For a periodical you can divide the bibliographical information
(Figure 10–11) into four parts: (1) author's name, (2) title of article,
(3) title of periodical, and (4) volume number, date, and page number.

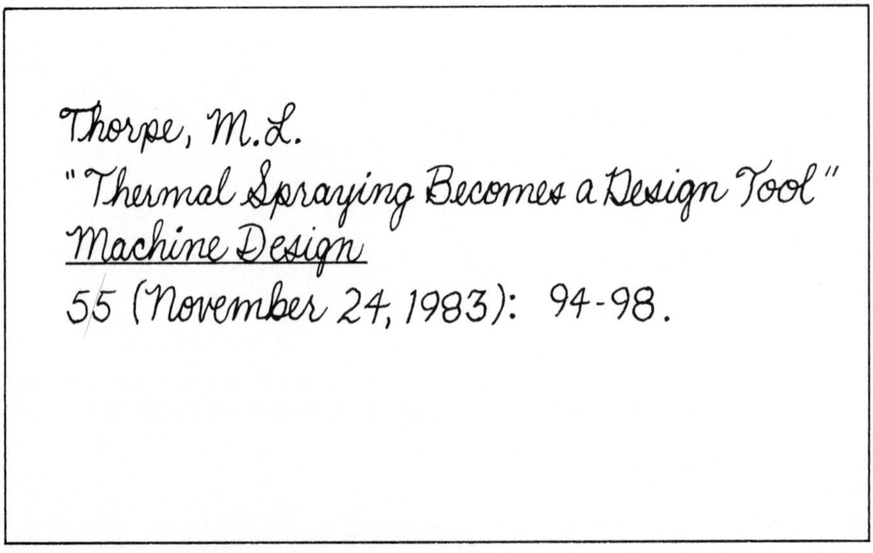

Thorpe, M. L.
"Thermal Spraying Becomes a Design Tool"
Machine Design
55 (November 24, 1983): 94-98.

FIGURE 10–11 Bibliography card for periodical

When you take notes during your reading, you'll make out note cards. Usually 4-by-6 cards are better than 3-by-5 cards for this purpose. Fill out a separate card for each note. As shown in Figure 10–12, you should put three kinds of information on each card: (1) a brief descriptive heading at the top to help you with sorting and arranging note cards as you organize your material, (2) the note itself, and (3) the author and page or pages used at the bottom to identify the source of the note. If there's more than one work by one author or more than one author with the same last name, indicate the title and author's initials as well as the author's last name and pages.

You should take three different kinds of notes—quotations, paraphrases, and summaries.

Quotations

Quotations are appropriate when you want to be sure not to misinterpret the author's opinions. They are fairly easy to do. Copy the passage word for word exactly as it's printed. Put quotation marks around the passage so there'll be no question in your mind later that the passage is a direct

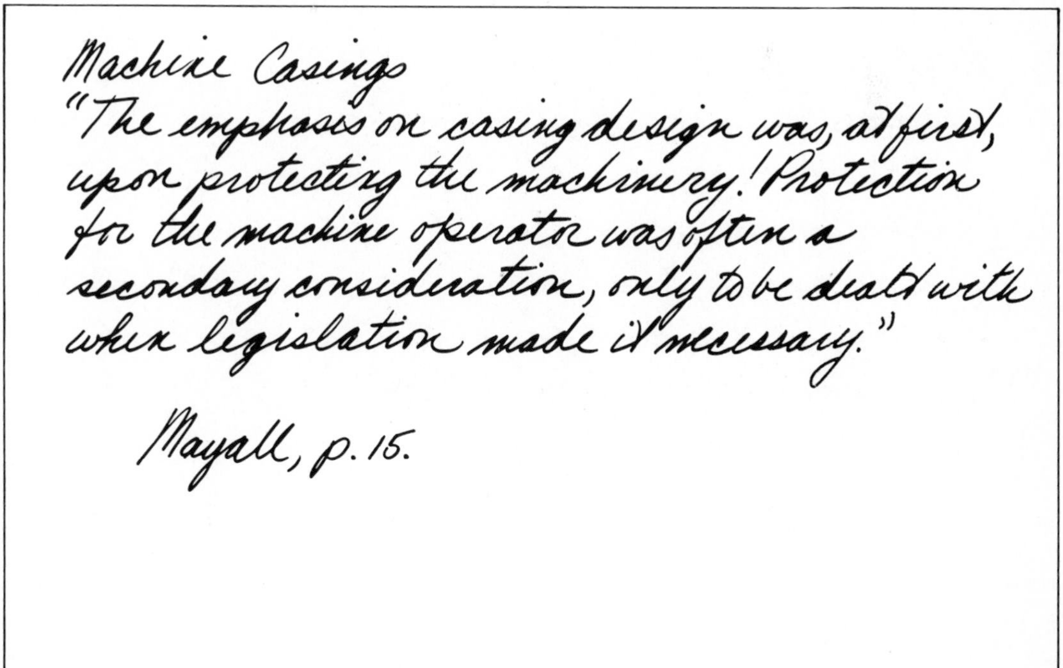

Machine Casings

"The emphasis on casing design was, at first, upon protecting the machinery! Protection for the machine operator was often a secondary consideration, only to be dealt with when legislation made it necessary."

Mayall, p. 15.

FIGURE 10–12   Note card

quotation. If you desire to omit part of the author's words, indicate the omitted part by ellipsis points (see Ellipsis Points entry in Writer's Guide, page 412). If you want to insert some explanatory word or phrase of your own inside the quotation, indicate the insertion by putting it inside brackets (see Brackets entry in Writer's Guide, page 404). Figure 10–13 shows an example of a clarifying statement inserted in brackets inside a quotation.

Paraphrases

Paraphrases are appropriate when you want to state facts taken from an author's writings. They require you to put the author's ideas in your own words, but they are also fairly easy to do. Just write *in your own words* what the writer wrote in the original. Avoid merely substituting words. Try to rephrase the whole passage in your own expression.

Let's illustrate the paraphrasing of a passage. An original passage is shown in Figure 10–14; a paraphrase in Figure 10–15.

Notice two important features of this paraphrased note. First, the notetaker has rephrased the information of the original *to fit a particular*

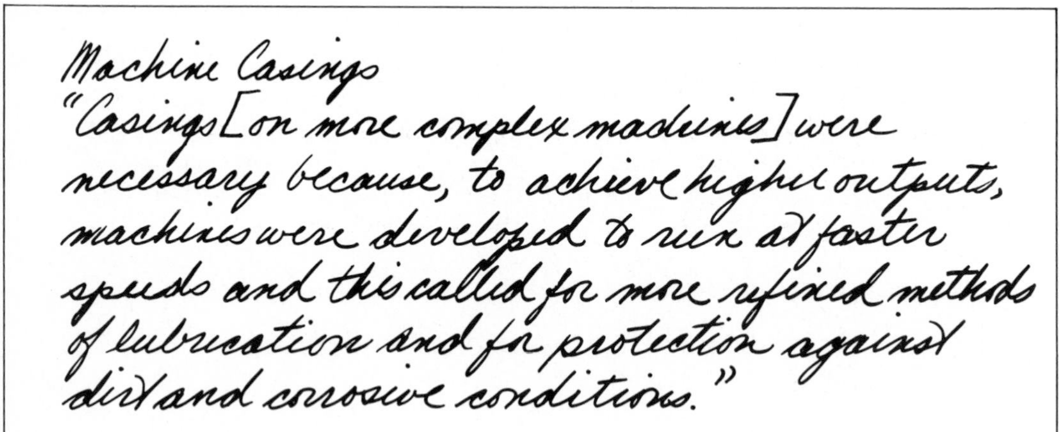

Machine Casings

"Casings [on more complex machines] were necessary because, to achieve higher outputs, machines were developed to run at faster speeds and this called for more refined methods of lubrication and for protection against dirt and corrosive conditions."

Mayall, p. 15.

FIGURE 10–13 Quotation with bracketed statement

> Most early machines were built for working man, not for leisured man. If we compare then with, say, the architecture and furniture of the periods in which they were built, we can readily see one considerable difference. The machines lack the shapes and decorative devices which, in architecture and furniture, were applied to heighten visual appeal. But when some machines found their way into leisured environments they often acquired currently stylistic forms. Today some of us may find these forms faintly ludicrous, while others would regard them as appropriate on the grounds that any product must be related to its environment.

FIGURE 10–14 Original passage (W. H. Mayall, *Machines and Perception in Industrial Design;* © 1968 Litton Educational Publishing, Inc.; reprinted by permission of Van Nostrand Reinhold Company)

need. The original passage emphasizes the historical development of machines changing their appearance as they become domesticated. The notetaker wants to retain only the idea that machines for the home are more esthetically shaped and ornamented than those for industry. Second, the notetaker has jotted a personal note below the paraphrased ma-

<u>Influence of Environment on Machine Design</u>

Although there may be little difference in operation and structure of a machine built for industry or the home, the machine built for the home is likely to become more esthetically shaped and ornamented.

[ex. sewing machines? lathes? food grinders? stoves?]

Mayall, p. 14.

FIGURE 10–15 Paraphrase card

terial as a reminder of examples as they must have popped into mind while reading and taking the note. This is an excellent practice to get into. If you don't write notes to yourself (bracket them to keep the notes separate from the paraphrased material), you run the risk of not being able to call back the ideas you had about a topic when you were working on it.

When we concentrate our attention on any particular object it is said to become "figural" while all surrounding features become "ground." Figure and ground effects are, of course, well understood in graphic design. Indeed much can be learned by studying graphic treatments to see how different features have been made figural according to the intentions of their designers. Perhaps the strongest cause for an object or a shape becoming figural depends upon whether it is regarded by the observer as meaning anything to him. In short we concentrate our attention upon what we want to see: which may be a fortunate tendency in some environments. Figural qualities also depend, however, upon the following additional factors:

degree of contrast between the perceived object and others, whether
  in terms of shape, tonal relationship or texture
relative sizes
degree of illumination

Generally speaking, a feature could be made figural if its shape and perhaps color and texture are made distinctly different from others in the visual scene. Larger relative size may help, and certainly the feature will be seen more clearly if the whole scene is well lit. All this may seem fairly obvious, but examine the dial gauge opposite. For the operator, the important features in this gauge are the scale and pointer together with an identification of what the gauge is measuring. Yet the most dominant element in the gauge is the central black circle surrounding the pointer mechanism. Almost certainly most observers will make this figural and so be distracted from what is really important. The modified gauge (below) shows how the scale and pointer have been made figural by making them more definite and by removing the black circle. The pointer, in particular, has been given greater significance by giving it a form more suited to its purpose; that is more meaning as a pointer. At the same time other distracting elements, such as the boundary lines about the scale markings, have been eliminated. We now have a gauge which is likely to be read more easily and probably more accurately.

FIGURE 10–16 Original two-paragraph passage (W. H. Mayall, *Machines and Perception in Industrial Design;* © 1968 Litton Educational Publishing, Inc.; reprinted by permission of Van Nostrand Reinhold Company.)

Summaries

Summaries consist of a few sentences in your own words to give the essence or major ideas of what you've read. Knowing how to paraphrase also equips you to write summaries of longer passages—something you may want to do so you can jog your memory about research material or provide your readers with a usable condensed version of a longer document. An original two-paragraph passage is shown in Figure 10–16; a summary of the two paragraphs in Figure 10–17.

As you can tell, the summary in this instance is similar to an extended paraphrase. When the original passage is lengthy, though, the summary becomes much shorter than a paraphrase, perhaps as short as one-fifth or less than the original. But the principle remains the same—get at the essential ideas, condense them, and put them in your own words.

Here are some tips on taking notes, regardless of whether they are in quotation, paraphrase, or summary form.

- Write down all the information you'll need, so you won't have to go back to the source.
- Write legibly so you can read your own handwriting. In paraphrasing

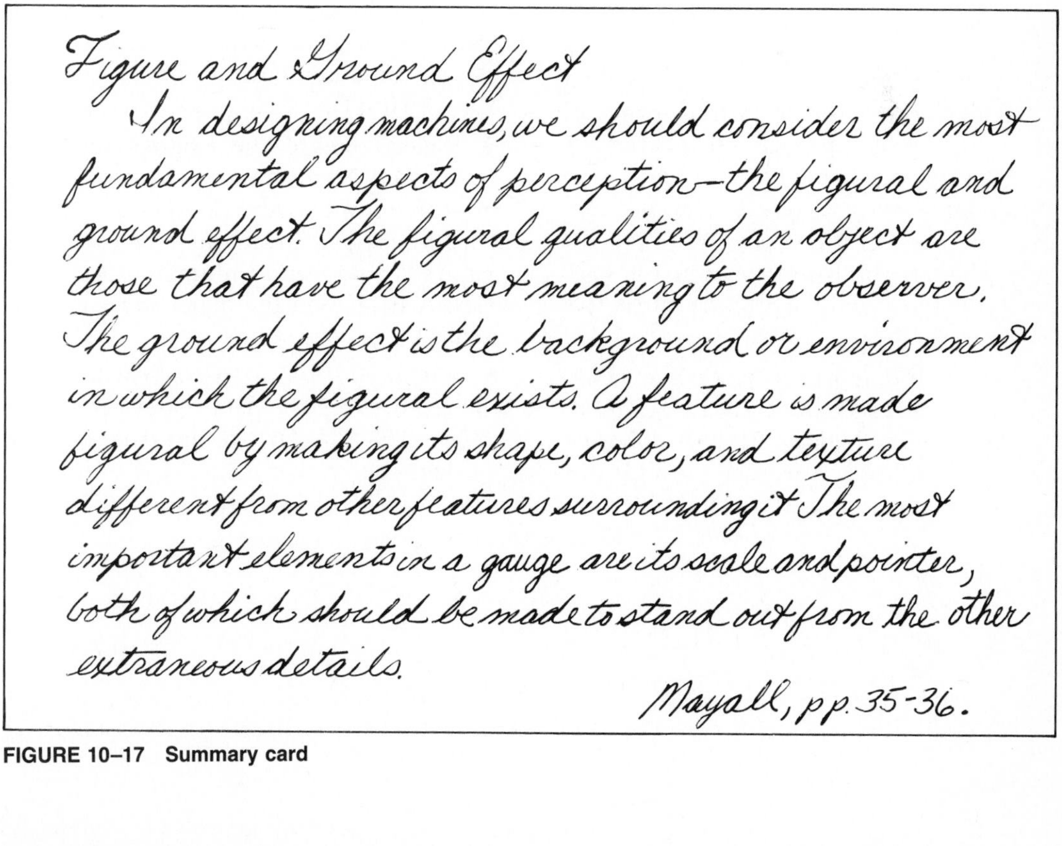

Figure and Ground Effect

In designing machines, we should consider the most fundamental aspects of perception—the figural and ground effect. The figural qualities of an object are those that have the most meaning to the observer. The ground effect is the background or environment in which the figural exists. A feature is made figural by making its shape, color, and texture different from other features surrounding it. The most important elements in a gauge are its scale and pointer, both of which should be made to stand out from the other extraneous details.

Mayall, pp. 35-36.

FIGURE 10–17 Summary card

or summarizing, don't use abbreviations and shorthand expressions that you won't understand later.

- Write one note to a card so you can rearrange them easily.
- Write on only one side of a card. If your note runs over to a second card, number the cards.
- Double-check to make sure you have included the page number(s) and author of the source the note comes from.

SUGGESTIONS FOR APPLYING YOUR KNOWLEDGE

1. Thumb through a dictionary, an encyclopedia, a periodical index—or any kind of subject index—from A to Z, jotting down terms that catch your interest. Choose three terms from the list and check your library's card catalog to locate any books listed under each term. Select one book under each term and find the book in the stacks. Write out the full bibliographical information for each book on separate bibliography cards (see Figure 10–10).

2. Check to see if there are any "see" or "see also" cards for the three terms. If there are, look up each cross-reference and locate one book under each. Select one book from each cross-reference and find the book in the stacks. Write out the full bibliographical information for each book on separate bibliography cards (see Figure 10–10).

3. From the types of reference books discussed in this chapter—almanacs, yearbooks, atlases, biographical dictionaries, and encyclopedias—search through the table of contents and the index of the most recent edition for information related to any of the three original terms or the additional cross-referenced terms. If you find material on any of the terms, make out a bibliography card for the appropriate references (see Figure 10–10).

4. Go to your library's periodical division and find at least one article that has been published since 1970 on a topic related to each of the three original terms and the cross-referenced terms. Fill out the full bibliographical information for each article on separate bibliography cards (see Figure 10–11).

5. Select one of the original or cross-referenced terms that interests you the most, read one of the periodical or reference items, and make out note cards (see Figure 10–12) and summary cards (see Figure 10–17) on the major ideas in each item.

6. See if your library has access to any of the computerized data bases listed on pages 217–218. If so, list the services available.

C H A P T E R

11

BIBLIOGRAPHIC REPORTS AND LITERATURE REVIEWS

There's no way you and your co-workers can know all the information you'll need to face the situations you come up against. Even your entire organization cannot hold all the information you need. Fortunately, though, it's not what you know that's important so much as knowing how to find out. You know whatever you can look up, for the chances are good that the information you'll need is in some published work.

To illustrate the value of knowing how to find published information, consider the case of an enterprising retailer trying to decide whether or not to give premiums with her merchandise to attract more customers. She needs information to make the decision. What's the cost of giving premiums? What percentage of retailers using premiums increased their volume of business with premiums? How much added volume is needed to meet the cost of giving premiums? Is it best to use nationally distributed premiums? Which premiums—nylons, cases of soft drinks, dishes, beach balls, other items that can be handled with small profit—increase business most? Are certain premiums more appropriate for certain products? Are there local, state, and federal laws that control or restrict the use of premiums?

The sources for answers to these questions are many. The retailer could rely solely on information from firms proposing to supply premiums to her. But the danger of depending only on the seller is obvious. The retailer could ask her business colleagues about their experience with premiums. She could hire—for a fee—a consultant. But she also could spend a little time in a library checking to see what information has been published on the use of premiums to improve business. If she spends 20 minutes looking *in the right places,* she'll find that dozens of articles have been published on the subject in a five-year period.

Under the subject headings *Coupons, Premiums,* and other related words in the 1981–1983 volumes of *Business Periodicals Index,* the retailer will find articles with titles like these:

- "Case against Coupons"
- "Coupons and Premiums: Turning Long Shots into Sure Things"
- "Coupons in Yellow Pages Draw Customers to Miami Contractor"
- "Demographic Profile of Coupon Users"
- "Incentives Move Products—and People"
- "On Generics and Coupons and Consumers' New Definitions of Value"
- "Purchasing Behavior of Customers"

If the retailer looks under the same subjects in the library card catalog, she might find entries on books. And in very little time she will be on the way to published material that will help her decide what kinds of bait to dangle before customers, if she should offer premiums.

As you can see, such a search develops many leads to published information on a particular topic. For a more detailed account of specific procedures for conducting library research, see Chapter 10, "Library Research."

You may want to keep a record of these leads to literature for yourself or for others. In this chapter, we concentrate on compiling four types of bibliographic reports. One is an information storage and retrieval file for your own personal use. The other three are for readers other than yourself: the bibliography, a selected list of readings on a specific subject; the annotated bibliography, a bibliography containing a summary or an abstract for each bibliographical entry; and the literature review, an analysis in essay form of the literature related to a particular topic.

PERSONAL INFORMATION STORAGE AND RETRIEVAL FILE

If the information you gather is for yourself, the end product might be an information storage and retrieval system designed for your own needs. Such a system would be kept up to date to keep you informed about current information on particular subjects. The system can be as elaborate as you want to make it, but a relatively simple and efficient one might consist of two separate files of 3-by-5 note cards. One file would include annotated bibliography cards—one for each item to be entered into the system—and key-word cards.

Each annotated card (see Figure 11–1) would contain bibliographical information and a summary of the book, article, or report. It would be filed alphabetically by the author's name.

Each key-word card (see Figure 11–2), arranged alphabetically,

Unklesbay, N., M.E. Davis, and G. Krause. 1983.

Nutrient retention in pork, turkey breast, and corned beef roast after infrared and convective heat processing.
Journal of Food Science 48: 865-868, 904.

Roasts were heat processed by infrared and convection to compare the effects of these alternative heating methods upon nutrient retention. In addition to proximate analyses, nutrients analyzed

included thiamin, riboflavin, seven fatty acids, 18 amino acids, ammonia, sodium, phosphorus, and iron. Convective heating of turkey breast and corned beef produced a higher product yield. Few significant differences between heat processed samples were revealed. After convection heating of corned beef, riboflavin was significantly higher than after heating. Similarly, arachidonic acid was higher in turkey breasts. After infrared heating of pork, aspartic acid, threonine, and serine were lower than after convective heating; ammonia was higher.

FIGURE 11–1 Annotated bibliography card

Nutrient Retention in Meat after Microwave Processing

Allen, N. et al.
Britto, C., and V. R. Garcia
Fulweiler, H. W.
Jones, P.
Unkleshay, N., M. E. Davis, and G. Krause
Vely, J. W.

FIGURE 11–2   Key-word card

would consist of a key word or words and a list of the authors whose publications deal with the subject of the key word. To find the information you're seeking, you'd consult the key-word file to identify the authors who have written on the subject, find the annotated bibliography card that contains the information, and pull it.

If the information is for others, you'll have to prepare a bibliography, an annotated bibliography, or a literature review. The potential value of bibliographies and literature reviews is not to be underestimated. Their purpose is to give readers the information they need to increase their own knowledge of a particular subject. Which type of bibliography or literature review you prepare will depend on the purpose the report is to serve.

BIBLIOGRAPHIC REPORTS

Happiness for our enterprising retailer would have been an up-to-date bibliographic report on merchandise premiums and coupons. With such a report, she could have bypassed most of the search and gone directly to the publications. A list of readings might have met her needs, or it might have served as a convenient beginning for further searching.

Bibliographic reports come in two types. If your readers want only a list of readings, a simple bibliography will do. If your readers want to know more specifically what the contents of the works are or which works are more relevant to their needs or how one work differs from another, an annotated bibliography will be especially helpful. An annotated bibliography is a list of readings accompanied by notes that give an idea of either the content or value, or both, of the works listed.

To be useful for readers, bibliographic reports must contain accurate and complete information in a consistent form. Most errors in bibliographies are generally minor, but the incomplete name of an author or editor, an incorrect title or volume number, or inconsistent form can be troublesome for users of bibliographic reports. So as you compile entries for your report, be especially careful when transcribing names, titles, and facts of publication. The form of entries depends largely on whether you used the humanities style or the science style. We covered these forms in Chapter 9, "Basic Principles of Reports." Here we will discuss the writing of an introduction that precedes the bibliographic entries.

The bibliographic entries, of course, are the basic information that most readers want. But the chief merit of many bibliographic reports is a helpful introduction that is concerned with such information as the following:

- The subject and purpose of the report.
- The scope and coverage of the bibliography, especially the principle of selecting the items.
- The arrangement of the bibliography.
- The form of the citations.

Most of the time, your readers will need to know this information to use your bibliography efficiently.

Subject and Purpose

You won't write a bibliographic report just because it's Thursday and you feel like doing one. Your report will be part of the solution to some subject or problem that you and your readers are interested in. One of the best ways to connect with the users of your bibliography is to state as explicitly as you can the subject or problem that your report relates to and what your purpose is in compiling the bibliography. Notice how clearly the authors of *A Guide to Minority Aging References*[1] define the situation that has led to their work and state their objectives.

They begin by describing the problem to provide background for their readers.

> By the year 2000 the current number of older minority persons in the United States will almost double. It is projected that the total number of minority individuals over the age of 65 will be well over five million. This represents an increase of 2.2 million over the 1978 figure and an increase of over 3.8 million over the 1960 census figures.
>
> This dramatic change in our demographic structure has stimulated a growing awareness of the need for better understanding of the condition and circumstances of older minority persons of different ethnic heritages. This volume is part of an effort to develop a systematic knowledge base

about older minorities upon which future planning efforts in both research and human service delivery policies and strategies can be based.

It is generally acknowledged that older minorities received much less research attention than any other aging segment during the formative years of gerontology. Only during the last two decades has the attention of gerontology been significantly focused on older persons in minority communities.

In the last ten years, the literature on minority aging has grown at an exponential rate. Yet, researchers and advocates, providers and practitioners, policymakers and planners, students and teachers, all have continued to lament the perceived paucity of information. This lack of readily accessible information has resulted in the transmission of inadequate and fragmented knowledge, which has impeded the development of viable public policies and program models, and hindered the opportunities for research by gerontologists among older minorities.

From this opening, readers learn the context of the authors' work. The writers want to establish that information about older minorities, developed by recent research, is not getting to the professionals who need it. We urge you not to take it for granted that your readers will understand the context of your bibliographic report. Ask yourself these two questions: What has caused me to compile this bibliography, and who is my audience? Then answer both questions early in your introduction.

The authors of *A Guide to Minority Aging References* go on to state their purpose in compiling the bibliography and connect the project to the work of the professionals who will be using it.

The general purpose of the project is to identify and codify research literature on older minority persons. The term *codify* means "arrange in a systematic way."

The basic goal is to establish the parameters of an organized body of minority aging knowledge. This body of minority group information is organized around the four major ethnic group classifications—American Indian/Alaskan Native, Black, Hispanic, and Pacific/Asia, and twelve subject categories—Health, Nutrition, Social Network/Family Relations, Income/Economics, Transportation/Mobility, Mental Health, Education, Leisure/Recreation, Literature Review/Overview. This classification permits identification of what is available, as well as what is not available, for each of the four major ethnic groups, and within each of the twelve major subject categories.

Your statement of the subject and purpose of your bibliography should be presented this clearly to enable readers to judge the significance of your work and to determine whether it is related to their interests. Get into the habit of defining your subject and stating your purpose. They are two important things your readers want to know. You might even be surprised at how much the practice will help you clarify your own thinking.

Scope and Coverage

When developing the bibliography, you will probably attempt a comprehensive list of works, even if you later decide to eliminate certain items. In your introduction you should state explicitly the kinds of works you include in the bibliography and, if necessary, the kinds of works you have excluded. Choosing the works to be included and excluded must be done carefully. You should explain the criteria for selection and perhaps even justify certain inclusions and exclusions. Here's the way the authors of *A Guide to Minority Aging References* explain their selection of works.

> Each had to have a significant focus on (a) aging or later life, and (b) on members of minority groups that have been subjected to collective discrimination, unusual treatment because of their racial or cultural characteristics. . . .
>
> Examples of materials appropriate for inclusion in the collection include (1) research publications; (2) research project preliminary and final reports; (3) assessments of public policies; (4) curriculum guidelines and training materials; (5) unpublished meeting presentations; and (6) dissertations and master's theses. Examples of material excluded include (1) letters, editorials, memos, and book reviews; (2) pamphlets, catalogs, and brochures; (3) annual reports of institutions, agencies, and organizations; (4) questionnaires or survey instruments; and (5) computer search outputs.
>
> All documents acquired were analyzed for minority *and* aging focus.

Notice how the authors had specific criteria for selecting and excluding material. The ideas that the authors are driving home are that they have searched thoroughly and selected carefully. They have included documents that are not widely disseminated, such as project reports, unpublished papers, and dissertations and theses. (Elsewhere in the introduction they describe the method of their literature search.) They point out that they have included no works that make only passing comment on the subject. They also reassure readers that entries have not been excluded because they were not available: "If it was not possible to acquire and/or analyze documents, due to project time constraints or availability, the reference was entered in the Uncodified Bibliography (see page 100)."

You must also use your introduction to explain clearly how you selected the works that are included in your bibliography.

Arrangement of the Bibliography

Like any report, your bibliography must be arranged in some order that can be easily recognized by and helpful to your readers—alphabetically by author's or editor's last name, chronologically, or by type of publication. The first and last arrangements are the most common.

As shown in Figure 11–3, a bibliography may be arranged alphabetically by author, surname first. If no author is given, the title of the

Barber, C.E. and A. Cook. 1980. Attitudes of Navajo youth
        toward supporting aged parents. Paper presented at the
        39th annual meeting of the Gerontological Society of
        America. San Diego, California.

Duke, F. C. 1980. The elder American Indian. San Diego,
        Calif.: Campanile Press.

Employment and the elderly. 1981. National Indian Council
        on Aging Quarterly 1:2-5.

Hanson, W. 1980. The urban Indian woman and her family.
        Social Casework: The Journal of Contemporary Social
        Casework 61:476-83.

National Indian Council on Aging. 1980. May the circle
        be unbroken: A new decade. Alburquerque, N.M.:
        National Indian Council on Aging.

Red Horse, J.G. 1980a. American Indian elders: Unifiers of
        Indian families. Social Casework: The Journal of
        Contemporary Casework 61:490-93.

_____. 1980b. American Indian elders: Needs and aspirations.
        In Minority aging: Policy issues for the '80's, edited
        by E. P. Standford, 61-68. San Diego, Calif.: Campanile
        Press.

FIGURE 11–3 Bibliography arranged alphabetically

work is used. If there's more than one work by the same author, they are arranged, usually, alphabetically by title, under the author's name. For the second and subsequent entries by the same author, an underscore of seven spaces may replace the author's name. If the author-year style is used, an author's works published in the same year are designated by lowercase letters after the author's name (1985a, 1985b, 1985c, and so on).

As shown in Figure 11–4, a bibliography may be arranged by publication (book, periodical, unpublished material, and so on). Each categorized list is placed under a separate heading. The entries under each heading may be arranged alphabetically by author or editor (Figure 11–4), chronologically, or by publisher (for books) or title of periodical.

Look at the following explanation of the arrangement of a bibliography dealing with fire safety in transportation:

> The bibliography is organized into two sections: a citation section (white pages) and an index section (blue pages). The citation section consists of complete publication information required for locating the work, and a brief summary or abstract of its contents. The citation section is further organized into these five categories: Agriculture and Wildlands, Commercial Facilities, Industrial Facilities, Institutional Facilities, and Public Facilities.
>
> The index section is the key for locating items in the citation section. The index section is comprised of three separate indexes that classify information according to subject, author, and year. A three-digit accession number is assigned to each citation. The subject index lists key words related to fire safety measures. The author section is an alphabetized list of all authors, whether principal or secondary, cited in the citation section.

Bibliographies are typical of other types of reference documents in that they are not designed to be read straight through. Readers want to gain access to material quickly, so you need to explain how your bibliography is arranged and how users can locate entries in which they are interested.

Form of the Citations

The citations should not be presented in any sort of incomplete, unusual, or inconsistent form. We discussed the forms recommended by *The Chicago Manual of Style* in Chapter 9, "Basic Principles of Reports," pages 173–185. Here we offer a few tips on how to make your citations more helpful to your readers and how to write annotations (notes) for an annotated bibliography.

Undoubtedly the biggest help you can offer users of your bibliography is that which prevents them from flipping around through the pages trying to figure out what some of the information means or from spending unnecessary time when they read the references in the bibliography. If space is not a problem, we recommend that you spell out the

BOOKS

Dukepoo, F.C. 1980. <u>The elder American Indian</u>. San Diego, Calif.: Campanile Press.

Hines, C. <u>Elderly Alaskan natives in Anchorage: A needs assessment for social services program planning</u>. Anchorage: University of Alaska Press.

CHAPTERS FROM BOOKS

Red Horse, J.G. 1980. American Indian elders: Needs and Aspirations. In <u>Minority aging: Policy issues for the '80's</u>, edited by E. P. Standord, 61-68. San Diego, Calif.: Campanile Press.

ARTICLES

Employment and the elderly. 1981. <u>National Indian Council on Aging Quarterly</u> 1:2-5.

Hanson, W. 1980. The urban Indian woman and her family. <u>Social Casework: The Journal of Contemporary Social Casework</u> 61:476-83.

UNPUBLISHED PAPERS

Barber, C.E., and A. Cook. 1980. Attitudes of Navajo youth toward supporting aged parents. Paper presented at the 39th annual meeting of the Gerontological Society of America. San Diego, California.

Manson, S.M. 1980. Cultural determination of mental health programming and service delivery to American Indians and Alaskan Native elderly. Paper presented at the Conference on Provision of Services to Minority Elderly,

FIGURE 11–4 Bibliography arranged by type of publication

full names of journals and books. Although you might be able to rely on readers recognizing abbreviations of well-known journals in their field, you cannot assume they know abbreviations of lesser-known periodicals or of periodicals outside their field. If space is a problem, causing you to resort to abbreviated titles, we recommend that you include a list of abbreviations. For periodicals appearing only once or twice in your bibliography, we recommend that you spell out the complete title to save readers from having to check the list of abbreviations.

We also recommend that you include the beginning and ending pages of cited passages. The abbreviations *f.* and *ff.* for "page(s) following" are not very helpful. Just list the pages where the subject is treated; it will save the user some time.

An annotated bibliography contains a description or summary of each item cited. Unless you are writing an evaluative report, you should avoid judgmental statements like "this important study," "an out-of-date article," and "an ill-conceived book." Users expect your annotations to be accurate, fair, and a complete summary of the work. Such an annotation might read like this:

> Rice, T. 1984. Determinants of physician assignment rates by type of service. Health Care Financing Review 5 (Summer): 33–34.
>
> In this article, the determinants of physician assignment rates under the Medicare program are examined separately for medical, surgical, laboratory, and radiology services. Data for this study include copies of all Medicare claims submitted by over 1,200 Colorado general practitioners, internists, and general surgeons during the periods both before and after they experienced a substantial change in program reimbursement rates. The results indicate that there is a significant positive relationship between changes in reimbursement and changes in assignment rates for medical, laboratory, and radiology services, but the relationship for surgical service is not significant. Furthermore, for laboratory and radiology services, only the change in medical service reimbursement is significant—reimbursement rates for laboratory and radiology services are not.

As you can see, the annotation describes the general coverage and summarizes the important ideas. The style is that of good prose. There is no telegraphic language that omits articles, conjunctions, and verbs. The summary is objective. The wording "The results indicate" states neutrally that the research results are convincing without stating judgmentally that the research *proves* anything.

Annotations may be only a sentence or two, or they may be an ample paragraph. If the annotations are paragraphs, they are set off in paragraph form, beginning two lines below the bibliographical entry, as in the annotation on physician assignment rates. If the annotations consist of only a sentence or two, they may be run in, beginning on the same line as the last entry of the bibliographical information, like this:

> Rice, T. 1984. Determinants of physician assignment rates by type of service. Health Care Financing Review 5 (Summer): 33–34. This article reports that there is a significant positive relationship between changes in Medicare reimbursement rates and changes in medical services rates.

It would be nice if we had specific rules for writing the introduction to bibliographic reports. But introductions must be keyed to the particular purpose and user of your bibliography. In Chapter 9, "Basic Principles of Reports," we point out that the main functions of an introduction are to explain your subject, purpose, scope, and plan and order of presentation. Those general functions are equally important in the introduction to bibliographic reports.

LITERATURE REVIEWS

In writing a literature review, you take a significant step beyond the annotated bibliography, because you analyze the contents of the various sources and then synthesize them into a new whole that gives the reader an understanding of the state of the art on a particular subject. Such a synthesis requires the form of an essaylike report, not a compartmentalized bibliography. Your synthesis is guided by your purpose and your reader's needs. Your synthesis may be to inform, to persuade, or both.

Following is a selection from a literature review that is part of a research proposal requesting authorization and funding to investigate further the scientific classification of Chara (a genus of freshwater algae) in North America. The writer's purposes are specifically as follows:

- To *inform* the reader of the previous work on the subject to provide a state-of-the-art perspective.
- To *analyze* the previous work to identify areas that need further research and to define the scope of the proposed study.
- To *persuade* the reader of the writer's credibility by demonstrating the writer's familiarity with, and response to, the earlier work, thus reassuring the reader that the writer is not "reinventing the wheel."

The following two-paragraph passage sets the stage for the writer's proposal to study further the taxonomy of Chara and to investigate the evolutionary process by which new species of Charophytes are formed. The writer organizes the passage with two principles in mind. The first is to give a chronological development of the state of the art. The second is to point out major areas of agreement and disagreement on the topic.

COMMENTARY

The writer begins this portion of the review by summarizing the results of work before 1950, concluding that the work had not identified the wide variety of Characeae. In the rest of this paragraph, the writer synthesizes her reading of seven studies conducted in the 1950s and 1960s that established the wide variety of Characeae. Identifying the studies by author and year, she describes their similarity of approach and identifies the scope of their research. The writer points out the consequences of the approach taken by Wood and Imahori and then describes the critical reaction to their studies.

In the second paragraph, the writer analyzes the results of three recent works, pointing out that these researchers used cytological and experimental techniques in addition to morphological analysis to determine the different species of Characeae. The writer identifies the "corrective" nature of the studies by Bell, Jones and Hayata, and Guiccone and Williams. The writer ends the paragraph by stating that these studies discovered the existence of more than two sets of chromosomes in algae and that further investigation will be valuable in the study of speciation in other lower plants.

Research on the taxonomy of the Characeae of North America before 1950 was based on relatively few specimens from widely scattered localities. Consequently, the charophyte taxonomy did not fully reflect the morphological plasticity of these plants. This extreme variability was brought to light as a result of a few significant investigations of North American species including Wood (1950), Wood and Meuncher (1956), Dalhousie (1953), Dalhousie and Kiner (1956), and Allen (1959). All of the above authors followed a similar approach to the problem of delimiting species and their respective interpretations of variability differed only slightly. However, no attempt was made to analyze and clarify this variation other than to synonymize certain species. The most drastic treatment of this type was presented by Wood and Imahori (1964, 1965). These authors presented a revision of the entire group, reducing the total number of species from 314 to only 76. In doing so they disqualified the use of several morphological features which had been utilized to distinguish species and even generic sections. Major objections to this treatment have been voiced by several workers. The most serious criticism to the revision is the fact that it was based completely on comparisons of general morphological features without any attempt to test the validity of utilization of recent findings which actually validate the use of these characteristics.

During the past few years several workers have carried out investigations on North American charophytes utilizing cytological or experimental techniques in association with detailed morphological analysis (Bell, 1966; Jones and Hayata, 1969; and Guiccone and Williams, 1970). Publications of similar studies on species from other continents are also available. Most of these works prove, to some extent, that many of the characteristics disregarded by Wood and Imahori actually represent important distinguishing features and that in many cases these characteristics are valuable not only for separating species but also for determining evolutionary relationships within the various genera. These studies have been especially successful in pointing out the importance of polyploidy as a mechanism of speciation. This is of special interest in that polyploidy in the algae is not well understood. Further investigation of the Characeae will doubtlessly be of considerable value in understanding other groups of lower plants.

We will not attempt to include every type of literature review. We have presented an excerpt from an informative and persuasive literature review that is part of a research proposal. To conclude our discussion of literature reviews, we present another one—the literature review section from a report entitled "Commuting and Migration Status in Nonmetro Areas."[2] Its purposes are *informative*—to establish the relationship of the current study to earlier work—and *persuasive*—to show by the historical analysis of earlier work that the writers have earned the right to conduct the present study.

COMMUTING AND MIGRATION STATUS IN NONMETRO AREAS*
Gladys K. Bowles and Calvin L. Beale†

COMMENTARY

The review, which is arranged chronologically into seven compact paragraphs, constitutes the introduction of the report. It summarizes the methodology and findings of previous research. The focus is on the scope of earlier research and what those studies have or have not accomplished. The first three paragraphs describe three stages of interest in data related to worker migration and commuting. The numbers in parentheses refer to items contained in the list of references at the end of the report.

The third paragraph ends by pointing out the lack of research on the current topic—

INTRODUCTION

The 1865 census of the State of New York provides the first evidence of official interest in the relationship between place of residence and location of employment. A question was asked "on the usual place of employment, if out of the city or town where the family resides." Unfortunately, the results were considered "too meager." Figures were published "only for the counties upon the Hudson and on Long Island and Staten Island," and a recommendation was made that the subject not be pursued (7).[1]

Only much later, when the automobile became the primary mode of transportation and contributed to the growth of suburbs, did commuting become a recognized research topic. In this century, the fifties saw a proliferation of studies based on traffic flows, management records, and special surveys; and the Federal Government measured intercounty commuting in a national sample survey (15). But, as Schnore points out, until 1960 "the United States census—long used as a model by other nations—[was] one of the few in the Western world which [had] never collected information on the places of work of employed members of the labor force as part of its full-scale operations" (8).[2] By 1960, a sufficient demand for commuting data existed that the Census of Population included questions on place of employment. Although these questions were repeated in 1970, neither census inquired about distance traveled.

Most commuting research appearing since 1960, whether based on the 1960 and 1970 Bureau of the Census publications, *Journey to Work (13, 14)* or on other sources has been confined to metropolitan areas. A bulletin based on the 1975 Annual Housing Survey (AHS) contains general

*Revised version of paper prepared for the annual meeting of the Population Association of America, April 26–28, 1979, Philadelphia. The paper is based on research conducted under Agreement No. 12-17-09-8-1663, between ESCS and the Institute for Behavioral Research (IBR), University of Georgia. The assistance of Susan S. Carley, Sam T. Davis, III, and Eva J. Miller of the IBR in the development of materials for the paper is gratefully acknowledged.

†The authors are demographers in the Economic Development Division, ESCS.

[1]Italicized numbers in parentheses refer to items in the references at the end of this article.

[2]Schnore's article contains an excellent bibliography of both published and unpublished works before 1960.

commuting patterns and migration in nonmetro areas and using current metro boundaries.

At this point the writers establish the relationship of the current study to earlier work and identify what agencies conducted the current study. This and the next two paragraphs identify the data base and explain the rationale for the current study.

commuting information for both metro and nonmetro populations, but it neither examines migration and commuting nor uses current metro boundaries *(10)*.

No national study of the intercounty commuting patterns of migrants and nonmigrants living in nonmetro areas had been published prior to this study, which was conducted cooperatively by the U.S. Department of Agriculture (USDA) and the University of Georgia *(3)*. Interest in the nonmetro aspects of commuting resulted from the substantial inmovement of people to nonmetro communities in the seventies after decades of net outmovement, growing questions as to the impact of energy costs and supply on settlement patterns, and earlier research findings on the characteristics of metro/nonmetro migrants. Data from the March 1975 Current Population Survey indicated that metro/nonmetro migrants did not have a negative impact on the nonmetro population as some people had predicted. A large number of migrants were in white collar occupations and industries, and their average income was not less than that of the total nonmetro population. The income of metro/nonmetro migrants was similar to that of persons moving in the opposite direction *(2)*.

These issues and findings raised questions about similarities and differences among the migrant and nonmigrant groups that had not hitherto been addressed. These questions involved the characteristics of nonmetro commuters, the association between migration and commuting, and comparative distances traveled by metro and nonmetro people. A key issue was the extent to which the recent nonmetro population growth resulting from metro/nonmetro migration is linked to commuting to jobs in metro areas.

The 1975 AHS, with its travel-to-work supplement containing information on previous and current places of residence and work for household heads, provides a data base for such investigation.

The introduction ends with the definition of key words in the study and a restriction of the current research to persons identified as "household heads."

In our study, *commuters* are defined as household heads who worked in different counties from those in which they lived at the time they were surveyed;[3] *migrants* lived in different counties in 1975 from those in which they had lived 5 years earlier; *household heads* were designated by survey respondents, except that married women were not reported as household heads if they were living with their husbands. The data, based on special AHS tabulations, reflect metro designations through 1975. Thus, they reflect nonmetro and metro commuting more accurately than other published AHS data, which were based on older metro boundaries *(10)*.[4] No data were available by migration *and* commuting status for persons who were not household heads.

---

[3]We recognize that, in addition to the comparative availability of employment, such geographic features as size, shape, and topography of counties are important determinants of commuting patterns. Intercounty commuting, by definition, always occurs in commuting between nonmetro and metro areas.

[4]Information on the reliability of AHS estimates and definitions of terms can be found in recent publications of the Bureau of the Census on the journey to work in selected metro areas and in the AHS *per se* *(10, 11, 12)*.

SUGGESTIONS FOR APPLYING YOUR KNOWLEDGE

1. You may have to do library research in conjunction with a report for your writing course or some other course. Prepare a bibliography of published material that relates to the subject of the report.

2. As part of a progress report on a research project, write an annotated bibliography on published material that relates to the project. Or in a periodical index, locate five articles on a topic that interests you, look up the articles, read them, and write an annotation on each.

3. Rewrite an annotated bibliography as a literature review that informs the reader of the state of the art on a particular topic. Arrange your synthesis of the material according to some useful pattern, such as by topics or by areas of agreement and disagreement.

C H A P T E R

12

Mechanism description explains the purpose, appearance, physical structure, and sometimes the operation or behavior of a mechanism. The word *mechanism,* as used here, applies to anything that takes up space and behaves in a predictable manner or performs work. In this sense a driver's license is as much a mechanism as is a clutch or an automobile. A mechanism can be small or large, simple or complex, man-made or natural. Hand tools (scissors, pen, nail punch), devices (oil pump, telephone, bicycle, tesla coil, artesian well, electric dust extractor), and natural objects (eggs, knee joint, flower, kidney, volcano) suggest the wide range of mechanisms. In addition, the layout of a waste water treatment plant or a post office and an abstract entity such as the Federal Reserve System might also be regarded as mechanisms.

A mechanism may even be something that is otherwise unseeable until you describe it. Scientists often work with things that cannot be seen by optical means. The shape and size of atoms, the double helix structure of DNA, the synaptic ends of nerves, and many concepts of modern physics cannot be seen directly, but they can be visualized from data that convince us that they are present. Mechanism description is an important means for conveying evidence of their presence.

Regardless of the mechanism to be described, the main problems confronting you when you describe it are (1) how much information to include, (2) how best to create a picture of the mechanism in your readers' minds, and (3) how to arrange the details of the description.

DECIDING HOW MUCH INFORMATION TO INCLUDE

Two familiar considerations face you immediately when you prepare to describe a mechanism: What is the purpose of your description? Who is your audience? Mechanism description is always selective. You would never describe a mechanism just to be describing it. What information you include about the mechanism depends on whether you're describing it to readers who will make it, buy it, ship it, operate it, or repair it.

Mechanisms have specially designed features built into them that are important to readers, and handling these features is one of your most important tasks. You don't want to burden readers with unnecessary information, but you also don't want to omit meaningful information. Sometimes it is difficult to determine when simply to state the feature and when to explain its significance. For instance, if it is important to point out that a certain element is made of tungsten, is it also necessary to explain the *so-what*—that tungsten is used because of its hardness and its capability to withstand corrosives and high temperatures? In a way, you will be walking the tightrope between the legal maxim that "the fact speaks for itself" and the often-proclaimed scientific principle that "a fact in itself is nothing."

Because you know so well the features of the mechanism you describe, it is difficult for you to remember that they might mean little or nothing to readers. What may be obvious and important to you may appear isolated and unimportant to your readers unless you explain the importance of the feature. Let's look at an example of how you can be sure you know enough about the features so that you can explain them to readers who need an explanation. Assume that you're describing an electric paper shredder that reduces paper to unreadable ¼-inch strips and that you want to point out several important features. In preparing your notes, you might find the following two-column format handy. The left column identifies the feature, and the right column identifies the significance of the feature—the *so-what*.

Feature	Significance
1. Built-in shredder continuously feeds paper through shredder.	Works automatically, without supervision.
2. ¾ h.p. motor	Has 70 percent more shredding power than most other models: shreds 14 sheets of 20-lb. bond at one time.
3. 12″ throat	Accepts computer printout pages.
4. Hardened cutter blades	Cannot be damaged by conventional staples and paper clips.

5. 10″ high × 21″ wide × 22″ deep	Compact and small enough to use on table or desk top.
6. Soft rubber feet	Won't mar furniture.
7. Brown, gray, or beige finish	Fits most office decors and color schemes.

When you mention the features in your presentation, immediately explain the significance of the feature so that the feature has meaning to your readers. The two-column format will do, or you can combine the information like this:

> The Shredmaster 180 has seven major features:

- Built-in shredder that continuously feeds forms through the shredder. It works automatically and without supervision.

- ¾ h.p. motor that has 70 percent more shredding power than most other models. It will shred 14 sheets of 20-lb. bond paper at one pass.

- 12″ throat that accepts computer printout pages.

- Hardened cutter blades that cannot be damaged by conventional staples or paper clips.

- Size—10″ high × 21″ wide × 22″ deep—makes it small enough to use on table or desk top.

- Soft rubber feet won't mar furniture.

- Brown, gray, or beige finish matches most office decors and color schemes.

When you review and revise your description, keep asking yourself if your intended reader is likely to need certain features translated into more meaningful terms. This way what you say about the mechanism will have some value to your readers.

Describing a Familiar Mechanism

If your purpose is to remind readers of the major features and parts of a mechanism with which they are somewhat familiar, you can rely on graphics to describe its appearance and on a few words to describe its materials, connections, and functions. Figure 12–1 is a description of a device provided by the manufacturer to acquaint customers with their purchase.

The description, appearing at the front of the customer's manual

Know Your

Osterizer.
LIQUEFIER-BLENDER®

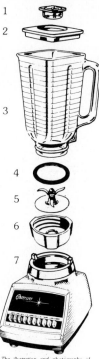

cover

The cover for your Osterizer blender consists of two parts, the plastic feeder cap (1) and the vinyl cover (2). The cover is self-sealing and is made of vinyl and resistant to absorption of odors and stains. The feeder cap is removable for use as a measuring cap and provides an opening for the addition of other ingredients.

container

The 5-cup container (3) for the Osterizer blender is graduated for easy measurement and is molded of heat and cold resistant material. The convenient handle and pouring lip permit easy removal of liquid mixtures, while thicker mixtures are more easily removed through the bottom opening.

agitator or processing assembly

Consists of three parts: (4) a sealing ring of neoprene used as a cushion between the container and the agitator; (5) agitator of high-grade stainless steel; (6) a threaded container bottom.

motor and motor base

The powerful multi-speed motor is the heart of the appliance and designed just for this unit. It is completely enclosed within the housing (7).

The Osterizer blender motor uses a "free-floating" feature to reduce noise and wear. This feature allows the square post which protrudes from the motor base to move slightly from side to side.

Your Osterizer blender contains a powerful food processing motor, but it can be overloaded. To avoid this possibility, closely follow the instructions and the quantities specified in the recipes in this book.

The illustration and photography of Osterizer blenders found in this book do not necessarily depict the particular model Osterizer blender that you have purchased. These photographs are merely a guide to illustrate the versatility of your Osterizer blender.

care and cleaning of your Osterizer blender

Never store foods in your Osterizer blender container. Always remove the agitator assembly and wash and dry container and agitator assembly thoroughly after you have finished blending. Re-assemble container after cleaning so it will be ready for future use. Never place processing assembly on motor base without the container. See page 2 for proper assembly and tightening instructions.

Osterizer blender parts are corrosion resistant, sanitary, and easily cleaned. Wash in warm, soapy water and dry thoroughly. DO NOT WASH ANY PARTS IN AN AUTOMATIC DISHWASHER.

NEVER IMMERSE THE MOTOR BASE IN WATER. It does not require oiling. Its outside can be cleaned with a damp cloth (unplug cordset first).

FIGURE 12–1   The first page of manufacturer's booklet describing a product (Courtesy Oster Corporation)

for the blender, is brief, yet sufficient for its purpose, and well organized. The mechanism is described in terms of its major parts and their functions. The two-column format, placing an exploded view of the blender to the right of the written description, enables readers to move back and forth from the writing to the pictures with ease. The headings and numbered parts help readers identify parts.

Describing an Unfamiliar Mechanism

Often your purpose will be to acquaint readers with mechanisms they are unfamiliar with. In such cases you'll need to explain more thoroughly the purpose, physical structure, and use or operation of the mechanism. Let's assume, for instance, that you're introducing a group of beginning drafting students to an instrument they'll have to know backwards and forwards—the adjustable beam compass. You'll need to blend as much functional description with visual description as you think is necessary to acquaint them with the mechanism.

THE ADJUSTABLE BEAM COMPASS
The adjustable beam compass is a drawing instrument used by draftspersons and technical illustrators to draw large arcs and circles that cannot be obtained with a regular bow compass. Depending on the number and length of beams, it can draw circles up to five feet or more in diameter. In spite of the variety of beams, the adjustable beam compass consists essentially of four major parts: (1) the beam, (2) the coupling attachment, (3) the center pin, and (4) the writing head.

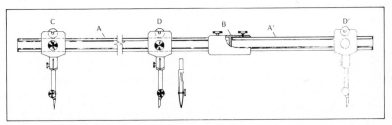

View of adjustable beam compass (Courtesy Betty L. Bradford, Drafting Instructor, Rowan County Vocational School, Morehead, Kentucky)

THE BEAM The beam (A) makes up the main body of the compass and forms the channel for the center pin (C) and writing head (D), which can be adjusted to obtain the desired diameter. Made of various types of metal or wood, the beam comes in several lengths—ranging from 6″ to 36″— which are graduated in inches to $\frac{1}{32}$″. Metal beams look like miniature I-beams, approximately $\frac{5}{16}$″ thick. Wood beams look like flat rulers, approximately $\frac{7}{32}$″ thick. The potential radius of the beam compass can be extended by connecting "extension" beams (A′) to the base beam with coupling attachments.

COUPLING ATTACHMENT   The coupling attachment (B) is a double-locking device that rigidly connects beams for desired diameter lengths. A rectangular opening, slightly larger than the beams, is cut into the ends of the coupling attachment so that the beams fit inside. Two knurled tension screws serve to hold the beams rigidly.

THE CENTER PIN   The center pin (C), consisting of an interchangeable leg assembly and a divider point, serves as a pivot for drawing arcs and circles. The interchangeable leg assembly (so called because it is identical to the one used to hold the drawing point) mounts on the beam by the beam passing directly through its rectangular center. The knurled thumb roller, which is like a geared wheel riding against the beam top, allows the leg to be minutely adjusted. The locking screws maintain the exact setting of the leg on the beam and hold the center pin in place. The center pin (like the writing head) extends only one inch below the beam.

THE WRITING HEAD   The writing head (D), as its name suggests, is the part of the compass that marks the desired curve. It consists of an interchangeable leg assembly (identical to the one on the center pin) that holds either a pen, lead, or scriber.

ADJUSTABLE BEAM COMPASS IN USE   The number of beams necessary to obtain the diameter are connected, the center pin and writing head are adjusted and locked into position, and the proper marking point is put in the writing head. The center pin is then set at the center of the arc or circle to be drawn. The remainder of the beam compass is rotated to draw the desired curve.

The description of the adjustable beam compass provides more detail than does the description of the Oster liquifier-blender in Figure 12–1. The extent to which a mechanism should be described (and consequently, the length of the mechanism description) depends on what readers need to know about the mechanism. If your purpose were to provide specifications so that someone could make the mechanism, you would need to include detailed information that would provide a pattern to be copied. Not even the most minor dimensions or features could be omitted. So it's important to establish in your mind the purpose of your description and what your readers need to know of the mechanism. Otherwise you won't know what to include in your description, sometimes putting in too much information, sometimes not enough.

HELPING READERS VISUALIZE THE MECHANISM

It's natural for you to want to show readers what a mechanism looks like. The three common methods of doing this are to use pictorials, analogies, and geometric shapes.

Pictorials

When visual understanding is involved, pictorials (photographs and drawings) are the most exact method of communication. Verbal language—written or spoken—simply doesn't measure up to visual language in showing physical appearance and spatial relationship.

The old saying that "one picture is worth a thousand words" is true only if the picture is a good one and if it communicates better than words. Unless you're skilled in photography and drawing, you'll need to get help in making pictorials. If you work for an organization that has a presentations department that will do your pictorial work for you—count your blessings. If you don't, you'll have to hire someone to do them. However, even when others prepare pictorials for you, you should know what makes a good pictorial. You may be required to supply preliminary sketches that are to be made into finished pictorials.

The choice, execution, and placement of pictorials should *not* take a back seat when you plan your description. Determine what aspects of the object you want to convey, so that you can decide which type of pictorial best illustrates what you want to show. The following information on photographs and drawings should help you make such choices.

PHOTOGRAPHS   Photographs present the exact appearance of actual objects. Realism is their greatest asset. They are often essential in showing the appearance of newly created objects, objects readers have never seen before, objects at the end of a particular stage of development, and worn or damaged objects. Photographs are also useful in comparing sizes of objects by scaling them against more familiar objects, such as a hand or coin, or an actual scale like a ruler.

Photographs are indispensable for showing the exact appearance to validate the condition of an object. Figure 12–2 illustrates how photographs contrast the appearances of strong, vigorous tobacco plants and damaged tobacco plants. Drawings would not be suitable in these instances, because they would not provide realistic appearances and would be time-consuming to prepare.

Take care in preparing a photograph for a report. It should be no larger than the other sheets of your report. Use rubber cement to attach the photograph to your paper. Don't use staples or paper clips. If you make notations on the back of a photograph, mark lightly or the marks might show through.

DRAWINGS   Like photographs, drawings show what objects look like. Unlike photographs, they can be made to show different aspects of an object. The four most commonly used views are external, cutaway, sectional, and exploded. They may be freehand or ruled, drawn to scale or not.

An external view, like a photograph, shows the outside of an object to give readers an idea of its appearance. The outline is a special kind of

FIGURE 12–2 Tobacco plants. *Top:* Strong, vigorous plants. *Above:* Cutworm injury in plant beds. (Courtesy Cooperative Extension Service, University of Kentucky College of Agriculture, Lexington)

external view that shows, as the name suggests, an object in outline form. The clear appearance of outline drawings avoids the realistic clutter of photographs and makes them useful for emphasizing significant features and for showing shapes and dimensions. Figure 12–3 is an outline drawing showing the shape, dimensions, and parts of a garden trowel.

Photographs and external views do not show the inside parts of objects, how parts fit together, or the transportation of material through a machine. Hidden lines, which may be used with any kind of view, help show features that can't be seen. The unseen features are represented by short dashes. Hidden lines are used in the drawing of the adjustable beam compass and in Figures 12–3 and 12–4.

When interior parts cannot be shown well by hidden lines, cutaway and sectional views are used. They are very useful when objects contain so much housing that all readers see is the outside covering.

A cutaway view, as the name implies, shows an object as if some part of its exterior nearest the viewer had been cut away. It's used to show both internal and external construction in the same drawing. Figure 12–4 illustrates the use of hidden lines and a cutaway view to show unseen rear parts and interior parts of the ammunition magazine of an M-14,

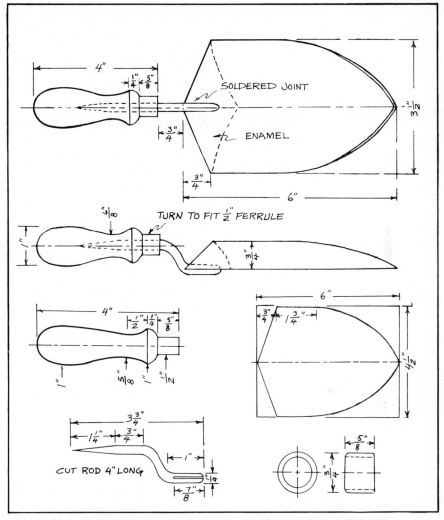

FIGURE 12–3   Outline drawing of a garden trowel (Courtesy Norman Roberts)

A-1 military rifle that would not be visible in an external view. Notice also the exploded view to show the bottom plate. In Figure 12–5 the door and the covering for the wave guide channel of a microwave oven have been removed.

A sectional view, as the name indicates, shows an object as if some section of the object nearest the viewer had been removed. The sectional view may be partial or full; that is, the sectional cut may be through just a portion of the object or may run completely through it. A cross-sectional view, which runs completely through the object, shows an object as if it had been split down the middle and the half nearest the viewer removed.

A phantom view suggests the way the object may look in an alter-

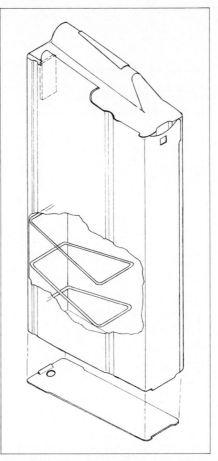

FIGURE 12–4   View of ammunition magazine M-14, A-1 military rifle (Courtesy Betty L. Bradford, Drafting Instructor, Rowan County Vocational School, Morehead, Ky.)

native position. The drawing of the adjustable beam compass illustrates many of the drawing techniques we've been discussing. Hidden lines indicate the existence of the beam inside the center pin and writing head. Break lines cut the beam in two to shorten the view. A partial sectional view shows the inside of the coupling device, indicating that the base beam and the extension beam are separated by a partition. (Notice that the portion of an object cut through in a sectional drawing is represented by diagonal lines.) A phantom view indicates where the writing head would be on the extension beam.

LABELING PICTORIALS   To make photographs and drawings as self-explanatory as possible, you need to label them informatively and neatly. Quality work is required here, because you don't want sloppy techniques

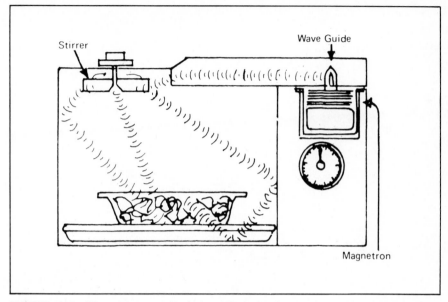

FIGURE 12–5   Microwave oven (Agricultural Extension Service, University of Minnesota, St. Paul)

to distract from an otherwise effective pictorial. Here are some suggestions to help you achieve uniform quality in labeling.

- Call a formal pictorial a *figure,* and furnish each with a figure number (Arabic) and a descriptive title.

Figure 1. The main components of the bolus gun

Figure 4. The diskettes (The diskette on the left is pictured in its protective paper jacket; the diskette on the right is not.)

Figure 9. Cessna 402 antenna distribution

As shown in these captions, run the figure number and the descriptive title on the same line. Place the caption beneath the pictorial.

- Identify the parts of the pictured object clearly and neatly. Labels should be placed in the background area of the figure and be neatly arranged and straight.

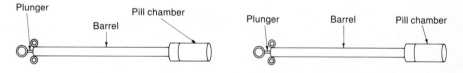

- Labels should be right-hand justified when the arrow comes from the right side of the label.

UNDESIRABLE   PREFERRED

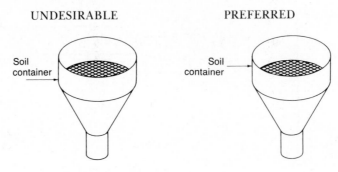

- Labels should be left-hand justified when the arrow comes from the left side of the label.

UNDESIRABLE   PREFERRED

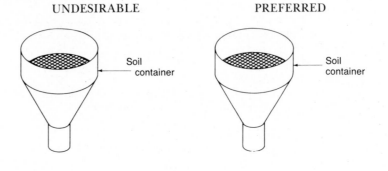

- Where there is adequate space, avoid the use of keys and label the parts directly.

UNDESIRABLE   PREFERRED

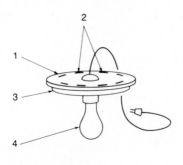
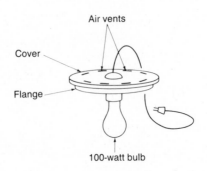

Legend: 1--Cover
          2--Air vents
          3--Flange
          4--100-watt bulb

- If labeling directly results in a cluttered and crowded pictorial, then a key should be used to identify the parts.

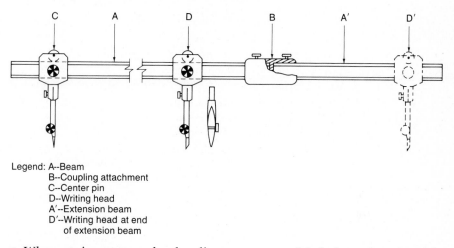

Legend: A--Beam
       B--Coupling attachment
       C--Center pin
       D--Writing head
       A'--Extension beam
       D'--Writing head at end
          of extension beam

- When main parts and subordinate parts are labeled on the pictorial, make the hierarchy distinctive.

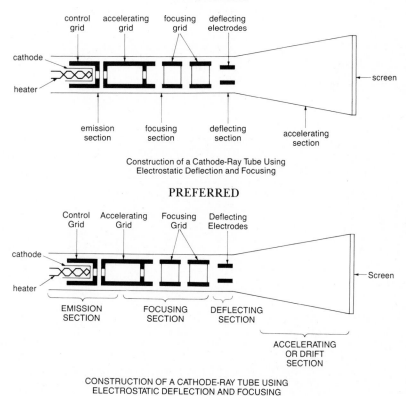

UNDESIRABLE

Construction of a Cathode-Ray Tube Using
Electrostatic Deflection and Focusing

PREFERRED

CONSTRUCTION OF A CATHODE-RAY TUBE USING
ELECTROSTATIC DEFLECTION AND FOCUSING

The labels on the preferred pictorial cue the reader to the hierarchical arrangement of information. The highest level is the title of the pictorial in oversized uppercase letters. The next highest level is the names of the main parts (Emission Section, Focusing Section, Deflecting Section, and Accelerating Section) in normal uppercase letters. The third level is the names of the subparts of the main sections (Control Grid, Accelerating Grid, Focusing Grid, Deflecting Electrodes, and Screen) in mixed upper- and lowercase letters. The lowest level is the names of elements of the subparts (cathode and heater are elements of the Control Grid) in all lowercase letters. The type size and capitalization are only two methods of using labels to indicate hierarchy. There are other ways to do this, but the important thing is to reflect the hierarchy. Otherwise the reader is forced to look elsewhere for that information.

- Use consistent nomenclature in pictorials and text. Don't call an antenna an *antenna* in the text and label it an *air terminal* on the pictorial. Don't refer in the text to an *elevator control channel* and label it an *elevator control system* on the pictorial. Inconsistent nomenclature can easily confuse the reader.
- Arrows which come from the top or bottom of the label should be centered, if possible.

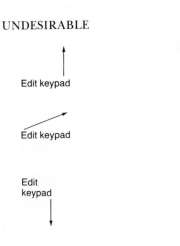

- Arrows should not touch the label.

UNDESIRABLE   PREFERRED

Edit keypad   Edit keypad

- Arrows should just touch the object.

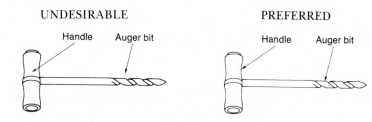

UNDESIRABLE   PREFERRED

Handle   Auger bit   Handle   Auger bit

- In exploded views, if it is necessary to illustrate how the parts fit together, lead lines should be used.

UNDESIRABLE   PREFERRED

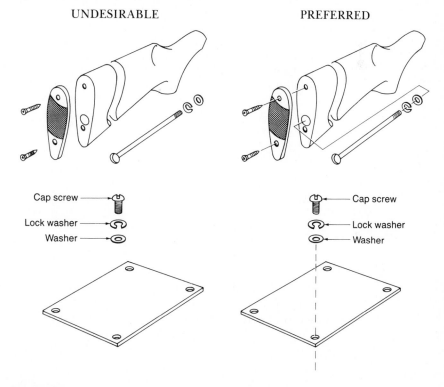

Cap screw   Cap screw

Lock washer   Lock washer

Washer   Washer

Analogies

Suppose we want to describe something that we've seen for the first time or our readers have never seen. How do we describe the unknown? Usually the best way is by comparing it to the known.

Can you remember the tremendous feeling of excitement when you first looked at things under a microscope? Those magnified images revealed a world that had been hidden from you before. In 1665 Robert Hooke, a seventeenth-century English scientist, constructed a microscope that allowed him to examine many things that had never been seen by the human eye. One of the things he looked at was a piece of outer bark of the cork oak. Part of his description of what he saw with his microscope is shown here as he recorded it in *Micrographia* (1665). We have modernized the spelling, so you should have little trouble reading the passage.

> I took a good clear piece of cork, and with a pen knife sharpened as keen as a razor, I cut a piece of it off, and thereby left the surface of it exceedingly smooth, then examining it very diligently with a microscope, I thought I could perceive it to appear a little porous; but I could not so plainly distinguish them, as to be sure that they were porous, much less what figure they were of. But judging from the lightness and yielding quality of the cork, that certainly the texture could not be so curious, but that possibly, if I could use some further diligence, I might find it discernible with a microscope, I with the same sharp pen knife, cut off from the former smooth surface an exceedingly thin piece of it, and placing it on a black object plate, because it was itself a white body, and casting the light on it with a deep plano-convex glass, I could exceedingly plainly perceive it to be all perforated and porous, much like a honeycomb, but that the pores of it were not regular; yet it was not unlike a honeycomb in these particulars.
>
> First, in that it had a very little solid substance, in comparison of the empty cavity that was contained between, as does more manifestly appear by the Figure A and B of the XI scheme, for the *interstitia,* or walls (as I may so call them) or partitions of those pores were nearly as thin in proportion to their pores, as those thin films of wax in a honeycomb (which enclose and constitute the sexangular cells) are to theirs.
>
> Next, in that these pores, or cells, were not very deep, but consisted of a great many little boxes, separated out of one continued long pore; by certain diaphragms, as is visible by the Figure B, which represents a sight of those pores split the long-ways.

Although Hooke's style may seem a little strange to modern readers, he used two conventional methods to convey impressions of what he saw. As his references to "Figure A and B" indicate, he used drawings. His comparison of the cells to "honeycomb" and "little boxes" shows that he relied on analogies to describe what the cells looked like.

Take a lesson from Hooke. When an object resembles something else your readers are more familiar with, analogies can be helpful in explaining its shape, size, and structure. A common way to do this is to use metaphors of shape based on the letters of the alphabet: A-frame, C-clamp, I-beam, O-ring, S-hook, T-square, U-bolt, Y-joint, and so on. Another way is to name parts of objects after parts of anatomy: head, eyes, ears, mouth, teeth, lip, throat, tongue, neck, shoulder, elbow, arm, leg, foot, and heel. Gears and saws have teeth; pliers and vises have jaws; needles have eyes. A third way is to use resemblances to other well-known objects: a mushroom-shaped anchor, a barrel-shaped container, a canister the size of a tube of lipstick.

Analogies also can be used to suggest structure and size.

• Each stair tread on an escalator is like a small four-wheel truck.

- Some bearing sleeves are porous and under a microscope look like very fine sponges, but are rigid.
- The simplest portable hair dryer looks a little like an oversized handgun in which a small fan blows hot air out of a screened nozzle.
- The tape-recording head is a small C-shaped electromagnet the size of a dime.
- The barometer case looks like a small metal shoe box with a glass lid.
- The islands hang like a loose necklace from the entrance of the bay.
- The combustion chamber is shaped like a fat figure eight.
- Our galaxy may be surrounded by an ultraviolet halo emmitted by Neutrinos.

If you can't make the comparison by using a well-known and easily visualized analogy, you can often compare a new mechanism with an older one or a more complex one with a simpler one.

- Disposable syringes are just like rubber ones except that they are made of plastic and can be discarded after use.
- An automobile battery is a much larger and chemically different version of the battery that powers a flashlight.

How good an analogy is depends on how well the comparison clarifies the object being described. It wouldn't do to describe something as looking like a pair of dividers or a lemur unless your readers could be expected to know what a pair of dividers or a lemur looks like. You'd be describing the unknown by the still more unknown. Furthermore, an analogy can mislead rather than clarify if it doesn't suggest the right features. For instance, comparing an object to a circle is ineffective if the object looks more like a wheel or a donut. Likewise, comparing an object to a funnel is misleading if it is only cone-shaped. So be sure your analogy is familiar, is appropriate, and reveals as many characteristics as possible.

Geometric Shapes

When an object has an easily identifiable geometric shape, you can refer to that shape—assuming that you and your readers know geometrical terminology. However, if your readers can't be expected to know what a rhombus or a parallelepiped is, don't refer to them. And if the object you're describing is three-dimensional, don't refer to a two-dimensional shape. For instance, if your readers look at a two-dimensional drawing of a three-dimensional object, they might mistake a cone for a triangle. You must either provide a three-dimensional view or explain that the object is conical.

Let's review some of those terms from your geometry class that you've put away because you thought you weren't ever going to use them. They are very useful terms in mechanism description.

TWO-DIMENSIONAL SHAPES   Two-dimensional shapes include angles, polygons, and circles.

Angles.   Angles are shapes formed by two straight lines that meet. When two straight lines meet at a 90° angle, the angle is said to be a *right* angle. Angles less than a right angle are called *acute* angles. Angles greater than a right angle are called *obtuse* angles (see the figures).

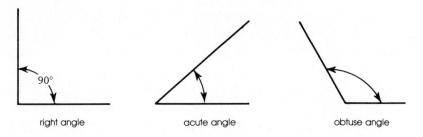

right angle   acute angle   obtuse angle

Polygons.   Polygons are two-dimensional shapes bounded by straight sides. The most usual kinds of polygons are illustrated as follows:

NUMBER OF SIDES   NAME OF SHAPE   SHAPES

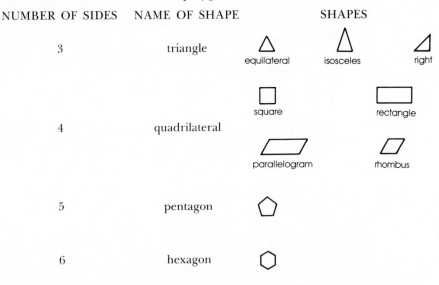

3	triangle	equilateral isosceles right
4	quadrilateral	square rectangle parallelogram rhombus
5	pentagon	
6	hexagon	

Most of these shapes exist around us. The face of an Egyptian pyramid is a triangle. A musical percussion instrument, the triangle, is an example of an equilateral triangle. If you fold a square sheet of paper diagonally so that two of its opposite corners meet, you've made a right triangle. The courthouse squares in county seats are laid out on a square parcel of land. The face of a length of board is a rectangle if the length exceeds the width. Home plate on a baseball diamond and the five-sided building in Arlington, Virginia, that is the headquarters for the U.S. armed forces are pentagons. The cells in a honeycomb are hexagons.

Circles.   A circle is a shape bounded by a curved line that is at all points at an equal distance from its center. A hula hoop, the face of a coin, and wedding rings are circular.

A half-circle, or semicircle, is half a circle with a diameter line connecting the end points. Half a circle without a diameter line is a type of arc.

An oval is a shape that looks like a stretched-out circle. The orbit of a satellite and the layout of a race track are examples of ovals.

THREE-DIMENSIONAL SHAPES   Technically speaking, a three-dimensional object is a solid object. For our purposes in mechanism description, however, the object doesn't have to be solid—it's the shape that we're concerned with. For example, a container or housing for a piece of machinery may be referred to as cubical or cylindrical even though the object is not solid. The most common three-dimensional shapes are polyhedrons, cylinders, cones, spheres, and ellipsoids.

Polyhedrons.   Polyhedrons are "solid" objects bounded by plane surfaces. The most familiar type of polyhedron is the cube. Children's blocks, dice, and even some kinds of ice "cubes" are cubes.

Cones.   Cones are shapes that look like tepees. The upper part of a funnel, the nose "cone" of a space capsule, cinder-coned volcanoes, and even some kinds of ice cream "cones" are examples of cones.

Cylinders.   Cylinders are shapes that look like jars, glasses, cans, and tubes.

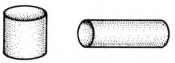

Spheres.   Spheres are "solid" objects bounded by a surface that is at all points the same distance from its center. Tennis balls, globes, and marbles are examples of spheres. A hemisphere is half a sphere.

Ellipsoids.   Ellipsoids are egg-shaped objects. An egg, a football, and various seeds and pills are examples of ellipsoids.

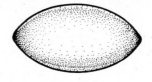

ARRANGING THE DETAILS OF THE DESCRIPTION

Because you have more than one thing to tell readers about a mechanism, and because a mechanism has more than one part, it is impossible to describe it all at once. Thus, you'll have to lead readers through a particular order of presentation. The following three-part arrangement will usually be satisfactory:

1. An introductory overall description of the function and appearance of the entire mechanism.
2. A description of the function and appearance of each major part of the mechanism.
3. An explanation of how the mechanism operates or is used.

What you're doing, in effect, is explaining what the mechanism does and looks like, what each part does and looks like, and how the mechanism as a whole works. Proportion of the description usually works out this way: For a mechanism composed of five major parts, the presentation will have seven main sections—an introduction, five sections describing the five functional parts, and a concluding section describing the operation of the mechanism. Figure 12–6 shows the basic organizational pattern.

The title is usually no more than the name of the mechanism being described: *Multipurpose Police Vehicle, Field-Effect Transistor, Underground Gasoline Storage Tanks,* and so on.

The Introduction

The introduction provides a frame of reference and an overview for the entire mechanism. It names the mechanism again, explains its function or

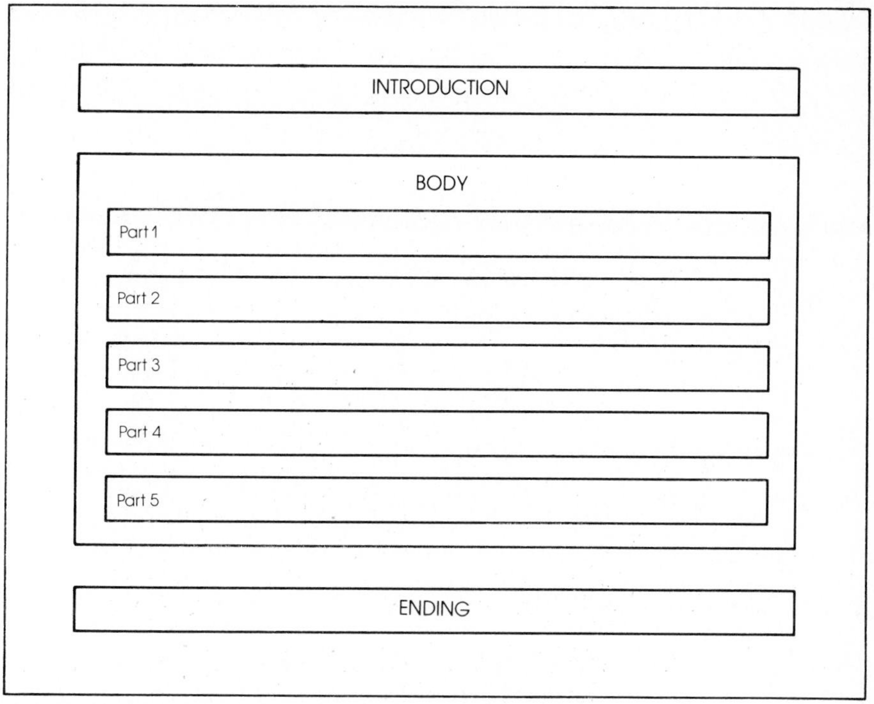

```
┌─────────────────────────────────────────────────────────────┐
│  ┌───────────────────────────────────────────────────────┐  │
│  │                      INTRODUCTION                       │  │
│  └───────────────────────────────────────────────────────┘  │
│  ┌───────────────────────────────────────────────────────┐  │
│  │                          BODY                           │  │
│  │   ┌─────────────────────────────────────────────────┐  │  │
│  │   │ Part 1                                           │  │  │
│  │   └─────────────────────────────────────────────────┘  │  │
│  │   ┌─────────────────────────────────────────────────┐  │  │
│  │   │ Part 2                                           │  │  │
│  │   └─────────────────────────────────────────────────┘  │  │
│  │   ┌─────────────────────────────────────────────────┐  │  │
│  │   │ Part 3                                           │  │  │
│  │   └─────────────────────────────────────────────────┘  │  │
│  │   ┌─────────────────────────────────────────────────┐  │  │
│  │   │ Part 4                                           │  │  │
│  │   └─────────────────────────────────────────────────┘  │  │
│  │   ┌─────────────────────────────────────────────────┐  │  │
│  │   │ Part 5                                           │  │  │
│  │   └─────────────────────────────────────────────────┘  │  │
│  └───────────────────────────────────────────────────────┘  │
│  ┌───────────────────────────────────────────────────────┐  │
│  │                        ENDING                           │  │
│  └───────────────────────────────────────────────────────┘  │
└─────────────────────────────────────────────────────────────┘
```

FIGURE 12–6   Organizational pattern of a mechanism description

behavior, describes its overall appearance, and lists its individual parts. Let's examine an introduction that does these things.

> A volcano is a cone-shaped mountain with a crater in the top that from time to time erupts, spewing gases, rock, ash, and molten lava. The main features of the volcano are its crater (the opening in the earth's surface) and the conduit connecting the opening to the interior of the earth, which contains magma (hot, molten lava). The largest active volcano in the world is Mauna Loa in the Hawaiian Islands, which towers more than 13,500 feet above the island floor.

The most important statements you make about a mechanism early in your description relate to its function, parts, and appearance. Since you'll be familiar with the mechanism, you'll probably take it for granted that your readers share your knowledge. But you'll have to remind yourself that most readers will need information about what the mechanism does, what it looks like, and what its major parts are. Let's look at a few more explanations of the function and listings of the parts of mechanisms:

> A hand hacksaw is a metal-cutting saw of three parts: a handle; a C-shaped frame; and a thin, narrow blade fastened to the open side of the frame.

An amoeba, a one-celled animal found in fresh water, consists of a nucleus, the surrounding protoplasm, and an enclosing outer membrane.

A cantaloupe is a small melon having a ribbed, netted rind; yellow, delicately flavored flesh; and seeds.

A microwave oven consists of a housing, power unit, magnetron, wave guide, and oven cavity.

The steering system of a sailboat consists of the rudder, the rudder post, and the tiller.

Venetian blinds, which are horizontal slatted window shades that can be adjusted to control the amount of sunlight that enters a room, from unimpeded sunlight to nearly complete darkness, may be divided into the following parts:
1. control cords to lift and lower the blinds;
2. control cords to control the tilt of the blinds;
3. slats resting on crosspieces between pairs of tapes.

A rifle cartridge consists of a bullet, a case, powder, and primer.

A miter box is a device used to guide a saw in cutting stock to form angle joints. The simplest form consists of a wooden trough having saw cuts through the sides, usually at angles of 45 degrees and 90 degrees.

The heart consists of four chambers (two atria for receiving blood and two ventricles for pumping blood), valves to prevent a back flow of blood, and numerous vessels that help this part of the circulatory system to work.

These examples partition the mechanism into main parts. You can provide a more extensive forecast of the parts and subparts by "nesting" the subparts with each main part, as in these examples.

The UJ 1000 Printing Calculator has three main parts:
1. the upper panel (composed of the display screen and the printer),
2. the control board (composed of the power, decimal, and printer switches),
3. the keyboard (composed of the function pad, the number pad, and the memory pad).

The cell, as shown in a magnified cross-section in Figure 1, includes three principal parts:
1. the membrane, which holds the cytoplasm together and separates the cell's internal parts from the external environment;
2. the cytoplasm, the substance between the nucleus and the membrane; and
3. the organelles, which are highly specialized components such as the nucleus, mitochondria, endoplasmic reticulum, golgi complex, and lysomes.

Such extended partitioning outlines for the reader the main parts and subparts of the object. Occasionally such detailed forecasting can be done, providing that it doesn't present too much information too fast. But if the overview of the main part and subparts is presented at a pace that is too fast to be absorbed by the reader, you should identify only the main parts in the introduction and introduce the subparts later.

Every mechanism is designed or has the form to fulfill a particular function. Sometimes you can explain that function in the first sentence of the introduction, as in the example of the hand hacksaw, venetian blinds, miter box, and heart. At other times you'll have to devote a sentence or more to explaining the function:

A draftsman's compass is designed for drawing circles, arcs, and ellipses.

A torque wrench is used to tighten bolts to a specified degree of tightness.

In explaining the function, be sure to describe all the important functions the mechanism is designed to perform. For instance, the function of an air conditioner is to do more than cool a space. Most air conditioners also circulate the air, remove moisture from the air, and filter the air. An explanation of the function of an air conditioner should fully reveal the kinds of "conditioning" the air conditioner is designed to do.

When the object you're describing is part of a larger mechanism—say, the ammunition clip or magazine of a rifle, the points in a distributor (or the distributor itself), or the speaker system of a stereo—you should explain how the mechanism relates to the larger whole. For example, readers unfamiliar with the distributor on an automobile would benefit from knowing that it, along with the battery, spark-plug wires, and spark plugs, is part of the ignition system of the engine.

Your reader always needs to have a notion of the size, shape, and general appearance of the mechanism. Size can be explained by giving dimensions (the metal plate is $2'' \times 3'' \times \frac{1}{4}''$) or comparisons (the film canister is about the size of a tube of lipstick). Shape can be expressed by geometric shapes (the book end is shaped like an equilateral triangle) or comparison to shapes of letters of the alphabet and numbers. A drawing that shows the entire mechanism is often placed in the introduction to give readers some idea of the general appearance of the mechanism as a whole and to orient them to the physical viewpoint from which they are viewing the mechanism.

Partitioning the mechanism into its major functional parts usually doesn't present any problems, unless the mechanism is extremely simple or complicated. In either instance you'll have to make some arbitrary decisions. Try to come up with not less than two parts and not more than five or six.

Every mechanism has at least two parts. Something as simple as a piece of chalk, when thought of as a mechanism, has two ends for marking on a chalkboard and a cylindrical body used for a handle (unless some kind of handle is provided). Just because the mechanism is in one piece is no sign that you should not look for at least two functional parts. Do not confuse a physical piece with a functional part. Similarly, if a mechanism has lots of parts, you should group several of them under one larger part. For example, an adjustable beam compass can be separated into as many as 30 pieces, but it can be regarded as having only three major functional parts: the writing head, the center pin, and the beam. The thirty separable pieces are grouped as subparts of these major functional parts.

The list of parts will indicate the order in which the parts will be discussed. The order may be one of three sequences:

1. *Function:* The parts are described in the order of their activity—Part A moves Part B, which moves Part C, and so forth.
2. *Space:* The parts are described from left to right, top to bottom, outside to inside, front to back, and so on.
3. *Importance:* The parts are described from the most significant to the least significant.

Random order of parts is seldom satisfactory.

The Body

The body of a mechanism description explains each major part in the order indicated by the list of major functional parts in the introduction. The parts description provides much the same information for each part that the introduction did for the mechanism as a whole. Simply think of the part as a miniature mechanism. Give at least one section of details for each major part. The following example[1] describes a bolus gun, which is used by veterinarians and other persons who work with livestock to administer medication in pill or tablet form. In the introduction (which is not included here), the writer explains the function of the bolus gun, compares it to a hypodermic syringe in design and use, indicates the different sizes it comes in, and provides an overview of the instrument by listing its three main parts (the plunger, the barrel, and the pill chamber) and providing this drawing:

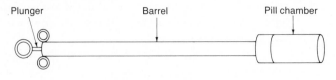

Figure 1. The bolus gun

In the body of the description, the writer devotes a section of details to each main part, explaining the part's function and appearance and identifying its subparts. In the rest of each section, the writer gives the details of material, finishes, weight, connections, and use needed to give readers a visual and functional understanding of the part.

THE PLUNGER

The plunger (Figure 2) fits inside the barrel and pushes the bolus out of the pill chamber into the animal's throat. It consists of a ring grip, stem, and knob. Located at the back of the plunger, the ring grip is used to maneuver the plunger. The stem is that part of the plunger between the ring grip and the knob. When the stem is pushed forward in the barrel, it causes the knob to move forward and eject the bolus from the pill chamber into the animal's throat. The knob is attached to the front of the plunger and fits inside the pill chamber. It is the knob, shaped like a disc measuring $\frac{3}{16}$ inch thick and $\frac{7}{8}$ inch in diameter, that ejects the bolus.

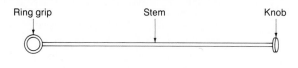

Figure 2. The plunger

THE BARREL

The barrel (Figure 3), which is 10-$\frac{3}{4}$ inches long and $\frac{1}{2}$ inch in diameter, is long enough to insert the pill chamber well into the animal's mouth and is large enough to enclose the plunger. Two ring grips, through which the operator's forefinger and middle finger are inserted, provide the necessary grip on the gun while administering the medicine.

Figure 3. The barrel

THE PILL CHAMBER

The pill chamber holds the bolus before it is ejected into the animal's throat. As shown in Figure 4, it consists of a base, clip, and cover. The base connects the pill chamber to the barrel and supports the clip and the cover. The clip holds the bolus steady while the gun is being positioned in the animal's mouth. It is 2 inches long and $\frac{1}{4}$ inch wide to accommodate large pills. The cover is made of pliable plastic to protect the animal's mouth and throat.

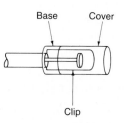

Figure 4. The pill chamber

The Ending

The ending explains how the mechanism works or is used. Here you divide its function or behavior into meaningful stages and explain what happens in each. For instance, if the writer who described the bolus gun had not provided such information in the introduction, he might have described its use like this:

> The bolus gun, designed like a hypodermic syringe, can be used with one hand. The operator grips the gun with one hand, opens the animal's mouth with the other hand, and inserts the end of the gun deep enough into the animal's throat to prevent the pill or tablet from being coughed up.

Another way to end your description is to explain briefly the principles involved in its action. For instance, a toaster "toasts" by broiling thinly sliced materials, such as bread; or an air conditioner cools a space by removing heat from it. (The next chapter discusses process description, of which mechanical processes are a major type.) If you have included this information in your introduction, you need not write a separate ending.

SUGGESTIONS FOR APPLYING YOUR KNOWLEDGE

1. Explain the visual analogy behind the name of each of the following:

alluvial fan	hammerhead
bandsaw	shark
claw hammer	hip roof
caterpillar gate	J-stroke
deadman	kangaroo rat
death's head moth	kettledrum
dining ell	kidney bean
disk brake	leaf spring
dovetail joint	monkey wrench
fiddlehead fern	needle-nose pliers
fiddler crab	organ pipe cactus
floppy disk	pineapple
forklift	rocker arm
foxhole	sea cucumber
gateleg table	T-hinge
hair spring	U-bolt
	wing nut

2. Explain the visual analogy behind the names of five items from your field of study.

3. Choose some mechanism you are familiar with, partition it into not fewer than two and not more than six major parts, and explain what order of parts you would use to arrange your description.

4. Write a description of some mechanism you are familiar with, and be prepared to explain to other students in the class the intended audience, the purpose and the arrangement of the description, and the methods to help readers visualize the object and its parts.

5. Form a panel with two others in your class to give an oral description of a mechanism all three of you are familiar with. Arrange to have a drawing or drawings or the mechanism itself in class. Decide who will make the initial introduction of the mechanism, who will describe its major functional parts, and who will describe the way it operates. Time: 10–15 minutes.

6. Analyze the description of the Osterizer and the adjustable beam compass for the use of *so-whats*. Divide a sheet of paper into two columns and list the features and their *so-whats*. If you find instances in which additional *so-whats* would be helpful, include them, too.

7. Analyze and discuss in class the description below of the Berlese funnel, a common collection device used by ento-mologists to collect and test samples for insect habitation.[2]

8. Write and illustrate a description of a mechanism you are familiar with for readers who need or want to know its function, its parts, and its operation or use.

The <u>Berlese</u> <u>Funnel</u>

You have several methods for sampling soil, leaves, or trash for insect habitation. You can simply pick out insects from a sample by hand, use a sieve to separate insects from a sample, or ''bake'' insects from a sample by using the Berlese funnel. The first two methods are not always satisfactory, because some insects will probably be overlooked. When an absolute count of the insects is required, use the Berlese funnel, named after the Italian entomologist who invented it in 1912. The Berlese funnel uses heat from an incandescent bulb to dry the sample and force the insects to burrow away from the heat source and ultimately drop through a funnel into a collection jar. Although Berlese funnels vary in size, depending on how large a sample needs testing, they all have the same parts and appearance and work the same way. As shown in Figure 1, the three main parts of a workbench-sized Berlese funnel capable of holding up to a half gallon sample are (1) the cover, (2) the container, and (3) the stand. Its overall height is 15 inches.

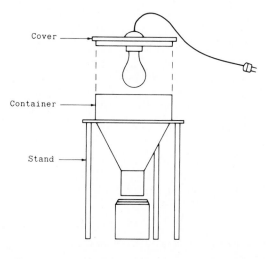

Figure 1. The main parts of the Berlese funnel
and the collection jar

The Cover

The metal cover (Figure 2) resembles a miniature trashcan lid. It covers the container and serves as a mount for the 100-watt bulb. Air vents in the cover allow excess heat to escape and enable you to observe the sample without removing the cover. A 1/2-inch flange holds the cover in place.

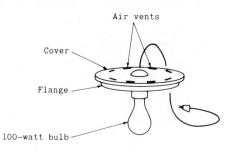

Figure 2. The cover

The Container

The container (Figure 3), which fits into the steel retaining ring of the stand, is divided into an upper and a lower section. The upper section is the 4-1/2-inch deep plastic reservoir that holds the sample, and the lower section is the plastic funnel through which the insects drop into the collection jar. A galvanized screen with a 1/4-inch mesh, upon which the sample is placed, separates the two sections. The container has an overall height of eleven inches and a diameter of 8-1/2 inches before narrowing to a diameter of 1 inch at the bottom of the funnel.

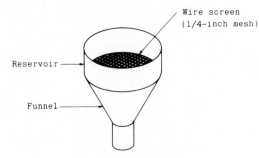

Figure 3. The container

The Stand

The stand (Figure 4) supports the container and allows room for the collection jar to be placed beneath the funnel. It is composed of a 1/2-inch

steel retaining ring with a 9-inch diameter into which the sample container is
placed and of three legs made of 1/2-inch steel cylinders 11 inches long. The
legs are attached to the retaining ring by screws, allowing the stand to be
disassembled for storage or transportation.

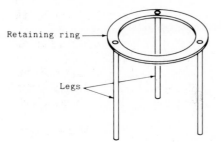

Retaining ring

Legs

Figure 4. The stand

Using the Berlese Funnel

The Berlese funnel works like an oven. The heat from the 100-watt bulb
''bakes'' the sample, forcing the insects to seek a moister area. As the top of
the sample dries, the insects burrow down toward the remaining moist sample. When
the entire sample is dry, the insects have passed through the wire screen and
dropped through the funnel into the collection jar. Depending on the size and
dampness of the sample, it takes approximately 24 to 36 hours for the sample to
dry thoroughly.

C H A P T E R

13

**PROCESS
DESCRIPTION**

A process is a specific series of actions that brings about a specific result. Process is essentially chronological or sequential—this happens, then this, then that. Because business and industry are concerned with processes, much of the writing and speaking you may do will be explaining processes. You may need to explain to a co-worker, a supervisor, or a customer the way something happened, the merits of a particular process, or the way a mechanism works. Or you may need to explain a natural process such as photosynthesis or how parasites change hosts or how peat bogs are formed. Almost any action can be regarded as a process.

Obviously, such explanations are useful only if they're clear. Thus, you'll have to plan your explanation carefully. In this chapter, we show you, through several examples and explanation, how to determine the purpose of your description and how to organize and illustrate your description.

DETERMINING THE PURPOSE OF THE DESCRIPTION

You'll have to decide first on the purpose of your explanation. You must distinguish between explaining a process and giving instructions for performing it. If you expect your readers to perform the process, you should write a set of instructions. (We take up writing instructions in the next chapter.) If you don't expect your readers to perform the process but only to understand it, you should write an explanation of it. After reading your explanation, your readers should know the process well enough to understand what happened during a chain of events, to evaluate the reliability or efficiency of a process, or to understand the operational sequence of a mechanism.

Explaining How Something Is Done Or Made

Much process description tells how something is done or made: how ships are mothballed, how coal is mined, how money is coined or printed, and how riots are controlled. Organizations use process description to tell the story of their product. Professional persons are often asked by their supervisors to explain how something was accomplished. For example, the report in Figure 13–1 was written by a supervisory mining engineer of a coal company to explain the work and costs in controlling a large fire in an abandoned mine. The intended readers are the engineer's superiors in the company: the director of mining safety, other senior administrators, and the board of directors. Read it over before you read the discussion that follows.

The report is organized into three major sections: Background (introduction), The Fire Control Plan (body), and Cost Summary (ending). The sections are set off by heads. The longest section of the report—The Fire Control Plan—is further divided into two subsections, each explaining a stage of the plan. The subsections are identified by subheads. The segments of the subsections are further marked off by subordinate heads.

Most of the well-known journalistic topics—*who, what, when, where, why*—are used throughout the report. However, the topic *who* is not emphasized. Most of the action taken by the company's fire control team is written in the passive voice, probably because the writer assumed that the readers already knew who did what or that they were primarily interested in what action was taken rather than in who performed the action. The report focuses on what was done and what it cost. The active voice is used, however, to explain additional information, for example, "Containment of the fire protected that important area." "The burning garbage probably ignited the coal . . . ." "Table I provides . . . ." "A gasoline-driven pump powered . . . ." "The second step under Stage 2 involved . . . ."

A review of the background section reveals the writer's use of the remaining journalistic topics:

- **What**—A fire in Bevo #3 mine.
- **When**—Discovered on July 11, 1980; initial action taken between October 1 and November 1, 1980.
- **Where**—The fire is close to a residential area and threatens an industrial park; the fire is in the Newcome bed and perhaps has invaded the Courtney bed just below it. Figure 1, which is not included in this sample, is a map showing the location of the mine, the fire, and the sur-

<u>CONTROLLING</u> <u>THE</u> <u>FIRE</u> <u>IN</u> <u>BEVO</u> <u>#3</u> <u>MINE</u>

<u>Background</u>

On July 11, 1980, a mine fire was discovered in the central portion of Bevo #3 Mine. Although situated about two miles east of the Sherman Township residential area, the site was only 300 yards north of the Armistead Industrial Park (Figure 1). Containment of the fire protected that important area.

The fire is believed to have started in a partly backfilled strip pit that had been used since 1965 as an ash and garbage disposal site. The burning garbage probably ignited the coal in some of the exposed portions of the pillar remnants in the highwall of the strip pit. The outcrops of both the Newcome and Courtney beds that had been strip-mined at this site are part of the abandoned Bevo #3 Mine.

From October 1 to November 1, 1980, some of the burning material in the strip pit was excavated and 10 exploratory boreholes were drilled. From the elevated temperatures in the pit and the boreholes it was concluded that the fire had spread to the Newcome bed and possibly to the underlying Courtney bed (Figure 2).

<u>The</u> <u>Fire</u> <u>Control</u> <u>Plan</u>

Because there was evidence that the fire would spread beyond the limits determined by our exploratory drillings, a two-stage plan to extinguish the fire was developed, as follows:

1. Drilling a sufficient number of boreholes from the surface to the mine voids to determine the extent of the fire in the Newcome bed and its possible existence in the lower Courtney bed; excavating and extinguishing hot material encountered above the floor of the Newcome bed; and restoring the surface, if it proved unnecessary to excavate to the Courtney bed.

2. If fire were present in the Courtney bed, excavating and extinguishing hot material to the floor of the Courtney bed and restoring the surface.

Ultimately, the second stage of the plan had to be performed.

<u>Exploratory</u> <u>Drilling</u> <u>and</u> <u>Trench</u>

<u>Excavation</u> <u>to</u> <u>the</u> <u>Courtney</u> <u>Bed</u>

<u>Drilling</u> <u>boreholes</u>. Drilling boreholes to determine the perimeter of the fire and the location of the proposed isolation trench was started on November 12, 1980. Temperatures obtained from boreholes drilled to the voids in the Newcome bed ranged up to 1000° Fahrenheit. Temperatures from boreholes to the Courtney bed were not high enough to indicate that the fire had spread to those mine workings at that time.

<u>Excavating</u> <u>the</u> <u>isolation</u> <u>trench</u>. The location and the shape of the isolation trench to the floor of the Newcome bed were planned to conform with the limits of the heat zone indicated by the temperatures obtained from the boreholes.

During excavation, a hot area was encountered, and this required widening the original trench at that location (Figure 3). Upon completion, the isolated "hot island" was bounded by a trench on two

1

FIGURE 13-1 Sample process report

sides, and on its third side by a natural deep gully south of the
Courtney bed outcrop in which Nifonger Creek flows.

Additional holes were drilled in the isolation trench from the
floor of the Newcome bed to the underlying Courtney bed. Elevated
temperatures up to 500 degrees Fahrenheit obtained from some of these
holes established that a fire was also burning in the Courtney bed in an
area northwest of the isolation trench in the Newcome bed.

At this time, it was decided to widen the original Newcome trench
at one point to overlie a cold area in the Courtney bed and then deepen
the entire trench to encircle the fire in the Courtney bed. The
resulting hot area was therefore considerably greater than originally
planned (Figure 4).

Work on the first stage was completed December 20, 1980. After this
work was completed, the active fire area in the Newcome and Courtney
beds had been successfully isolated.

Table I provides detailed data on the extent and cost of work
conducted during this stage. Appendix A contains copies of invoices,
contracts, and work orders related to work performed during this stage.

Table I. Cost of Exploratory Drilling
and Trench Excavation, Stage 1,
Bevo #3 Mine Fire, October 1–
December 20, 1980

Item	Quantity	Cost per unit	Total cost
6-inch drilling	893.0 linear ft.	$2.00	$ 1,786.00
3-inch drilling	718.5 " "	1.85	1,322.25
6-inch casing	450.0 " "	2.50	1,125.00
Excavation	70,288.0 cubic yds.	.55	38,658.40
Excavation	18,197.0 " "	1.25	22,723.75
Recasting spoil	18,197.0 " "	.25	4,549.25
Bulldozer rental	12.0 hours	30.00	360.00
Total			$70,524.65

Removing Remaining Hot Material and

Subsequent Backfilling of Project Area

The work planned under the second stage involved the following
three steps: (1) sealing off the hot area, (2) excavating all the
material that had been isolated, quenching the hot or burning material,
and (3) backfilling and regrading the surface in the project area to its
approximate original configuration.

Sealing off the hot area. Work was started January 4, 1981, by
placing a seal of wet sand on the exposed Newcome and Courtney beds
along the cold side of the entire isolation trench (Figure 5). This seal
was intended to prevent any hot material thrown during blasting in the

2

FIGURE 13–1 Sample process report *(cont.)*

fire zone from igniting carbonaceous material in these beds. The seal at the Courtney bed level also acted as a dam to impound water used in quenching and cooling the fire area. During the course of the work, a pool of water approximately 6 feet deep on the floor of the Courtney bed was created. During January and February 1981 the pool of water froze, indicating that no fire existed in an unmined thin leader bed a few feet below the Courtney bed. Water for quenching extremely hot or burning material was obtained from nearby Nifonger Creek, across which a temporary impounding dam was built. A gasoline-driven pump powered the two 6-inch water cannons which sprayed constant streams of water on the excavation and disposal area.

Excavating material in the isolated hot zone. The second step under this stage involved excavating all material in the isolated hot zone that covered the floor of the Courtney bed. The operation consisted of blasting and quenching a total of 45,000 cubic yards of material.

Recasting spoil and restoring the surface. The third step consisted of recasting spoil, which had been excavated from the trench during the first stage, back into the excavated area. Finally, the surface was graded to its former contours (Figure 6).

A final inspection of the completed work was made May 1, 1981. Table II provides detailed data on the amount and cost of work during the second stage. Appendix B contains copies of invoices, contracts, and work orders related to work performed during the second stage.

TABLE II. Cost of Excavating and Backfilling,
Stage 2, Bevo #3 Mine Fire,
January 4–May 1, 1981

Item	Quantity	Cost per unit	Total cost
Excavation	45,000.0 cubic yards	$1.00	$45,000.00
6-inch drilling	113.0 linear ft.	2.00	226.00
6-inch casing	50.0 linear ft.	2.50	125.00
Recasting and grading	150,000.0 cubic yards	lump-sum payment	75,000.00
Total			$120,351.00

Cost Summary

The total of the fire control project is summarized as follows:

Stage 1	$ 70,524.65
Stage 2	120,351.00
	$190,875.65

During excavating operations, marketable coal from the relatively few pillars that remained in the various beds was recovered. The money received for the coal ($65,000) was used to help defray the total cost of controlling the fire. Appendix C contains copies of sales contracts for the recovered coal.

3

FIGURE 13–1 Sample process report *(cont.)*

rounding area. Figure 2, which is also not included, is a cross-sectional view of the mine showing the Newcome and Courtney beds.

- **Why**—Proximity of the fire to the residential area and the industrial park makes it important to contain the fire.

The *why* topic is a version of the *so-what* principle that we discussed in Chapters 2 and 12. This report contains many *so-whats* that explain the purpose or importance of the actions or the significance of the facts. For instance, the writer explains the purposes of containing the fire, drilling the boreholes, widening the original Newcome trench and deepening it to the Courtney bed, and constructing the wet-sand seal. In addition, the writer explains the significance of facts given: the elevated temperatures, the water freezing in the Newcome bed, and the recovery of coal during the operations. Where the writer does not provide *so-whats,* the action or the facts are self-defining or obvious: extinguishing the hot material, restoring the surface, drilling boreholes from the Newcome bed into the Courtney bed, the 1,000°F temperature in the Newcome bed, and the 500°F temperature in the Courtney bed.

Process description also explains how research or tests were conducted. Research reports often contain a section describing the work done so that readers can evaluate, even reproduce, the methods. Thus, the explanation should be complete and clear enough that readers could use it as a guide to repeat the original investigation or experiment. Such a section is shown in the following excerpt from an article that describes the results of an experimental process to improve the baking characteristics of frozen par-fried French fries.

PREPARING THE PRODUCT

To evaluate the baking characteristics of the surface-treated fries, the product was prepared as follows:

- PREPARATION Russet Burbank potatoes (commercial processing quality, specific gravity 1.086–1.096) held at 45°F were cut into ⅜-in.-square and ¼-in.-square × 3½-to-4-in.-long strips with a hand-operated French fry cutter. Shorter strips ⅜-in.-square × 1½-to-2-in.-long were also cut for use in precooked frozen dinners. The cut strips were washed and held briefly in tap water until used.

- SURFACE FREEZING The potato strips were placed on a dripping rack and then immersed and agitated in R-12 held in a Dewar flask (Nonaka et al., 1972). The immersion time in R-12 ($-21.6°F$) was standardized at 7 sec.

- LEACHING The ⅜-in.-square surface-frozen strips were leached in 125°F water for 15 min. and the ¼-in.-square strips for 10 min. The strips were immersed in heated water contained in a steam-jacketed kettle and agitated with a rotating propeller-type stirrer. The strips were not rotated.

- PAR-FRYING   A Wells fryer using 5 qts. vegetable oil heated at 365°F was used for par-frying. The duration of par-frying was varied depending upon whether the French fries were to be baked on a cookie sheet or in a frozen dinner such as a TV dinner. Duration was also varied to change the degree of final crispness.

  For the product to be baked alone, a par-fry time of 1 min. at 365°F was used to more or less duplicate the conventional practice of the industry. However, durations of 1 to 2½ min. will increase the crispness of a ⅜-in.-square fry. For a ¼-in.-square fry, a most desirable product was obtained with a 1 min. 15 sec. par-fry.

  For the product to be baked with a precooked frozen dinner, the par-frying time was lengthened to 2, 3, and 4 min. to produce varying degrees of crispness. Frozen dinners are cooked for a specified length of time under conditions of steam heating, and the French fry must withstand this environment and still maintain the quality of a desirable fry.

- FINAL FREEZING   The par-fried French fry was frozen in a tunnel blast freezer for 15 min. at −34°F and held at −10°F until used.

- BAKING   The surface-treated fries were baked in the usual manner—placing the fries in a single layer on a cookie sheet and baking them in an oven. The ⅜-in.-square par-fries were baked 7 min. at 450°F, then turned and baked an additional 8 min. The ¼-in.-square par-fries were baked 4½ min. at 450°F, then turned and baked an additional 4½ min.[1]

Each of the six steps in preparing the potatoes for evaluation is set off by a heading. The writers discuss the materials, equipment, and methods in enough detail so readers know exactly what was done. Notice the writers' use of passive verbs:

"Russet Burbank potatoes . . . were cut. . . ."

"The cut strips were washed and held briefly. . . ."

"The potato strips were placed. . . ."

The passive voice is used often in research reports to focus attention on the action, not the researcher. Readers assume that the researcher performed the action.

Explaining How Something Works

Process description also explains how mechanisms work: how a laser measures inaccessible, and sometimes invisible, points; how an image is telecast; how a CB radio communicates; how an inclinometer works. When you explain mechanical processes, you emphasize the interaction of parts and the underlying principles of those interactions that take place during a cycle of the mechanism's operation. Figure 13–2 is the description of how the parts of a tire pressure gauge work together. Notice how the

Tire Pressure Gauge

Correct tire pressure for varying vehicle loads in all seasons can improve tire performance and decrease wear. To assure this, a pencil-size gauge accurately measures tire pressures in pounds per square inch. And the gauge is designed to fit all standard tire valves. Its operation principle is simple: A hollow tube in the gauge head depresses the spring-loaded valve pin in the tire. This taps pressurized air from the tire into the gauge. Within the gauge, a plunger is driven by the inrushing air much the way a piston is driven during the power stroke in an internal combustion engine. This thrusts a bar indicator out into view and provides a reading. The "magic" factor about the tire gauge is that the indicator stays in the "out" position until it is manually pushed back inside the gauge.

When the gauge is at rest, a coil spring holds the plunger next to the head and serves to sleeve the indicator bar. Inside the gauge head is a central hollow pin surrounded by a gasket that ensures a tight seat when the pin depresses the tire valve.

As the tire's pressurized air rushes into the gauge's chamber, the tire and the gauge become a sealed unit. Inrushing air forces the gasketed plunger along the gauge's cylindrical lining. This compresses the spring and thrusts the indicator bar into view. The increasing spring resistance finally stops the plunger when the pressures within the tire and gauge are equal.

As the gauge is removed from the tire valve, the pressurized air within it escapes, and the spring returns the plunger to the gauge head. But the indicator bar, held by the friction of the base cap, remains extended until it is read and then manually pushed back inside the gauge, ready to take the next reading.

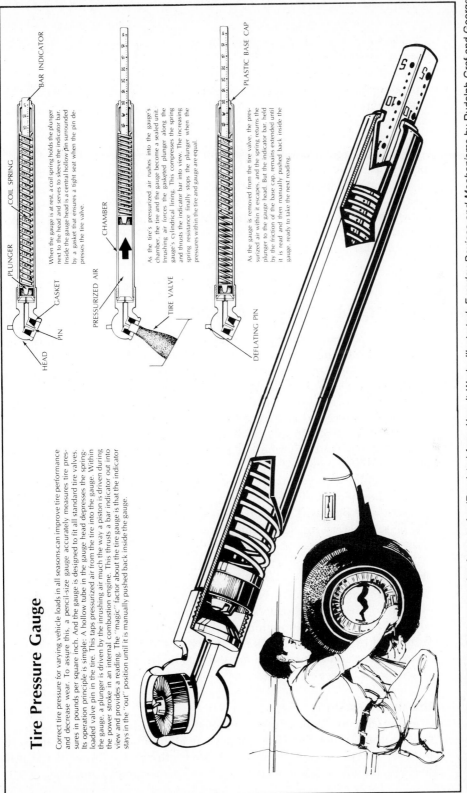

Labels: BAR INDICATOR, COIL SPRING, PLUNGER, GASKET, PIN, HEAD, CHAMBER, PRESSURIZED AIR, TIRE VALVE, PLASTIC BASE CAP, DEFLATING PIN

FIGURE 13–2 Description of how a mechanism works (Reprinted from *How It Works Illustrated: Everday Devices and Mechanisms* by Rudolph Graf and George J. Whalen; published by Popular Science Books)

explanation concentrates on the operation, not on the physical hardware. Pictorials, not words, carry visual features.

The description of how the pressure gauge works consists of an introductory paragraph and three paragraphs of descriptive details. The introduction explains the importance of the pressure gauge, its appearance, and its overall operation. Each of the other paragraphs explains the movement of the gauge's parts as it operates.

The large cutaway drawing, placed diagonally across the illustration, helps familiarize readers with both the external and internal features of the gauge. The drawing of the person using the gauge is an effective use of "window dressing" to attract readers' attention. The cross-sectional drawings, showing what happens in each step of the gauge's operation, illustrate the changing positions of the expanding chamber of air, the plunger, the spring, and the bar indicator.

ARRANGING THE DETAILS OF THE DESCRIPTION

As you have seen, process description is the method of the storyteller. You have to do more than merely explain a process. One of the biggest problems readers have in following the explanation of a complex process is being thrust into the first stage of the process without orientation. So it is not always best to explain the initial stage without first giving readers some information to help them get their bearings. If you move too quickly, you're likely to lose readers.

To help you describe complex processes that require more than just a "then-this-happens" story, let's study the arrangement and the kinds of information that will aid readers in following your explanation.

The following three-part arrangement (Figure 13–3), which is very similar to the one used in mechanism description (see page 267), will usually be satisfactory for describing a process.

The Title

Your title doesn't have to be terribly snappy, but it should be specific enough to identify the process. If submerged welding techniques is the subject of your explanation, include those words in the title. "Liquid Fuels from Coal by the SRC-11 Process" and "Using Helium to Trace Gases in Oilfields" are good descriptive titles of process reports.

The Introduction

The introduction, which may run one paragraph or several, prepares readers for the details of the process. It identifies the process, states its purpose and significance, and traces briefly the main course of the process by naming its main stages. A well-written introduction may be the

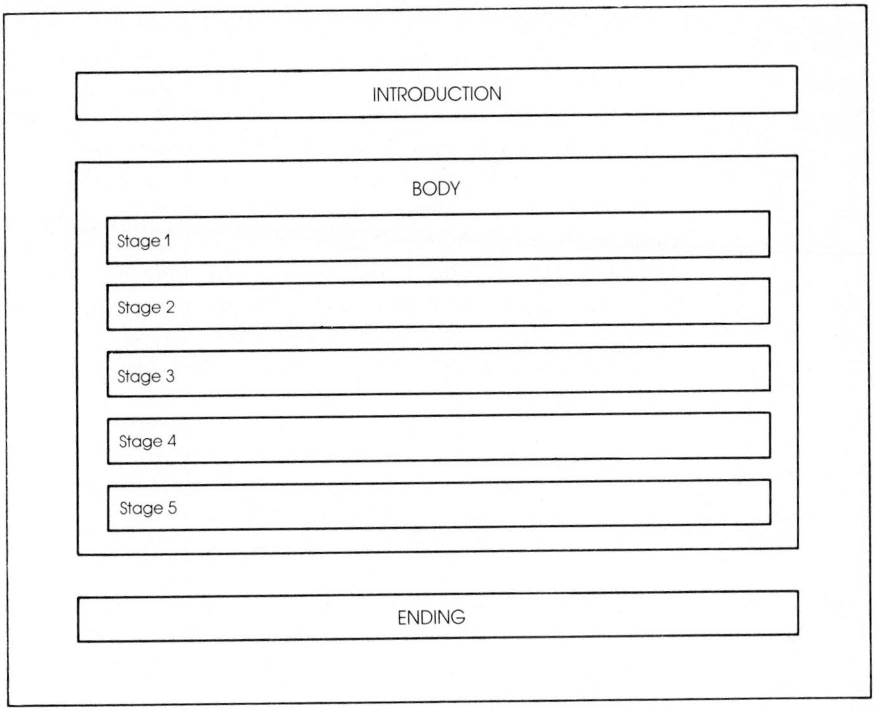

```
┌─────────────────────────────────────────────────────────────┐
│  ┌───────────────────────────────────────────────────────┐  │
│  │                    INTRODUCTION                        │  │
│  └───────────────────────────────────────────────────────┘  │
│  ┌───────────────────────────────────────────────────────┐  │
│  │                       BODY                             │  │
│  │   ┌─────────────────────────────────────────────────┐ │  │
│  │   │ Stage 1                                         │ │  │
│  │   └─────────────────────────────────────────────────┘ │  │
│  │   ┌─────────────────────────────────────────────────┐ │  │
│  │   │ Stage 2                                         │ │  │
│  │   └─────────────────────────────────────────────────┘ │  │
│  │   ┌─────────────────────────────────────────────────┐ │  │
│  │   │ Stage 3                                         │ │  │
│  │   └─────────────────────────────────────────────────┘ │  │
│  │   ┌─────────────────────────────────────────────────┐ │  │
│  │   │ Stage 4                                         │ │  │
│  │   └─────────────────────────────────────────────────┘ │  │
│  │   ┌─────────────────────────────────────────────────┐ │  │
│  │   │ Stage 5                                         │ │  │
│  │   └─────────────────────────────────────────────────┘ │  │
│  └───────────────────────────────────────────────────────┘  │
│  ┌───────────────────────────────────────────────────────┐  │
│  │                      ENDING                            │  │
│  └───────────────────────────────────────────────────────┘  │
└─────────────────────────────────────────────────────────────┘
```

FIGURE 13–3 **Organizational pattern of a process description**

key to your readers' understanding of the process, so spend some time working on it.

IDENTIFYING THE PROCESS Often just naming the process is adequate (taping an ankle, how sediments build up on the ocean floor, recruiting personnel). Sometimes, though, you'll have to use a sentence or more explaining the nature of the process:

> Like a refrigerator, an air conditioner cools a space by removing heat from the air and pumping it elsewhere.

> Dew is the result of the condensation of moisture from the air. As air cools, it is able to hold smaller and smaller amounts of water vapor. At a certain low temperature—the dew point—the air is saturated with water vapor, and dew begins to form as water droplets on cool surfaces, such as grass.

Remember to remind or inform your readers of the general principle behind what's familiar to you but little understood by them.

GOING THROUGH THE MAIN STAGES Readers will always find it easier to follow the explanation of a process when they have been given an overview of the process first. The process is divided into its main stages, which are listed in the order they occur. The process may involve many separate actions, so to keep your readers from getting lost in the forest of little steps and to protect them against a monotonous "and-then" sequence, group closely related steps as a single main stage. For instance, preparing burley tobacco for market involves dozens of activities, but the main stages of the process are five: (1) removing the tobacco from the barn, (2) stripping and sorting the leaves, (3) pressing and bulking the stripped leaves, (4) loading the stripped leaves, and (5) unloading the stripped leaves at the warehouse. Each main stage consists of several substeps. The second stage—stripping and sorting the leaves—consists of sorting the plants, grouping the leaves, and tying the leaves into "hands."

You may present the overview two ways—by list or flow chart.

Let's first look at a few examples of sentences that list the major steps of a process:

> Executive recruitment consists of six steps: (1) making the position opening known to potential applicants, (2) screening the applicants, (3) interviewing qualified applicants, (4) selecting the best qualified applicant, (5) offering employment, and (6) responding to the candidate's decision.

> A fuse "blows" when the electrical current through the fuse becomes too great, creating heat that melts away the narrow center strip of the fuse, thereby interrupting the operation of the electrical circuit.

> Making paper consists of four major stages:
>
> 1. preparing the pulp;
> 2. removing impurities from the pulp;
> 3. turning the pulp into paper strips;
> 4. wrapping the paper around a roller or cutting the paper into separate sheets.

> Making a jigsaw puzzle consists of three main steps—mounting the picture on a sturdy material, cutting or sawing the mounted picture, and finishing the pieces.

> Barbecuing chicken consists of four steps: preparing the fire, preparing the chicken, preparing the sauce, and broiling the chicken.

> The formation of salt deposits occurs in three stages: (1) deposit of alkaline earth metals in bodies of water, (2) concentration of salt in waters with limited inflow, and (3) sedimentation of carbonates into layers of salt.

> Mitosis, the process by which the nucleus of a cell divides into two parts, consists of four separate stages, known as the prophase, metaphase, anaphase, and telephase.

> The shield budding method of grafting involves five steps:
>
> 1. A bud is cut from a twig.
> 2. A T-shaped cut is made in the bark of the stock.

3. The bark is raised to admit the bud.
4. The bud is placed in the cut.
5. The stock and bud are wrapped.

The relationship of the RITE 1000's three main components is as follows:

1. Copy is typed into the screen from the keyboard.
2. The copy is then transferred from the screen to the disk for storage.
3. The disk is then removed from the RITE 1000 and taken to a RITE 9200, where the copy is justified and typeset.

As you can easily see from some of these examples, listing the main stages in a column makes them easier to see, to remember, to refer to—primarily because of the attention drawn to them by the surrounding white space. Notice also that the sample processes range from three to six main stages. That's about the right number. There's really no simple rule about how many stages to divide the process into, but too many stages (or too many steps within a stage) can give readers trouble. There is some evidence that *seven or fewer* stages is pretty good. For example, George Miller, in his article "The Magical Number Seven, Plus or Minus Two," suggests that there is a limit to the bits of information that the human mind can retain at any one time, and that the human mind apparently deals efficiently with sets of seven or fewer bits.[2] We don't want to be too rigid in recommending that you use the "seven plus or minus two" rule in every instance, but when you find that you have more than nine stages in a process or more than nine steps in a stage, consider repartitioning to reduce the number.

To make a list:

Make the items in the list grammatically parallel; that is, use groups of words of the same grammatical type. (See also Parallelism, pages 423–425.) Following is an ungrammatical list of the steps in forming laminated wood bowls and plates:

1. making a plastic form
2. the veneering is then cut to fit the form
3. build up the laminations
4. to cure the laminations
5. finishing the laminations

A grammatically parallel list would read like this:

1. making a plastic form
2. cutting the veneer to fit the form
3. building up the laminations
4. curing the laminations
5. finishing the laminations

Single-space each item in the list. If any item is more than a line long, double-space after each item in the list.

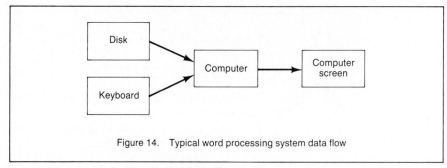

Figure 14.   Typical word processing system data flow

Figure 13–4   Example of a simple block diagram

In addition to listing the main stages of the process, you can also use a flow chart to give in relatively few words an overview of the general activity. The block diagram (Figure 13–4), the simplest of flow charts, shows the main stages of a process by means of labeled blocks connected by arrows. The arrows indicate the direction of the activity flow. Almost any simple geometric shape can be used as long as the shape is consistent. For instance, the circles in Figure 13–5 are the "blocks" that represent the levels of the food chain.

Simple block diagrams like these are easy to understand and easy to remember. But using different geometric shapes to indicate the same activity creates inconsistencies that can confuse the reader. Of course, specialized shapes are used in certain kinds of flow charts to indicate specific kinds of actions, such as the standard computer template symbols for computer documentation in Figure 13–6. Even here, though, the same symbol must be used from one diagram to another. If *start* and *end* of a

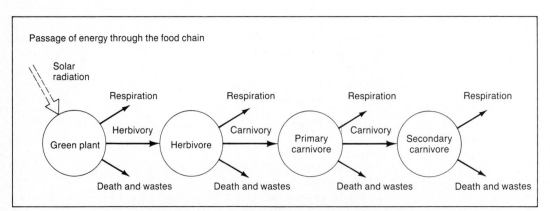

Figure 13–5   Example of a simple block diagram using circles (Source: W. B. Clapham, Jr., "The Animal Kingdom and the Way We Look at It," *1982 Yearbook of Agriculture* [Washington, D.C.: U.S. Department of Agriculture, 1982], 57)

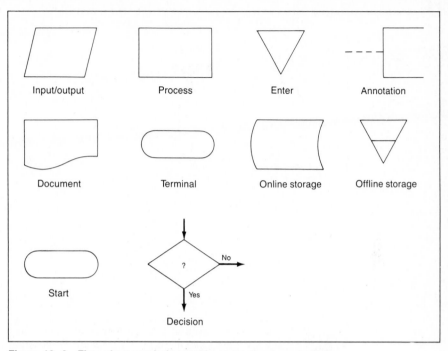

Figure 13–6   Flow chart symbols used in computer documentation

procedure are represented by ovals in one diagram, they should not be circles in the next.

Most flow charts are designed to be read from left to right, and if more space is needed, from first row to second row to third. A flow chart that illustrates a cyclical process might be represented better as a circle, designed to be read clockwise. The circular flow chart in Figure 13–7 compares the gradual and complete metamorphic life cycles of insects.

Some flow charts use pictorials or schematic symbols to indicate activity at specific points in the process. Pictorial flow charts, such as those illustrated in Figure 13–7 and Figure 13–8, are interesting ways to provide concrete images as well as a broad overview of a process. But flow charts consisting of schematic symbols and formulas should be used only if your readers can understand them. For example, $2H_2 + O_2 \rightarrow 2H_2O$ may be an efficient way of summarizing a chemical process. But if your readers can't read the formula, you'll have to use language that they understand, such as, "When two molecules of hydrogen react with one molecule of oxygen, two molecules of water are formed."

We've emphasized throughout this book that your writing must be easy to understand. The same holds true for flow charts. There's just no reason why a flow chart should not be drawn clearly.

You should know how to make a block diagram—the simplest kind

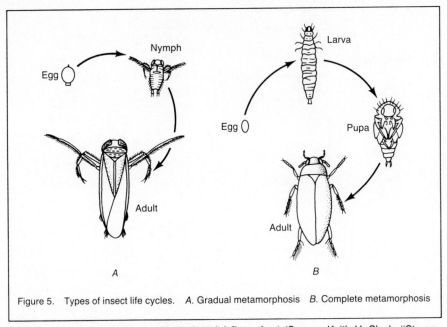

Figure 5. Types of insect life cycles. *A*. Gradual metamorphosis *B*. Complete metamorphosis

Figure 13–7 Example of a cyclical pictorial flow chart (Source: Keith V. Slack, "Stream Biology," in *Biota and Biological Principles of the Aquatic Environment,* edited by Phillip E. Greeson [Alexandria, Va.: U.S. Geological Survey, 1982], A13)

of flow chart—because it is relatively easy to make and to read. Here's the way to make it:

1. Draw geometric figures to represent stages in the process. Make each one large enough to hold the name of the stage it represents.
2. Label each geometric figure with the name of the stage it represents.
3. Connect the geometric figures by using straight lines with arrows that show the direction of activity flow.
4. If desired, rule a boundary around the flow chart.

The diagram in Figure 13–9 is a block flow chart that illustrates the preparation of dried fruit. The process consists of five main stages for most fruits (sorting, washing, dicing and slicing, drying, and packaging). However, notice that for some fruits, such as prunes, two additional stages (blanching and pitting) are necessary between washing and dicing and slicing.

The Body

The body of the process description describes each main stage in the order given by the list of stages or the flow chart in the introduction. The stage-by-stage description provides much the same information for each

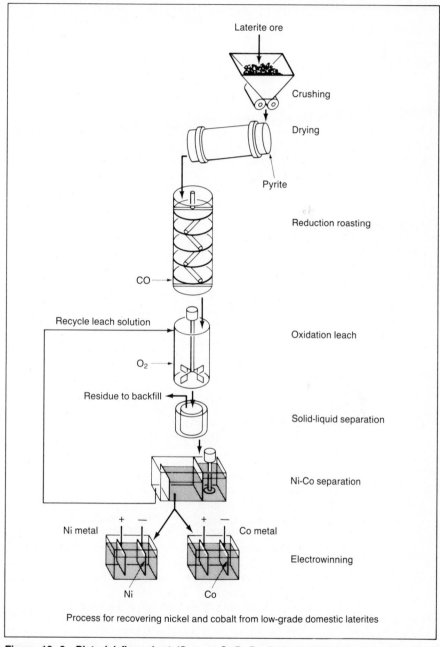

Figure 13–8 Pictorial flow chart (Source: C. B. Daellenback, "Nickel-Laterite Pilot Plant Testing," *Bureau of Mines Research, 1981* [Washington, D.C.: U.S. Department of the Interior, 1981], p. 14)

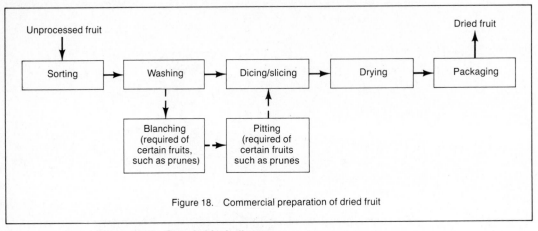

Figure 18.   Commercial preparation of dried fruit

Figure 13–9   Sample block diagram

stage that the introduction did for the process as a whole. Again, as we suggested when we discussed mechanism description, simply think of a single stage of the process as a miniature process.

If the stages of the process are complex or lengthy, introduce them with headings. Give each stage proper emphasis by devoting at least a paragraph or section to it. Early in each paragraph or section explain what the stage is and what happens. If the stage is complex and the detail is necessary, provide an overview of its substages just as you did for the process as a whole. Topic sentences should explain what the result of each stage is or what takes place in that stage. The topic sentences of a series of paragraphs describing the preparation of text for letterpress printing might read like this:

> First, the manuscript goes to the Linotype operator, who types the text into individual, justified lines. . . .
>
> Second, each assembled, justified line goes to the casting section of the Linotype machine, where it is cast into metal as a single unit. . . .
>
> Third, the lines so cast are stacked and then "locked up" in a metal frame called a *chase on a stone,* a flat granite or steel table, by the compositor. . . .
>
> Fourth, the press operator mounts the chase on the bed of the press, where inked rubber rollers run over the raised type and leave a coat of wet ink wherever the type stands high. . . .

And so on to the end of the process. Each of these sentences starts a paragraph that may be expanded to the length and degree of detail the writer feels the reader should have.

As you describe each stage of the process, you can continue to use flow charts to partition each stage visually into substages or steps. One way to do this is to provide a multilevel diagram that shows the main stages and their substages. Such a flow chart is illustrated in Figure 13–10, which explains the marketing chain for beef cattle. The first level

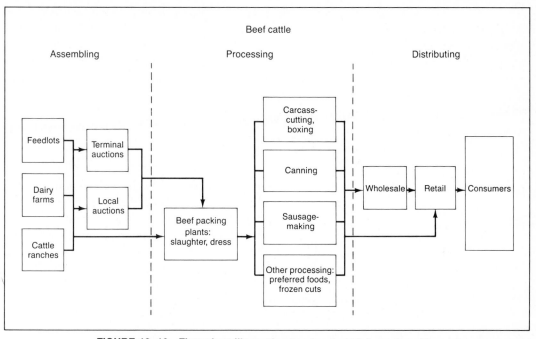

FIGURE 13–10   Flow chart illustrating two levels of information: The major stages and their constituent steps (Source: Modified from Joseph N. Uhl, "Who Does What in the Marketing Field," *1982 Yearbook of Agriculture* [Washington D.C.: U.S. Department of Agriculture, 1982], 145)

of the flow chart identifies the three main stages—assembling, processing, and distributing. The second level of the flow chart identifies the sub-stages of each main stage. The vertical broken lines arrange the substages under the appropriate main stage.

Block flow charts that describe processes as complicated as the marketing chain for beef cattle usually leave much to be desired because they use a poor format or present too much information for the limited memory of most readers. However, the visual segments of the flow chart in Figure 13–10 make the process easy to follow. Readers don't have to grasp more than five activities at a time: at first, the three main stages, then the substages of each stage (five at the most in the assembling and the processing stages). Thus readers are able to see the entire process and keep the "big picture" in mind while reading about the stages and substages.

Another way to illustrate multiple levels of a process is to use a series of flow charts—one depicting the main stages and subsequent ones detailing the substages of each main stage. The following simple one-level flow chart identifies the three main stages of a community relations plan developed as part of an organization's management program. The three blocks provide an overview of the entire process. As each of the three main stages is described in more detail in the body of the process description, a flow chart shows that stage in greater detail, as shown in Figures 13–11, 13–12, and 13–13. The interrelated flow charts work together to emphasize visually the key information in each stage and how it is related to the rest of the process.

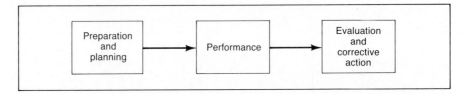

The decision of whether to describe the process in a series of interrelated flow charts or to use one multilevel flow chart, such as the one illustrated in Figure 13–10, depends on your analysis of your readers. Readers who are familiar with the process or similar ones should have little difficulty following multilevel flow charts. Readers who are not so familiar with the process will probably find the series of interrelated flow charts easier to read. For some readers you might want to provide both a full-page, multilevel flow chart that shows all levels of the process (see Figure 13–14) and a series of diagrams that detail the steps of each main stage.

The important thing is to use flow charts. They take up space, but if they are easy to read they minimize reading time and help readers keep track of how each activity fits into the overall process.

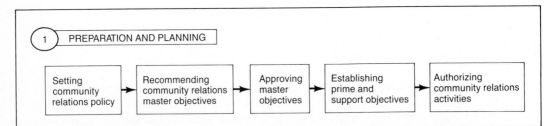

FIGURE 13–11   Flow chart showing the first stage and its substages of a community relations plan

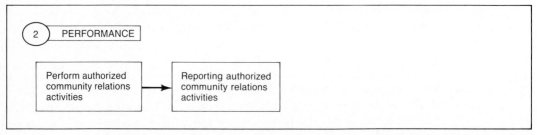

FIGURE 13–12   Flow chart showing the second stage and its substages of a community relations plan

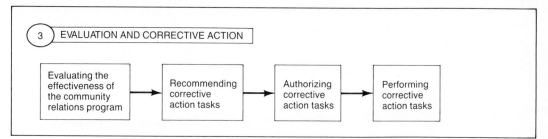

FIGURE 13–13 **Flow chart showing the third stage and its substages of a community relations plan**

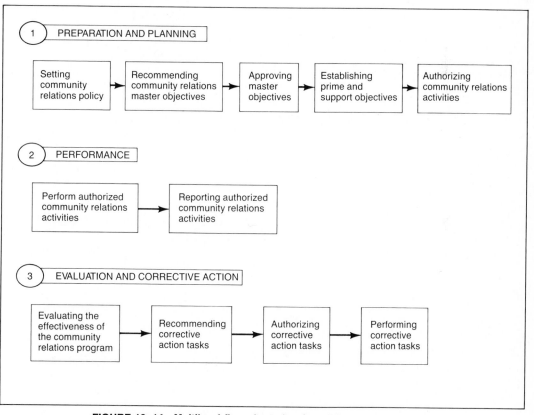

FIGURE 13–14 **Multilevel flow chart showing all levels of the process**

The Ending

There is no set way to end the process description. It might simply end with an explanation of the last main stage, like this:

> The gases have lost almost half of their velocity and about one-third of their temperature before entering the turbine. As the gases pass through the turbine, they move through the converging exhaust nozzle (see Figure

5) and out of the engine. By going through the venturi-shaped tail pipe, the exhaust gases gain velocity to increase the propulsion of the craft.

The description might end with a brief summary of the main stages:

The process—from the time the dough is placed in the hopper until the finished product is ready for shipment—takes only two minutes and fifteen seconds.

Or the process might end with additional comments on the process as a whole:

When a metal is cold worked—is shaped at normal temperatures—it nearly always ends up harder because the force that changed the shape of the piece also caused some changes inside the metal. Although the increased strength is useful for finished parts, it makes further cold working of unfinished pieces more difficult. Cold-worked metal can be made soft again by heating it, a process called "annealing."

SUGGESTIONS FOR APPLYING YOUR KNOWLEDGE

1. Analyze the use of *so-whats* in the descriptions in this chapter of the experiment to improve the baking characteristics of frozen par-fried French fries and of the tire pressure gauge. Divide a sheet of paper into two columns and list the actions or facts in the left column and the *so-whats* in the right column. If you feel that additional actions or facts require *so-whats*, add them to the list and identify the *so-whats*.

2. Analyze and discuss in class the description, at the end of this section, of the filtration of domestic water supplies by use of a rapid sand filter.

3. Choose a process you are familiar with, partition it into its main stages and the main stages into substeps. Submit for your instructor's evaluation: (1) a sentence listing the main stages; (2) sentences listing the substeps for each main stage; (3) a flow chart depicting the main stages.

4. Team up with a classmate to give an oral explanation of a process both of you are familiar with. Prepare the necessary graphic aids large enough to be seen by the rest of the class. One of you make the initial introduction of the process; the other describe the main stages and steps in the process.
Time: 10 minutes.

5. Write an explanation of a process you are familiar with:

A. Explain how something is made:

beer	nylon
bricks	paint
butter	paper
clay flower pots	pencils
coins	printed circuits
glass	shingles
honey	soap
nails	wire

B. Explain how something is done:

an auction is conducted
a beginning driver is taught to drive a
  vehicle
a credit rating is checked
a letter goes through the mail
an organization hires an employee
a student registers for courses at your
  school

C. Explain how a mechanism works:

chain saw
circuit breaker
drill
EKG machine
fireplace
gall bladder
heart
light bulb
odometer
optical scanner
pancreas

pump
remote controller
rotary engine
sewage-treatment
    plant
solar heating
    system
speedometer
telephone-answer-
    ing machine
toaster

vacuum cleaner
vise grips

water cannon

D. Explain how some natural process occurs:

digestion of
    proteins
earthquake
fog
hurricane
growth of a
    particular plant

growth of a
    particular animal
lightning
pollination
sound
volcano
yawning

The Operation of a Rapid Sand Filter

Domestic water supplies can be filtered simply and efficiently by a rapid sand filter. A rapid sand filter, as illustrated in Figure 1, consists of a rectangular concrete box, open at the top, with a depth of 8-1/2 feet. The depth must be adequate to accommodate a water depth of 3 to 4 feet, beds of sand and gravel, and the underdrain system. The sides of the filter are roughened to prevent water from streaming between the walls and the sand. The process comprises three main stages: (1) filtering the raw water, (2) draining the filtered water into storage tanks, and (3) washing the filter.

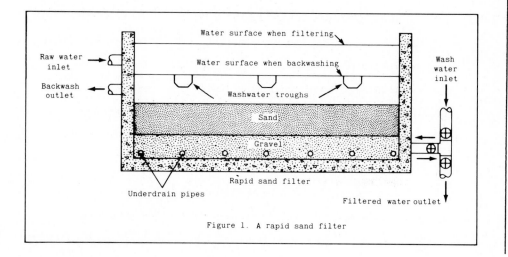

Figure 1. A rapid sand filter

Filtering the Raw Water

The filter consists of a bed of sand 24 inches deep, supported by gravel 12 inches deep. The raw water comes into the filter from primary sedimentation at the raw water inlet. As the water seeps through the pores of sand, the bacteria, finely divided clay, and other foreign particles in the water come into contact with the sand surfaces and are retained. The process is aided by the curved flow paths around the grains, throwing the particles against the sand grain surfaces. As the pores fill, the velocity of the water increases through the porous sand, and some of the deposited material is removed and washed farther down into the bed of sand. Most of the particles are collected on the first 3 to 4 inches of the sand bed.

Since much of the filtration is accomplished in the upper portion of the sand, the rest of the sand and the gravel bed catch any particles which fail to stick in the upper 3 to 4 inches. The depth of the additional sand and gravel also gives a more nearly uniform rate of filtration over the entire bed at all times. Without the uniform flow throughout the bed, some parts of the bed might dry and crack, causing the water to stream through without proper filtration.

Draining the Filtered Water

After the filtered water passes through the gravel, it collects in the underdrain system, which is a series of 16-inch diameter manifold pipes running lengthwise along the bottom of the rapid sand filter. Extending at right angles to the manifold pipes are 4-inch diameter pipes with 1/2-inch diameter holes spaced every 6 inches. The holes are located near the bottom of the lateral pipes to prevent clogging. Filtered water seeps through the holes and flows through the lateral pipes to the manifold pipes. The water then travels through the manifold pipes to the filtered water outlet, where it flows into storage tanks.

Washing the Filter

After 24 to 72 hours of continuous filtration, the filter beds become clogged with an accumulated mass of particles. To free the bed of these particles, the filter beds must be washed. Washing consists of passing filtered water in at the wash water outlet and through the underdrain system at such velocity that it causes the sand bed to expand to 50 percent greater than during the filtration process. The sand grains move through the turbulent water, rub against each other, and are cleaned of the accumulated particles. The rising washwater, after passing through the sand, flows into the washwater troughs and is wasted through the backwash outlet.

After the backwash, the filter is then ready for another filtration cycle.

C H A P T E R

14

INSTRUCTIONS

Learning how to do something new can be either enjoyable or frustrating. The key is how clear and complete the instructions are. Some instructions, written by persons who do not know how to do the job themselves, are full of misinformation. Other instructions, written by persons who know very well how to do the job and assume that everybody else does too, contain general directions that are hazy to readers. Good instructions are written by people who know the job inside out and who know how much detailed instruction their readers need.

When you become good at giving instructions, you also become one of your organization's most valuable people. For good instructions can aid your organization in two ways: They can be an effective customer-relations tool, helping customers use the goods they purchase; they can also be useful in helping employees learn to do many jobs. Instructions can be oral or written, but they should be put in writing when a mistake in a procedure is likely to be serious or when it is inconvenient or impossible to communicate orally with your audience.

Written instructions come in all sizes. They range from terse directions on bottle caps and the sides of packages to longer forms like manuals and books. It's impossible, of course, to cover every conceivable kind of written instruction. Nevertheless, in this chapter we discuss the more frequently used written instructions—instructional panels on packages, instructional sheets and leaflets, instructional booklets and manuals, and trouble-shooting procedures. But before we get to the written instructions, we describe how to gather the information you'll need to prepare them.

COLLECTING THE INFORMATION TO WRITE INSTRUCTIONS

Since readers of instructions expect you to write with *authority,* you must know the procedure inside out before you try to tell how to do it. To identify and record the essential information you'll need to include in the instructions, we suggest that you use the following task analysis sheet (see Figure 14–1), which is similar to those used by directors of training in writing vocational training materials.[1]

A. The job objective is a statement of what the reader should be able to do when he or she finishes reading the instructions. A good objective should complete a "how-to" statement:

[How to]   replace a fuel pump.

[How to]   check the credit rating of a customer.

[How to]   enlarge a drawing.

[How to]   identify igneous rock.

[How to]   conduct a presentence investigation.

[How to]   calibrate a centrifuge with a tachometer.

[How to]   conduct an audit.

B. List the materials and equipment that will be needed to perform the procedure. Materials are those items that are consumed during the procedure. Equipment is the "hardware." In baking bread, the ingredients (flour, yeast, water, salt) are the materials; the measuring cup, mixing bowl, spoon, breadboard, loaf pans, and oven are the equipment. Be specific. Be complete. Don't tell the reader to get a fishing pole and line and hook if a 2-foot pole, 15 feet of 2-pound-test monofilament line, and a

Task Analysis Sheet				
(A) Job Objective:				
(B) Equipment and Materials:				
(C) No.	(D) Steps in Performing the Procedure	(E) Precautions	(F) Graphics	(G) Learning Difficulty

FIGURE 14–1   Task analysis sheet

size 10 or smaller hook are needed for ice fishing. If raw sunflower seeds are needed for a recipe, don't simply tell the reader to get sunflower seeds, or the reader may get salted, roasted, barbecue-flavored, or garlic-flavored sunflower seeds. Tell the reader exactly what to get.

C. Number the steps in Arabic numerals (1, 2, 3, . . .) so the reader will know the exact sequence of steps and be able to follow cross-references to other steps.

D. State each step in terms of what the reader *does* when performing the step. Use a specific imperative verb (one that states a command) to tell the reader the statement is *instructional:*

Instructional   Disengage the clutch. (Use this style for instructions.)
Descriptive   The clutch is disengaged.
Subjunctive   The clutch should be disengaged.

E. According to the National Safety Council, approximately 1,900,000 disability accidents occur each year in the United States. Approximately 500,000 of these happen on the job. Giving precautions is one of your most important responsibilities. Place precautions into one of these three categories:

Caution: to prevent damage to tools, equipment, and materials.

Warning: to prevent injury to the person doing the job or to others nearby.

Danger: to warn of life-threatening situations to the person doing the job or to others nearby.

Highlight precautions to make them visibly distinctive from the surrounding text. Any of the following formats may be used.

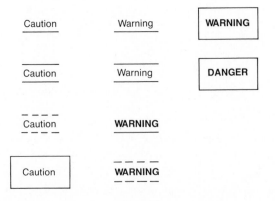

Examples of caution, warning, and danger statements are given in Figure 14–2. Use a consistent format for precautions throughout the set of instructions.

Caution: Tighten the nut to 25-30 pounds per inch. If
         you tighten the nut too hard, you will strip
         the threads.

Caution: Oil rags are combustible. Wash or destroy them
         immediately.

WARNING

Do not get under vehicle held up by a jack or by concrete
blocks. The jack might slip and a concrete block will
not hold the car. Use jack stands or ramps.

DANGER

ELECTROMAGNETIC RADIATION

Do not stand in the direct path of the antenna while
the power is on. Do not work on the wave guide while
the power is on.

High frequency electromagnetic radiation can cause
fatal internal burns. If you feel the slightest
warming effect while near the equipment, move away
quickly.

FIGURE 14–2 Examples of caution, warning, and danger statements

Ideally, readers should follow precautions exactly. Unfortunately, many readers ignore them because they do not understand their implications. To persuade readers to do exactly as a precaution says, you will have to explain the *how-comes* (a statement similar to the *so-what* principle discussed in Chapters 2 and 12). The *how-come* principle is illustrated in the following passage:

> Put out all cigarettes and flames. A spark can ignite hydrogen gas from the battery.

"Put out all cigarettes and flames" is the precaution. "A spark can ignite hydrogen gas from the battery" is the *how-come* statement that explains why the instruction should be followed. Such explanations help persuade the reader that it is reasonable to heed the precaution.

F. Graphics should be used as equal partners with words. Keep the following in mind when you write instructions: I have *told* the reader *what* to do. Have I *shown* the reader *how* to do it? Use this column to remind yourself of the types of graphics you will want to use to illustrate the written instruction.

G. Some tasks are more difficult to learn than others. As you fill out this column, try to indicate how easy or difficult the task is to learn by using words like *difficult, moderate to difficult, moderate, moderate to easy, easy,* and so on. Such analysis will help you decide how detailed your instruction for the task should be. You can also use this column to remind yourself of any special knowledge that may be needed by the reader to perform the task. For instance, if the reader has to make a miter joint, you have to decide whether to assume that the reader already knows how to use a miter box or whether you have to explain how to use it.

Figure 14–3 is an example of what your task analysis sheet might look like when it is completely filled out. Moving from the completed task analysis sheet to the first draft of your instructions should go fairly smoothly. The job objective and the list of materials and tools give you the core of the introduction. The numbered steps, safety precautions, and graphic notations give you the blueprint for the step-by-step instructions. In fact, your entries for Steps in Performing the Procedure will be very close to the language you'll actually use in writing the instructions. As you examine the examples of different kinds of instructions in the rest of this chapter, you will notice that the completed task analysis sheet gives you the important information in the order in which you will use it in writing the instructions.

Once you have completed the task analysis sheet, review it carefully to make sure there is no misinformation, irrelevant information, vague instructions, or logical gaps. Leave nothing to chance.

Now let's analyze the first of three types of instructions listed earlier—instructional panels on packages.

Task Analysis Sheet

Job Objective: Build a silkscreen frame (first stage of six stages in printing your own T-shirts)

Materials: Two 20" lengths of 2"x2" pine } To make the frame
Two 16" lengths of 2"x2" pine
One sheet of medium grit sandpaper to smooth the wood
Eight corrugated fasteners to secure the corners of the frame
Wood glue (such as Elmer's)

Equipment: Carpenter's square and pencil to mark wood
Handsaw to cut wood
Miter box to cut 45° angles at the ends of the wood pieces
Table saw with a dado blade to make groove in the wood pieces
Hammer to drive corrugated fasteners

No.	Steps in Performing the Procedure	Precautions	Graphics	Learning Difficulty
1	Using the handsaw and miter box, cut the ends of wood pieces to make miter joints.	Cut the wood at the correct angles so that everything will fit correctly.	drawing to show how each corner should be cut	must know how to use miter box
2	Using the carpenter's square and pencil, draw a line down each piece of wood 3/8" from the edge away from the point or long side of the wood.	none	drawing to show where the line is to be drawn	easy
3	Using the table saw with a dado blade, carefully cut a 3/16" groove in each piece of wood as shown.	Wear safety goggles to protect eyes from flying wood particles. make sure the measurement is exact, because the groove is used to secure the 1/4" cotton cord that will attach the cloth screen to the frame in a later stage.	drawing to show cross-sectional view of the board cut	must know how to use table saw with dado blade
4	Go over all pieces of wood with the medium sandpaper to remove splinters. Smooth just enough to remove splinters and rough edges; the frame will not be painted.	Pieces of wood should be smooth and safe to handle.	none	easy
5	Glue the joints with small amount of wood glue.	none	drawing to show the assembled frame	easy
6	Carefully pound the corrugated fasteners into place as shown.	none	drawing to show how the fasteners are centered in each corner	easy

FIGURE 14–3   Part of a completed task analysis sheet

INSTRUCTIONAL PANELS ON PACKAGES

Instructions frequently appear on the sides of containers, as illustrated by these brief directions for putting a mantle on a kerosene lamp.

DIRECTIONS
+ Without touching fabric, remove mantle from box by wire frame and handle by ears. NEVER TOUCH FABRIC.

+ Fit mantle to burner gallery and lock by turning clockwise.

+ Taking care that match does not touch mantle, apply light to base of mantle to burn off protective coating. TAKE CARE THAT MATCH DOES NOT TOUCH MANTLE.

+ Lock chimney in burner gallery by turning clockwise. DO NOT FORCE.

The instructions for installing a mantle on a kerosene lamp are written in the imperative voice. That is, the reader is ordered to perform some action, as in "Remove mantle from box" and "Fit mantle to burner gallery." Notice that the imperative is simply the "You" sentence form— "*You* remove mantle from box"—with the "you" missing. Imperative sentences sound a bit brusque when taken out of context as we have done here, but they don't really trouble anyone. You've read imperative-voice sentences many times in instructions, we suspect, and we're sure you've never been disturbed by them. Remember that instructions tell how to do something. Your readers rely on you to tell them what they're expected to do and how to do it.

Notice, also, that the sentences are short and to the point. They run from a low of 3 words to a high of 19. They average about 10 words each. From 9 to 14 is probably about the average you want in instructions.

Each step is emphasized by being separated from the others by paragraphing, plenty of white space, and the little plus marks.

Capital letters are used to warn or caution the reader about potentially troublesome or dangerous phases of the procedure. Notice, however, that the *how-comes* are missing from the precautions. The precautions with the *how-comes* added might read like this:

NEVER TOUCH FABRIC. If fabric coating is disturbed before it is burned off, fabric may not light properly.

TAKE CARE THAT MATCH DOES NOT TOUCH MANTLE. Direct contact of match will cause a quick flash of fire and will destroy mantle fabric.

DO NOT FORCE. Force may break chimney or jam burner gallery.

How-comes help persuade the reader to follow the precautions and should be included in even the briefest instructions.

INSTRUCTIONAL SHEETS AND LEAFLETS

Instructions also appear on sheets or leaflets enclosed with goods, as shown by the material in Figure 14–4, which tells how to mount decorative ceiling hooks for hanging flower pots, chimes, or chains for swag lamps.

Usually the first thing readers see when they look at an instruction sheet is the title. (In fact, that's usually what they're looking for.) The title should be specific enough to assure readers that they have the right in-

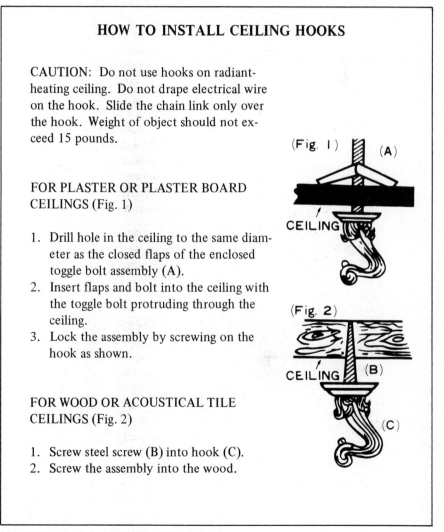

HOW TO INSTALL CEILING HOOKS

CAUTION: Do not use hooks on radiant-heating ceiling. Do not drape electrical wire on the hook. Slide the chain link only over the hook. Weight of object should not exceed 15 pounds.

(Fig. 1) (A)

CEILING

FOR PLASTER OR PLASTER BOARD CEILINGS (Fig. 1)

1. Drill hole in the ceiling to the same diameter as the closed flaps of the enclosed toggle bolt assembly (A).
2. Insert flaps and bolt into the ceiling with the toggle bolt protruding through the ceiling.
3. Lock the assembly by screwing on the hook as shown.

(Fig. 2)

CEILING (B)

FOR WOOD OR ACOUSTICAL TILE CEILINGS (Fig. 2)

(C)

1. Screw steel screw (B) into hook (C).
2. Screw the assembly into the wood.

FIGURE 14–4 Sample of instructional sheet

formation for the right job. Words like *directions, instructions, procedures, how to . . .* signal the type of document it is. Also, it helps to name the procedure in the title, as "How to Install Ceiling Hooks." Warnings and cautions should be placed where they cannot be overlooked easily.

If there are several steps or series of steps, a numbered system can replace bullets (●), dashes (—), or other marks. As readers look over the instructions, they should see down the left margin each instruction beginning with an Arabic numeral and period (or some other mark).

Graphics that help readers understand and follow a direction should be placed as close as possible to the direction. Call-outs (references to graphics) and captions should be included to identify graphics and relate them to the text. Otherwise, readers may not refer to them at all.

INSTRUCTIONAL BOOKLETS AND MANUALS

As you can see from the samples in this chapter, the layout and design of instructions are important. You must think carefully about the amount of space they will occupy. Sometimes instructions have to be squeezed into small panels on the side of the box. Sometimes they fill a manual. Instruction manuals share many characteristics with briefer forms of instructions: Directions are given in short imperative sentences; are separately paragraphed; are emphasized by surrounding white space, numbering, and different typeface; and are supported by graphics.

To see these characteristics in more detail, we include two types of instructional booklets and manuals. The first, which we call *workbench* instructions, are to be followed by readers while they are actually performing a procedure. The earlier examples in this chapter are examples of workbench instructions. The second type, which we call *armchair* instructions, teach new techniques and skills to readers in the calm of their offices or homes.

Workbench Instructions

Read the instructions for installing a Dayton Elite sink (Figure 14–5), and then let's analyze its format, arrangement, and style.

FORMAT Notice the heavy reliance on graphics, bold type, and headings. Graphics *show* the reader how to do the work. The two-column format allows the graphics to be placed next to the written instructions they illustrate. (One of the most common faults in preparing instructions is to place graphics where they are not immediately useful.) Heads and subheads help readers keep their place as they look back and forth between their work and the instructions.

ARRANGEMENT Many instructions contain only the steps of the procedure, as illustrated in earlier examples given in this chapter. However,

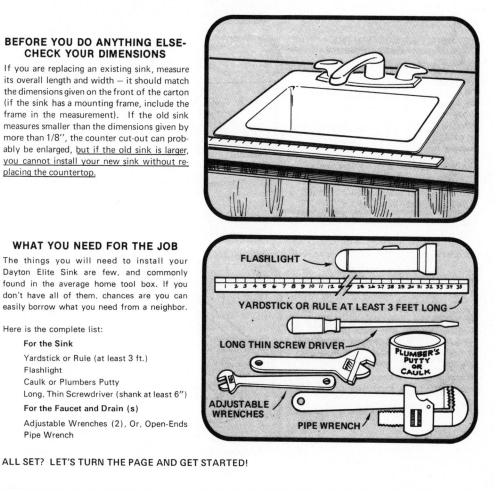

DAYTON *Elite* ILLUSTRATED INSTRUCTIONS

CONGRATULATIONS! You Have Just Purchased The Last Sink You Will Ever Need To Install In The Location You Have Selected!

We're delighted that you have chosen our quality product, and we're confident that it will prove to be one of the best values-for-the-money you have ever received. We feel that we have made the following installation instructions extremely clear and simple to follow. Read them through once now to get the "big picture," and then go back to the beginning and start the actual, step-by-step procedure. We would wish you "good luck", but you really won't need it — just follow the instructions, and you'll sail through the project like a pro!

BEFORE YOU DO ANYTHING ELSE-CHECK YOUR DIMENSIONS

If you are replacing an existing sink, measure its overall length and width — it should match the dimensions given on the front of the carton (if the sink has a mounting frame, include the frame in the measurement). If the old sink measures smaller than the dimensions given by more than 1/8", the counter cut-out can probably be enlarged, but if the old sink is larger, you cannot install your new sink without replacing the countertop.

WHAT YOU NEED FOR THE JOB

The things you will need to install your Dayton Elite Sink are few, and commonly found in the average home tool box. If you don't have all of them, chances are you can easily borrow what you need from a neighbor.

Here is the complete list:

For the Sink

Yardstick or Rule (at least 3 ft.)
Flashlight
Caulk or Plumbers Putty
Long, Thin Screwdriver (shank at least 6")

For the Faucet and Drain (s)

Adjustable Wrenches (2), Or, Open-Ends
Pipe Wrench

FLASHLIGHT

YARDSTICK OR RULE AT LEAST 3 FEET LONG

LONG THIN SCREW DRIVER

PLUMBER'S PUTTY OR CAULK

ADJUSTABLE WRENCHES

PIPE WRENCH

ALL SET? LET'S TURN THE PAGE AND GET STARTED!

FIGURE 14–5 Workbench instructions for installing a sink (Dayton Products, Inc. A Subsidiary of Elkay Manufacturing Co. Reprinted with permission.)

STEP NO.1 OUT WITH THE OLD

Taking out an old sink really isn't too hard a job, because you can leave the "toughest nuts" in place — the faucet and drain outlet — and simply lift them out right along with the sink itself. (Then, if you _do_ want to remove those parts for use on your new sink, you can do so in a much easier position.) Here then, is what you do to remove the old sink:

1. Shut off the water supply valves
2. Disconnect the faucet supply fittings
3. Disconnect the drain fittings
4. From the underside of the sink, loosen and remove the frame or rim fasteners
5. Lift the entire sink out of the counter-top

STEP NO. 2 CONFIRM THE MEASUREMENTS

Next, check the dimensions of the cut-out opening to be sure that it is sized properly. The easiest way to do this is to simply set the new sink into the opening to see that it fits. If the sink won't insert properly (rim won't set uniformly on the countertop), enlarge the cut-out opening with a sabre saw or keyhole saw according to the following dimensions:

Sink Model	Dimension	
	A	B
Double-Bowl Kitchen Sink	32-3/8''	21-3/8''
Single-Bowl Kitchen Sink	24-3/8''	21-3/8''
Bar Sink	14-3/8''	14-3/8''

NOTE: Follow directions on page 5 for corners.

STEP NO. 3 ATTACH FAUCET, DRAIN FITTINGS, ACCESSORIES

If you are installing a new faucet and/or drain, garbage disposer or other accessory, follow the directions provided with those products. If you are re-installing the fittings you had on the old sink, mount them on the new sink, using putty or caulk under the faucet base, and top flange of the drain, to protect against seepage. Attach your supply riser tubes to the faucet at this time (these connections are more difficult to make after the sink is in place).

NOTE: FOR NEW COUNTER TOP SEE PAGE FIVE (5).

CAULK

2

FIGURE 14–5 Workbench instructions _(cont.)_

STEP NO. 4 ASSEMBLE AND INSERT FASTENERS

Assemble the "speed screws" into the clamps, as shown. (NOTE: Screws are designed to insert into the clamps with <u>backward threading</u>, so that in mounting, they will turn the normal direction.) Assembled fasteners can be inserted into the mounting channels at either end, or in a special opening in the middle. It will simplify mounting if you insert and position the clamps <u>before</u> putting the sink into the counter. Locate the fasteners in the positions shown in Step #5, using the following "trick" to permit clearing the sides of the cut-out when you insert the sink into place: <u>Hand-tighten each fastener onto the channel so that the clamp "teeth" point in the same direction as the channel</u>. NOTE: An undersize cut-out will not permit this method—instead, you will have to insert fasteners after the sink is in place.

STEP NO. 5 POSITION FASTENERS IN CHANNELS

Using the method described in Step #4, locate the fasteners in the positions shown. (The number of fasteners varies between models, but in any case, the key is to locate one approximately <u>in the middle</u> of each side.) Distribute other fasteners uniformly around the sink.

STEP NO. 6 CAULK AROUND RIM— DROP SINK INTO CUT-OUT

Place a continuous bead of putty or caulk around the entire perimeter of the rim (between the channel and the edge) to serve as a water seal against possible seepage down into the cabinet below.

Now, pick up the sink and set it into the countertop cut-out opening. Square up the positioning by lining up the front rim with the front edge of the countertop.

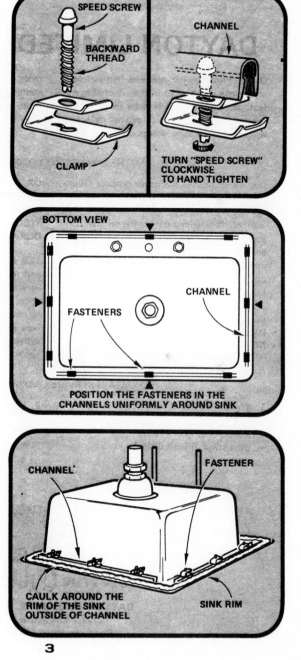

SPEED SCREW

BACKWARD THREAD

CLAMP

CHANNEL

TURN "SPEED SCREW" CLOCKWISE TO HAND TIGHTEN

BOTTOM VIEW

CHANNEL

FASTENERS

POSITION THE FASTENERS IN THE CHANNELS UNIFORMLY AROUND SINK

CHANNEL

FASTENER

CAULK AROUND THE RIM OF THE SINK OUTSIDE OF CHANNEL

SINK RIM

3

FIGURE 14–5 Workbench instructions *(cont.)*

STEP NO. 7   ENGAGE AND TIGHTEN FASTENERS

With your flashlight and long screwdriver, get under the sink to tighten the fasteners. First, twist the clamps so that their teeth swing under the counter (pushing them with a screwdriver is an easy way to do this). Next, push the speed screw upward to engage the clamp flange with the channel, and tighten, beginning with the fasteners located in the middle of each side. Finally, tighten the remaining fasteners, until the entire rim is seated with no gaps. (Occasionally, it is necessary to loosen a fastener and slide it to a different position to compensate for an uneven counter.) NOTE: Be careful not to over-tighten. It is only necessary to draw the rim down snugly to the counter — additional turning of the screws will not make it any better fitting, and could result in damage to the rim.

STEP NO. 7A   *FASTENING TO EXTRA-THICK TOP*

Our standard fastener screw will fit standard countertops with thicknesses up to 7/8''. (Measure the thickness at the cut-out area, not along the front edge of the counter.) If you have a counter which is thicker than 7/8'' (up to 1-½'' thick), you may still install your sink, using this alternate method: Instead of using the speed screws furnished, obtain some #8-32 round head screws, 2'' long (one for each clamp), and a lock washer and nut for each screw. Rather than threading into the clamps, these screws simply fit through the openings, with fastening accomplished by tightening the nut against the bottom of the clamp. NOTE: In some cases, a counter will be thicker at the front only, due to the cabinet attachment, which would require longer screws for the front clamps only.

STEP NO. 8   CONNECT FAUCET SUPPLIES AND DRAIN FITTINGS

In reverse order of Step #1 — connect the drain trap fittings, connect the faucet supply fittings, and turn on the water supply. Check for possible supply leaks at these locations: (1) Supply riser tubes to faucet, and (2) Supply riser tubes to shut-off valves (or, lower connections). Next, fill the sink bowl(s) with water and check for possible leaking around the drain flange(s) (this would show up as dripping into the cabinet below). Release water from sink and check for possible leaks at drain connections. Tighten any joints which leak.

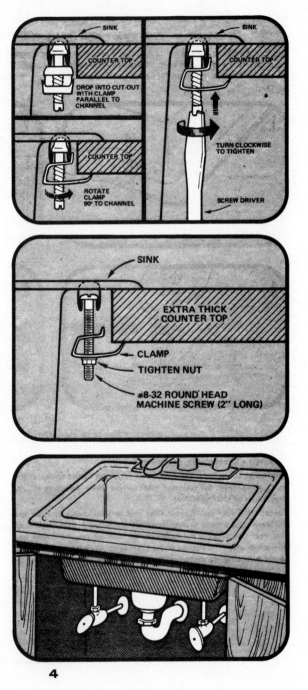

4

FIGURE 14–5 Workbench instructions *(cont.)*

FOR NEW COUNTER INSTALLATIONS ONLY

The following instructions are to be used if you are installing a new countertop along with your new sink. NOTE: If the countertop has not yet been anchored to the cabinets, you will find it much easier to make the cut-out and install the sink first, while it is in an "easier-to-work" position.

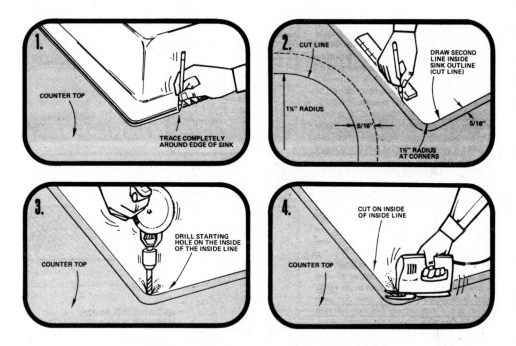

CARE AND CLEANING OF YOUR DAYTON ELITE SINK

Dayton Elite is made of the lifetime material — solid stainless steel. Because of this, your new sink will never chip or crack, and will never rust, corrode or tarnish.

Don't be afraid to "use" your new sink. You don't need to use protective mats — in fact, they may create unsightly marks and prevent the stainless steel surface from "breaking-in" and reaching its mellow satin lustre from use (a patina similar to sterling silver).

You will find your new Dayton Elite sink to be a breeze to keep sparkling clean. Ordinary kitchen soap or detergent and water, and a good rinsing, is all that's needed — then, wipe it dry with a cloth or dish towel, and it will shine like new. Feel free to scour the compartment areas of your sink with your favorite cleanser from time-to-time, but just be sure to rub with the direction of the grain lines. Unlike enamel surfaces, stainless steel will not become porous with continued scrubbing, so don't feel that you have to "baby" it — your Dayton Elite sink will probably outlive all of us!

5

FIGURE 14–5 **Workbench instructions** *(cont.)*

instructions for complicated procedures may contain an introduction, a body (the step-by-step instructions), and an ending section—essentially the same arrangement as for a description of a mechanism or a process.

At the beginning of the Dayton instructions is a one-page introduction that "resells" the product, reassures that the procedure will be easy with these instructions, shows what to do first (check the dimensions of the countertop cutout), and lists the equipment and material for the job. Not all instructions need to resell or reassure (especially if they are written for the technician—the person who makes a living doing this kind of work), but such information is appropriate for the do-it-yourselfer. If you're writing for a mixed audience—both technicians and do-it-yourselfers—we suggest that you include the resell and reassurance; the technician can skip them, but the do-it-yourselfer may be nervous without them. Don't be afraid to do a little hand-holding with beginners. But regardless of the audience, the introduction has the important function of showing the reader how to get started.

The body of the instructions—the step-by-step procedure for installing the sink—is given on the next three pages. Each step is emphasized by a numbered heading and by being stated in the imperative. (The only step not written in the imperative is step 7A, which is a contingency step—to be followed only if the thickness of the countertop is more than 7/8 inch.) Notice how the writer handles step 1 by breaking it down into a subroutine.

The end section of the instructions (page 5) explains an alternative procedure ("for new counter installations only"), does a bit more reselling, and advises about caring for the sink after installation.

STYLE   Keep three stylistic considerations in mind when you write instructions. The first is to avoid writing in a telegraphic style. As we mentioned earlier, you want your sentences to be short and to the point, but you still should write in natural, grammatical expression.

NATURAL EXPRESSION USED IN THE DAYTON ELITE INSTRUCTIONS	TELEGRAPHIC STYLE
From the underside of the sink, loosen and remove the frame or rim fasteners.	From underside of sink, loosen/remove frame/rim fasteners.
If you are reinstalling the fittings you had on the old sink, mount them on the new sink, using putty or caulk under the faucet base, and top flange of the drain, to protect against seepage.	If reinstalling old sink fittings mount them on new sink, using putty/caulk under faucet base, and top flange of drain, to avoid seepage.

Although most readers can understand the telegraphic style, many will not be willing to work with it because it looks different from natural prose. Telegraphic style is too choppy and doesn't save you all that much space anyway.

A second stylistic consideration is to know when to use the imperative voice. Use the imperative when you are writing an instruction. For example, you should write

> Shut off the water supply valves.

not

> You should shut off the water supply valves.

not

> The water supply valves are to be shut off.

not

> The water supply valves must be shut off.

The last three sentences are not imperative. They don't tell the reader what to do, and there's a good chance that the reader will not recognize them as instructions. However, if you are explaining a general principle or providing descriptive information, use nonimperative sentences. For example, notice the first two sentences of step 2: The first sentence is an instruction written in the imperative; the second is useful information written in the indicative. You will probably be giving instructions and useful supplemental explanations throughout your set of instructions. Notice how the writer of the Dayton instructions uses style to keep instructions and descriptive information distinct.

A third stylistic consideration is related to explaining contingencies. A contingency is a possible situation that the reader must be prepared for. The third sentence of step 2 is an example:

> If the sink won't insert properly (rim won't fit uniformly on the countertop), enlarge the cutout opening with a sabre saw or keyhole saw . . . .

As you can see from other parts of these instructions, the structure for a contingency explanation is "if this . . . then this. . . ." If such-and-such happens, do this. . . .

Armchair Instructions

About the only differences between workbench instructions and armchair instructions are the more leisurely pace and longer introduction of the latter. Armchair instructions also often look more like essays. Such a pace, introduction, and format often appear in informational pamphlets, such as the passage in Figure 14–6, which is from a U.S. Coast Guard publication, *(Almost) Everything You Ever Wanted to Know About Boating—But Were Ashamed to Ask* (Washington, D.C.: U.S. Coast Guard, February 1972).

The first five paragraphs of this passage make up the introductory section of this particular set of instructions. The writer works primarily

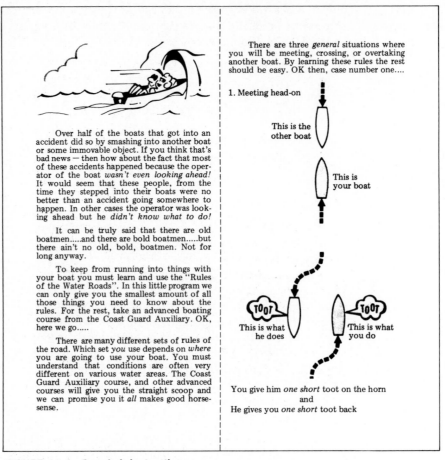

Over half of the boats that got into an accident did so by smashing into another boat or some immovable object. If you think that's bad news — then how about the fact that most of these accidents happened because the operator of the boat *wasn't even looking ahead!* It would seem that these people, from the time they stepped into their boats were no better than an accident going somewhere to happen. In other cases the operator was looking ahead but he *didn't know what to do!*

It can be truly said that there are old boatmen.....and there are bold boatmen.....but there ain't no old, bold, boatmen. Not for long anyway.

To keep from running into things with your boat you must learn and use the "Rules of the Water Roads". In this little program we can only give you the smallest amount of all those things you need to know about the rules. For the rest, take an advanced boating course from the Coast Guard Auxiliary. OK, here we go.....

There are many different sets of rules of the road. Which set *you* use depends on *where* you are going to use your boat. You must understand that conditions are often very different on various water areas. The Coast Guard Auxiliary course, and other advanced courses will give you the straight scoop and we can promise you it *all* makes good horsesense.

There are three *general* situations where you will be meeting, crossing, or overtaking another boat. By learning these rules the rest should be easy. OK then, case number one....

1. Meeting head-on

This is the other boat

This is your boat

This is what he does

This is what you do

You give him *one short* toot on the horn
and
He gives you *one short* toot back

FIGURE 14–6 Armchair instructions

on motivating readers to follow these directions by describing common mistakes and dangers. If you think that your readers need to understand why they are to do something in a certain way, explain why. But keep the instruction and the explanation distinct. It's particularly important when giving instructions to analyze the job from the point of view of readers unfamiliar with—perhaps even totally ignorant of—the job. This advice also applies when you give a specific command. Ask yourself whether a general command such as "Remove the oil filter" is clear enough, or whether the action of removing the oil filter will have to be broken down into a subroutine—into the smallest possible steps. Remember, just as some people who have boats don't know anything about maneuvering them, some people who have cars don't know how to remove an oil filter. Spell things out; don't be afraid of being too simple.

The writer of the Coast Guard manual ends the introduction by providing an overview of the series of directions to come, by mentioning the conditions or circumstances in which certain procedures are to be fol-

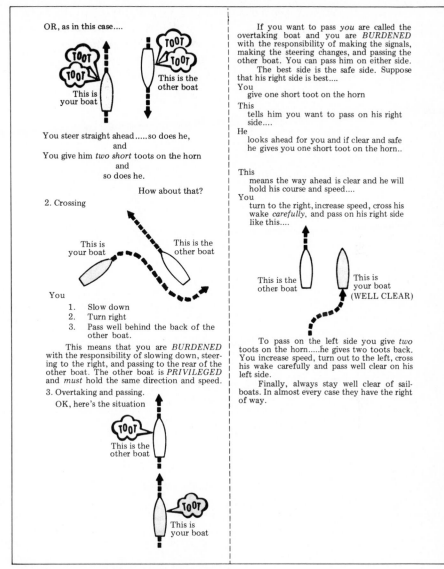

FIGURE 14–6 Armchair instructions *(cont.)*

lowed, and by leading into the first circumstance. The remainder of the passage is divided into the three series of commands to perform the maneuvers.

Troubleshooting

When something goes wrong during a procedure, the reader hopes that the instructions contain troubleshooting procedures to aid in isolating and correcting the problem. A three-column table with headings such as

"Problem," "Probable Cause," and "Solution" is apt to be the easiest way to lead the reader quickly from the symptom of the problem to the solution with a minimum amount of information. Figure 14–7 shows a typical troubleshooting table. List the most frequent problems first. For any one problem, there may be several possible causes. List the possible causes and solutions in order from most frequent to least frequent occurrence.

TROUBLESHOOTING TABLE

Note: Many tape player problems are caused by defective cassettes. Check the cassette by substituting a known good cassette.

PROBLEM	PROBABLE CAUSE	SOLUTION
Motor does not run when cassette is inserted.	1. Micro-actuating arm is bent or broken.	Bend the actuating arm far enough to actuate the micro-switch when the cassette is inserted, or replace.
	2. Micro-switch is defective.	Replace.
	3. Motor is defective.	Replace.
Poor tape drive, wow or flutter.	1. Cassette is defective.	Check by inserting a known good cassette.
	2. Drive surfaces are dirty.	Using isopropyl (rubbing) alcohol, clean and wipe dry the outer edge of the flywheel, motor drive pulley, capstan shaft, and tape head.
	3. Drive belt is defective or incorrectly installed.	If the drive belt is stretched, replace. If the belt is not installed with the stripes on the outside, reinstall. If the drive belt rides too high or low on the motor pulley, readjust.

FIGURE 14–7 Troubleshooting table

SUGGESTIONS FOR APPLYING YOUR KNOWLEDGE

1. Your textbooks probably contain many examples of instructions. Bring one example to class to examine in the light of the information provided in this chapter.

2. Discuss a hobby procedure that you recently learned. Who instructed you? Were the instructions oral or written? Did you have any initial problems in following the instructions?

3. Provide the *how-comes* for the following safety precautions in instructions on how to jump-start a car.

Make sure the cars don't touch.

Do not jump-start unless both batteries are the same voltage.

Do not jump-start if the battery is frozen.

Wear goggles.

4. Analyze the set of instructions for loading a diskette drive, which comprise the third part of a training manual for computer operators.[2]

5. Complete a task analysis sheet for a procedure from your field of study, from your work, or from one of your hobbies.

6. Using your task analysis sheet, write a set of instructions for either a do-it-yourselfer or a technician.

PART THREE

LOADING THE DISKETTE DRIVE

In the previous two sections, you learned how to provide power to the computer and to ready it for processing data. But no system is complete without a means to also save data. The diskette provides that means. In this section you will learn how to load the diskette onto the diskette drive, a simple operation that takes less than a minute. Loading the diskette drive involves (1) opening the diskette drive door, (2) removing the diskette from its protective jacket, (3) aligning the diskette with the slot on the diskette drive, (4) inserting the diskette, and (5) closing the diskette drive door.

> Caution
>
> To prevent possible damage to the diskette be sure that the red power light of the diskette drive is on. If the light is not on, refer to the power-on procedure.

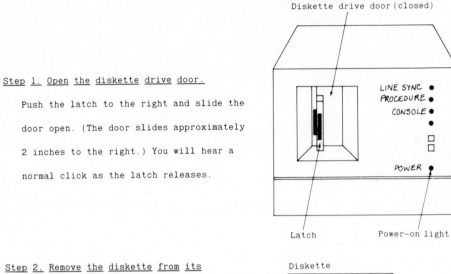

Diskette drive door (closed)

Latch   Power-on light

Step 1. Open the diskette drive door.

Push the latch to the right and slide the
door open. (The door slides approximately
2 inches to the right.) You will hear a
normal click as the latch releases.

Step 2. Remove the diskette from its
protective sleeve.

Caution The diskette has three exposed
surfaces on front and back. To prevent
possible damage to the diskette, do not
touch these surfaces.

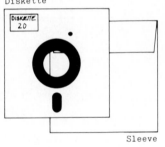

Diskette

Sleeve

Step 3. Align the diskette with the slot on
the diskette drive. Hold the diskette
vertically with the label to your right
and the oval cut-out toward the diskette
drive.

Step 4. Insert the diskette. Gently slide
the diskette into the slot.
Caution Do not rub the exposed surfaces
of the diskette against the door.

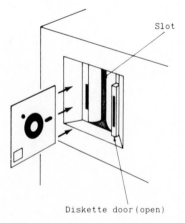

Slot

Diskette door (open)

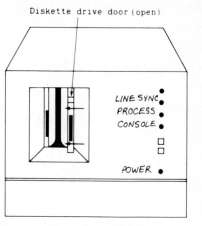

Diskette drive door (open)

<u>Step 5</u>. <u>Close the diskette door.</u> Slide the
diskette door to the left until you hear
the latch click. <u>Note</u>: If the door rubs
against the diskette when closing, the
diskette is not seated in the slot. Slide
the door open, push the diskette in some
more, and close the door.

    The diskette is now loaded and the computer is ready to process and save
data. In the next section you will learn how to access a menu and select a
procedure for execution.

CHAPTER

15

PERIODIC REPORTS, ACCIDENT REPORTS, TRIP REPORTS, AND MINUTES

S omebody once joked that Charles Lindbergh's nonstop solo flight across the Atlantic was relatively easy. A more difficult task, according to the joke, would have been to have five persons aboard, with each one partly responsible for flying the airplane.

Perhaps there is no other feature in which individual work and organizational work differ more than in the need to coordinate the activities of several individuals and to keep everybody informed of what's happening. When Charles Kettering, the American inventor and automotive manufacturer, worked in his backyard developing an electrical starter for his automobile, he kept no records of materials, labor, or progress. He simply worked until he achieved what he had set out to do. He knew exactly what his objective was, he didn't have to coordinate the work of others, he built what he needed, and he didn't have to tell somebody else what his costs were or how he was spending his time.

But the work of an organization is different. Its activity, like Lindbergh's and Kettering's, is directed toward the achievement of objectives. However, its objectives are achieved through the coordinated efforts of several individuals. As we mentioned at the beginning of Chapter 9, "Basic Principles of Reports," successful organizations achieve their goals by getting information to those who need it. A knowledge of the types of reports discussed in this chapter—periodic reports, accident reports, trip reports, and minutes—will help you write the effective reports your organization needs to achieve coordination.

PERIODIC REPORTS

Periodic reports are records of work over a specific period of time—a day, a week, a month, and so on. Their intervals are determined by managerial needs or customers' requirements. Such reports frequently build up from workers' daily logs or job reports to their supervisors' weekly, monthly, or quarterly reports. Higher-level periodic reports pull together these other reports to present information to organizational officers or customers.

These reports are vital documents that give an organization the necessary information on which to base decisions. If they are not used or are not well written, organizations can have many problems. Persons responsible for the work, but perhaps removed from the actual work, can find it difficult to keep abreast of expenditures of time, money, and materials and to evaluate work. Persons responsible for long-range planning can be deprived of valuable records of their organization's capabilities and performances.

Because periodic reports are often preliminary to other reports and are important as references, they should be designed so that readers can retrieve information from them easily. And although no set format exists for periodic reports—they may be transmitted as memos, letters, or informal or formal reports—they are often so routine that their arrangement can be regularized into printed forms.

Printed Periodic Report Forms

Printed periodic report forms are useful because the type of information to be included in them seldom varies. New data is simply put in the existing categories. For instance, monthly periodic reports on the activities of a government agency contained the following categories: (1) Liaison with Department of Transportation, (2) Assistance to County Planning Commissions, (3) Assistance to Bureau of Recreation, and (4) Supervision of Youth Conservation Corps Programs. Since the work of the agency was restricted to these four categories, a printed form was a great convenience in making monthly periodic reports. Any time the activities of an organization change significantly, the printed periodic report form can be changed accordingly.

Figure 15–1 shows a printed form used by truck drivers after each trip to report routine information periodically. As you can see, the information filled in consists mostly of numbers and phrases. Sometimes, as in the "Remarks" space in Figure 15–1, the information is presented in phrases, sentences, or paragraphs. All printed periodic report forms have two advantages: The organization of a particular report is always the same, and the spaces encourage complete reporting of essential data.

WILLIAMS-NICKELL TRANSPORT CO., INC.

MOREHEAD, KY. 40351

Driver *Arthur Baldridge*		Date *February 22, 1985*		
Out *12:50 pm*	In *7:95 pm*		Delay	
Louisville	✓	Gasoline	✓	Straight Load	✓
		Oil		Split Load	
Ashland		Fuel Oil		Straight Load	
		Oil		Split Load	
Route		West Liberty		Town	
#5 Fuel		Destination *Morehead*		

Truck Number *#4*		Fuel Used	
		Number of Gallons	*60 gal.*
Beginning Mileage *204,697*		Ending Mileage *204,987*	

Remarks *I-64*

1650 gal. Super Regular
2500 gal. Super Shell
Morehead Car Wash 2500 gal. Shell Regular
Plant 1650 gal. Super Shell

FIGURE 15–1 Printed form to be filled in by truck drivers after each trip (Courtesy Agnes Williams)

Progress Reports

If you've ever had something repaired or built, you've probably had a keen interest in keeping posted on how the work was going. And probably, as long as you didn't make too big a pest of yourself, the contractor very cordially kept you up to date. That same desire to know accompanies almost every endeavor, large or small: Knowing what's happening on a project that's underway, but not yet completed, is essential.

The pressing need to know is satisfied by a special kind of periodic report—the progress report. The obvious purpose of progress reports is to record work completed and to outline work planned so that everybody who needs to know (managers, customers, co-workers) will know just what the situation is at the time of the report. Thus, a lot of important persons need to have progress reports available to them.

There are three ways of scheduling progress reports. First, like periodic reports, they may be submitted at specified time intervals—weekly, monthly, quarterly, or whatever regular interval has been decided on—until the project is completed. Second, they may be submitted when major stages of work have been completed rather than at definite time intervals. Third, they may be submitted in response to requests by persons who want to know what progress is being made on a project.

Like other periodic reports, progress reports have no set format and are usually multilevel. That is, in projects of long duration there may be different formats for different levels of progress reports. A work log may be submitted each day; a letter or memo or informal report may be submitted each quarter or semiannually. Such a report schedule accumulates information at different times and uses different formats for different audiences.

ORGANIZING AND DEVELOPING PROGRESS REPORTS Regardless of the submission schedule or format, progress reports tell how a project is going, how much has been completed, and how much remains to be done. To report these three things, the following arrangement is quite suitable:

- An introduction explains the period of work covered by the report, the work that had been planned, and if appropriate, the authority to do the work. If expected by readers, the introduction may also assess the progress to date.
- A discussion section (body) provides a detailed account of what has been accomplished, and if appropriate, how.
- An ending explains what work is planned for the future and gives an overall appraisal of the progress to date.

This three-part arrangement may suggest the actual headings in some progress reports: Introduction, Discussion, Ending. What arrangement and headings are used will depend on two important factors: the practices of the organization, and the data-submission plan that may be part of the contract with a customer or sponsoring agency. To appreciate how varied headings may be, consider the following headings gathered from just four progress reports:

Statement of Problem	Introduction
Current Progress	Job Description
Future Work	Work Completed
Assessment of Progress	Work Remaining
	Overall Appraisal

Period of Report   Introduction
Discussion of Work Completed   Project Progress
Roster of Personnel   Project Problems
Expenses Incurred   Logistics
Work of the Next Period
Conclusions and Recommendations

In these four report outlines you can readily see that time is the major arrangement. The sample progress report in Figure 15–2 uses time as the major organizing principle. The report, written by the person in charge of a large commercial poultry farm, is an example of a simple, straightforward progress report that evaluates the progress, covers each task in the detail necessary, and then looks ahead and tells what the plans are for the future.

Although the progress report on the poultry plant expansion is arranged chronologically (work completed, work to be completed) with subsections on specific tasks (laying house, brooder house, processing room, drying yard), progress reports are sometimes arranged according to specific tasks, with subsections arranged chronologically. Organized by tasks, the report outline looks like this:

    I. Laying House
       A. Work Completed
       B. Work to Be Completed
   II. Brooder House
       A. Work Completed
       B. Work to Be Completed
  III. Processing Room
       A. Work Completed
       B. Work to Be Completed
   IV. Drying Yard
       A. Work Completed
       B. Work to Be Completed
Conclusions

Most of the progress reports you'll write will use a straight time arrangement, but if the tasks you're reporting on are large enough to be regarded as miniprojects in themselves, you might consider arranging your report by tasks.

The degree of detail included in progress reports will depend on your readers' needs. For most simple projects, brief statements like those in the progress report on the expansion of the Medina poultry plant sufficiently inform readers of what's been done and what will be done. In more complex projects it may be necessary to use tables and charts to report a mass of data, especially numbers. But don't interrupt your discussion with too many charts and tables. Place them in an annex at the end of your progress report, commenting on them and referring to them in your discussion.

PROGRESS REPORT
EXPANSION OF THE MEDINA POULTRY PLANT
MARCH 1–MARCH 31, 1985

During March we made good progress toward completing the expansion of the poultry plant. The addition to the processing room has been completed. We should complete the entire expansion project by May 15, nearly two weeks ahead of schedule, which will give us additional time to review our late summer and fall production schedules, and will allow us to conduct a tour of the plant for the Farm Advisory Committee at its annual meeting.

Work Completed

Laying House

1. The new 150′ × 34′ laying house has been completed.
2. 4500 hens (2500 leghorns and 2000 New Hampshires) were added to the laying flock and were housed in the new laying house. Pockman cages (12″ × 16″) were installed to hold two hens each. The New Hampshires were housed at the front of the building because they are less easily frightened than the leghorns.

Brooder House

1. The new 150′ × 40′ brooder house has been completed, except for installing the automatic feeding and watering system.
2. A portable sprayer has been ordered.

Processing Room

1. The 25′ × 40′ addition to the processing room has been completed.
2. A new Eggomatic sorting machine has been installed to handle the anticipated increase in egg production.

Drying Yard

1. The drying yard has been doubled in size.
2. The yard has been regraded so that no liquid runoff goes onto adjoining property or into underground water.

Work to Be Completed

Laying House

1. During the first week of April, we will cull the nonlayers from the new hens. We anticipate approximately 300 to be culled and marketed.
2. Experiments will be conducted to determine the best lighting.

Brooder House

The automatic feeding and watering system should arrive about the middle of April, and it will take about three days to install.

Processing Room

The processing room is complete.

Drying Yard

1. Marion Harris, Assistant Poultry Plant Supervisor, will visit the Poultry Experimental Stations at State University and Western University, April 14 and 15, to study the work at these stations in controlling flies and maggots in large manure drying yards. He will make recommendations on further environmental control of our drying yard. Until then, we will continue spraying every two weeks.
2. Invitations for bids to remove manure on a monthly basis will be announced April 27, 28, and 29. Bids will be opened at 2 p.m., May 10, in the poultry office.

FIGURE 15–2 Sample progress report

ACCIDENT REPORTS

Unlike periodic reports, the remaining three reports discussed in this chapter are written when special situations require them.

Accident reports are written when failures, breakdowns, accidents, or anything that interferes with normal work occurs. Such reports are important for two reasons. First, they are indispensable for persons who are reponsible for the performance and operation of personnel and machinery. Second, they are often required as legal documents for reporting injuries, deaths, and damage. Regulations of various state and federal agencies and state and federal law (worker's compensation law, for example) provide reporting guidelines that explain what accidents should be reported to what authorities, who is required to report, what reports are required, and the penalties for failure to report.

Regardless of what kind of accident is being reported, certain information must be reported objectively and specifically:

- What the accident is.
- When and where the accident occurred.
- Who was involved.
- If there was injury, what was done to provide medical treatment, where, and by whom.
- Who reported the accident, and when.
- What caused the accident.
- What has been done to correct the trouble.
- What recommendations or suggestions are given to prevent a recurrence of the accident.

Information required for accident reports has become so standardized that an accident report form can be designed to handle most routine situations. Figures 15–3 and 15–4 show two such forms. Figure 15–3 is to be filled out by hospital employees who are injured, so that the proper insurance claims can be filed on their behalf. Figure 15–4 is to be filled out by a physician or nurse when an accident happens to a patient in a hospital or nursing home.

If accident report forms are not available, or if the situation requires you to write the accident report from scratch, the following will be a suitable pattern to follow:

- Description of the accident. Get right to the point: Explain what happened, to whom, when, and where. Explain how you learned of the accident.
- Explanation of what was done to correct the situation. Explain how the injured were treated or cared for, how the damage was repaired, and how the troublesome situation was corrected.
- Discussion of the situation. Analyze what happened, trying to explain reasons for the accident.

ST. AGNES MEDICAL CENTER
Stillman, Kentucky

EMPLOYEE's FIRST REPORT OF INJURY

Hospital personnel who are injured while working must complete this form
and turn it in to the Personnel Office. This form is for the protection
of the employee, that he or she may report an injury and the proper
insurance claims can be filed for the employee's benefit.

Name of injured employee _____

Home address _____

Home phone number _____

Date of injury _____Time of injury_____a.m. or_____p.m.

Where were you when injured? _____
_____

Describe what you were doing when injured _____
_____
_____

What caused the injury? _____
_____

Describe your injury (e.g., cut on rt. index finger, etc.) _____
_____

Did you receive medical treatment? If so, where and by whom? _____
_____

Were X-rays taken or lab work done? _____

Were you paid in full for the day of injury? _____

Did you report this injury to your supervisor? _____E.R. nurse? _____

Date of report _____ Signed _____
                                                    Employee
NOTICE: If you are unable to work because of the injury on any day after
        the day of injury, you must contact the Personnel Director.

FIGURE 15–3 Injury report form

ST. AGNES MEDICAL CENTER

ACCIDENT OR INCIDENT REPORT

Name: last   first   middle   Age   Sex   Room No.   Adm. No.

Date of accident or incident_____ 19_____ Time_____ a.m.
                                                                         p.m.

Diagnosis_____

Name of attending physician_____ Name of nurse in charge_____

Was physician notified?_____ Time of notification_____ Notified by_____

Describe accident or incident _____

_____

_____

_____

_____

Was there apparent injury?_____ Was treatment rendered?_____

If yes, describe _____

_____

_____

Answer the following with "Yes," "No," or "N/A" (not applicable):
  BEFORE THE ACCIDENT:
Was patient in bed?_____ Was patient in chair?_____ Was floor
dry?_____ Was patient restrained?_____ Was call light on?_____
Were side rails up?_____ Was patient on sedatives?_____ Was patient
confused by nature of illness or condition?_____ Was patient post-op
under 24 hours?_____ Record any factors pertinent to cause or
environment of incident_____

_____

_____

Were corrective measures taken to prevent a further accident or incident
of this nature?_____

Describe_____

_____

Date report written_____ 19_____ Signed_____
                                                Physician or Nurse

FIGURE 15-4 Accident report form

- Recommendations. If called for, explain what corrective measures should be taken to prevent a recurrence of this particular accident.

TRIP REPORTS

Trip reports, often called travel reports, are records of business or work trips. They are primarily used to keep supervisors, managers, directors, and sometimes customers informed on the progress of projects, work done, or meetings attended out of town. Trip reports also share information with fellow workers on a project. This is especially helpful if the project is later transferred to another person or group.

Trip reports are written all the time, and the circumstances that call for them are endless. A large company with several branches or offices frequently sends employees from the home office to other branches to exchange information about projects with their counterparts. A company may send a technician to train customers to operate a system that has been sold to them. Or an employer may send an employee to a two-week school or to a convention.

The observations you make, the information you gather, and the work you do during a trip do not always fall into clear categories or are not always relevant to the purpose of the trip. Your job is to select only that information relevant to the trip and to organize it in some helpful way for the reader.

Trip reports don't usually follow any predesigned format. They may be in the form of a memo, a letter, or a formal report. However, certain features should be kept in mind when you write trip reports:

- Use headings to show your organization.
- Record accurately dates, times, places, and the names and titles of people you met.
- Emphasize what was covered during the trip that was relevant to its purpose.
- Include conclusions, recommendations, and evaluations, if appropriate.

As you'll see in the trip report in Figure 15–5, these features are arranged much in the order listed.

The example trip report (Figure 15–5) is a fairly common report required by instructors to get feedback about class trips. The information in the report is arranged under three headings: Purpose, Agenda, and Evaluation of Trip. The first section identifies the site of the visit, the purpose of the trip, and a brief summary of the visit (which even in this brief memo provides a handy overview of the visit). Notice how the subheads and paragraphing guide the reader through the report. The third section, which evaluates the trip, transmits two recommendations made by the writer as a result of the trip.

November 6, 1985

To: Professor Essie Payne
    Department of Corrections and Social Work

Reed Grant

From: Reed Grant
      Corrections Major—Junior

Subject: Visit to Bryson City Training Center,
         November 1, 1985

Purpose

    As a member of the SW 429 class, I visited the Bryson City Training
Center (BCTC) to learn how a typical juvenile correctional facility
operates. BCTC is one of six such facilities under the jurisdiction of
the State Division of Human Resources.

    The visit included a briefing by Dr. James Mitchell, Superintendent
of BCTC; a tour of the inmate dormitories; lunch with staff and inmates;
and a tour of classrooms and workshops.

Agenda

    9 a.m. to 10:30 a.m.: Dr. Mitchell gave us a brief history of the
establishment of juvenile correctional facilities in the state and the
history of BCTC. He also discussed the charges leading to inmates
incarceration at BCTC and described a typical inmate's stay at BCTC.

    10:30 a.m. to noon: Mr. Stan Fralex, a resident counselor at BCTC,
gave us a thorough tour of the dormitory area.

    Noon to 1:00 p.m.: Lunch in mess hall with staff and inmates.

    1:00 p.m. to 1:30 p.m.: Mr. James Morrow, BCTC Coordinator of
Education and Training, briefed us on BCTC's educational and training
programs, which consist of classes in English, arithmetic, mechanical
drawing, automotive maintenance, and woodworking. All inmates take
English and arithmetic and one of the vocational classes every day. A
new water pumping station and sewage disposal plant are planned for the
facility, and a course in water resources technology is to be added to
the curriculum.

    1:30 p.m. to 2:30 p.m.: Mr. Weaver led us on a tour of the
educational and training area. We visited classes in session.

    2:30 p.m. to 3:30 p.m.: Mr. Raymond Bissell, a BCTC Counselor,
explained how Positive Peer Culture was used as part of the
rehabilitation process at BCTC. All inmates are assigned to a group that
meets daily to work on the personal problems and conflicts of the
members of the group.

FIGURE 15–5 Sample trip report

2

Evaluation of Trip

I learned a lot from the visit. I had never witnessed peer group counseling sessions before, and I now understand how skillful the group counselor must be to allow the inmates to engage in the process and yet still maintain reasonable control of the group. I also was surprised that of the 212 inmates, most had been charged with larceny, burglary, auto theft, and other felonies. I had assumed that most of the inmates would have been jailed for violations of the juvenile code. Dr. Mitchell said that it was his opinion that juvenile courts were tending to regard juvenile code violations as "predelinquent behavior" and not incarcerating violators. He also said that he believed that only those guilty of "serious" misdemeanors such as possession of weapons, contempt of court, and vandalism, or of felonies were being incarcerated.

The BCTC staff was very courteous and helpful in explaining the way the facility operates. However, I would recommend that two additional items be added to the agenda of future trips.

1. An opportunity to visit privately with some of the inmates. The subject of inadequate recreation and sports programming came up during lunch, but most of the inmates were reluctant to say much about it since the staff members were present.

2. An opportunity to discuss more thoroughly the responsibilities of resident counselors at BCTC. Since I am considering serving my practicum at one of the juvenile correctional facilities, I believe such a discussion would help prepare me better for such service.

FIGURE 15-5 Sample trip report (cont.)

MINUTES

You will take part in many types of meetings. Occasionally you may be called on to serve as secretary to take the minutes of the meeting—the official record of action taken by the group. Although groups may set up their own rules for conducting meetings and recording their actions, most groups follow the suggestions in *Robert's Rules of Order*.

When you serve as secretary, you should sit near the chairperson. Most of the discussion and all official motions will be aimed toward the chair, making it easier for you to hear what you need to record. Record the meeting as well as you can. When the meeting is over, write out the minutes fully from your notes (conferring with the chairperson if you're not sure of a particular item of information), and give the minutes to the chairperson for distribution.

A fairly well-established format for minutes has developed, so your biggest concern will not be how to organize or lay out the minutes. What may prove bothersome, though, is determining the degree of detail required to make the minutes complete. But even here the solution is fairly simple. Remember that minutes are *the official record of action taken by the group during its meetings*. It is mainly a record of what was done, not what was said by the members. Sometimes, however, especially in the case of reports by group members or of debates on an important issue, you may be required to summarize what was said. What you record should be written down objectively and factually, without reflecting your opinions.

The minutes of a meeting should contain the following information, in the following order:

1. Name of the group holding the meeting.
2. Kind of meeting (regular, special, and so on).
3. Date (and place, if not always the same) of the meeting.
4. Subject of the meeting.
5. Names of persons attending, including the fact that the regular chairperson and secretary were present, or in their absence, the names of those persons who substituted for them.
6. Time the meeting was opened.
7. Whether the minutes of the previous meeting were read and approved (as read or as corrected).
8. Reports of members of the group.
9. Action of the group, with special attention to stating exactly what motions were made and their disposition (carried, defeated, tabled, and so on). It is conventional to include the names of persons making motions, seconding motions, or making amendments to motions. It is also conventional to explain the voting on a motion—how the vote was conducted and so on. If a roll call vote is conducted, the minutes should include a roster of members and how each voted. Going beyond this information may be recording too much. How-

G. G. WARREN AND ASSOCIATES—HOTELIERS

Minutes of Regular Meeting of the Committee on New Construction
May 19, 1985

SUBJECT: Review of Items of Work on The Flowers House,
Houston, Texas

ATTENDEES: Howard Dickinson, Chairman   Don Jones
           William Drummond,   Charles Meiners
           Willoughby Fulweiler   Wanda Smith
           Richard Hudson, Secretary

AGENDA:

1. The meeting was opened by the chairman at 1:15 p.m.

2. The minutes of the previous meeting were accepted as read.

3. Charles Meiners briefly summarized the status of work on The Flowers House project. The basic situation is as follows:
   A. The project is ahead of schedule.
   B. Cooperation has been excellent between the general contractor, his superintendent, and the major subcontractors.
   C. An adequate work force has been maintained. No appreciable delays or work stoppages have occurred.
   D. All items have been delivered on schedule. There are no anticipated delays. Some difficulty was encountered in obtaining shop drawings on the marble and granite facing material for the exterior of the building. But that problem has been resolved and the first phase of the material has been released for shipment.

4. Don Jones stated that he now believes the wood veneer to be applied to the drywall panels in the dining room is too thin. He said that the subcontractor told him that the specified wood veneer might buckle, because he had seen it happen before on other jobs. After some discussion, it was moved by Wanda Smith and seconded by William Drummond that Charles Meiners check with the subcontractor on changing the work order to include a heavier wood veneer if the cost were not more than $9 per panel. Motion carried.

5. Willoughby Fulweiler reported that an incandescent downlight over the head table area in the banquet room has been incorrectly connected to the circuit supplying the fluorescent lights in the area He said that the problem was not observed until this week, and therefore has not appeared on any previous work–change order. It was moved by Willoughby Fulweiler and seconded by Don Jones that Charles Meiners check with the electrical subcontractor to have the light corrected. Motion carried.

6. The chairman reported that all the documents needed to close the contract on The Flowers House, with the exception of the general contractor's statement concerning the full payment of accounts, are in the hands of the architect. After some discussion, it was moved by Wanda Smith and seconded by Richard Hudson that the chairman request the architect to attend the next meeting of the group to discuss the procedure for closing the contract. Motion carried. The chairman said he would notify the architect by telephone.

7. There being no other business, the chairman closed the meeting at 3:00. The next regular meeting is scheduled for May 26 at 1:15.

Richard Hudson

Richard Hudson, Secretary

FIGURE 15–6   Minutes of a meeting

ever, the group should decide how much detail the minutes should include.

10. Time of adjournment and the time and place of the next scheduled meeting.

11. Signature of the secretary (as well as the chairperson, if so desired).

Minutes of a meeting are shown in Figure 15–6.

SUGGESTIONS FOR APPLYING YOUR KNOWLEDGE

1. Collect samples of different types of periodic reports and study the format and types of information that have been categorized by headings. Design a periodic report form that would be suitable for reporting recurring kinds of information.

2. Write a progress report to your advisor showing your progress toward completing a degree or receiving a certificate or license.

3. If you are working on a project in a course, write a progress report to your team leader or instructor showing your progress.

4. Collect samples of different types of accident reports and study the format and types of information that have been categorized by headings. Design an all-purpose accident report form that would be suitable for reporting almost any kind of routine trouble an organization might have.

5. If you take a field trip in a course, write a trip report addressed to the teacher of the course.

6. Take complete notes on a class meeting and write a report explaining what was done during the class period.

7. If you belong to an organization that holds regular formal meetings, attend a meeting, take notes of the business conducted, and write a set of minutes. If you don't belong to such an organization, attend a meeting of an organization that holds such meetings, take notes of the business conducted, and write a set of minutes.

C H A P T E R

16

RECOMMENDATION REPORTS

A frequent task for people in the world of work is reporting and explaining recommendations and decisions. Such recommendations and decisions, usually growing out of a problem-solving situation, must be explained and justified. The resulting reports—for simplicity's sake, we'll label them all *recommendation reports*—present the results of exercises in practical logic. Before we get to the reports themselves, let's pause for a moment and talk about what we mean by practical logic.

PRACTICAL LOGIC

You may or may not have taken a course in formal logic, but you have been practicing practical logic and coming to decisions since you were a child. When you stood before a candy showcase weighing the merits of buying four licorice sticks for ten cents against buying five jawbreakers, also for ten cents, you were analyzing a problem. You were comparing and contrasting alternatives. You were doing a cost analysis—four for ten cents versus five for ten cents. You remembered the flavor of the two candies and realized that the licorice in your estimation was superior. You weighed quantity versus quality. You reached a series of conclusions:

- The jawbreakers were cheaper.
- Each piece of candy lasted ten minutes.
- The jawbreakers would give you fifty minutes of pleasure.
- The licorice would give you forty minutes of pleasure.

- However, the flavor of the licorice was superior.
- For you, forty minutes of superior pleasure were better than fifty minutes of inferior pleasure.
- Therefore, for you, the licorice sticks were a better buy.

If you proceeded to plunk down your dime for the licorice, you were backing your conclusions with a decision.

As you grew older, your analyses became bigger and more complicated. Perhaps you had to buy a bicycle. You considered cost, naturally. You also considered the comparative weights of bicycles. You compared ten-speed bikes against three-speed bikes. You made these comparisons not in an abstract way but by considering them against your own needs. If you were a serious biker who planned long trips through hilly country, a lighter, expensive ten-speed might be the answer. On the other hand, if you were an occasional bike rider who simply wanted to combine some exercise with transportation around the flat streets of town, you probably would have chosen a heavier, less expensive, three-speed bike.

In such analyses you were following the processes of induction and deduction that we describe for you on pages 24–35. You were drawing upon information that you already possessed or that was easily obtainable. Analyses you will conduct in the world of work are different in degree but not in kind. That is, the process will be more complex and involve more information but will still draw on essentially the same practical logic you have frequently used. We'll look at the process in more detail. With some variations, practical logic is likely to follow a course similar to this:

- Define the problem.
- Create solutions.
- Test the solutions.
- Choose a solution.

Defining the Problem

A problem can be considered as either a question or a situation. In the candy and bike examples, the problem is a question: Should I buy licorice sticks or jawbreakers? What sort of bike should I buy?

A situation that is a problem will always be a situation that deviates from the norm. For example, you're cruising smoothly down an interstate highway. Your car is performing in its normal manner. Suddenly, you hear a loud whooshing sound and see clouds of steam pouring out through the hood. You have a problem.

In defining the problem, the approach is approximately the same whether you are dealing with a question or a situation. In defining a problem, you have to both relate it to the environment that surrounds the problem and break it down into its components. You have to be clear-eyed about your objectives in solving the problem. Finally, you have to recognize any limitations placed on you in solving the problem. We'll illustrate these points by using a problem that a student, Scott Pahl, recently dealt with.[1]

Scott looked at a problem in our state department of transportation. In the last few years, the department's grass-mowing budget has been getting out of hand. In a recent year, mowing costs came to almost $4 million. What was to be done?

RELATING TO THE SURROUNDING ENVIRONMENT   Where does grass mowing fit into the total picture of the department's responsibilities? As big a chore as mowing the grass on the state's highways is, it's only one of many things done by the department. It's a small part of a budget that exceeds $600 million. Considerably more important to the state are the maintenance of existing highways and the construction of new ones. Although the citizens of the state expect the grassy areas near their roads to be neatly kept, they would not want money taken away from road building and maintenance to achieve this neatness. Solving the grass-mowing problem is important, but it is not a problem of crisis proportions.

In this manner, Scott looked at the grass-mowing problem in relation to the surrounding environment of the department's other tasks and problems. Any problem has to be seen in proper perspective before you begin seeking its solution. Consider again the loud whooshing sound coming from your automobile. If that occurred at 3:00 A.M. on a lonely country road, it would be a totally different problem than if it occurred at 3:00 P.M. at a spot 100 feet from a full-service gas station.

BREAKING THE PROBLEM DOWN   In defining your problem be very specific about its elements. What are its components? If you don't analyze your problem carefully at the beginning, you'll find yourself out of your depth when trying to find a solution. In analyzing your problem, you have to get beneath the surface problem, high costs in Scott's problem, and look for the causes of the surface problem. The solution almost certainly will attack these subproblems and not the surface problem as such. In breaking down your problem, you will often find the journalist's questions of *who, what, when, where, why,* and *how* to be valuable. Using these questions, Scott came up with such facts as these:

- *Mowing season:* 15 May to 1 October.
- *Total miles mowed:* 9,910 miles, broken down into metro areas, the interstate system, and the nonmetro state highways.
- *Number of mowings per season:* 10 in metro areas, 6 on interstates, 3 on state highways.
- *Cost:* $3,855,000 in 1983. Costs include wages, equipment operating and maintenance, equipment replacement, storage, workers' compensation, and insurance.
- *Associated problems:* The work is tedious and dangerous. Mowers tip over on steep slopes; motorists throw things at the mower operators. Every

year workers are seriously injured, and over the years several have been killed.

Scott found much more, but you get the idea. Look at all the possible causal factors in your problem. If there are related problems (for example, the danger to the mower operators), get them out into the open. As you examine these factors, write your findings down. The more you get on paper early, the better off you'll be later.

SETTING OBJECTIVES   Knowing your objectives is an important key to solving the problem. The solution to our bicycle problem rests on the objectives. The objective of cross-country travel calls for a different solution than the objective of riding a few miles to work each day. You have to be absolutely clear-eyed about what you want the outcome of the solution to be. You should have one major objective. You may have other objectives of lesser importance. State them all clearly, preferably in writing. Know the priority you set on each.

Scott's major objective was clear: Lower the cost of grass management on the state's highways. He had lesser objectives as well, including lowering the operators' accident rate and freeing the operators for other kinds of maintenance work.

KNOWING THE LIMITATIONS   Almost always there will be limitations you must observe in solving a problem. They will include such things as available funds and technology, people's attitudes, environmental problems, time, and so forth. One of the tests for any solution will be that it can be accomplished within the limitations.

The limitations in the grass-maintenance problem were these:

- Citizens expected grass bordering the highways to be maintained neatly.
- Any solution had to be ecologically safe.

Creating Solutions

Creating solutions and the next step, testing solutions, are understandably closely related. Given the speed with which the human mind makes connections, it's likely that most of us, at least some of the time, test a solution almost as quickly as we form it in our minds. However, we separate the steps here for two reasons. First, we want to suggest that if you make snap decisions about solutions, you may overlook the solution that would ultimately be best. Second, if you are seeking solutions in a group, you may do better if the group creates solutions without the pressure of immediately testing them. By doing so, group members can present solutions, even silly-sounding ones, without fear of someone immediately jumping on their ideas. It's not at all unusual for a solution that at first glimpse seems ridiculous to prove to be the best one.

Obviously, creating solutions calls for the problem solver to possess knowledge relevant to the problem. Someone with no knowledge of the appropriate subject matter is going to have difficulty in forming solutions. For example, in our simple bike problem, a problem solver who didn't know about the various kinds of bikes available would be in no position to frame an answer to the question, "What bike should I buy?" If you do not already have the needed knowledge from your education and experience, you have to seek it as part of the problem-solving process. As you'll see, it was Scott's knowledge as an agronomy student that enabled him to come up with the solution that he ultimately chose.

Wherever your knowledge comes from, begin creating solutions. Put down all your ideas, even the outlandish ones. Scott's possible solutions were these:

- Leave the situation as he found it.
- Stop mowing the grass.
- Mow the grass at less frequent intervals.
- Pave over some or all of the grassy areas.
- Stop the grass from growing.

When he was satisfied he had thought of all the possible solutions, Scott was ready to test them.

Testing Solutions

Solutions may be tested logically and empirically. To test a solution logically, you'll work with the objectives and limitations you have already stated. These objectives and limitations lead you to the criteria—the standards of judgment—you'll use to measure the effectiveness of the proposed solutions. In the bike example, let's consider the major objective to be buying a bike suitable for cross-country travel. Let's also assume a cost limitation of $500. Such an objective and limitation might lead to these criteria. The bike should

- be lightweight,
- have gearing suitable for long hills,
- have an effective braking system,
- be sturdy and easily maintained, and
- not cost more than $500.

Think your criteria through carefully. Without proper standards of comparison, you'll find yourself unable to test your solutions. You should also set priorities for your criteria. Which of the preceding criteria is the most important? It may well be the $500 limitation. If that is the case, no matter how lightweight a bike is and how effective its gearing system, if it costs more than $500 it will not be considered.

Once the criteria are set, testing the solution becomes fairly simple. You gather information on the relevant attributes of bikes in the below—

$500 range. You compare their weights, gearing systems, and so forth, much in the manner that Consumers Union compared the attributes of electric drills in the example in Chapter 2 on pages 28–31. The bike that best meets the criteria will emerge as the choice.

In Scott's grass-management problem, his objectives and limitations led him to several criteria. A proposed solution had to

- lower the cost of grass management,
- be aesthetically pleasing,
- be ecologically safe, and,
- if possible, lower the exposure of workers to danger and free them for other jobs.

His first priority was lowering the cost. However, no solution that did not also meet the other criteria could be seriously considered. Scott was then ready to examine his solutions by his criteria.

- Leaving the situation as it was, although it met all the lesser criteria, obviously did not lower the cost.
- Stopping the grass mowing lowered the cost but would not be aesthetically pleasing.
- Mowing the grass at less frequent intervals lowered the cost but also failed the aesthetic test.
- Paving all the grassy areas was too expensive to consider and would not be aesthetically pleasing.
- Stopping the grass from growing was possible. Scott was an agronomy student and knew of a product manufactured by the 3M Company, Embark,[2] that would retard grass growth. He examined this solution thoroughly and found that it passed all his criteria. It lowered costs. It left the grass in good enough condition to be aesthetically pleasing. It was ecologically safe. The necessary spraying took much less time than the mowing; therefore, workers would be less exposed to danger and would be free for other work.

Logically, Scott had his solution. He also considered empirical testing. By empirical testing, we mean the testing of a solution's effectiveness through either physical means or social scientific means such as polls or questionnaires. For example, if you read the directions that come with a carpet cleaning fluid, you'll find they tell you to test the fluid in some inconspicuous place. If the cleaner removes all the color from your carpet under the couch, you'll know not to use it on the rest of the carpet. That is the empirical physical test. If your solution might affect people, perhaps the workers in some section of a plant, a questionnaire polling their attitudes toward the change might be advisable. This would be the empirical social scientific test.

Scott knew that Embark had been empirically tested by 3M and had proven to be effective. That fact had entered into his logical testing. However, he was not prepared to recommend on the strength of 3M's testing that the state spray the grass along 9,910 miles of highway. Obviously, further large-scale testing was called for. Scott decided that his recommendation would be that the department conduct a major test of Embark on several hundred miles of state highway. Furthermore the testing should be in several spots in the state. Parts of the state are warmer and dryer than others, and cities have microclimates of their own different from the nearby suburbs and rural areas. If the testing proved successful, then the state could consider a grass-management program that included the use of Embark.

Scott had arrived at his recommendation. It was time for him to report it.

REPORTING THE SOLUTION

When you have followed a reasoning process similar to the one just described, most of your work lies behind you when it is time for you to write your report. You have your problem defined. You know what solutions you have seriously considered and the criteria you have used to compare them. You know what your conclusions are and what recommendations they lead to. Your task now is to plan the organization and format of your report and write it in a prose understandable to your readers.

A complete recommendation report may consist of all of the following:

Letter of transmittal

Title page

Table of Contents

List of Illustrations

Introduction

Body

Summary and Conclusions

Recommendations

List of References

Here we tell you only about the introduction, body, summary and conclusions, and recommendations. For the other parts we refer you to Chapter 9, "Basic Principles of Reports," where they are thoroughly discussed.

Introduction

In describing a typical introduction on pages 148–149, we tell you to explain your subject, purpose, scope, and plan to your readers. The introduction to a recommendation report follows this basic format. In a recommendation report, your subject is the problem you are working with. Your purpose is to present your solution and show how you have arrived at it. Your scope includes the definition of the problem, the solution or solutions you are considering, the evaluation of the solutions, your conclusions, and your recommendations. Your plan is how you plan to present your material. Scott's introduction demonstrates all the basic parts of a successful introduction.

Last year, the Department of Transportation spent almost $4 million, out of a total budget of slightly over $600 million, on mowing the grassy areas along the state's highways. This grass mowing is a major summertime chore for state highway crews. In the struggle to keep the many miles of highway medians, ditches, and embankments mowed, other important projects are delayed and limited budgets are depleted.

Under contract to the Department, I studied the problem. I considered four possible solutions:

- Leaving the situation as is

- Lowering the frequency of mowing or stopping it altogether

- Paving over the grass

- Retarding the growth of the grass

The major criteria used to evaluate the solutions were that the acceptable solution had to lower the cost of grass management, be aesthetically pleasing, and be ecologically safe. Lesser criteria were lowering the exposure of the workers to danger and freeing them for other jobs.

Only the solution of retarding the growth of the grass met all the criteria. Therefore, it is the only one considered in this report.

Immediately following this introduction, I present a summary of my data and major conclusions followed by my recommendations. Following my recommendations are three annexes in which I describe the problem fully, present a solution to it, and evaluate the solution.

We draw your attention to several things in this introduction. First of all, in it, Scott disposes of all his solutions but one. This is advisable only when one solution clearly stands out as the best. When the solutions are more balanced, you may have to carry over a consideration of the alternative solutions to the body. We say more about that in a moment. Second, Scott's plan reveals that he has chosen what is frequently called an *executive format* for his report. That is, he presents his summary, conclusions, and recommendations *before* he presents the body of his report. We discuss the rationale for doing so when we discuss the summary and conclusions.

Body

The body of your recommendation report should display your reasoning in complete enough detail to allow your readers to judge for themselves if your analysis has been adequate. You should in your report, as in your reasoning, describe the problem, present your solutions or solutions, and evaluate them. With only one solution your organization might look like this:

- Definition of problem
- Presentation of solution
- Evaluation of solution by criteria

If the problem can be simply defined, that task may sometimes be done in the introduction. In that case, the body would consist of only the last two items on the list.

When you have two or more solutions to evaluate, your organization will be slightly more complicated:

- Definition of problem
- Presentation of solutions
- Evaluation of solutions
    - Criterion A
        - Explanation of criterion A
        - Evaluation of solutions 1 and 2
    - Criterion B
        - Explanation of criterion B
        - Evaluation of solutions 1 and 2
    - (And so forth)

You can also organize the evaluation of solutions by solution rather than by criteria, in this manner:

- Definition of problem
- Explanation of criteria
- Solution 1
    - Presentation of solution 1
    - Evaluation by criteria

- Solution 2
    Presentation of solution 2
    Evaluation by criteria

We find that most people can demonstrate the differences among their solutions more sharply when they organize by criteria. No matter which plan you choose, be sure both criteria and solutions are carefully explained before you begin your evaluation. Scott's table of contents, reproduced in Figure 16–1, illustrates how he used the general plans we have shown you for his purposes.

In defining his problem, Scott discusses the existing mowing program, its costs, and its associated problems. Here is Scott's description of the mowing program:

> The state normally starts its mowing season May 15, about one month after the grass begins to green up, and ends it on October 1. The state's mowing responsibilities can be divided into three major groups of roads: the metro area roads, the nonmetro interstate highways, and the nonmetro trunk highways. The crews attempt to mow the metro highways every two weeks. Some metro areas will be mowed ten times during a season. The areas along the nonmetro interstates are mowed, on the average, six times per season. The nonmetro trunk highways receive three mowings per season.

In presenting his solution, Scott begins with a clearly stated overview of his solution in the grass-management problem:

> Embark, a plant-growth regulator, developed and released by the 3M Company, shows a good deal of promise in the area of chemically assisted turf grass management. Embark works by suppressing cool-season grasses' vegetative and reproductive development. The plants remain a healthy, normal green color. With proper application, grass growth can be suppressed for up to eight weeks, eliminating the need to mow.

The overview allows the readers to grasp the solution in its entirety before they are hit with the details. It's a good technique. Scott follows the overview with technical descriptions of Embark's chemistry and mode of action. He concludes by describing how Embark would be applied.

You must be careful in describing your solution not to provide too much detail. Executives, who are the usual readers of recommendation

TABLE OF CONTENTS

FIGURE 16–1   Table of contents

reports, are not likely to want the same detail that someone carrying out the solution would need. In other words, executives would not want a full set of instructions. On the other hand, executives do need enough detail to understand how the solution will work. It's a fine balance you must maintain. Also, be careful to use language that your readers can understand. Define any technical terms you must use and that your readers are not likely to know. Here is how Scott explained the application of Embark:

> The product should be applied after the grass greens up and is actively growing but before the seedheads start to emerge. This normally occurs in late April. Applied in this manner, applications of Embark will give vegetative and reproductive growth suppression for up to eight weeks.
>
> In situations where full-season grass suppression is needed, Embark may be applied more than once per season. To avoid plant injury, there should be a six-week wait between applications.

As you will see when we discuss the summary and conclusions section, Scott is including material that will be useful in supporting his conclusions.

In evaluating his solution, Scott applies his criteria of cost, aesthetics, ecological safety, and solution of associated problems. Here is part of his evaluation of the ecological safety of Embark:

> Embark is a safe compound. It is nonirritating to either whole or abraded skin and only slightly irritating to eyes. Its toxicity to fish and birds is quite low. However, it should not be sprayed on lakes or streams, and animals should not be allowed to graze on treated areas. As with any chemical, care should be taken to avoid prolonged or unnecessary contact with Embark.
>
> Melfluidide, the chief component of Embark, is unstable in the soil, with a half-life of only two days. It is rapidly broken down by soil microbes. Therefore, it will not build up in the soil or cause serious problems for birds or other wildlife.

In evaluating your solution, you are making a scientific argument (see pages 23–35). You do not need to show your reasoning in every detail, but you must show enough so that the readers can judge the validity of your argument. Also, if there are any risks involved in your solution, you should draw them to your readers' attention. They will need to weigh them in their decisions. Scott, for example, pointed out that, despite Embark's safety, animals should not graze on grass treated with it. Also be careful to point out *so-whats* to your readers, as Scott has done in his statement, "Therefore, it will not build up in the soil or cause serious problems for birds or other wildlife."

Summary and Conclusions

The summary and conclusions section often may be the only part of the report many readers read. Therefore, it must be well done. Also, most of the time, executive readers will find the summary and conclusions and read them before they read anything else in the report. When read in this sequence, the summary and conclusions become the overview of the report that helps readers to understand the report. Furthermore, this section helps the readers to select those parts of the report they may wish to read more thoroughly.

For example, an executive reader might be satisfied with Scott's summary statements concerning ecological safety. Consequently, she may not bother to read the body section, where greater detail about ecological safety can be found. On the other hand, she may doubt Scott's cost figures and choose to read the body section on cost with great care. For these reasons, in many modern reports, summaries, conclusions, and recommendations immediately follow the introduction. The feeling is that as long as the executives read them early, these parts might as well be up front where they are easily found. Scott's Table of Contents, reproduced in Figure 16–1, shows that is the format he chose. Generally, when the body parts are removed from the center of the report, they become known as *annexes*. Again, Scott's Table of Contents reflects that change.

To write a good summary, you must read through your body (or annexes), selecting those key facts that have led you to your conclusions. Generally, such key facts will be surrounded by supporting details. To summarize, you leave out the details and report only the key facts. Furthermore, you are not merely piling up facts in a random way. Rather, you are placing facts together in a context that allows you, through induction and deduction, to demonstrate how you reached your conclusions. Figure 16–2 illustrates the sequence that leads you from facts through conclusions to recommendations. We can illustrate these principles by comparing the material in several sections of Scott's annexes with his use of the same material in his Summary and Conclusions.

In his evaluation, Scott showed some of his cost calculations:

The per-gallon cost of Embark is $79.00. At the recommended

application rate of 1½ pints per acre, the chemical costs per acre

would be $14.80. To this must be added the average application cost

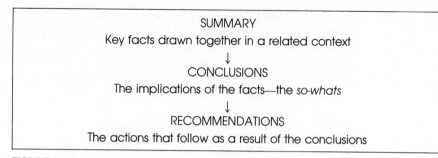

FIGURE 16–2 Logic sequence

of $5.00 per acre, for a total cost per acre of $19.80. By comparison,

mowing costs, on average, are $13.00 per acre for each mowing.

One mowing costs less than one application, but two mowings at a

total cost of $26.00 exceed the cost of the application by $6.20.

Earlier in his annexes, while describing the state's grass-mowing program, Scott described the different number of mowings used in the state, depending on the type and location of the highway (see page 346. In his annex section on the solution, Scott, in discussing the application of Embark, said that one application would retard grass growth for up to eight weeks (see page 346). Now, read through Scott's Summary and Conclusions and see how these key facts and others are condensed and properly related to one another, allowing Scott to reach his conclusions and state them in a convincing way.

SUMMARY AND CONCLUSIONS

The state's current highway grass-management program is costly

at $3,855,000 a year. It is also dangerous. Every year workers

mowing grass are injured, and fatalities have occurred. A possible

solution to this problem of high costs and injuries is the use of

Embark, a plant-growth regulator manufactured by the 3M

Company. A single application of Embark retards the growth of

grass for up to eight weeks. Although its growth is retarded, the

grass retains its natural healthy green color. Embark is ecologically

safe. It is noncorrosive to machinery and, if used properly, nontoxic

to human beings and wildlife. However, the manufacturer does

recommend that animals not be allowed to graze on grass sprayed

with Embark. Embark breaks down quickly in the soil, having a half-life of only two days. Because Embark is rapidly broken down by soil microbes, it will not build up in the soil and cause serious problems for wildlife.

A comparison of the costs involved in mowing and in applying Embark shows that a grass-management program using Embark can be worked out that will lower costs. Currently, the mowing season runs from May 15 to October 1. During that time, the metro roadways are mowed, on average, 10 times, nonmetro interstates 6 times, and nonmetro trunk highways 3 times. Each mowing costs, on average, $13.00 per acre. The comparable cost for each Embark application is $19.80 per acre. The break-even point in cost for using Embark thus comes between the first and second mowing. Given the 8-week period of retardation following each Embark application, two applications—one before the spring grass-growing season and one before the late-summer grass-growing season— would be cost effective on the metro and interstate areas. For the trunk highway areas, a single Embark application in early spring coupled with a fall mowing would be the most cost effective. Because the combined number of mowings and applications under the Embark program would be considerably lower than under the current all-mowing program, the workers' exposure to danger would be greatly reduced, and they would be free for other maintenance work.

3M Company's testing of Embark has been thorough, but it would seem prudent for the Department to run a series of tests of its own before launching a statewide program. Climatic conditions vary throughout the state. Also, metro areas have microclimates different from surrounding areas. Therefore, any testing should include both metro and nonmetro areas and enough locations in the state to test Embark's performance under the state's various climatic conditions.

Notice that Scott's final conclusions form a bridge to the recommendations that follow. In fact, your conclusions should always be written so that the recommendations can be anticipated by the reader. The recommendation section of a report is no place for surprises.

Recommendations

Recommendations are action steps. The recommendation section is the place in your report where you tell the readers what they *ought* to do. (If you're writing a decision report rather than a recommendation report, this is the place where you tell your readers what *is* going to be done.) The recommendation section should be short. Your reasoning has been displayed elsewhere in the body and in the summary and conclusions. You need not repeat any of it in the recommendations. Confine yourself to action statements.

The first recommendation should always answer the key question of the problem. What is the solution to the problem, the answer to the chief question asked? Later recommendations, if any, will supplement the first recommendation and show how it should be implemented. In our bicycle example, the first and only recommendation might be simply "Buy Brand-X bicycle." In Scott's report, the recommendation section is necessarily more complex, but the principles stated here are well demonstrated.

RECOMMENDATIONS

1. The Department of Transportation should begin a statewide test on the state's highways of the effectiveness of 3M's Embark in grass management.

2. The testing should be conducted in both metro and nonmetro areas. Enough testing areas should be chosen to reflect the varied climatic conditions in the state.

3. The test grass-management program should be as follows:

   a. Apply Embark twice per season, spring and late summer, on interstate and metro right-of-ways.

   b. Apply Embark once in the spring on nonmetro trunk highway right-of-ways, and follow with a late-summer mowing.

When the recommendations are stated, your report is done. You have studied your problem, found a solution for it, and reported your reasoning and your solution.

SUGGESTIONS FOR APPLYING YOUR KNOWLEDGE

Are there problems in your school or community? Almost certainly there are. A glance at a local paper will reveal community problems ranging from potholes in the streets to child abuse. Most schools perennially have problems such as inefficient use of energy, poor food service, and long lines at registration time. You may already be at work and be aware of job-related problems. Perhaps your office is trying to decide what brand of word processor to buy.

Choose such a problem. Be sure to choose one that suits your interests and knowledge. After a preliminary study of the problem, propose to your instructor that you do a recommendation report presenting a solution. (See pages 369–371 for advice on how to make such a proposal.)

When you and your instructor agree on the project, analyze your problem by using the logical method described in this chapter:

- Define the problem
- Create solutions
- Test the solutions
- Choose a solution

When your analysis is complete, report the results in a recommendation report.

C H A P T E R

17

PROPOSALS

One excellent essay on the proposal defines it this way:

> A proposal is simply a formalized proposition. Written out in rather elaborate detail, the proposal merely says, in effect, "Here's what we will do for you at this time for this price." In this sense it is no different from the proposition of the horse trader who says, "I'll tell you what I'll do: I'll throw in the saddle and the bridle with the horse, just to make a deal today."[1]

Proposals are made for many purposes and come in many sizes and formats. An insulation contractor, for example, called in to examine an old house, may make a proposal to the house's owner. He may outline the quantity and type of insulation needed and describe how the job will be done. He'll estimate how soon the job can be done and set a price for it. If he's a good salesperson, he may give the names and phone numbers of satisfied customers. He may give an incentive for quick action: "For the rest of August, we can give you our summer discount of 10 percent. In September our prices go back up." The whole proposal, or bid, as it may be called in this instance, may be contained on one page. At the other end of the scale, an aircraft manufacturer, proposing to build a new airplane for a large airline, may submit a proposal that fills several books. The aircraft proposal will contain information on plans, facilities, schedules, costs, key engineering and management personnel, and much more.

The specific information contained in a proposal is the work you or your organization want to do for someone, including details about the need for the work, methodology, schedule, price, and personnel. The specific audience is made up of the people you are trying to convince to have the work done. Your purpose is to get your audience to select and pay you to do the proposed work.

The proposal is a persuasive document. Achieving credibility will help you as much in a proposal as it does in a sales letter. Observe the you-attitude. How will your proposal benefit the people footing the bill? Clearly state your *so-whats* in a proposal. Usually, the major *so-what* is the relevance of your work in solving some problem of concern to the organization to which you are making the proposal. (See Chapter 16, pages 337–343.)

Proposals fall into two general categories—solicited and unsolicited. A solicited proposal is an answer to a request for a proposal. The RFP, as it is called, is usually made by some branch of government or a large company. An unsolicited proposal is made on the initiative of the proposer. We look at both types and also at a useful classroom project, the proposal for a paper.

SOLICITED PROPOSALS

A request for a solicited proposal will state carefully what goods or services are wanted. It will specify how the proposal should be organized. You can learn a good deal about how to organize and write a proposal by looking at such requests. To that end, we reproduce in part, and slightly modified, a National Science Foundation (NSF) solicitation that requests proposals for student-originated studies. Most of the information found in proposals of any size at all is requested in this NSF solicitation—information on cost, people, facilities, and schedule. NSF wants to know precisely what will be done and why, and it is particularly interested in the value and significance (the *so-whats*) of what is to be done.

STUDENT-ORIGINATED STUDIES

GUIDE FOR PREPARATION OF PROPOSALS

1. INTRODUCTION In conducting a competitive program for the support of student-originated studies, the National Science Foundation is pursuing three closely related goals:

(1) to provide talented students with science learning opportunities above and beyond those normally available in most science education programs in the Nation's universities and colleges.

(2) to increase the variety of instructional modes and of institutional patterns of instruction by demonstrating to both students and faculties the capacity of students to be motivated by independence and thus to accept greater responsibility for planning and carrying out their own learning activities, and

(3) to encourage college students to express in productive ways their concern for the well-being of our Nation by applying their scientific and

technological expertise to the study of significant societal problems.

To request Foundation support through Student-Originated Studies, student groups will submit proposals that describe the scientific or technological studies they wish to carry out and that give details as to the funds required for that purpose. In almost every academic institution there are faculty members who are familiar with this "proposal process" who can provide information to interested students. There are also officials in the institution's business office who are experienced in estimating the cost of projects. Although the competition requires that proposals be developed by students, the Foundation recognizes their need for faculty and business office advice, and has no objection to applicants' obtaining this sort of assistance.

Guidelines for the Student-Originated Studies Program are being kept as brief and straightforward as possible to encourage diversity and flexibility in the supported projects—within the general framework outlined below:

- Each project proposed is to be problem-oriented—to deal with a local problem (or set of associated problems) that has immediate relevance to society, and that poses yet-unanswered questions of a scientific or technological nature on which the student group can collect meaningful data. Ideally, a prospective user's needs become a relevant consideration in the design and conduct of the project.

- The approach to understanding the problem(s) and the search for solutions are to be *interdisciplinary* or *multidisciplinary* in nature, hence,

- Each proposed study or set of studies is to be conducted by a group of students (a minimum of 5 students, but usually not more than 12)—primarily made up of undergraduates, although some graduate students may be included within each group.

- Projects proposed are to be *student*-originated, *student*-planned, and *student*-directed, and are to be carried out under the leadership of one of the students in the group (hereinafter referred to as the *Student Project Director*).

- In discharging his duties, the Student Project Director may be assisted by a Steering Committee chosen from and by the group of participants. The extent to which each group seeks consultation with one or more college faculty members or members of the community at large is a matter for decision by the students, but it is required that there be associated with each grant a specifically-named *Project Advisor* who is a member of the science faculty of the host institution.

- Projects are to be planned to occupy fully the time of the student investigators (predominantly undergraduates) for an uninterrupted period of 10 to 12 weeks. This means that most projects will be conducted during the summer, although projects may be conducted at other times in institutions with schedules that provide 10 to 12 uninterrupted weeks for individual work or independent study during the academic year.

When you answer a solicited proposal, pay careful attention to the guidelines. For instance, in this case there would be no use in submitting a proposal for study by a single student. The request specifies a study to be made by a group of from five to about twelve students. Nor would you want to ignore the advice that the project is to last "for an uninterrupted period of 10 to 12 weeks."

The NSF solicitation also lays out with care the content of the proposal and how it should be organized:

CONTENT OF PROPOSAL

A proposal consists of the following items arranged in the order given: (A) Cover Sheet, (B) Summary Budget Page, (C) Budget Explanations, (D) Abstract, (E) Narrative, (F) Appendices.

(A) Summary Cover Sheet—prepared in strict accordance with the sample on page 15.

(B) Summary Budget Page—see format, page 16.

(C) Budget Explanations—This section must provide a brief but convincing justification for all direct costs listed on the Budget Summary Page (except participant stipends). Items should appear in the same order as entries in the Budget Summary, with corresponding numbering. In drawing up the budget, only essential costs should be included.

(D) Abstract—a not more than one-page summary of the problem(s) to be investigated and the proposed experimental approach(es) or study plan(s).

(E) Narrative—the following points should be addressed in the order indicated: (Although there is no limit on number of pages, proposers should remember that a concisely written document will present a stronger case for support than one distinguished primarily by its wordiness.)

(1) A one-paragraph description of the host institution and its science program, including local experience in project-type studies, if any.
(2) A brief description of the institution's surroundings (natural and social), if these are relevant to the proposed problem(s).
(3) A description of the problem or group of problems, and of the methodologies to be employed in the study. The several coordinated disciplinary approaches that are to be applied must be outlined in all proposals. Provide any maps or other aids needed by reviewers seeking to understand the project plan. This analysis of the problem and the detailed discussion of the students' plan for attacking it form the core of the proposal. It is here that a merely "good idea" is fleshed out into a competent strategy. *Sufficient detail must be provided* to enable reviewers to reach an affirmative finding as to the adequacy and scientific merit of the proposed study.

COMMENTARY
The NSF guidelines for content and organization are fairly standard. See Figure 17–1.

See Figure 17–2. Budget information is high in importance. What will the proposal cost, and what will the money be spent for?

Abstracts are needed in all but the shortest proposals. Proposals are often read by busy executives who want to get the big picture early.

In describing the work to be done, the proposal writer has to strike a nice balance that provides enough detail without being wordy.

Notice the call for any graphics that may be needed.
The sales skill required in writing good proposals is pointed up by NSF's call for "evidence that the project's findings hold promise for utilization by civic, governmental or industrial entities responsible for planning and/or decision-making in matters related to the

COVER SHEET

1. Program: STUDENT-ORIGINATED STUDIES

2. Descriptive Title of Study: _____
   (Maximum: 12 words)

   _____

3. Host Institution: _____

   Address: City _____ State _____ Zip Code _____

   Grant to: _____
                        (Full official name of institution to which grant should be made)

4. A. _____ _____ _____
      Student Project Director's name   Social Security No.   Department

   Telephone: _____ _____
                    Summer Office Number   Number where you may be reached during current academic year

   B. _____ _____ _____
         Faculty Advisor's Name   Social Security Number   Department

   Telephone: _____ _____ _____ _____
              Area Code   Office Number   Department Number   Home Number

5. A. Major Disciplinary Code: IN

   B. Field of Science and Engineering: 9900000, OTHER NEC

   C. Field(s) of Interest and Application*: _____

   D. Type of Project: NEW

6. Period of Full-time Participation: _____ 197 ____ to _____ 197 ___
                                              Starting Date   Ending Date

7. Does the host institution intend to grant academic credit in appropriate amounts and levels for work
   on this project?
                    (   ) Yes   (   ) No

8. Participants and Cost of Proposed Project:

              FULL TIME
   No. of Weeks   No. of Participants   Amt. Requested

   _____   _____ $ _____
                          (Budget Item 32)

9. Signatures:

   _____   _____
   Signature of proposed Student Project Director   Signature of authorizing official

   _____   _____
   Signature of proposed Project Advisor   Typed name and title of official authorized to sign
                                                                for institution

10. Date of Submission: _____

   _____
   *List 1 to 3 codes with their abbreviations, in descending order of importance. See pages 13, 14.

   15

FIGURE 17–1   Summary cover sheet

SUMMARY BUDGET PAGE

Institution:_____

_____

Project Director:_____

_____

NUMBER OF PARTICIPANTS	
Full Time	Acad. Year
19____	
19____	
19____	

A. PARTICIPANT SUPPORT

_____ Participants for_____weeks @ $_____/wk.
(Minimum 10 weeks; Maximum 12 weeks); (Maximum $90/wk.)

10. Total Participant Support . . . .

B. OPERATING COST
Salaries and Wages
12. Staff* *(Faculty Advice)* . . . .
13. Assistants and Technical Personnel* (No._____) . . . . .
15. Secretarial and Clerical* . . . .
16.   TOTAL SALARIES AND WAGES (12, 13 & 15) . . . . . .
17. Staff Benefits *(When charged as direct costs)* . . . .
18.   TOTAL SALARIES, WAGES AND STAFF
          BENEFITS (16 & 17) . . . .
20. Staff *(Faculty Advisor's)* Travel* . . . .
21. Field Expenses* . . . .
22. Laboratory and Field Materials* *(Consumables)* . . . .
23. Office Supplies, Communications, Publicity* . . . .
24. Fees† . . . .
25. Insurance, Health Services & Activities Fees* . . . .
26. Permanent Equipment* *(Note Restrictions)* . . . .
27. Publication Costs and/or Miscellaneous Expenses* . . . .
28.   TOTAL DIRECT OPERATING COSTS
          (18 thru 27) . . . .
29.   INDIRECT COSTS_____% . . . .

30.   TOTAL OPERATING COSTS (28 & 29) . . . .

C. TOTALS
31. Total Budget *(Participant Support (10) + Total Operating*
Costs (30)) . . . .
32.   TOTAL REQUESTED FROM NSF
          (Round to nearest $50) . . . .

_____
* *Itemize in "Budget Explanations", with adequate justifications.*
† *Justify in "Budget Explanations". Other operating costs (lines 12–29) must be reduced to fully offset this item.*

FIGURE 17–2 Summary budget page

project," NSF's *so-what.* In writing a proposal, keep your eye on what your work will do for the people paying the bills. Try to find and show something unique about the goals or service you can provide—something that your competition can't duplicate.

In many proposals you are really selling the services of people. Therefore, it's important to provide details about previous education and relevant experience. (The term *curriculum vitae* used here refers to such significant biographical data.) Buyers of services are often willing to pay more for people they feel sure they can trust to do a job properly and on time.

Time and work schedules are important. They show that you know where you're going and how you intend to get there.

More personnel information.

Facilities are important. If you can't prove that you have the facilities and equipment to do the project, your proposal is not likely to be accepted. See Figure 17–3.

Detailed information about personnel, facilities, and other aspects of the proposal is often presented in an appendix. Note, too, the possibility of including testimonials, again a good selling

(4) Evidence that the project's findings hold promise for utilization by civic, governmental or industrial entities responsible for planning and/or decision-making in matters related to the project. This evidence should be as specific as possible, naming persons and organizations contacted, quoting or attaching to the Appendix (see F below) their expressions of interest and the like.

(5) A description of the student group that organized the group submitting the proposal and how this was accomplished. (Was it, for example, a science club, an individual, an informal group of concerned students, or who?); how the topic or topics were selected:

—the number of participants for whom support is being requested (with any special justification required);

—who has already been selected to participate in the project (a brief curriculum vitae for each principal participant should be included in the Appendix, emphasizing any previous experience in research or project-oriented studies);

—the disciplinary distribution and balancing of skills to be sought in filling remaining vacancies on the SOS team, by what criteria the remaining participants will be chosen, methods for recruiting participants from other institutions if this is to be done (or if not, the factors that decided the group against it); the function of the student Steering Committee or reason for not having such a committee;

—any other details that will assist reviewers to understand the personnel aspects of the project. (Curricula vitae should appear in the Appendix.)

(6) Pre-summer preparation of individuals and coordination of their efforts prior to formal initiation of the study.

(7) A time schedule for the project in outline form, sufficient to convince reviewers that realistic consideration has been given to the amount of work contemplated relative to available time and manpower.

(8) The Project Advisor—name; description of the process by which he was nominated by the students; statement of institution's confirmation of the nomination; curriculum vitae showing highlights of his academic training, scholarly productivity, and other qualifications for advising the group.

(9) A description of the institutional facilities (including the library) and equipment, specifically identifying what is to be available for use in the SOS project, and its adequacy for the project's needs.

(F) Appendix—

(1) Curricula vitae of Student Project Director and other principal participants already selected, following the format set forth on page 17.

(2) Supportive statements or materials that bear on the expected quality of the proposed project. This evidence should be as specific as possible. Testimonials are useful only if written by local authorities who possess detailed factual information concerning the problem and current efforts to deal with it. Broad, general statements of support from officials remote from the problem or policy issue under investigation are of little value.

(3) Bibliography of sources consulted in background research during preparation of the proposal. The inclusion of key references here will

CURRICULUM VITAE FORMAT FOR
STUDENT PROJECT DIRECTORS AND PARTICIPANTS

Name: _____
             (Last)   (First)   (Middle)

Present Institution: _____

Other Institutions Attended: _____

Major Field(s): _____ Minor(s): _____

Class: _____

Courses already completed which are relevant to proposed project (Faculty advisor will please submit in confidence grades for students in those institutions where policy prohibits their being shown to students.):

Course Title	Grade	Course Title	Grade

Additional relevant courses to be completed before project begins:

Previous experience in research or project-oriented studies:

Skills, hobbies, interests pertinent to the proposed study:

Please note briefly why you wish to participate in the projected studies:

FIGURE 17–3 Curriculum vitae format

technique.
In many instances a bibliography can be a good way of showing that you have done your homework. (See pages 234–242.)

assure reviewers as to the thoroughness of the group's preliminary study.

Remember that the proposal is a sales document. Emphasize the value and quality of your own products and services. Point out the unique advantages offered by the experience and education of your people. If possible, provide testimonials covering your previous work. Use scientific argument and problem-solving techniques in a proposal. (See Chapter 16 and pages 23–35.) Present your facts and the implications of those facts in a thorough and attractive manner.

When preparing a solicited proposal, take care to follow the required organization precisely—even if you don't like it. The requesters will be looking for information in the places where they have specified they want it. When preparing an unsolicited proposal, you can devise your own organization.

UNSOLICITED PROPOSALS

Unsolicited proposals are very much like solicited ones. Essentially the same information is required, with one major difference. In a solicited proposal the solicitors recognize a need. Therefore, you don't have to sell them on the need, only on your ability to understand and interpret the need and to meet it. In an unsolicited proposal you must first convince the audience that the need exists. If you can't, they will have no particular interest in your goods or services.

For example, a roofing contractor called in by a homeowner to bid on reshingling a roof does not have to establish the need for the job. But an enterprising contractor who sees a roof in need of repair may have to convince the owner that reshingling is really necessary. Often establishing a need calls for a problem-solving organization. The problem establishes the need. Your goods or services supply the solution.

A small, simple, unsolicited proposal might fall into six parts:

1. *Summary*—provides a concise statement of the proposal.
2. *Introduction*—establishes need.
3. *Overview section*—defines the process to be followed or describes the goods to be furnished, or both.
4. *Work and management plan*—outlines the tasks to be done and schedules their accomplishment.
5. *Detailed budget*—gives precise information on costs.
6. *Personnel section*—briefly gives the relevant qualifications of the people involved.

Very often, short proposals are drafted in the form of a letter or memorandum. Even so, headings and applicable graphics should be used—particularly easy-to-read informal lists and tables.

The proposal in Figure 17–4, modeled after an actual successful proposal, follows the six steps just outlined. Take time to read it now. The bracketed letters in the model proposal refer to the following comments.

A. *Project Summary.* The proposal is set up in a memorandum format commonly used for short proposals. It includes, as do most proposals, a summary of the proposal. Executives like to have a concise statement of a proposal before they study it in detail. You will impress them favorably if you compress the major points of your proposal into a short summary.

B. *Introduction.* The beginning of the introduction defines the subject, peer advising, and points out its successful use elsewhere. The survey presented shows that early and careful planning has taken place. The results of the survey do not show that an outright problem of student dissatisfaction exists. But they do show that students might feel more comfortable with another approach. The survey results also set to rest the thought that the faculty might object. The statement about more faculty time and possible innovative advising techniques presents significant *so-whats*.

C. *Methodology.* The methodology section outlines the strategy and some of the timing of the operational experiment. Again it shows that a good deal of thought has gone into the proposal. The final paragraph again suggests that the money spent for the proposal may result in a new and more desirable advising procedure than currently exists. Such a development is likely to please the Center for Educational Development, an organization charged with developing innovative methods to improve the college's educational process.

D. *Facilities.* Facilities have to be explained somewhere. In a simple report like this one, the work and management plan is a good location. If facilities are extensive, they would rate a section of their own.

E. *Task Breakdown.* The tasks to be accomplished are presented in a chronological sequence. A simple graph shows the time relationship of the tasks.

F. *Management.* Proper management is always a concern. People want to know that the spending of their money will be overseen by experienced, responsible managers.

G. *Detailed Budget.* The budget is presented in a simple table form. Don't overlook any possible expenses. Figure 17–2 provides a good checklist. If appropriate, specify the time and method of payment. Tell how the money will be accounted for.

H. *Personnel.* In a simple proposal, a short narrative biography that gives relevant education and experience is usually enough. But use your sales skills here. The facts chosen for the student's biography emphasize his maturity and experience. The two courses listed establish an interest in counseling that is a real selling point for the project. The information

Battle Creek College

Kellogg, Michigan 48108

DEPARTMENT OF CRIMINAL JUSTICE STUDIES

10 December 1984

TO: Janice H. Grumbacher, Director
           Center for Educational Development
           317 Clark Library
           Battle Creek College
           Kellogg, MI 48108

FROM: Martin A. Doyle, Student, Criminal Justice Studies

SUBJECT: Request to Center for Educational Development for funding a
           Peer Advising Program for Criminal Justice Studies Students.

PROJECT SUMMARY **[A]**

A survey shows that students and faculty in Criminal Justice
Studies (CJS) favor the concept of peer advising. Peer advising is
being successfully used in other colleges in the United States. This
proposal requests $2,718.00 to set up an operational experiment in peer
advising in CJS. The experiment would run for 13 months from May 1985
through May 1986. The experiment will be monitored by senior CJS
faculty. Evaluative reports will be written and disseminated at the end
of the experiment.

INTRODUCTION **[B]**

A new development in many two- and four-year colleges is the
successful use of students for advising their fellow students regarding
course registration, program development, and job opportunities. Called
peer advising, this new development supplements but does not replace
normal faculty advising.

In the fall of this year, I surveyed the faculty and students of
the Department of Criminal Justice Studies (CJS) regarding their
opinions about peer advising. A complete copy of the survey results,
"Response to Peer Advising in the Department of Criminal Justice
Studies," is available from me upon request. But the results can be
summarized briefly:

    -Rightly or wrongly, many students feel they are imposing upon
     their advisers' time by seeking assistance. Some students view
     their advisers as having more important matters to contend with.

    -Students feel that peer advisers will be better able to relate to
     the problems of their fellow students.

FIGURE 17–4   Model proposal

Janice H. Grumbacher   2   10 December 1984

　　　　—Students stated frequently that they would feel freer and more
　　　　comfortable in bringing their problems to peer advisers.

　　　　—Faculty acceptance of peer advising was high. Most felt it would
　　　　be a welcome addition for both faculty and students.

　　The study showed such strong support for peer advising among
faculty and students that such a program seems to have a good potential
for success. If successful, peer advising will remove a significant
burden from the CJS faculty, freeing them for additional time to pursue
their teaching and professional development. The experiment may lead to
similar innovative advising techniques in other departments of the
college.

　　In the remainder of this proposal, I'll present a methodology for
establishing the program, a work and management plan, a detailed budget,
and the qualifications of the key personnel involved.

METHODOLOGY **[C]**

　　If instituted, peer advising will be conducted for 13 months as an
operational experiment. A peer advising unit of two students will be set
up in the spring of 1985. Mr. William Morrell, Chief Adviser for CJS,
has agreed to train the two peer advisers and to supervise the program
through the year. Beginning in the fall of 1985, regular office hours
will be maintained with one or both peer advisers present at all times.

　　The peer advising unit will deal with

　　　　　　—registration and scheduling difficulties
　　　　　　—guidance on classes and instructors
　　　　　　—sequence of classes and prerequisites
　　　　　　—recommended classes
　　　　　　—questions on the CJS program
　　　　　　—information for potential majors
　　　　　　—information on jobs and placement
　　　　　　—information on University services and agencies

　　The peer advising unit will work closely with:

　　　　　　—current faculty advisers
　　　　　　—the Head of CJS
　　　　　　—Admissions and Records

　　The peer advising unit will collect statistics and information on

　　　　　　—number of students helped
　　　　　　—types of problems dealt with
　　　　　　—where/who solved problems
　　　　　　—feedback from CJS students and faculty

FIGURE 17–4 Model proposal *(cont.)*

Janice H. Grumbacher   3   10 December 1984

    In the spring of 1986, the peer advisers will prepare a full
evaluation consolidating all the data collected and presenting
conclusions concerning the potential of peer advising in CJS.
Mr. Morrell will prepare a separate evaluation of the program. Both
evaluations will be submitted to Dr. Carlos Montoya, Head, CJS;
Dr. Mary Baker, Dean of the College; and your office.

    Dr. Montoya and Dean Baker will arrive at a decision concerning
the continuance of peer advising in CJS. Dean Baker will also consider
the possibility of peer advising in other departments of the college.

WORK AND MANAGEMENT PLAN

    This section provides detailed treatment of facilities, the task
breakdown, and management.

Facilities **[D]**

    Dr. Montoya has agreed to provide an office for the peer advising
unit. The office will be located in an area easily accessible to CJS
students. CJS will furnish the office with a desk, telephone, filing
cabinet, bookshelves, a swivel desk chair, three straight chairs, a
typewriter, and a typewriter table. The peer advisers will have the use
of CJS office supplies including stamps and stationery. CJS secretaries
will furnish clerical assistance not to exceed three hours a week.

Task Breakdown **[E]**

    There will be three major tasks: training, maintaining office
hours, and evaluating the program. The accompanying graph shows the task
timetable.

    Training. May, 1985. Mr. Morrell will give the two peer advisers 10
hours of training in advising procedures to include filling out
registration forms and procedures for adding and dropping courses. He
will provide information concerning other college programs, particularly
those that provide aid in needed study skills such as note-taking,

FIGURE 17–4 Model proposal *(cont.)*

Janice H. Grumbacher   4   10 December 1984

reading, listening, and library research. He will aid the peer advisers
in learning the interpersonal communication skills needed for effective
advising.

Office hours. 3 September 1985–28 May 1986. Office hours with at
least one person present will be scheduled from 11 a.m. to 2 p.m., five
days a week, holidays and school breaks excluded. During each of the
heavy advising months of September and January, an additional 20 hours
of advising time will be scheduled to allow two advisers to be present
during peak hours.

Evaluation. 1–30 April 1986. During April 1986, the two peer
advisers will consolidate the information they have gathered throughout
the year and write their evaluation report. A total of 16 hours is
scheduled for this task.

Management [F]

Mr. Morrell will supervise the entire peer advising experiment as
part of his duties as Chief Adviser for the CJS program. He will be
readily accessible to the peer advisers. He will monitor their
procedures and provide advice and counsel when needed. Throughout the
year he will provide informal reports to Dr. Montoya. At the end of the
experiment he will provide an evaluation of the peer advising program.

DETAILED BUDGET [G]

Because CJS is furnishing office space, office supplies, and
clerical help, the entire budget needed is for salary for the two peer
advisers. The normal student hourly wage of $4.50 per hour is requested.
The budget breaks down in the following manner.

Training time:	Salary for 2 peer advisers, a total of 20 hours	90.00
Office hours:	Salary for 3 hours of peer advising a day for 176 days, a total of 528 hours	2,376.00
	Salary for 40 additional advising hours in September and July	180.00
Evaluation time:	Salary for 16 hours	72.00
	TOTAL	$2,718.00

The budgeted $2,718.00 would be divided approximately equally
between the two peer advisers. If this grant request is approved, your
office is requested to transfer $90.00 to the CJS budget in April of
1985 and the remaining $2,628.00 in September 1985. Normal college
accounting procedures will be used by CJS to account for expenditures.

PERSONNEL [H]

I request that I be one of the peer advisers. In March of 1985 the
other peer adviser will be chosen from among applicants for the job by a
secret ballot of the CJS students.

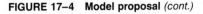

FIGURE 17–4 Model proposal *(cont.)*

Janice H. Grumbacher   5   10 December 1984

My qualifications are as follows. After graduation from high school in 1973, I served four years in the U.S. Air Force as an air police officer, leaving the service with the rank of sergeant. From November 1978 to the present I have been a sheriff's deputy in Bad Axe County. I am currently working half-time while I complete my CJS studies. I have a special interest in counseling. To develop myself in this area, I have taken Social Science 1104, Dynamics of Small Groups, and I am currently taking Social Science 2111, Interpersonal Communication. My current grade point average is 3.2.

Mr. William Morrell, who will supervise the experiment, is Chief Adviser for CJS. Before taking his degree in Criminal Justice Studies at the University of Washington, Mr. Morrell was a police officer with the Seattle, Washington, Police Department for eight years. He also has a Master's Degree in Educational Administration from the University of North Dakota. With CJS for the past six years, Mr. Morrell has been Chief Adviser since 1983.

CONCLUSION [I]

Evidence gathered at other schools indicates that peer advising is successful—a positive benefit to students, faculty, and the school. I have reports concerning established programs at two major universities that I will send to you at your request. Preliminary studies here indicate that both faculty and students favor peer advising in CJS.

I will be happy to discuss this proposal with you at your convenience. And I will be open to any modifications in the plan you might suggest.

Sincerely,

Martin A. Doyle

Martin A. Doyle

cc: Mr. William Morrell
    Dr. Carlos Montoya
    Dean Mary Baker

FIGURE 17–4   Model proposal *(cont.)*

on Mr. Morrell establishes his credibility as a supervisor and points out that the project will have high-level direction.

I. *Conclusion*. The conclusion resells the proposal. It emphasizes previous successes for peer advising and offers to provide evidence for this claim. Indicating flexibility and the willingness to negotiate is also important. Often proposals can't be carried out exactly as proposed.

Proposals are unique documents. They combine the skills needed for information-giving, analysis, and persuasion. Remember, too, they are legal documents. Whatever you say you are going to do, you can be held legally accountable for doing. But the satisfaction of writing a successful proposal is considerable. When someone gives you money on the strength of a proposal you have written, you have direct evidence of your writing and persuasive skills.

THE PROPOSAL FOR A PAPER

Frequently teachers ask students to propose what they intend to do for their major term report. Many of the principles used in writing business proposals can be applied equally well in such proposals for papers. In your proposal for a paper, present information on the following:

- subject, purpose, and audience of the proposed paper
- your methodology and resources for researching and producing the paper
- your schedule of work
- your credentials for doing the paper

Such a proposal will assure your teacher and you, too, that you know where you are heading and will not waste time and energy following dead-end paths. Also, it is an excellent rehearsal for the larger proposals discussed in this chapter. See Figure 17–5 for a model of a proposal for a paper.

SUGGESTIONS FOR APPLYING YOUR KNOWLEDGE

Proposals provide a rich field for both long and short writing assignments and for class discussion.

- You could submit a proposal for a paper such as the one illustrated in Figure 17–5.
- Short proposals can be essentially bids. You can bid to furnish products or services in construction, research, interior

design, food service, health services, and so forth. You could bid to build a porch, install track lighting, furnish carpets or drapes, or cater a party. The possibilities are enormous. The proposals can come from schoolwork or off-campus work or some combination of the two. Just include the information absolutely relevant to the bid, such as

MEMORANDUM

Date: 2 February 1985

To: Professor Richard Ferguson

From   Scott Pahl *Scott Pahl*

Subject: Proposal for a report on the feasibility of lowering annual grass—
            mowing costs for the State Department of Transportation

I propose to conduct and report on a study to determine if the State Department
of Transportation can lower the cost of its annual grass—mowing budget, currently
about 4 million dollars a year. Although the total Department budget is over 600
million dollars, mowing the grass on the State's highways is a significant item
in that budget. The current high cost takes money away from other needed
maintenance work.

The audience for the report will be Mr. James Orwin, Supervisor of Environmental
Services, Department of Transportation. Mr. Orwin has an M.S. in landscape
architecture and 15 years of experience in environmental matters.

<u>Methodology</u> <u>and</u> <u>Resources</u>

My preliminary research into the problem shows that the costs of the Department's
grass—mowing program include wages, equipment, operating and maintenance costs,
equipment replacement, storage, workers' compensation, and insurance. The
Department mows over 9900 miles of right—of—way a year. Depending on location,
grass areas are mowed from 3 to 10 times a year. Besides being costly the work is
dangerous. Workers are injured every year and fatalities have occurred.

I propose to look at several solutions, including lowering the frequency of the
mowings, paving over some or all of the grassy areas, and retarding the growth of
the grass. In testing my solutions, I'll consider not only cost but aesthetics
(How pleasing would be the appearance of the areas if the solution is applied?)
and ecological safety. If the solution can also lower the workers' exposure to
danger, so much the better.

My preliminary search for information has turned up good sources in the
literature as well as people with knowledge that will be helpful. My sources
include the following:

Bloomberg, J. R., and L. M. Wax. 1978. Absorption and translocation of mefluidide
        by soybean (<u>Glycine</u> <u>max</u>), common cocklebur (<u>Xanthium</u> <u>pensylvanicum</u>), and
        giant foxtail (<u>Setaria</u> <u>faberii</u>). <u>Weed</u> <u>Science</u> 26: 434—440.

FIGURE 17–5 Student's proposal for a paper

Professor Richard Ferguson   2   2 February 1985

Field, R. J., and A. R. Whitford. 1981. The retardation of grass growth by
    synthetic plant growth regulators. The chemical manipulation of crop growth
    and development. Ed. J. S. McLaren. London: Butterworth.

Green, R. F. 1984. Trimming mowing costs. Public Works Magazine. January, 102–
    104.

Hagman, Jerry L. 1983. Growth regulators can cut maintenance costs. Park
    Maintenance. January, 66–68.

Orwin, James. 1984. Supervisor of Environmental Services for State Department of
    Transportation. Interviews and correspondence.

Tautvydas, Kestutis J. 1984. Product Development Supervisor and Plant
    Physiologist for Agricultural Products Division of 3M. Interviews and
    correspondence.

Schedule

I should have completed my research by the 5th week of the quarter. I will submit
an organizational plan for my report during the 6th week. With your approval of
my plan, I will draft the paper in the 7th week and polish and submit it during
the 9th week.

Credentials

I am a student in agronomy. My course work has made me familiar with grass growth
and management.

cc. Mr. James Orwin

Figure 17–5   Student's proposal for a paper *(cont.)*

what is to be furnished, by whom, and at what cost. You might also include a few sales touches like experience and testimonials.

- Long proposals could be a term project. Like short proposals, they could relate to major fields of study or to off-campus work. They could relate to community problems. They could involve extensive research in the area involved, perhaps even including surveys and interviews, as in the model proposal about peer advising. In long proposals you would have more sections, such as facilities, equipment, schedules, and personnel. You would have to establish the need for the product or service offered. You would have to sell your ability to fulfill the terms of the proposal. You would have to devise an organization and a format that present your proposal in the best way possible.

- Long proposals can also be team or even class projects. There are certainly enough sections to go around. You could even try a proposal that is real and not just an exercise. Most colleges have an office that deals in grants. You could go to the grants office in your college and see if they have any student-oriented requests. The NSF solicitation used as an example in this chapter was just such a request. If you find such a solicitation, it might be a stimulating group project that could end in real accomplishment.

- Long proposals can often be combined with speeches. Proposals often have to be sold orally as well as in writing. They provide good applications of persuasive speaking skills.

- A good deal of material can be gathered for class discussion. Your grants office will likely have on hand out-of-date requests for proposals they would be happy to let you have. These requests can furnish material for good class discussions as you analyze the types of information, organization, and format they call for. They provide fine examples of our constant theme: Writing provides specific information for a specific purpose. Compare and contrast the organizational plans and formats called for. You can learn from all of them, but try to decide which ones are best, and why. You may also find it possible to obtain actual proposals submitted by various units of your college or by companies in your area. Discussion of how they were researched, organized, and written can be a good way to learn how to do your own proposals. The originator of the proposal might be willing to enter into the discussion.

C H A P T E R

18

peaking at a convention, Robert T. Oliver of Pennsylvania State
University said:

Winston Churchill with a rifle in his hand, crouched behind an earthen
rampart along the Dover coast, might have repelled two or three Nazi
invaders. But the same Winston Churchill, speaking with his matchless
oratory, was able to marshal the global resources and inspire the will to
victory that toppled Hitler's empire and preserved the democratic civiliza-
tion of the Anglo-American world.[1]

Professor Oliver's point is important. Through communication you
can enlarge your own resources many times over. You can teach others
to know what you know and to do what you can do. You can persuade
others to help you to do what you do. You can seek understanding for
your beliefs. The people we communicate with become extensions of ourselves. Because of its personal, live nature, spoken communication is
something rather special. Even in an age of technology, speechmaking is
still a highly effective way of communicating, necessary in almost every
professional occupation. It's worth doing well.

Our purpose in this chapter is to guide you from the moment you
know you have to give a speech to the moment you step from the rostrum
after completing your successful speech. We talk about how to prepare a
speech, how to integrate visuals, and how to deliver it.

PREPARATION

Preparation is much more than gathering material for a speech and even more than organizing that material. Successful preparation involves, first, considering whom you're talking to and where. What is the occasion for your talk? After you know the audience and the occasion, you can consider your purpose. When you know audience, occasion, and purpose, then you can select the right material to satisfy all three and organize that material. It's these important matters that we discuss in this section.

Context

Conversations differ depending upon where you are, what you're doing, and whom you're with. A conversation between a man and a woman in a dimly lit restaurant differs from a conversation between two men at a football game. A conversation with a potential employer is not the same as a conversation with your girlfriend or boyfriend. You don't use the same tones or language at a noisy party as you do in church or in a library. As the context changes, so do the content of your conversation and the manner of its delivery.

So, too, do speeches differ with context. Specifically, we refer to occasion and audience.

OCCASION   When you are invited to speak, find out as much about the occasion for your speech as you can. What is the purpose of the occasion? Is it social, business, or some mix of the two? Are you the only speaker? If there is a program of speakers, where do you fit in? Why were you specifically invited to talk? What is expected from you? These are the questions you should try to get answers for. Without knowing the answers, you can be led into terrible traps. A speech entirely suitable for one occasion may be utterly unsuitable for another.

> CASE IN POINT   Teachers from colleges around the country gather at a major university for a three-day conference. The first meeting of the group occurs at an evening social hour and a dinner. The group meets, drinks, and eats a heavy meal. A dean of the university is introduced to give the group a welcoming talk. He proceeds for forty minutes to deliver an excellent, informational talk about programs at the university, complete with statistics, success-failure ratios, and so on.
>
> How successful was the dean on this occasion? He was a complete flop. He was at a social occasion, but he treated it like a business meeting. He put half his audience to sleep and made the other half too annoyed to sleep. He delivered a speech that would have been successful and appropriate on another occasion—say, the annual report to the board of regents. What was called for at the dinner was a short, light talk of perhaps five to ten minutes' duration in which he welcomed the group and told a humorous anecdote or two.

It is also important to know the physical location where you are going to talk. What size is the room? Does the room fit the number of people in the expected audience? It can be more depressing than you may think to talk to 40 people in a room meant to hold 200. Conversely, it's often exciting and successful to talk to an overflow crowd of 40 in a room meant for 30 people. What kind of equipment is available? Is there an overhead projector or a blackboard if you need it? Will you have a lectern and a light?

> CASE IN POINT A prominent writer is invited to give an after-dinner speech to a group of writing teachers. It's expected that the talk will be fairly serious. The writer is respected, and the teachers want her opinions about writing. The writer comes with her speech written out. The banquet room is dimly lit. There is neither lectern nor light at the writer's place. While she gives her speech, she holds her manuscript about ten inches from her face in order to see it. She gives up trying to read in the dim light and tries to give the speech extemporaneously. However, she has quotes she has to read, and when she tries to find them from the manuscript, she loses her place. Finally, in frustration, she sits down to light, polite applause.
>
> What should have been an excellent talk was ruined by a lack of equipment. One of two preparatory actions would have prevented the disaster. The writer could have let the dinner's organizers know that she had to have a light and a lectern. If, for reasons beyond control, light and lectern were not available, she should have been warned in ample time. She could then have prepared an extemporaneous speech. Speaking from a brief outline, as one does in extemporaneous speech, she could have survived in the dim light. Her quotes could have been typed in large type on separate, numbered cards and placed in the order she needed them.

The moral in these tales is clear. Know beforehand what you are getting into and plan accordingly. If you have any control over the situation, ask for needed changes: the right-sized room or the necessary equipment, for example. If you can't get the changes you want, at least you will be forewarned. You can probably make appropriate plans that will give the proper results.

The occasion also has much to do with the mode of speech you choose—impromptu, memorized, written, or extemporaneous.

- *Impromptu* As the name implies, impromptu speeches can't be prepared. Or rather, you can't plan the specific speech. Your preparation is knowledge of the subject matter. At a social occasion you may be asked to give a little impromptu speech to introduce yourself. Or at a business meeting you may be called upon to stand up and discuss an arrangement, a contract, or the operation of your shop. At a school board meeting you may stand up to protest or support an action. Some of the things we say about content and organization later will help some, but to deliver a good impromptu speech, you had better know your subject thoroughly.

- *Memorized* Memorized speeches have extremely limited uses. They probably serve best when you have to repeat a speech many times. For instance, the guides at places like Disneyland memorize their patter: "Good afternoon, ladies and gentlemen, we're about to enter darkest jungleland. If you are fainthearted . . . ." Experienced lecturers, actors, and politicians go about the country giving the same speech over and over. In the late nineteenth century, Dr. Russell Conwell earned over $7 million by giving a speech he called "Acres of Diamonds" more than 6,000 times. That was a speech worth memorizing. But for most of us it's not worth memorizing a speech. It's too much effort and can get us into trouble. When you learn something word for word and forget a word, the whole speech can depart from your mind—instant blank.
- *Written* Written speeches are quite suitable for some occasions. People running for political office often write their speeches. Having the speech written prevents them from making misstatements of fact or overheated spur-of-the-moment statements that may plague them later. People in business often write their speeches for the same reasons. But rarely should speeches for social occasions be written out. Usually, the desired light, ad lib effect is destroyed by a written speech. And often, as in the case of the writer in the dimly lit room, conditions are not right for reading.
- *Extemporaneous* The most suitable speech for the widest variety of occasions is the extemporaneous speech. This mode calls for a good deal of preparation. You organize, outline, and rehearse it, but you do not write it or memorize it. You know what ideas and facts you're going to work with and have them well in hand. But the actual wording of the speech is left for each delivery of it. It's a good speech mode—sound, safe, flexible. It's the primary mode that we consider.

AUDIENCE Find out as much about your audience beforehand as you can. First, how many people will there be? For 20 people you might plan an informal speech that is mainly discussion—a short talk followed by an extensive question-and-answer period. For a large group meeting in an auditorium, discussion might be unwieldly, so you would plan for a longer well-organized speech. But most of your decisions based on audience, regardless of its size, will be based on the social context and the audience's knowledge and expectations.

How closely do you relate to your audience? For instance, is it composed mainly of friends and co-workers? Is it an audience with which you have many shared interests? Are you a student talking to students? A nurse to nurses? A computer programmer to computer programmers? If so, in some ways your job is easier. Your language can be a bit casual, your speech patterns relaxed. You can leave some things unsaid, because everybody knows them anyway. On the other hand, speaking to this group can be tough. They are likely to question your expertise. The old notion that prophets are not listened to in their own countries is often true. People know them too well to take them seriously. So you may need more evidence to prove your points with this audience than with another that doesn't know you as well.

Groups that don't share your experiences present different kinds of problems. They may expect less relaxed, more formal language from you. They may not take you seriously because you are too young or too old. When you move out of your normal social context, expect difficulties. Your speech will have to be well prepared to overcome them.

What does the audience know about your subject? If they already know all the basics, you can start at a more advanced level. If not, you may have to give background information. We all learn a vocational vocabulary with the jobs we are educated to do. Sometimes we forget that others don't share that vocabulary. An engineer speaking about horizontal and vertical curves may forget that nonengineers would call the first simply *curves* and the second *hills*. When you can, use simple expressions for a nonexpert audience. If you can't, define the needed terms.

But judge your audience correctly. An audience that doesn't need background, simple language, or definitions will feel talked down to if you do supply them.

What does the audience expect of you? In occupational situations most audiences can be classified as management, technical, or nontechnical. By technical we mean those people who work closely with whatever it is you're talking about.

Suppose you develop a new process in an auto shop for taking off old tires, putting new ones on, and balancing the wheels. If you were talking to the management about this new process, they would expect cost data. Will this new process cost more or less than the old? Will it require fewer or more mechanics? Are safety problems involved? The technicians would also want to know some of these same things. But they would also want more details about the process itself. How do you do it? What are the major steps in the process? Does it require new equipment? The nontechnicians primarily expect to be told how the process relates to them. In the case of new tire-changing techniques, the nontechnical customers of the garage would want to know two things: Will the new process be cheaper, and will it get cars in and out of the garage faster?

So it goes. You have to know your audience to do your best. For you can't get through to an audience unless it lets you get through. In that sense the audience is in control, not you. But don't despair if you can't always analyze an audience perfectly. Remember that Aristotle said that credibility is inspired by a speaker having good sense, good moral character, and good will. With these three qualities you'll get along with most audiences. Without them all the analysis in the world probably won't do you much good.

Purpose and Content

Purpose and content are closely related, and both are closely related to occasion and audience. In broad terms you would normally wish to speak socially or to inform or persuade. Or you may have in mind some mixture of the three. For a specific speech to a specific audience you would narrow a broad purpose down to a specific one:

- I propose to welcome and amuse for a few minutes a group of 20 visiting salespeople.
- I propose to inform 20 visiting salespeople how the new billing system works.
- I propose to persuade 20 visiting salespeople that the new billing system is better than the old.
- I propose to inform 20 visiting salespeople about the new billing system and to persuade them that it is better than the old.

When you have your specific purpose clearly in mind, you have completed the criteria you need to choose your content. You should ask four questions about anything you intend to include in your speech:

- Will it meet the needs and expectations of my audience?
- Will it move my purpose forward?
- Does the occasion call for it?
- Does accurate presentation of the topic call for it?

Don't include any item that doesn't meet at least one of these criteria. Your best items will meet all four. The more criteria that each item meets, the more economical you will be of both your and the audience's time.

Time is always a problem. Accuracy may say to include an item. Time may say to leave it out. It's a conflict that goes on in all speaking and writing. Also, you must set priorities among your criteria because they will often be in conflict. For instance, an item that your audience really doesn't expect may be needed for accuracy. Which of these two criteria is your highest priority? In this instance you might be wise to remember Aristotle's comment about good moral character. Go for accuracy.

What sort of material makes up the content of speeches? Let's analyze a few excerpts from actual speeches to see.

In our first excerpt, the speaker began by generalizing that "advances in film technology . . . have intensified and broadened sense stimulation."[2] He than began a series of examples to illustrate the point, first with examples of visual stimulation:

> Various wide-screen photographic and projection techniques expand the area of visual stimulation to include peripheral vision and more. One such technique is Cinemascope. Twentieth Century Fox produced the first Cinemascope picture, *The Robe,* in 1953. A host of other wide-screen techniques soon followed, for example, Cinerama, Todd-AO, VistaVision, Panavision 70, and Omnimax.

After more examples of visual stimulation the speaker gave examples of sound stimulation, then turned to odor stimulation and what he termed *senture,* stimulation of the tactile sense:

> Odor for olfactory stimulation was added by several processes in the late 1950s and early 1960s. All were without commercial and aesthetic success, and without longevity. In 1959 it was AromaRama for the documentary film *Behind the Great Wall.* Smell-O-Vision was it in 1960 for Mike Todd, Jr.'s motion picture *Scent of Mystery.* Finally, *Pink Flamingos* was released in Odorama.
>
> Sensurround is the process that adds senture to film. Released in 1974, *Earthquake* was the first motion picture that effected tactile stimulation. Rocking devices under theater seats caused them to sway in syncronization with earthquake scenes on the screen. Other motion pictures released with Sensurround are *Midway* and *Rollercoaster.* Not much has been seen of, heard of, or felt from Sensurround since 1977.

In this next example, another speaker used an anecdote to illustrate a point:

> These informal relationships—upward, downward, sideways—are the channels of influence from which women in most instances are excluded . . . the ties of loyalty, the team experience, the sharing of information, the masculine jokes, the locker-room style. The way the old-boy system operates to exclude women from full participation is illustrated by the following experience of mine.
>
> After several months of telephone conversations, I established an appointment for dinner with a New York publisher with whom I was interested in having my company do business. I sent a memo to that effect to my boss before leaving for New York on a four-day business trip. The day before the prospective dinner, my office notified me at the hotel that my boss would be in New York the next day and would like to be included in the dinner arrangements. We were to meet him in the men's bar at his private club at 7:30 P.M. It was obvious that the old-boy system was fast at work, to exclude me from a meeting I had set up. Because I was not allowed in the men's bar of a private men's club, nor in the dining room for that matter, the publisher and I met briefly for 15 minutes or so and I waved him off in a taxi to the club, while I had a solitary meal in my hotel.[3]

Speakers may appeal to authority and define terms to support their points, as in this example:

> In using the term *rule,* I have relied on the definition of Susan Shimanoff, who, in *Communication Rules: Theory and Research,* defined rule as a "followable prescription that indicates what behavior is obligated, preferred, or prohibited in certain contexts." She casts rules in the *if-then* format, the *if* clause specifying the scope condition (context) of the rule, and the *then* clause stating the behavior indicated (and whether it is obligated, preferred, or prohibited).
>
> For example, we might state a rule thus:
>
> *If* you are in church,
> *then* you should not applaud after the soprano sings.

Here the *if* clause specifies the context, and the *then* clause indicates the behavior. In a different context, we could frame the rule differently:

If you are at a concert,
then you probably should applaud after the soprano sings.[4]

Speakers may use research results to support generalizations, as in this excerpt from a talk reporting on some consumer research:

And what do consumers say about sales help—the front line of the retail store? Shoppers have little good to say about the sales personnel they encounter in most stores: "poorly trained, "uninterested," "uninformed." That's how customers describe salespeople, and I can tell you it's not the fault of the salespeople. It is the fault of the retail managers who have failed to train sales personnel effectively and who have not set the proper expectations.[5]

The pattern is clear, we hope. General statements, such as "These informal relationships—upward, downward, sideways—are the channels of influence from which women in most instances are excluded," are made and then supported. The support can be almost anything and everything—facts, numbers and statistics, authoritative opinions, comparisons, examples, anecdotes, and so forth. All are suitable as long as they pass through the screen of your four criteria—audience, purpose, occasion, and accuracy.

Recognize that general statements need support unless they're widely accepted. But there is a limit to the amount of support you can supply or be reasonably expected to supply. When you reach the point where your material is adequate to satisfy a reasonable person, stop. We recognize, naturally, how subjective the word *reasonable* is, but speaking is a subjective business. Perhaps Mark Twain's story about his encounter with a fund-raiser speaking in his church will help illustrate the meaning of *reasonable*. When the fund-raiser had reached what Twain thought was a reasonable place to conclude, Twain was convinced he should give him ten, maybe even twenty, dollars. Finally, though, when the man talked on for half an hour longer, Twain took fifty cents from the collection plate.

Organization

After you have considered context, purpose, and content, the next step is organization. In looking at the content of speeches, we saw that most moved back and forth between generalizations and support for the generalizations. Indeed, this general-to-particular or particular-to-general development is a good overall organizational plan. (See pages 23–35.) Also, we discuss a great many other organizational plans in this book. We talk, for instance, about mechanism and process descriptions (in Chapters 12 and 13), good- and bad-news approaches (pages 101–103), and problem solving (Chapter 16). Most of the organizational schemes good for writing are also good for speaking, so don't overlook any of them. Choose the plan or combination of plans that best fits the same criteria we have discussed for content: audience, purpose, occasion, accuracy. One of your organizational chores is to prepare your speaking manuscript or notes. If you were to write your speech, you would first outline it (see pages 421–422) and then write it, much as you would any other piece of writing. Knowing it was meant to be read aloud, you would be careful about a few things. You would take care to use shorter sentences than usual and try for a higher percentage of sentences that begin with the subject. You would avoid putting complicated phrases or clauses between subject and verb. You would use contractions except when you wanted emphasis.

If you are going to speak extemporaneously, stop at the outline stage. We recommend that two outlines be made, actually. The first one would look like the outline for written work, complete with subdivisions and sub-subdivisions. You'll need this complete outline to bring all your material into order. But such an outline is too complex to speak from. You'll depend on it too much and be forever peering at it and losing your place, thus throwing away the whole graceful effect of extemporaneous speech.

Cut the first outline down to fit onto several 4-by-6 cards. You don't need to go as far as did a history professor that one of us once had. One afternoon he lectured knowledgeably for two hours about the ancient Greeks. He had a small card before him that read, "Talk about the Greeks today." Make one card for each major division of your speech. Put just enough on each card to keep you on track, following the main points in the order you have planned. Print your outline in rather large letters (but not all capitals; they're hard to read) on the card. It might look like Figure 18–1.

With such simple notes, you must rehearse your speech before-

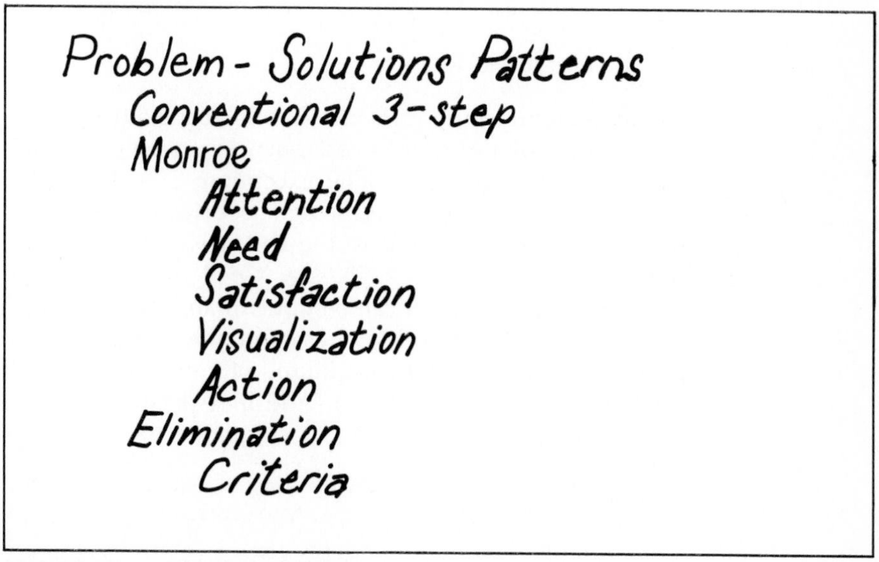

FIGURE 18-1   Speaking notecard

hand. But such notes enable you to see at a glance where you're going. Thus, most of the time you can keep your eyes where they belong—on your audience.

INTRODUCTION AND CONCLUSION

Both the introduction and conclusion are very important to your speech; they should be well prepared.

INTRODUCTION   Actually, most successful introductions come in two parts. The first part is often called the *icebreaker*. You want to slip gracefully from the introduction of you to the introduction of your speech. Various devices can be used. You can open with a quotation or an anecdote that illustrates your major point. The quotation about Winston Churchill that opens this chapter is an example of an icebreaker.

You can get audience participation in some manner. Ask for a show of hands: "How many people have had a hamburger in Larry's Diner in the last two weeks?" You can compliment the occasion or the audience. You have many options. We have only two warnings. Your quotations and stories should apply to your topic. Don't let them seem dragged in. Second, be careful of humor. If you can't handle it, don't touch it. And if the occasion for the speech is a serious one, humor would likely be seen as inappropriate.

After your icebreaker, state your purpose and plan plainly and clearly:

> In the next twenty minutes, I'll explain to you why the national speed limit should be kept at 55 miles per hour. It saves gasoline, highway maintenance, and lives.

In this statement the audience is told the main purpose and the major subdivisions of the speech. All purpose statements, with one exception, should be this complete. The exception: If your purpose involves bad news, use the bad-news approach (see pages 102–103). That is, build through a factual analysis to the bad news. Keep it out of the introduction.

Two other things can be done in an introduction. If your speech is going to include several key terms or theories not known to your audience, explain them at the beginning of your talk. Don't make people suffer from a lack of knowledge. And in a persuasive speech the introduction is often a good place to seek common ground with your audience:

> I'm sure we all agree on the need to conserve energy, money, and lives. Where we perhaps don't agree is on how to go about it. Let's consider . . . .

CONCLUSION Conclusions also come in two parts, sometimes three—all short. Once you move into a conclusion, move through it quickly. It should not take over a minute, even for a long speech.

Summarize your major points in a sentence or two:

> Driving at 55 miles per hour cuts gasoline use by 10 percent and cuts down highway maintenance by as much as $700 million a year. Most important of all, it saves over 10,000 lives a year.

Note the repetition of the key points of the introduction, but with the addition of some important support data.

If your speech has been persuasive, you may wish to add a call to action to the summary, much as you might in a sales letter (see pages 120–121):

> If I have persuaded you of the need for a 55-mile-per-hour speed limit, write your member of Congress today. You can be sure that the truck lobbies are bringing pressure to bear to raise the limit.

Sometimes you may also want to have something like an ice-breaker—a memorable quotation or story—to close your speech. If you do use a story, keep it brief.

VISUALS

As in writing, visuals are often indispensable in speaking. Think of the words saved in describing how to tie a square knot by a simple illustration like the one here.

Even when visual aids are not absolutely necessary, they add variety and interest to your presentations. They support, clarify, and expand your points. They can snap a wandering audience to attention. They increase understanding and retention of your information.

What exactly is a visual? As in writing, it can be a graph, drawing, table, photograph, and so forth. But in speaking, the field broadens. Visuals can be models. Your pictures can be animated. And you can use objects—even people and animals. In this section we give some criteria for selecting effective visuals and a rundown on some of the most-used visual tools.

Criteria

Good visuals enhance speeches; bad ones detract. In a valuable book, James Connolly of the University of Minnesota has laid down some criteria for judging the worth of visuals—visibility, simplicity, clarity, and control.[6]

VISIBILITY The notion of visibility in visuals seems obvious enough, but it is all too often overlooked. If your audience can't see your visual, it's worthless. A 9-by-12-inch photograph held in your hand and waved about does nothing for your audience. Because of the ease with which transparencies can now be made, speakers are tempted to reproduce printed pages and to show them on overhead projectors. Unfortunately, the print is usually so small that it's unreadable beyond the first few rows.

For printed material we can give you a simple rule. To be read, letters should be at least 1-inch high for each 25 feet between the visual and the audience. If you project a transparency on a screen, the letters on the screen should follow the same 1-inch-to-25-feet ratio. This means that you will have to prepare the originals for your transparencies by using oversized type.

For other visuals, such as drawings, photos, graphs, and objects, the rules are not so easily laid down. You may have to experiment a bit. You should know beforehand how far the last row of your audience will be from your visuals. Stand that far yourself and see if you can understand the material presented. If you can't, it's too small. Don't use it. It is frustrating to an audience to have a speaker point knowingly to a visual that they can't see well enough to comprehend.

CLARITY AND SIMPLICITY Visuals that are suitable in printed work may be too complicated for use in speaking. The reader, after all, can stop and study a visual. But in speeches the listener has only a limited time to take in the visual before the speaker sweeps it away and goes on to the next point. Therefore, the rule for speech visuals is to simplify and then to simplify again. Cut down to only absolutely vital information. The audience should be able to take in a visual's meaning at a glance. Use graphs to show the shapes of trends without worrying overmuch about the actual numbers. Break up tables and extract only needed information. Eliminate all unneeded features from maps. Use block diagrams rather than schematics.

The graph in Figure 18–2 is too complicated for use in a speech. Viewers must refer back and forth between the key and the surfaces to orient themselves. And a surface graph is difficult for many readers to interpret, let alone for a viewer who may have only a short glimpse of it. The graph in Figure 18–3 is more suitable. Here viewers can easily grasp the trends whether they absorb the dollar figures or not. Labeling the graph directly instead of using a key makes understanding the information even easier. And the speaker can easily draw attention to the dollar figures if they are important.

Figure 18–4 shows the layout of the interstate highway system in Minnesota. It would make a good transparency or poster. The lines are

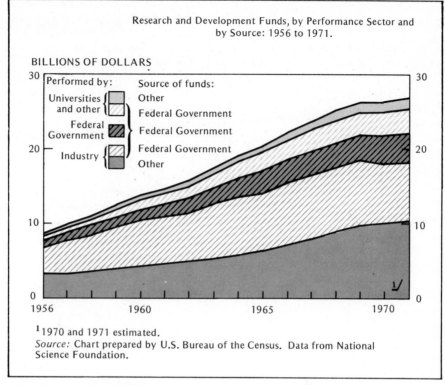

Research and Development Funds, by Performance Sector and by Source: 1956 to 1971.

¹1970 and 1971 estimated.
Source: Chart prepared by U.S. Bureau of the Census. Data from National Science Foundation.

FIGURE 18–2 Complicated graph

bold and the print large. The interstates, major cities, and state boundaries are clearly located. All other detail has been eliminated.

The table in Figure 18–5 is far too complex to be of any use in a speech. The simplified, large-print table in Figure 18–6 would work well if made into a transparency.

What is obvious here is that few visuals found in books are satisfactory for use in speaking. So resist the temptation merely to reproduce them. You will usually have to redesign them first. You will need to eliminate unneeded material and to provide bold lines and large lettering.

CONTROL As a speaker, you should control your audience as much as you can. You don't want their minds wandering from you and your speech. Properly made and used, visuals can increase an audience's concentration. They draw attention when you want them to and are invisible when you are through with them. Poorly made visuals distract an audience by drawing attention when you don't want them to.

For instance, large models or mockups of equipment are often excellent visuals. But they have the disadvantage of sitting there on the rostrum like a lump after you are done with them. The audience may stare

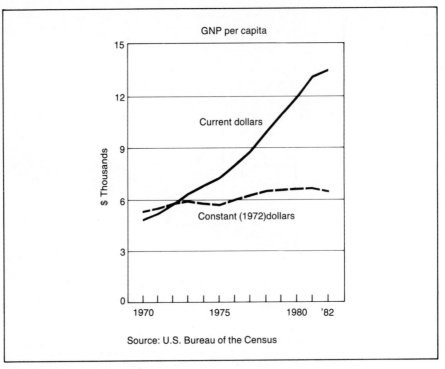

GNP per capita

Current dollars

Constant (1972)dollars

Source: U.S. Bureau of the Census

FIGURE 18–3   Simple graph

at them, running over their operation, instead of attending to you. If possible, arrange to have them removed or at least covered when they are not in use.

Small exhibits passed through the audience are deadly for proper concentration. Members of the audience get involved in the mechanics of passing them about. They examine them when they receive them, ignoring the speaker. Passed-around objects are perfect examples of visuals you can't control.

For proper control, then, you should be able to show or remove a visual at will. You'll be even farther ahead if you can easily change it by adding or deleting material.

Visual Tools

You have a wide range of visual tools to choose from—movies, 35mm slides, models, blackboards, flannelboards, and many others. We deal here with four such tools, all recommended for their effectiveness and ease of use: blackboards, posters, flipcharts, and overhead projectors.

BLACKBOARDS   Blackboards have the major advantage of being easy to use. They do not normally require extensive preparation beforehand.

FIGURE 18–4 Minnesota interstate system (Minnesota Department of Transportation, St. Paul)

They also provide eye-appealing action as you move about, writing and drawing on them. Their major disadvantage is slowness. It takes time to produce your drawings, lists, or whatever, on the board. You can, of course, put your visuals on the board before you talk. If you do, cover them until you use them and erase them as soon as you are done with them.

Write or print legibly and in large letters. Drawings can be crude but must be understandable. It takes experience to draw and talk at the same time. Do try not to talk to the board exclusively. Remember that you have an audience out there.

In an age of technology the old-fashioned blackboard's effectiveness is often underrated. It meets the important criterion of control excellently. You don't have to draw your visuals until the moment you need them, you have all eyes on you as you are drawing them, and you can erase them whenever you like.

No. 1. Population and Area: 1790 to 1980

[Area figures represent area on indicated date including in some cases considerable areas not then organized or settled, and not covered by the census. Total area figures for 1790–1970 have been recalculated on the basis of the remeasurement of States and counties for the 1980 census. The land and water area figures for past censuses have not been adjusted and are not strictly comparable with the total area data for comparable dates because the land areas were derived from different base data, and these values are known to have changed with the construction of reservoirs, draining of lakes, etc. Density figures are based on land area measurements as reported in earlier censuses. For additional area data, see tables 5 and 339.]

CENSUS DATE	RESIDENT POPULATION				AREA (square miles)		
	Number	Per square mile of land area	Increase over preceding census		Gross	Land	Water
			Number	Percent			
CONTERMINOUS U.S. [1]							
1790 (Aug. 2)	3,929,214	4.5	(x)	(x)	891,364	864,746	24,065
1800 (Aug. 4)	5,308,483	6.1	1,379,269	35.1	891,364	864,746	24,065
1810 (Aug. 6)	7,239,881	4.3	1,931,398	36.4	1,722,685	1,681,828	34,175
1820 (Aug. 7)	9,638,453	5.5	2,398,572	33.1	1,792,552	1,749,462	38,544
1830 (June 1)	12,866,020	7.4	3,227,567	33.5	1,792,552	1,749,462	38,544
1840 (June 1)	17,069,453	9.8	4,203,433	32.7	1,792,552	1,749,462	38,544
1850 (June 1)	23,191,876	7.9	6,122,423	35.9	2,991,655	2,940,042	52,705
1860 (June 1)	31,443,321	10.6	8,251,445	35.6	3,021,295	2,969,640	52,747
1870 (June 1)	[2]39,818,449	[2]13.4	8,375,128	26.6	3,021,295	2,969,640	52,747
1880 (June 1)	50,155,783	16.9	10,337,334	26.0	3,021,295	2,969,640	52,747
1890 (June 1)	62,947,714	21.2	12,791,931	25.5	3,021,295	2,969,834	52,553
1900 (June 1)	75,994,575	25.6	13,046,861	20.7	3,021,295	2,969,565	52,822
1910 (Apr. 15)	91,972,266	31.0	15,977,691	21.0	3,021,295	2,969,451	52,936
1920 (Jan. 1)	105,710,620	35.6	13,738,354	14.9	3,021,295	2,977,128	45,259
1930 (Apr. 1)	122,775,046	41.2	17,064,426	16.1	3,021,295	2,977,128	45,259
1940 (Apr. 1)	131,669,275	44.2	8,894,229	7.2	3,021,295	2,974,726	47,661
1950 (Apr. 1)	150,697,361	50.7	19,028,086	14.5	3,021,295	2,968,054	54,207
1960 (Apr. 1)	178,464,236	60.1	27,766,875	18.4			
UNITED STATES							
1950 (Apr. 1)	151,325,798	42.6	19,161,229	14.5	3,618,770	3,552,206	63,005
1960 (Apr. 1)	179,323,175	50.6	27,997,377	18.5	3,618,770		74,212
1970 (Apr. 1)	[3]203,302,031	[3]57.4	23,978,856	13.4	3,618,770	[3]3,540,023	[3]78,444
1980 (Apr. 1)	226,545,805	64.0	23,243,774	11.4	3,618,770	3,539,289	79,481

X Not applicable.   [1] Excludes Alaska and Hawaii.   [2] Revised to include adjustments for underenumeration in Southern States; unrevised number is 38,558,371 (13.0 per square mile).   [3] Figures corrected after 1970 final reports were issued.

Source: U.S. Bureau of the Census, *U.S. Census of Population: 1920* to *1980*, vol. I; and other reports and unpublished data. See also *Areas of the United States, 1940*, and *Area Measurement Reports*, series GE–20, No. 1.

FIGURE 18–5   Complicated table

POSTERS   Words, drawings, and graphics can be displayed on posters prepared ahead of time. Display the poster on an easel. Keep the poster a convenient size: 2 feet wide by 3 feet high is a common dimension. Be sure that all lettering is at least 1 inch high for every 25 feet from your audience. Do not use all capital letters. A normal mixture of capital and lower case letters is easier to read. Check to be certain that all drawings and graphs are easily visible from the back row.

Population	Unit	1970	1975	1980	1981	1982
Total, incl. Armed Forces abroad	Mil.	204.4	216.0	227.1	229.8	232.1
Resident population	Mil.	203.3	215.5	226.5	229.3	231.5
Per square mile	No.	57.4	60.9	64.0	64.8	65.4

Source: U.S. Bureau of the Census

FIGURE 18–6   Simple table

Posters are controllable and quite effective if you keep their contents visible and simple. Put them on the easel only when you need them. They require a good deal of advance preparation, but the wide range of brightly colored felt-tipped pens available today has speeded up the process considerably.

FLIPCHARTS The flipchart in its simplest form is a large tablet (about 2 feet wide by 3 feet high) securely fastened to an easel. When you are through with one page, you flip the page over and reveal the next. When a blackboard is not available, the blank pages of a flipchart can be used instead. Of, if you want to prepare ahead, you can construct each page as you would a poster.

A combination of the two approaches is to draw your visuals lightly on the flipchart before your talk. (If you do it lightly enough, your audience won't see your sketches, but it won't matter particularly if they do.) Then, during your presentation, you cover the light lines with bold strokes of a felt-tipped pen. This method effectively combines action with accuracy.

You have good control with a flipchart. Be sure to leave the top page blank, so that you can cover visuals when not using them.

OVERHEAD PROJECTORS At the risk of sounding like salespersons for overhead projectors, we have to say that they are probably the most effective visual tool ever devised for speakers. This simple machine that allows you to project transparencies on a screen or wall has numerous advantages.

- *Ease of preparation* Most of the photo reproduction machines readily found in offices and libraries make transparent copies as well as opaque ones. These transparencies are your visuals. It's so easy to reproduce almost anything for a transparency that you must guard against reproducing inappropriate material, such as pages of small print or complex graphs.
- *Ease of operation* With your projector in the front of the room, you can remain in front of your audience and easily control your own visuals. You lay transparencies directly on the machine in a position that allows you to read them. Turn on the machine, focus the image, and you're in business. There are no trays of slides to jam. Room lights can remain on. You can project on either a light-colored wall or a screen. About the only thing that can go wrong with an overhead projector is a burnt-out light bulb. Keep a bulb handy and know how to change it.
- *Ease of control* Overhead projectors offer more control over your visuals than any other tool. You can prepare transparencies ahead of time. Or you can put a blank transparency on the projector and use it like a blackboard. You can prepare a transparency partly and finish it with a felt-tipped pen or a crayon while you talk. By sliding a piece of paper around on your transparency, you can reveal as much or as little

of your visual as you like. You can prepare other transparencies to superimpose over a first transparency adding material as you go along. You can shut off the entire visual with a flip of the switch.

In preparing your transparencies, keep our criteria in mind. Keep transparencies visible, simple, and clear. Your projected image must be of sufficient size to be seen in the back row. For printed material this generally means your letters have to be about twice the size of ordinary typewriter print. Many schools and offices now have oversized-print typewriters or reproduction equipment that allows the duplicate to be expanded or reduced from the original. There is also a way to use ordinary typewriter print. You can move the projector farther back from the screen wall and thus enlarge the letters. But by so doing you may lose the option of changing and controlling your own visuals, one of the major advantages of the overhead projector.

A modern overhead projector is small enough not to block anyone's view. Place it in front of your audience and stand slightly to the side. Face your audience while you talk and work with your visuals. You may point to material on the transparency with a pencil. The pencil's shadow will point to the image on the wall. Always turn the projector off immediately when you are not using it.

Because of their effectiveness, overhead projectors are used in many schools and businesses. You almost certainly have the opportunity to see them in action. Observe carefully how they are used. Learn what to do from the people who use them well, and what not to do from those who use them poorly.

PERFORMANCE

Let's assume you have made all the preparations we have suggested. You've organized your speech and either written it or made up a speaking outline for it. You've planned your visuals and integrated them into your speech. You now have only one task left—the performance of the speech itself. And make no mistake about it—standup speaking is a performance. Whether you choose a low-keyed conversational style or a more wide-open orator's style, you're giving a performance. In this section we talk about the preperformance period, the delivery of your speech, and the question-and-answer period that often follows a speech.

Preperformance Period

No matter whether you plan to give your speech from a manuscript or extemporaneously from cards, you must rehearse it. If you can find a sympathetic but critical audience of one or two persons, fine, but rehearse even if it's only in front of a mirror and, if possible, to a tape recorder.

Play back the tape and listen critically to your pace and delivery. Listen for effective use of the techniques we'll discuss shortly. Timing is critical. Tailor your speech to fit precisely into whatever time is allotted you. Running seriously under or over your allotted time can greatly inconvenience a good many people and gain you nothing but bad marks from your audience. Pay attention to the pronunciation of words. Rehearsal is the time to discover the words that you can't pronounce or that you feel shaky about. Look them up; practice them until you have mastered them. You will know your rehearsals are adequate when you can run through a speech comfortably—on time, with no major hesitations, and with all the words properly pronounced. You should feel comfortable in your movements and know how you're going to work with your visuals.

On the day of your speech pay some attention to your appearance. Dress for the occasion, whatever it is. Some occasions are shirt-sleeve affairs; others are more formal. But unless there are exceptional circumstances, you should be neat and well groomed for your speech. The simple truth is that people feel better about themselves when they feel attractive, and proper dress enhances whatever nature gave us to work with.

Delivery

The moment arrives. You have done all you can to get ready. You are introduced, and it's time to make your way to the front of the audience. For many people this is an absolutely terrifying moment. For others it's a stimulating, enjoyable experience. In either case, however, the right delivery techniques will enable you to do a better job. Specifically, we tell you here about the beginning of a speech, some general techniques, and the ending.

THE BEGINNING Rule number one: Don't hurry your beginning. Walk slowly to the lectern. Place your manuscript or notes in front of you and arrange them the way you want. Incidentally, don't try to hide the fact that you're speaking from notes or a manuscript. Use them openly. Pause; survey your audience pleasantly. If water is available, pour some and take a sip. All this business may take only twenty seconds, but if you're an inexperienced speaker, it may seem like an hour. This unhurried approach is essential. It gives you time to prepare yourself, and it relaxes your audience. It tells them they are about to listen to a calm, composed individual, and they will be glad of that.

Begin by greeting your audience in whatever manner is appropriate for the occasion. Perhaps a simple "Good evening, ladies and gentlemen" will do. On more formal occasions you may need to acknowledge the person who introduced you and greet important people in the room: "Thank you, Mrs. Robinson, for that kind introduction. President Weaver, Dean Goodding, faculty, students. . . ."

Now begin firmly and authoritatively with your icebreaker. At this moment adrenaline will be pouring into your bloodstream. You will be experiencing what physiologists call the fight-or-flight response. You can't fly, so let the response carry you not into fight but into vitality and enthusiasm.

At the beginning of a speech never apologize for conditions or set up a rationale for failure: "Despite having driven over a thousand miles in the pouring rain to be here with you today. . . ." No, have your icebreaker and the rest of your introduction well in hand and get on with your business.

TECHNIQUES   The expressions *good vibes* and *bad vibes* are familiar to most people. When you have good vibes about someone, you feel comfortable and rate the person highly. With bad vibes the reverse is true. Researchers in communication are well aware of good and bad vibes. And they have found that they are produced by very subtle interactions between people. Body motions, or body language, and the way people's voices sound may be more important in producing good or bad vibes than what is actually being said. For instance, a man may be addressing you as a friend, but the extreme tension of his body, the stiffness of his neck, may be shouting his hostility toward you. You will instinctively trust what his body says rather than believe his words. A great many politicans have ultimately failed over the years because, say what they would, they were never able to project sincerity through their bodies and voices. So proper body actions and voice sounds are important for success in speaking.

A stiff, motionless speaker comes across as a frightened speaker. Motion is important in convincing people—and even yourself, for that matter—that you are relaxed and assured. Use all the normal body motions while you are speaking. Shake your head yes and no. Indicate size with your hands and arms. Clench a fist for determination or righteous anger. Point for emphasis. Almost every gesture you would use in normal conversation, perhaps broadened a bit, is appropriate in speaking. Have a mobile face. Smile or frown as you feel like it. Move about the rostrum if you can. The use of visuals is important here; they encourage natural movement as you draw or write or move a poster or transparency.

Eye contact is an important part of body language for two reasons. First, people really don't feel that you're speaking to them unless they feel your eyes on them. They will feel you're insincere if you fail to meet their eyes. Second, if you are really looking at people, you can read their body language. You get feedback. People sitting alertly with faces pleasantly composed are giving you positive feedback. You can continue as you are. People slumping down, yawning, or looking away from you are giving you negative feedback. If that happens, don't panic, but recognize that something needs to be changed. The change might be a different speech rate, more motion, or more explanation. If it's a problem you can do something about immediately, do it. Perhaps curing the problem is beyond you for the moment. Then file it away as a lesson for next time. After the speech, analyze what you did wrong and try not to do it again.

The very sound of your voice carries part of your message. Obvious as it may seem, pay attention to whether or not you're being heard. Early in your speech look carefully at the back rows. If people there are frowning, stop and ask them if they can hear you. If not, crank up the volume. Besides volume, you can also control pitch and rate. High pitch and high rate both suggest excitement and enthusiasm. But too high in either one suggests hysteria. Low pitch and rate suggest confidence and stability. Too low, however, and boredom sets in. Practice varying volume, pitch, and rate to get the effects you want.

Be careful to say your words clearly. A slovenly style of speech tells people you don't care; therefore, why should they care? Avoid what *New Yorker* writer John Davenport labeled "Slurvian." An example of Slurvian is the man who brings his "sweet as surp" wife "flars" for their anniversary. Or some human "beans" go to "Yerp" to visit "forn" countries.[7]

How can we sum all this up? Simply. Stand up straight, move freely, speak loudly and clearly, and look directly at the faces of the people in front of you. If you seem both vital and composed, people will take their cues from you and get good, not bad, vibes.

THE ENDING   As we have said elsewhere, once you suggest you are going to end, end quickly. Have your final summary or quote or whatever firmly in mind or handy on a card so that you won't miss a beat when it's time to conclude. Close firmly, but don't hurry from the rostrum. As you did at the beginning, pause. Hold eye contact with your audience for five seconds. In certain situations applause can be expected and will come. Wait for it and take it standing on the rostrum, not back in your seat. In situations such as a classroom session or a company briefing, applause is unlikely. But hold eye contact for five seconds anyway and then look away as you gather up your notes and move from the lectern.

Question-and-Answer Period

In many situations you will have a question-and-answer period following your prepared talk. In some business situations the entire talk, after a brief introduction, could be questions and answers. Sometimes a chairperson will take the questions; in other situations you will. In any case be sure everyone in the audience understands the question before you begin your answer. We can sum up what your behavior should be during the question-and-answer period with five C's: You should be *courteous, correct, complete, concise,* and *careful.*

COURTEOUS   Give everyone in the audience a fair chance. Look around and answer questions from different parts of the room. Don't zero in on one area or let one person monopolize you. Sometimes questions may indicate hostility to you or your ideas. Don't rise to the bait. Be polite and objective in your answer. But don't take abuse either. If someone is obviously more interested in harassment than information, say something like "Under the present circumstances, I cannot answer that question objectively," and move on to the next question. Whatever you do, don't play for laughs at the expense of someone who may have innocently asked a foolish question. You embarrass the person needlessly, probably make a lifelong enemy, and lose the rest of the audience.

CORRECT   Be sure your answers are accurate. Quite frankly, in the excitement of playing expert, speakers sometimes get carried away. They make up facts or give dubious answers rather than appear ignorant. Answer a question only if you can do so accurately. If you can't, don't be afraid of saying, "I don't know." Or get the questioner's name and address and promise to send the information. If you do, keep your promise.

COMPLETE AND CONCISE   *Complete* and *concise* are obviously somewhat in opposition. Answer as fully as time allows and the question deserves. Questions often indicate that major points in your talk have not been understood or, worse, have been misunderstood. Elaborate as needed until you reach a correct understanding, In many situations you would be wise to bring additional material with you for the question-and-answer period—reports, tables, charts, and so forth. Take enough time to look up the answers needed if you have such material with you. Be complete, but keep your eye on the clock. Don't get carried away into a whole new talk. When you really have answered the question, stop.

CAREFUL   Keep your head when answering questions. If you're not careful, you can be trapped into many unhappy situations. Be careful not to be angry or sarcastic. Be careful not to let playing the expert lead you into inaccurate answers or into giving authoritative answers to questions outside your field. Be ready to say, "My opinion on that matter would be no better than anyone else's." Be careful not to make elaborate promises to people. In other words, be careful to be courteous, correct, complete, and concise.

SUGGESTIONS FOR APPLYING YOUR KNOWLEDGE

If there is time for it, speaking can be tied into many of the course writing assignments. A sales letter can easily be made into a persuasive talk. Descriptions of processes and mechanisms can be given orally as well as in writing. Proposals are often accompanied by briefings that cover their major points. The possibilities are wide.

Often the major report of the term is given orally as well as in writing. Because the major term report is usually based on the information of a specific discipline, it furnishes a good opportunity for cooperation with other departments of your school. Teachers who are experts in the subject matter can be brought into the class to help evaluate the speech. Their presence in the classroom assures a combined audience of experts and nonexperts, a situation common in real life.

Try to go beyond the schoolroom situation of a student talking to other students. Create a context for the talk, such as a sales meeting, a proposal briefing, a demonstration of a new process or mechanism to its users. Students can even role-play, becoming executives, technicians, members of community groups, and so forth.

Create a real-life situation in other ways. Have a lectern for the speaker. Put out a pitcher of water and some glasses. Invite guests. Schedule time for a question-and-answer period.

Speeches should not be considered complete without visuals. You can create transparencies if an overhead projector is available. Flipcharts and posters are easily assembled. A blackboard is almost always available.

UNIT IV

A WRITER'S GUIDE

The "Writer's Guide" is a handbook containing a series of little essays on various writing techniques, conventions, and problems. To see a complete list of what it contains, look at the inside back cover. We have arranged the handbook alphabetically to make it easier for you to find your way around.

If you're in a writing class, your instructor may use the symbols on the inside back cover in marking your papers. In this way your instructor will refer you to entries that should show you how to correct a problem in your paper.

ABBREVIATIONS

Abbreviations are often used in business and technical writing. However, they must be used with some care. Remember that abbreviations are primarily for the convenience of the writer. If they are likely to inconvenience the reader, they should not be used. Use without explanation only those abbreviations you are absolutely certain your reader will understand correctly. If you have any doubts at all, spell out the full expression the first time and follow it with the abbreviation in parentheses: *Trunk Highway (TH)*.

Any college-level dictionary will list the abbreviations you are likely to need. In most dictionaries the abbreviation will be listed twice—once as an abbreviation in normal alphabetical order, and once behind the word for which it is an abbreviation. Another excellent source for standard abbreviations is *The Chicago Manual of Style*.

Guidelines concerning the acceptability of abbreviations vary from place to place, but the following rules are usable unless you have instructions to the contrary.

Accepted Abbreviations

Some abbreviations are generally known and accepted, even preferred, in all writing. The following is a representative list of such abbreviations:

Titles

Dr.   Mrs.
Mr.   Ms.

These abbreviated titles are used only before the name, as in *Dr. Smith*. By themselves, of course, titles are spelled out: The *doctor* drove a black car.

Time

a.m.   B.C.   C.S.T. (Central Standard Time)
p.m.   A.D.

Academic Degrees

A.A.   M.A.   M.B.A.
B.A.   M.D.   Ph.D.

In most of your writing you may also abbreviate the names of organizations and countries when the names are long and unwieldy. Be careful to use a standard abbreviation and to spell it out the first time if it is unfamiliar to the reader:

CBS	Columbia Broadcasting System
FBI	Federal Bureau of Investigation
NASA	National Aeronautics and Space Administration
USAF	United States Air Force
U.S.A.	United States of America
U.K.	United Kingdom

Notice that the abbreviations of countries include periods. The abbreviations of organizations generally do not.

Some commonly known measurements expressed in two or more words are usually abbreviated in capitals without periods:

MPG
MPH
RPM

Certain common Latin terms, if used instead of their English equivalents, are always abbreviated:

etc.   (and so forth)
e.g.   (for example)
i.e.   (that is)

Abbreviations Accepted in Specialized Writing

Abbreviations are much more widely used in transactional writing, particularly scientific and technical writing, than in general writing. Terms of measurement of two or more words, such as *Brinell hardness number* (Bhn), *British thermal unit* (Btu), and *cubic foot* or *feet* (cu ft), will be abbreviated both in lists and tables and in the textual prose. Business writers will use such abbreviations as *C.O.D.* (collect on delivery) and *f.o.b.* (free on board, meaning the receiver pays the transportation charges).

But even in technical writing some restraint is called for. A page that bristles with abbreviations intimidates the reader and slows understanding. Therefore, many technical writers do not abbreviate one-word measurements, such as *ounce* or *pound,* in their text. However, they may abbreviate them in lists and tables. (See "Metric Conversion Tables," which includes the abbreviations for many metric measurements.)

Internal consistency is important. Once you abbreviate a term, continue to do so throughout your text. A typical piece of engineering prose might look like this:

> The horizontal and vertical alignment of the highway is consistent with a freeway designed for 70 MPH. The maximum mainline curve is 3°00′; steepest mainline gradient is 3%. Maximum speed on the frontage roads will be 30 MPH.

Abbreviations to Be Avoided

In any text, general or specialized, there are many abbreviations that you should avoid. We specify text because some of these abbreviations are suitable in lists, tables, illustrations, and addresses, where space may be limited. In your text, you should spell out

Titles

Colonel, *not* Col.

First Names

Charles, *not* Chas.

Geographical Locations

France, *not* Fr.
New York, *not* N.Y.
(Long names such as
U.S.A. are an
exception.)

Geographical Terms

street, *not* st.
road, *not* rd.
mountain, *not* mt.

Seasons, Months, Days

winter, *not* wtr.
January, *not* Jan.
Monday, *not* Mon.

Common Words

government, *not* gov't.
Protestant, *not* Prot.

APOSTROPHE

The apostrophe has three major uses: (1) to form the possessive case of nouns and indefinite pronouns; (2) to replace omitted letters and numerals; and (3) to form the plurals of numerals, letters, and symbols.

Forming the Possessive

Observe the following rules in forming the possessive case.

SINGULAR NOUNS   To form the possessive of singular nouns, including proper nouns, add an apostrophe and *s*. This is true even for nouns that already end in *s* or another sibilant sound such as *x* or *z*:

woman's
horse's
table's
lynx's
Jones's

There are a few exceptions to this rule. When adding an apostrophe and *s* results in an *s* or *z* sound that is hard to pronounce, add only the apostrophe:

Moses'
conscience'
appearance'

Try these pronunciations for yourself. Notice that *lynx's* is easy to pronounce, whereas *conscience's* is awkward to say.

PLURAL NOUNS   Form the possessive of plural nouns by adding an apostrophe plus *s* to words that do not end with *s* or another sibilant. Add the apostrophe only to plural words that do end in *s* or a sibilant:

women's
alumni's
advisors'
actresses'

PRONOUNS   For indefinite pronouns add an apostrophe and *s* to form the possessive:

> anyone's
> everyone's
> everybody's
> nobody's
> no one's
> other's
> neither's

Form the possessive of all other pronouns without the apostrophe:

> my (mine)
> your (yours)
> his, her (hers)
> its
> our (ours)
> their (theirs)
> whose

JOINT POSSESSION   When there is joint possession, add the apostrophe or apostrophe and *s* only to the last member of the group:

> Mary and John's house

When there is separate possession, add the apostrophe and *s* to each member of the group:

> Mary's and John's houses

Replacing Letters and Numerals

In contractions we omit letters, and in numerical expressions we sometimes omit numerals. In both these uses the apostrophe replaces the missing element:

> He doesn't work here now.
> It's Mary at the door.
> He graduated in '82.

Forming Plurals

Use the apostrophe and *s* to form the plural of letters and symbols:

> *Omitted* is spelled with one *m* and two *t*'s.
> There are four +'s in that equation.

This use of the apostrophe is for clarity—to prevent, for example, someone from confusing *a*'s with *as*.

You may also use the apostrophe plus *s* to form the plural of numbers, but frequently the *s* is used alone:

> The 1930's (*or* 1930s) were depression years.

BRACKETS

The major use you are likely to have for brackets is to insert material of your own into a quoted passage. Such insertion is sometimes necessary for various reasons: (1) to add a date or fact not obvious from the passage; (2) to indicate by the use of *sic* (Latin for *thus* or *so*) an error of fact or usage in the original and therefore not your error; (3) to straighten out the syntax of a sentence you may have disturbed through the use of ellipses (see entry on Ellipsis Points). Brackets are the accepted signal to the reader that the inserted material is not part of the original. Therefore, do not use parentheses for this purpose.

Many keyboards do not have a key for brackets, so you'll probably have to ink them in neatly. (Remember to leave space for them.) You can also make them by a combination of diagonals and underscoring:

In that month [January], the GNP fell.

He fell to erth [sic] from a plane.

I was encouraged to engage in others [partnerships] . . . on the same terms with that in Carolina.

CAPITALIZATION

Rules for capitalization vary from organization to organization, but the following general rules are fairly standard.

Proper Nouns

Capitalize proper nouns and the words that derive from them.

People

Charles Darwin, Darwinism

Geographic Entities

England, English
Minnesota, Minnesotans
East 40th Street
the Ohio River
Mount Everest

Languages

French
Russian
Swahili

Religious Terms

God	Judaism
the Bible	Jews
the Old Testament	Jewish
Protestant	Muslim
Catholic	

Days of Week

Monday
Tuesday

Months

January
February

Holidays

Easter
Independence Day

Specific Buildings

Empire State Building

Organizations

United States Senate	United States Air Force (USAF)
United Nations	American Legion

Certain Historical Terms

Magna Carta	Revolutionary War
Constitution	Renaissance

Brand Names

Chevrolet	Ivory Snow
Polaroid	Xerox

Companies

International Business Machines (IBM)

Course Titles

Scientific and Technical Writing

Ships

U.S.S. *San Pablo*

Titles of Books, Articles, Plays, Movies

Capitalize the first and last word of every title. Capitalize all other words except prepositions of fewer than five letters, articles, and conjunctions:

Maxims and Instructions from the Boiler Room
"Getting Inside Your Camera"
"What's a Camera For?"

Official Titles

Capitalize an official title when you place it before a person's name or use it to refer to a specific person:

Congresswoman Smith
Colonel Peter R. Moody
The President is in his office.

Do not capitalize a title used in a general way:

Most professors enjoy teaching.

See also entries for Colon and Quotation Marks.

COLON

The colon is a mark of introduction. You can use it to introduce quotations (particularly long quotations) and lists.

Quotations

The Environmental Impact Statement for I-35E clarifies the impact on wetlands as follows: "The most significant impact to water resources would be the direct displacement of wetlands. Of approximately 2,300 acres of wetlands in the study area, 28 acres would fall within the corridor of the proposed action and would be filled or altered."

Lists

There will be three final steps: a location-design hearing, a final EIS, and a Design Study Report.

The Metropolitan Council's long-range planning indicates that expansion of the urban service limit should involve the following areas:
Existing urban service area
Addition to the urban service area
Freestanding growth centers

Do not place a colon between a verb or a preposition and the objects that follow. Both the colons in the following examples are *incorrect* and should be removed:

Incorrect   The three steps are: a location report, a final EIS, and a design study report.

Incorrect   Public hearings have been scheduled for: Apple Valley, Eagan, and Mendota.

Place no punctuation at all after a verb or preposition:

Correct   The three steps are a location report, a final EIS, and a design study report.

Correct   Public hearings have been scheduled for Apple Valley, Eagan, and Mendota.

Following colons you may use a capital or a lowercase letter. Generally, a complete sentence would start with a capital, a subordinate clause or a phrase with a lowercase letter.

Conventional Uses of the Colon

Dear Mr. Rose:
6:22 p.m.
8:4:1 (expression of proportion)

COMMA

Commas have so many uses that it's little wonder people despair of using them correctly. In this elementary guide we'll keep things as simple as we can and still cover the major rules.

Compound Sentences

When two independent clauses are joined by a coordinating conjunction *(and, but, for, nor, or,* and *yet),* use a comma before the conjunction:

Building the highway on the present alignment would have little impact on the north bluffs, but building it on the new alignment would create a severe impact.

See also the entries for Run-on Sentences and Semicolon.

Introductory Elements

We begin about 25 percent of our sentences with an introductory word, phrase, or subordinate clause. After such an introductory element, a comma is never wrong:

> Unfortunately, the bridge will be seen as a man-made object.
>
> Of the 36 Indian mounds, only 12 were well preserved.
>
> As speed increases, foreground details fade rapidly.

Sometimes, when the introductory element is short, you would not be incorrect if you omitted this comma. Do so with care, however. Make sure you don't cause your reader to overread. Look at the following sentence:

> Because foreground objects do not block viewing, bridge structures can provide an opportunity for outstanding vistas.

Remove the comma after *viewing* and readers will mistakenly read that the bridge structures are being viewed. When they realize their error, they have to back up and begin again.

Unless you're quite sure of what you're doing, you may always want to use the comma after introductory elements. Be careful, however, not to confuse a long, complete subject with an introductory element. This error could cause you to put a comma incorrectly between subject and verb. You would want no punctuation at all at the spot we have marked with brackets in this example:

> Planned recreational development of the area [] includes a river valley trail system.

You may, however, have a parenthetical element between the subject and the verb that would call for two commas, one on each side of the element:

> This game refuge, as proposed, would cross the entire area.

Final Elements

Subordinate clauses or phrases that follow a main clause present more of a problem than do introductory elements. Generally, if they are not closely tied to the thought of the main clause, they are preceded by a comma. Definitely use a comma when the final element presents a turn of thought:

> Railroads and highways have contributed to the area's urbanization, although much of the area is still undeveloped.

However, when the final element is closely tied into the preceding main clause, you are better off without a comma:

> The highway will cross Indian mounds that have already been disturbed.

In this sentence the clause beginning with *that* is essential to the thought; therefore, a comma is not wanted. Reading aloud will usually help in this situation. If you pause before the final element while reading aloud, it's a good sign that a comma is needed.

Parenthetical and Interrupting Elements

When a word, phrase, or clause is parenthetical to the main thought of the sentence or interrupts the flow of the sentence, set commas around it:

> The cultural features, mainly Indian mounds, are to the west of the highway.

The inserted phrase, *mainly Indian mounds,* adds information to the sentence, of course, but it's an aside. It interrupts the flow of the main clause. See also the entries for Dash and Parentheses.

The phrase *of course* is usually set off by commas. So are conjunctive adverbs such as *consequently, however, nevertheless,* and *therefore:*

> The bridge is so high, of course, to allow river traffic to pass underneath. However, the most expansive vistas are to the east.

Nonrestrictive Modifiers

Nonrestrictive modifiers are set apart from the rest of the sentence by commas. Restrictive modifiers are not. Sometimes, determining which is which is a puzzle.

A restrictive modifier is essential to the meaning of the sentence. For instance,

> The design choices *for the Cedar Avenue Bridge* are all costly.

The italicized modifier defines and identifies which design choices, among all the possible design choices the writer could be talking about, are meant. The writer is not talking about the design choices for the Brooklyn Bridge or the Golden Gate Bridge. The writer is talking specifically and exclusively about the design choices for the Cedar Avenue Bridge. The modifier is therefore restrictive—it is essential to the meaning of the sentence. Look now at a nonrestrictive modifier:

> Old Shakopee Road, *which is a two-lane asphalt highway with narrow shoulders,* will be obsolete by 1990.

In this case the italicized modifier adds important and useful information, but it is not essential to the sentence. The road's name provides the limits or restrictions needed: It's not any road; it's the Old Shakopee Road. Therefore, the modifier is *nonrestrictive.*

If in doubt, try reading your sentence aloud. You will probably pause quite naturally at the breaks around nonrestrictive modifiers. These pauses are your clues to insert commas. See also the entries for Dash and Parentheses.

Series

Commas are the normal punctuation used when you are constructing a series:

This seepage emerges as natural springs that feed *tributary streams, lakes, and marshes.*

The components of the recreation system range from *miniparks, neighborhood playgrounds, and community playfields to multipurpose parks, park reserves, and historic parks.*

For lists with internal punctuation see the entry for Semicolon.

Conventional Uses

The comma is the conventional mark of punctuation in several situations:

Informal Salutation

Dear Dave,

Dates

November 13, 1959, is my birthday.
(But 13 November 1959 and November 1959 are both written without commas.)

Addresses

1269 River Valley Drive, Eagan, Indiana, is . . . .

Titles and Degrees

Charles E. Norad, Dean, is . . . .
Charles E. Norad, M.D., is . . . .

DASH

The dash is essentially a mark of separation. On a keyboard a dash is made with two unspaced hyphens:

For all three models--XL, XM, XN--you have your choice of over 40 lenses.

The dash is a rather peculiar but also rather useful mark of punctuation—as long as it is not overused. It is peculiar because it can be substituted for many other marks of punctuation, particularly the comma and parentheses. And, of course, it's this peculiarity that makes the dash useful.

When substituted for a comma, the dash indicates that the writer meant to be emphatic about the separation.

The table lists the total acres of wetlands within the project—all of which would be eliminated.

Placing dashes around parenthetical material indicates a degree of formal separation greater than the comma would indicate and less than parentheses:

> Several protective measures—wood fiber mats, mulches, and special seed mixtures—will prevent erosion.

You may also use the dash to emphasize items in a list or occasionally, instead of a colon, to introduce a list:

> Several antierosion measures are available:
>
>   —wood fiber mats
>   —mulches
>   —special seed mixtures
>   —berms and dikes
>
> Several antierosion measures are available—wood fiber mats, mulches, special seed mixtures, and berms and dikes.

The dash's versatility may tempt you to overuse it. It would quickly lose its emphatic value if you substituted it too freely for other marks. Used discreetly, the dash is a useful—even powerful—mark of punctuation.

DICTION

You have good diction when you choose words and expressions suitable to the occasion and express your thoughts as simply and clearly as possible.

Most people recognize that words suitable for some occasions are not suitable for others. The happy slang of locker rooms and poker games would be inappropriate in an annual business report. A paragraph from an annual report on student housing, for instance, reads this way:

> Dormitories were full and dorm waiting lists long as students began fall classes this year. More than 250 students were waiting to be assigned rooms. In some instances, students were temporarily housed in local hotels and motels.

The language is simple and serious and quite adequate to the occasion of the report. It's neither slangy nor heavy and pompous. Don't let the desire to be more formal lead you into windy pomposities like *viable interface* and *at this point in time* or tired clichés like *grim reality* or *Mother Nature*. Your cleaned-up, everyday language, supported by whatever professional vocabulary both you and your readers need and understand, will probably serve you well. You don't have to *ascertain reality* to write formally. *Finding out the facts* will serve just as well.

Your ear, as it is so often in writing, is a good guide. Read your work aloud. If it *sounds* foolish or pompous, it probably is. If you're sure you would not say something the way you have written it, don't write it that way either.

Faulty diction can also be caused by a lack of precision in choosing the words needed to express your thoughts. You may be *communicating* when *talking* is the more precise word. You may have confused *enormity* with *enormousness*. Perhaps you wrote the nonstandard *irregardless* for *regardless*. Perhaps you used *good* as in "Johnny played good" instead of "Johnny played *well*." You may have windily talked about *factors* when what is needed are some specific words to express what the factors really are.

You won't learn about good diction by reading about it. Rather you learn it by reading and listening to people who have it and by practicing what you have learned. And don't forget your dictionary—*diction* is its first name. (See also Chapter 3.)

ELLIPSIS POINTS

Ellipsis points consist of three spaced periods. They have several uses in transactional writing.

Use ellipsis points to indicate that you have omitted something from a quoted passage. Use four periods rather than three when the omission comes at the end of the sentence, the first period of the four being the period of the sentence. For example, the preceding sentence could be quoted as follows:

> Use four periods . . . when the omission comes at the end of the sentence. . . .

Notice that we have removed supplemental material from the sentence but have been careful not to change its meaning.

On occasion you might use ellipsis points to substitute for *and so forth* or *etc.*:

> After the semicolon you often see one of the conjunctive adverbs: *consequently, however, therefore*. . . .

In a brochure or ad you might use ellipsis points as an emphatic mark of separation between statements:

> Be sure to get your copy . . . ORDER NOW . . . Mail the coupon below with your check or money order for the full amount.

EXCLAMATION POINT

The exclamation point is placed after a statement to emphasize the statement. Its presence indicates that the information in the statement is particularly impressive, unusual, or emotional:

> The project engineer recommended the building site despite knowing it was unsafe!

If you don't have an exclamation point on your typewriter, make it with an apostrophe over a period.

The exclamation point has very limited use in transactional writing. Use it sparingly, and certainly never use more than one after a statement.

FRAGMENTARY SENTENCES

If you inadvertently punctuate a piece of a sentence as a complete sentence, you have written a fragmentary sentence. Fragmentary sentences most often lack a complete verb or are introduced by a relative pronoun or a subordinating conjunction.

Incomplete Verb

> **Incorrect** The glaciers forming three striking and different natural features.

Correct this sentence by correcting the verb:

> **Correct** The glaciers formed three striking and different natural features.

Relative Pronouns

The relative pronouns are *who, that, what, which, whoever, whatever,* and sometimes *as.* They signal that the clause they introduce needs to be connected to a complete sentence. When you make this connection, you have corrected the error.

> **Incorrect** The Minnesota River is an underfit river. That is too small for its valley.
> **Correct** The Minnesota River is an underfit river that is too small for its valley.

Subordinating Conjunctions

Subordinating conjunctions, as the name implies, connect a subordinate clause with a main clause. Therefore, their presence at the beginning of clauses marks the clauses as subordinate and unable to stand alone. Common subordinating conjunctions are *after, although, because, since, though, unless,* and *when.*

As with the relative clause, the answer here is to join the subordinate clause to the main clause.

> **Incorrect** Although the area is largely undeveloped. It does have some light industry.

Correct Although the area is largely undeveloped, it does have some light industry.

Sometimes writers will deliberately write fragmentary sentences to gain some special effect. In the following example the writer attempts to catch the feeling of conversation:

Unbelievable? Not really. In *Highway to Life* you'll find out how modern, safe, multilane divided highways are reducing traffic fatalities by as much as 90 percent.

The source of the example is an advertising letter where such use is appropriate. But use such devices with care, and be sure your deliberate use is so obvious it can't be mistaken for an error.

GRAPHICS

Graphs and tables play an important role in occupational writing. Whenever you have statistical data to present, consider presenting them graphically. Graphical presentation is particularly useful when you need to show comparisons and trends. We have integrated discussions of graphs and tables into our chapters in the places where we think they would be most useful to you. However, our major discussions of them are on pages 10–13, 185–196, 251–261, 288–295, 308–314, 383–390.

HYPHEN

Hyphens are used in word division and in numbers. For these two uses see the entries for Word Division and Numbers.

Here we are concerned with the use of the hyphen to combine two or more words to make them function as one word. Some publisher's or newspaper style manuals devote dozens of pages to the use of the hyphen. We suspect that madness lies in that direction. We attempt to simplify matters by considering hyphens used in compound words and in compound modifiers.

Compound Words

In English we form many new words by compounding two existing words, as in *wristband, wrist-drop,* and *wrist shot.* We have no trouble speaking such compounds, but we do have problems as soon as we attempt to write them. As our three examples rather maddeningly demonstrate, sometimes they're written as one word, sometimes hyphenated, sometimes as two words. There are no rules observed uniformly enough to be much help to us here. And most of us are not going to keep such fine distinctions in our heads.

What's the answer? When the piece of writing you are doing is important—perhaps a report or a letter of application—use your dictionary if you're not absolutely sure of the spelling. There is really no other way.

Compound Modifiers

Compound modifiers are obviously compound words also, but here our problems are somewhat eased. Most compound modifiers, whether in the dictionary or of our own invention, are hyphenated when used before the words they modify. For example:

> a coarse-grained texture
> a close-mouthed man
> a light-blue coat
> the ready-to-go-to-college woman

In informal writing we might see all these examples and similar modifiers written without the hyphen. But in transactional writing it's a good idea to use the hyphen to avoid confusion. Take the example of *light-blue coat*. A *light-blue coat* is light in color. A *light, blue* coat is light in weight. If the hyphens were omitted, consider the possibilities for confusion in *heavy-machinery operator*, *used-car buyer*, and *pink-skinned pig*.

Note that we have specified that a compound modifier is hyphenated when it is placed *before* the word it modifies. In constructions where the modifier appears as a predicate adjective—that is, after a linking verb—it is usually not hyphenated:

> For the ready-to-go-to-college woman . . . .
> For the woman who is ready to go to college . . . .

If in doubt about the hyphenation of compound words, whether they are used as modifiers or not, consult your dictionary. If you don't find an entry for the compound, use your own judgment and the principles given here. Remember, your goal is to avoid confusing the reader.

ITALICS

In print, italics are a special typeface, like this: *Modern Photography*. When you type or write you italicize by underlining:

> Modern Photography

Emphasis

You can emphasize a word or several words by italicizing them:

> Do not place a colon between a verb or a preposition and the objects that follow.

Like all emphatic devices, italics quickly lose their value if you over-use them.

Foreign Words

We sometimes incorporate foreign words into English. When they have been completely accepted—like *rendezvous,* for instance—we do nothing to make them stand out. But if they are still considered exotic, we italicize them:

> The officer in charge of a firing squad has the unpleasant task of giving the coup de grâce.

If in doubt about how to handle a word, use your dictionary. Its entry for the word will indicate whether or not you should italicize it.

Italicize the scientific terms for things:

> American chars belong to the genus Salvelinus.

Words as Words

When you use words as words and letters as letters, italicize them to prevent misunderstanding. There are frequent examples of such uses in this book, for instance:

> Omitted is spelled with one m and two t's.

Titles

Italicize the titles of books, journals, magazines, newspapers, films, and television programs:

> The Compact Edition of the Oxford English Dictionary
> Newsweek
> Wide World of Sports

MISPLACED AND DANGLING MODIFIERS

Modifiers are words, phrases, or clauses that limit or restrict other words, phrases, or clauses. *Green* modifying *coat* limits the coat to that color. "The bridge *that fell down*" can't be a bridge that remained standing. "A boy *moving downhill*" can't at the same time also be a boy *"moving uphill."* For the most part we all use modifiers with little difficulty, seldom thinking about them. But if we become careless in their placement, we can create sentences that can be vague or misunderstood or, on occasion, accidentally funny.

Modifiers that are in the wrong position to modify the words that the writer intended to modify are called *misplaced.* Modifiers that have nothing in the sentence to modify are called *dangling.*

Misplaced Modifiers

To correct a misplaced modifier, place it as close as possible to the words it modifies. Let's look at some examples:

> **Incorrect** The report about the resident students *of July 6, 1985,* reached me today.

Here the italicized modifier is located properly to modify *students* but incorrectly to modify *report.* If *report* is to be modified, move the phrase:

> **Correct** The report *of July 6, 1985,* about the resident students reached me today.

Another example:

> **Incorrect** Many researchers are attempting to identify factors that contribute to student development *in residential college life.*

If we move the italicized modifier, we have quite a different statement:

> **Correct** Many researchers are attempting to identify factors *in residential college life* that contribute to student development.

You the writer are in charge of the sentence. Put the modifier next to the words modified and say exactly what you mean.

Dangling Modifiers

Unlike misplaced modifiers, which modify the wrong word, dangling modifiers have nothing to modify:

> **Incorrect** *Analyzing change during the first year of college,* students who lived at home participated in fewer extracurricular activities.

At first impression this sentence leads us to believe that the students were analyzing change. But the sentence doesn't make sense that way. Looking at the sentence again, we realize that the word meant to be modified by the italicized modifier is not in the sentence. Let's say the missing word is *she.* We can now correct the sentence:

> **Correct** *Analyzing change during the first year of college,* she found that students who lived at home participated in fewer extracurricular activities.

Any time you begin a sentence with a phrase of the type represented by "Analyzing change" or "To analyze change," be alert. Be sure you include the words you intend to modify.

NUMBERS

The point at issue in writing numbers is whether they are written as a figure (26) or a word (twenty-six). The rules we give you are generally, though not universally, accepted. Whether you use these rules or others, be consistent throughout any piece of work.

Figures

Most style and usage books call for a number to be written as a figure in the following instances:

Addresses

1262 Pater Road, Dayton, OH 45419

Dates

July 27, 1985, or 27 July 1985

Time (with a.m. or p.m.)

6:20 p.m.

Exact Sums of Money with $ or ¢

$106.52
26¢

References to Pages, Figures, etc.

Page 6
See Figure 10.

Units of Measurement

10 meters   42 feet
20 amperes   9 tons

Identifying Numbers

His telephone number is (212) 626–6934.
His Social Security number is 010–18–7806.

Decimals

6.42 kilometers
3.5 liters

Percentages

61 percent
61%

Fractions Connected to Whole Numbers

42¼
6½

Tables and Illustrations

For reasons of space and clarity, all numbers in tables and illustrations are normally written as figures:

Table 3. Historical Population Growth

Area	1870	1920	1950	1960	1970	1975
Apple Valley	216	361	337	5,143	8,502	15,315
Burnsville	361	419	583	2,716	19,940	31,274
Eagan	670	857	1,185	3,381	10,398	17,686
Mendota Heights	444	757	2,107	5,028	6,168	7,258
Study Area Totals	1,691	2,394	4,252	16,268	45,008	71,533
Metro Area Totals	109,340	759,518	1,185,694	1,523,956	1,874,380	2,031,000

Source: U.S. Bureau of Census

Words or Figures

The general trend in business and technical prose is to use figures more than words. However, in some instances a word is still preferred or optional.

NUMBERS OVER 10   In most business and technical prose all numbers under 10 are written in words, and numbers 10 and over are written as figures:

> We have three choices in how to cross the valley.
> Only 36 Indian mounds are well preserved.

Large numbers are written with commas every three numerals, counting from the right:

> 3,126,400,000

If numbers under and over 10 are linked together in a series, write them all as figures:

> Historical sites in the area include 36 Indian mounds, 2 Indian villages, and 3 pioneer cemeteries.

NUMBERS OVER 100   Contrary to the previous rule, some organizations and publications write textual numbers under 100 as words and over 100 as figures. Under this system, hyphenate the two-word numbers between twenty-one and ninety-nine. If numbers under and over 100 are linked in a series, all are written as figures.

> Only thirty-six Indian mounds are well preserved.
> In 129 historical sites, only 36 Indian mounds are well preserved.

APPROXIMATE NUMBERS   Very often, numbers used in an approximate way are written as words, regardless of their size. The notion is that written as a figure the number might imply an exactness that is not meant:

> The bookstore sold over three thousand hand calculators during the fall term alone.

NUMBERS AT BEGINNINGS OF SENTENCES   Do not write any number that begins a sentence as a figure. This is a sensible rule. In certain circumstances a hurried reader might connect the number to the period of the preceding sentence and so read the number as a decimal. If writing the number as a word will be cumbersome, rework the sentence:

> Five hundred and ten insurance policies were sold in September.
> In September, 510 insurance policies were sold.

FRACTIONS   Fractions connected to whole numbers are always written as figures:

> 42¼, 6½

Small fractions are often written as words; if the fraction stands alone, write it as an unhyphenated compound:

> one fourth
> two thirds

Hyphenate a fraction written as an adjective:

> one-third speed

If the numerator or denominator of a fraction already is hyphenated, omit the hyphen between the parts:

> forty-two thousandths

This last circumstance will seldom occur because large fractions are usually expressed as decimals.

TIME (WITH *O'CLOCK*)   We normally use the term *o'clock* only with the hour. And we generally write the hour as a word:

> eleven o'clock

COMPOUND-NUMBER ADJECTIVES   In transactional writing two numbers frequently function together as a compound adjective. When such is the case, to avoid confusion write one as a number, one as a word:

3 two-lane highways
two 12-foot driving lanes

Be very careful about hyphenating number adjectives. There's considerable difference between 100 gallon drums and 100-gallon drums. In fact, it would be far safer to write the first as 100 one-gallon drums.

OUTLINES

To help you construct a formal outline, we present here an outline of a report you can see in final form in Figure 17–4, pages 364–368. To emphasize the rules of outlining, we have annotated the outline and followed it with a few comments.

Sample Outline

Peer Advising Proposal **Title**

The purpose of this report is to request funding for a peer advising program to be established for Criminal Justice Studies students. The report will be sent to Janice H. Grumbacher, Director of The Center for Educational Development **Purpose and audience statement**

I. Methodology **1st-level head, capital Roman numerals**
   A. Creation of peer advising unit **2nd-level head, capital letters**

   B. Duties of unit **No punctuation needed after any head**

   C. Evaluation of unit

II. Work and management plan **Capitalize only first letter of all heads and proper nouns**
   A. Facilities
   B. Task breakdown
      1. Training **3rd-level heads, arabic numerals**
      2. Office hours
      3. Evaluation
      4. Management
         a. Supervision **4th-level heads, lowercase letters**
         b. Reporting

III. Detailed budget
   A. Training time
   B. Office hours
   C. Evaluation time
IV. Personnel
   A. Martin A. Doyle
   B. William Morrell

Comments

- Normally, you don't include heads in the outline for your introduction or conclusion. The organization of the body of your report is what concerns you. Some version of your purpose and audience statement is likely to end up in your introduction, however.
- Make your heads statements of substance. That is, use words that will give the reader of your outline a true idea of your material. Heads such as "Cause 1," "Cause 2" or "Example 1," "Example 2" are of little use.
- Put parallel heads into parallel grammatical form. (See also the entry for Parallelism.) All parallel heads must have the same phrase structure. They must all be noun phrases, for example, and not a mixture of noun phrases and infinitive phrases. Use whatever phrase structure best suits your needs, but stick to it. Our sample outline uses parallel structures. An example of *improper* form would be

  A. Creation of unit
  B. To accomplish duties of unit
  C. How to evaluate the unit

- Logically, you can't divide anything without ending up with at least two pieces. This rule of logic holds true in outlining. Don't put just one subhead under any other head; you must have at least two. An outline entry like the following would be *incorrect*:

  4. Management
     a. Supervision

If you have I, you must have II; if an A, you must have a B; and so forth.

PARAGRAPHS

A typical paragraph is a central statement followed by opinions and facts that relate to or support the central statement—as in this example:

> Saint Anthony Falls, the only major cataract on the Mississippi and the original reason for the existence of Minneapolis, is the focal point of this historic district. Father Louis Hennepin, the first European to see the falls, viewed it and named it in 1680. In 1823, soldiers from the recently established Fort Snelling harnessed its powers for grist and lumber mills. The first dam was built in 1847, the first big sawmill in 1848. Within another 10 years, four flour mills were in operation, and Minneapolis was on its way to national leadership in both lumber and flour milling.

Generally, the central statement comes first in the paragraph, as it does in this example. In this position it fulfills two jobs: It introduces the paragraph and provides necessary transition from the preceding paragraph.

Sometimes, however, the central statement may be placed last:

A check of auto-deer collisions recorded by the Department of Natural Resources within the Study Area showed 60 auto-killed deer in 1983 and 64 in 1984. Several locations had a high incidence of deer-auto collisions. These locations are within linear bands of vegetation extending from the river valley to various woodlots and agricultural fields within the Study Area. Deer follow these vegetational bands in their movements between the valley and the higher ground. The proposed highway bisects several of these bands. Therefore, it seems likely that auto-deer accidents will continue and perhaps increase.

Placing the central statement last is useful in persuasion. You allow the facts to convince the reader before you draw the conclusion. It's a device to be used sparingly, however. Used too often, it can leave readers wondering why they have to plow through so many facts without proper guidance.

Paragraphs come in many lengths. On occasion a paragraph may be used as a transition between longer units. Such a paragraph might be only a sentence or two long. On the other hand, a fully developed paragraph in a scholarly book might be 250 words long.

Paragraphs also vary in length depending upon where they are going to appear. Paragraphs in newspapers run about 50 words long, in magazines about 100 words. These lengths relate to the narrowness of the columns being used. Newspaper and magazine editors don't want long columns of print without a break. Therefore, they break the paragraphs at fairly slight shifts of thought. Nonfiction books of a general nature have paragraphs that run 100 to 150 words long. Probably for most transactional reports an average of about 100 words per paragraph would be appropriate. In typed work this would be about 2½ paragraphs to a page.

Paragraphs run shorter in letters and memos than in printed work. A one-page letter that was all one paragraph would appear hard to read. Therefore, paragraphs in letters and memos may run only two or three sentences long—sometimes only one sentence.

Think of paragraphing as a way of guiding your reader through your material. Well-constructed paragraphs help the reader to spot your generalizations, usually the key to your organization. And, normally, your generalizations are your major statements—the ideas and opinions you want your reader to retain. Don't forget the visual impact of paragraphing. Large blocks of unbroken print may frighten off the reader. But too-short paragraphs may suggest a lack of organization. A middle road of paragraphs of varying lengths will probably present most material best.

PARALLELISM

When you start a series of sentence elements that serve the same function, put them into the same grammatical form. For instance, you will use many lists in transactional writing. Place all the elements of the list in the same form, as in this example:

> Always consider the following factors in designing an exhibit:
>
>> Distance of viewers from exhibit
>> Average viewing time
>> Material to be used
>> Lighting conditions
>> Visual acuity of viewers

In this example, each item on the list is based on a noun—*distance, time, material,* and so on. The writer would have had faulty parallelism if he had switched grammatical forms, as in this faulty list:

>> Distance of viewers from exhibit
>> To consider viewing time
>> What material should be used?

In this faulty list the writer went from a noun phrase to an infinitive phrase to a complete clause.

Use any grammatical form in your lists that is convenient for you. But stick to the same form throughout.

We have many paired constructions in English, such as *both . . . and; either . . . or; neither . . . nor; not . . . but;* and *not only . . . but also,* that call for parallel forms after each part of the pair. Look at this example:

> **Correct**   Design your exhibit *either for* a technically skilled audience *or for* the general public.

Both elements are based upon prepositional phrases and are correctly parallel. You would have faulty parallelism with this next structure:

> **Incorrect**   Design your exhibit *either for* a technically skilled audience *or to* please the general public.

Here the parallelism breaks down with the introduction of the infinitive phrase *to please* in the second element.

In most compound sentences you'll be wise to keep both clauses in the same voice—active or passive (see the entry for Sentences). In this example both sides of the compound sentence are in the active voice:

> **Correct**   People want to excel, construct, and imitate; and they seek pleasure, recognition, friends, and security.

The reader would be disturbed if we switched to the passive voice in the second clause:

> **Incorrect**   People want to excel, construct, and imitate; and pleasure, recognition, friends, and security are sought by them.

The following two main clauses read easily despite their length (36 words) because all the elements in both clauses are carefully balanced:

Speeding drivers passing a billboard off the highway will be able to read nine words at most, but slow-moving students passing a sign in a cafeteria line will be able to read several hundred words.

Any time you have elements in any kind of series, take a hard look at them. Be sure you have them in parallel grammatical form.

PARENTHESES

Of the three marks of punctuation used to enclose parenthetical material (commas, dashes, and parentheses), parentheses are the "heaviest." They separate the inserted material more definitely and can enclose longer elements—up to several sentences, if necessary—than the other marks. Look at several examples. Pay particular attention to the punctuation inside and around the parentheses:

Norway spruce *(Picea abies),* a native of Europe, is similar to white spruce in most characteristics. The model tree would have a straight central stem, normal taper (forming a cone the base of which is 70 to 80 percent of its height), and foliage that would be progressively less dense going from the bottom of the tree to the topmost whorl.

The primary purpose of shaping is to control height and width and to develop uniform taper. (Other purposes are to correct deformities, to remove multiple leaders, and to prune lower branches to form a handle and a complete base whorl.) A variety of tools may be used in the shaping process.

- Place no punctuation before the first parenthesis.
- Delay any punctuation needed after the last word before the first parenthesis until after the second parenthesis.
- Use any capitalization and punctuation required by the sentence structure inside the parentheses.
- Use no special punctuation around parentheses placed between sentences.

A special conventional use of parentheses is to enclose figures or letters used in lists:

The two main steps in shearing any species with a regular whorled branching habit are (1) regulation of the terminal whorl and (2) clipping or shearing of the side branches.

See also the entries for Comma, Brackets, and Dash.

PERIOD

Periods have the following conventional uses:

Abbreviations   Mrs., etc., Jr.
Decimal Point   .00236, $13.45
End Stop   He bought the farm.
Initials   John H. Doyle
Leaders   A series of periods to lead the eye are sometimes used in tables and tables of contents:

TABLE OF CONTENTS

See also the entry for Ellipsis Points.

PRONOUNS

Take care with pronouns in regard to agreement, reference, and case.

Agreement

Make a pronoun agree in number and gender with its antecedent—singular with singular, plural with plural, male with male, female with female, neuter with neuter:

John monopolized the meeting, but *he* . . . .
The *woman* walked through the lobby; then *she* . . . .
Set the *table* down and put the lamp on *it.*
The *group members,* when *they* meet . . . .

Traditionally, when we could be referring to either a man or a woman, we have used the male pronoun:

The *student* first gets a class card, then *he* . . .

The women's movement has made many people feel that this construction is unfair or at least insensitive. One way around the problem is to use a plural construction when you can:

The *students* first get a class card; then *they* . . . .

But English still lacks a neutral pronoun for such situations.
Be particularly careful with collective nouns (see the entry for Verb Agreement). They can be considered either singular or plural, depending on meaning. Make your pronoun agree with whatever number and verb you choose for the collective noun:

The *committee* is having *its* last meeting tonight.
The *committee* are arguing intensely among *themselves;* they . . .

See also the material on Collective Nouns, page 442.

Reference

Make sure your reader can tell without the slightest hesitation which word or word group your pronoun refers to. If you suspect any confusion, rewrite your sentence:

Despite the distance between the nouns and pronouns, the references are quite clear.

The speaker should place the notes on the lectern provided. *He* should not wave *them* about.

This reference is unclear. It could go back to either leader or secretary. In cases like this repeat the needed noun: "The *secretary* should keep an accurate record."

Both the group leader and the secretary are responsible for the proper recording of motions. *He* should keep an accurate record.

In this case *this* clearly refers to the broad concept of considering all contributions worthwhile.

Group members should believe that all contributions are worth considering. *This* in itself will prevent many arguments and unhappy members.

In this instance *this* is an unclear reference. We don't know what will not occur. We have three choices: (1) a faulty fact being identified; (2) a faulty fact being placed next to an accurate statement; (3) an accurate statement being made. A clear rewrite would be "But *this identification* may not occur."

A faulty fact can usually be identified when placed next to an accurate statement. But *this* may not occur.

As the last example demonstrates, you need to examine every reference for the possibility of misunderstanding. Remember that references clear to you may not be clear to your reader. Lean over backward to be clear. Be particularly careful whenever you are using *this, that, which,* or *it*.

Case

A brief lesson from the history of English is appropriate here. At one time—about 1,400 years ago—all nouns in English had case. A noun used as the subject of a sentence was in the nominative case, an indirect object in the dative case, and so forth. Thus, a hound eating a bone was a *hund,* but a hound given a bone to eat was a *hunde.* Except for the possessive case—*a hound's bone*—these cases did not survive in nouns. Today word order and prepositions tell us whether a noun is subject (S), object (O), or indirect object (IO):

> John gave the bone to the hound.
> S   O   IO

But case did survive in pronouns. Correct case is seldom necessary for understanding. If someone incorrectly says, "John and me went fishing," we understand that person as well as if he or she had correctly said, "John and I went fishing." If not necessary for understanding, however, case is still important. Quite frankly, status is involved. People who keep their pronouns sorted out correctly are considered by many other people to be more educated and cultured than those who do not.

A pronoun used as the subject of a sentence is in the nominative case—*I, he, she, we, they, who.* Pronouns used as objects of verbs and prepositions are in the objective case—*me, him, her, us, them, whom.* The pronouns *you* and *it* are the same in both cases.

Let's look at some examples:

> He hit *me.*
> *We* are going to *him* at once.
> *He* gave *her* the hat.
> *She* bought the car for *us* boys.
> *We* women want equality.
> *Who* is going to the fair?
> *He* gave the car to *whom*?

Many people have no trouble sorting out pronouns until they have to use a double object. Then they go to pieces and use the nominative case rather than the objective, perhaps because it sounds more elegant to them. The following forms are *correct:*

> He gave the book to *my brother and me.*
> It's a matter between *him and me.*
> She sent *them and us* an invitation.
> Between *you and me,* I think I understand it.

If in doubt about a double object, try it in a singular. Few people would say, "He gave the car to *I.*" Therefore, "He gave the car to *my brother and I*" would be equally incorrect. "He gave the car to *my brother and me*" is correct.

There is only one tricky place in the whole sorting out of pronouns—the seldom-used predicate nominative. After any form of the verb *to be* (*is, are, was,* and so on), we use the nominative case rather than the objective:

> It is *she.*
> Is it *she?*

Despite this rule almost everyone says "It's me," not "It's I." As we say, this construction is seldom used, particularly in writing. And if you get it wrong, most people will not notice. But do pay attention to your other pronouns. They may be more important to you than you think.

QUESTION MARK

If you write a direct question, place a question mark at its end:

How far must you drill to reach stable bedrock?

Polite requests may be punctuated with a question mark or a period:

Will you please send me the noise analysis report before Tuesday? [or] . . . before Tuesday.

Do not use a question mark after an indirect question:

The Sierra Club asked what the impact of the larger dam would be.

QUOTATION MARKS

Use quotation marks to set off quotations and certain titles. You may also use them to set off words used as words. (For additional information on making and documenting quotations see pages 159–160.)

Quotations

Use quotation marks to enclose a passage repeated from an earlier statement, whether written or spoken. The quotation marks signal that you have reproduced the passage word for word:

Zoo director John Sikes wrote, "The Zoo Board believes that most of the traffic will originate from the metropolitan area and will use the major freeways to reach the zoo."

You may make small, properly marked additions and omissions in quoted material, as explained in the entries for Brackets and Ellipsis Points.

If your quotation runs over three lines, don't put it inside quotation marks. Instead indent it on the page in the following manner:

In a letter to the Highway Department, the Chairman of the

Rockport Environmental Council expressed the Council's major

concern about the new route:

The proposed route would cut a path across the marsh, destroying valuable habitat. Even though the new bridge would be supported by piers, the piers themselves and the associated construction activities would leave permanent scars and damaging effects on the landscape.

Note that in this example the quoted passage is not only indented but also single-spaced, in order to contrast it with the double-spacing of the text. Use a colon to introduce indented quotations.

Titles

Titles of works shorter than book length, such as magazine articles, short stories, and poems, are set inside quotation marks:

> "Comparing Your Options in Home Insurance"
> "An Episode of War"
> "Frankie and Johnny"

Words as Words

Words used as words may be italicized (see the entry for Italics) or set inside quotation marks:

> What is meant by the term "shaping"?

Whichever method you choose, be consistent within a piece of work.

Quotation Marks with Other Marks of Punctuation

Fairly definite rules govern the use of other punctuation marks with quotation marks.

INTRODUCTORY MARKS   Quotations that need an introduction are preceded by commas or, in more formal circumstances, by colons:

> The Rockport mayor said, "No major conflicts with the plans for existing development are anticipated."

> The Rockport mayor supported alternative C with this statement: "All Rockport land use planning has anticipated the construction of alternative C. Therefore, we strongly recommend this alternative."

See also the entry for Colon.

When a quotation is closely integrated into a sentence, use no introductory mark of punctuation:

> The zoo director supports the building of the freeway because he feels "that most of the major traffic will originate from the metropolitan area. . . ."

The use of the lowercase letter at the beginning of the quote tells the reader that the preceding part of the sentence has been omitted. Therefore, no ellipsis is needed. However, an ellipsis is needed to signal the omission of the material at the end of the sentence. See also the entry for Ellipsis Points.

QUOTATION MARKS WITHIN OTHER QUOTATION MARKS When you use quotation marks within other quotation marks, use single quotes for the inside marks. When typing, use the apostrophe.

> In objection, the councilwoman said, "We question your use of the terms 'prudent and feasible' in this regard."

COMMAS AND PERIODS A period or comma at the end of any words set inside quotation marks is always set inside the marks, even when logic indicates it should go outside:

> The councilwoman questioned our use of the terms "prudent and feasible."

COLONS AND SEMICOLONS When a colon or semicolon is needed at the end of a quotation, always set it outside the marks:

> The councilwoman questioned our use of the terms "prudent and feasible"; we agree that the issue is open to interpretation.

DASHES, EXCLAMATION POINTS, AND QUESTION MARKS Dashes, exclamation points, and question marks follow the logic of the sentence. When they belong to the quotation, they go inside the marks. When they belong to the sentence, they go outside:

> Many new tree growers ask, "Why should trees be shaped?"
> What is meant by the term "shaping"?

Note that in the first example the question mark also serves as end punctuation for the sentence.

RUN-ON SENTENCES

The rule for avoiding run-on sentences is simple enough: Don't join two independent clauses with only a comma or with no punctuation at all. Normal punctuation between two independent clauses is one of the following:

1. a period
2. a semicolon
3. a comma and a coordinating conjunction (*and, but, for, nor, or, yet*)

The trick is to recognize an independent clause when you see one. The following are all independent clauses. If you have difficulty with run-on sentences, memorize these patterns:

> Overhead projection is a dramatic method of presenting facts and ideas clearly, concisely, and effectively.
> The instructor controls the equipment with a switch of his fingertips.

Put your overhead visuals on a transparent base.
Most inks can be washed off easily.
They are safe to use.

Placing a conjunctive adverb before an independent clause does not make the clause subordinate. Nor does the conjunctive adverb serve as a strong connective. Therefore, you must use normal punctuation as defined in this section before an independent clause beginning with a conjunctive adverb. The major conjunctive adverbs are *accordingly, also, anyhow, besides, consequently, furthermore, however, indeed, likewise, moreover, nevertheless, then, therefore.*

Observe carefully these examples of correct punctuation:

Most inks can be washed off easily. Therefore, they are safe to use.
Most inks can be washed off easily; therefore, they are safe to use.
Most inks can be washed off easily, and, therefore, they are safe to use.

See also the entries for Colon, Comma, Fragmentary Sentences, Period, and Semicolon.

SEMICOLON

The semicolon is used in certain situations between independent clauses and when internal commas make it necessary in a series. It really has quite limited uses. Don't confuse a semicolon with a colon. Don't use it to introduce lists or quotations, and don't use it after the salutation in a letter. See the entries for Colon and Run-on Sentences.

Independent Clauses

You can use the semicolon between two independent clauses at any time instead of the more normal period; however, the semicolon is most widely used when the link between the two clauses is one of the conjunctive adverbs: *consequently, however, nevertheless, therefore,* and so on. In this situation the comma is not considered strong enough punctuation, and the period is perhaps too strong:

The outlet will be below water level; therefore, it will be entirely submerged and not visible from the bank.

Sometimes, independent clauses between which you would normally use a comma and a coordinating conjunction already have strong internal commas. In this case substitute a semicolon for the comma:

The buildings, mainly flour- and sawmills, are gone; but foundations, penstocks, tailraces, and some machinery remain.

Series

When the elements of a series have internal commas, substitute a semi-colon at the breaks where you would normally use commas:

> The schools examined were Normandale, a two-year public community college; Hamline, a four-year private school; and the University of Illinois, a four-year public school.

SENTENCES

Elsewhere in this Guide we tell you about various sentence faults (see the entries for Fragmentary Sentences, Misplaced and Dangling Modifiers, Run-on Sentences, Parallelism, and Verb Agreement). In this section we give some positive advice about writing better sentences. Specifically, we discuss choice of the proper voice, sentence length, sentence order, and directness.

Voice

English sentences are in either of two voices—active and passive:

> **Active** The glaciers formed three striking and different natural features.
>
> **Passive** Three striking and different natural features were formed by the glaciers.

In the active-voice sentence the subject acts; in the passive-voice sentence the subject is acted upon. Active-voice sentences use fewer words and state more directly what you have to say. With the passive voice you run the risk of forgetting the final prepositional phrase—*by the glaciers*—and leaving the doer of the action unknown.

For simple instructions the imperative mood of the active voice is clearly superior to the passive. A passage in a safety brochure reads this way:

> Keep your distance. Never operate a crane beneath the power lines without adequate clearance. Play it safe. Leave more than the minimum six feet required. Remember, too, a boom may rebound when a load is released.

The passage is crisp and direct, and clearly says, "This means you!" Compare the active version to the passive:

> Distance should be kept. A crane should not be operated beneath power lines without adequate clearance. More than the minimum six feet should be allowed for safety reasons. It should be remembered that a boom may rebound when a load is released.

The second version is flabby, indefinite, and needlessly long.

> **Compare** It is requested that you send me a copy of your speech.
> **With** I would appreciate a copy of your speech.

The second, active-voice version is far closer to normal speech and far more polite than the impersonal passive voice version.

However, the passive voice has many uses. Use it when the person or thing acted upon is more important than the actor or when you wish to deemphasize the actor. But don't use the passive voice by accident. Know it when you see it, and use it only when it is clearly better than the active-voice version of the same idea. (See also pages 44–46.)

Sentence Length

Professional writers average about 21 words a sentence whether they're writing for high school graduates or Ph.D's. For an audience with less than a high school education they might scale down their sentences to 14 to 18 words. You should take a lesson from the professional writer and work for similar averages. Remember that we're talking about averages. Don't cookie-cut a series of 21-word sentences. Rather, let your sentences range over a spread of about 5 to 35 words. Being conscious of your sentence length will prevent the two extremes of poor writing—too-short sentences and too-long sentences. The former results in disconnected, primer-like sentences:

> The glaciers formed the topography of the study area. They left an accumulation of glacial drift. This drift is from 100 to 500 feet thick. [25 words in 3 sentences]

Smoothly connecting the ideas, we get this result:

> The glaciers, leaving an accumulation of glacial drift from 100 to 500 feet thick, formed the topography of the study area. [21 words in 1 sentence]

At the other extreme, too-long sentences are too complex for the reader to follow. And sometimes, as in this example from a government document, the writer loses control over the material:

> As of the effective date of this memorandum, projects which have received design approval (as defined in PPM 90–1) may receive PS & E approval, if otherwise satisfactory, on the basis of past state highway submissions which identify and document the economic, social and environmental effects previously considered with respect to these advanced projects, together with a supplemental report, if necessary, covering the consideration and disposition of the items and not previously covered and now listed herein in paragraph 4.b.

Seventy-eight words of gobbledygook!

Keeping track of your average sentence length is one easy thing you can do to improve your writing. (See also pages 38–39.)

Sentence Order

Normal English sentence order is subject first, verb second. Following the verb a wide range of objects, modifiers, subordinate clauses, and additional main clauses is possible:

> Actual shearing *techniques differ* among growers.
>   S   V
>
> *Some prefer* to begin trimming at the base of the tree and work upward to
> S   V
> the terminal leader.

Research shows that professional writers begin about 75 percent of their sentences with the subject.[1] Another 23 percent of the time they begin the sentence with a simple adverbial opener, followed by the subject:

> *In the terminal whorl,* the grower will encounter some common situations that require corrective action.
>
> *However,* these are dangerous tools, and you should take extra precautions.

Less than 2 percent of the time professional writers begin with a subordinate clause or verbal phrase:

> *When the operation is repeated annually,* it has the effect of developing a shorter, well-shaped, and compact tree.
>
> *To use any herbicide safely,* follow the exact instructions on the label.

Sentence openers before the subject usually serve as transitional devices, linking the sentence to a previous idea.

We appreciate professional writing because, being cast in normal sentence patterns, it puts no roadblocks between us and the thought. Follow the professional pattern and you'll put your main idea first most of the time. You'll avoid the difficulties of sentences like the following:

> If it appears logical to use the same shoulder width and surface type as that in place on adjacent projects, or if aspects of traffic growth or traffic assignment splits would justify a different selection, or if stage construction is a consideration, it may be desirable to deviate from standards.

This sentence, poor on several counts, puts its main idea—permissible deviation from standards—last. Readers wander through the conditions, wondering why they are reading them. Reverse the order and use a list, and the result would be a far better statement:

> You may deviate from standards under these conditions:
>
> 1. If it appears logical to use the same width and surface type as that in place on adjacent projects.
> 2. If aspects of traffic growth or traffic assignment splits would justify a different selection.
> 3. If stage construction is a consideration.

Directness

Write directly to your thought. Write to express ideas, not to line up words in a row. Don't follow old formulas that are word wasters. Don't *make application to;* simply *apply.* Don't *make contact* with people; instead, simply *see* them or meet them. Do you begin thank-you notes by saying, "I want to thank you for . . ."? Why not simply say "Thank you for . . ."? It sounds faintly pompous to say or write *at this point in time* rather than *now.* If something happens *due to the fact that,* simply say *because.* If something is *in accordance with the regulation,* it is really only *under* or *by the regulation.* The list of such tired, indirect ways of saying things is unfortunately all too long. You'll avoid most of them if you think about what it is you want to say and say it in the most direct way you can.

We also waste a good many words by not recognizing the value of the verb in English:

> **Compare** What is the conclusion to be drawn from this research?
> **With** What can we conclude from this research?

The second sentence saves three words. How was this achieved? By taking the action idea in *conclusion* and putting it in the verb *conclude,* where it belongs.

Besides using fewer words when you put your action into verbs, you'll make your writing more vivid. This first version of a sentence is pallid and indirect:

> A blockage of debris in the conduit could cause a flood in the upper pool.

By putting action into verbs, we have this far better sentence:

> Debris blocking the conduit could flood the upper pool.

Look at the use of verbs and verb forms in the opening paragraph of an advertising letter (the italics are ours):

> *To help prevent* highway deaths, engineers *may* someday *control* traffic with computers. For long distances, the computer *may steer, accelerate,* and *brake* the car as *needed.* The driver will *lounge, read, play cards, even sleep* while *being whisked* safely down the highway.

The professional writer of this paragraph knew that verbs snap people to attention. He used verbs to express ideas vividly and directly. He did not hide his ideas behind a smokescreen of needless words. (See also pages 44–46.)

SPELLING

Spelling correctly is important. Many people are quick to judge your competence and intelligence by how well you spell. A misspelled word or two in a letter of application may block you from a job as quickly as would lack of experience or education. This may be unfortunate and even unwise, but it is one of the facts of life.

For many historical reasons, such as changes in pronunciation and the introduction of foreign words, English is a difficult language to spell. Nevertheless, there are certain rules to follow. Numerous books explain these rules. Look for them in your library—under either *spelling* or *orthography*—or in your bookstore. The rules really do help and are worth mastering.

If you have a dictionary handy, you'll probably spell the difficult words correctly. That is, you know you can't spell them, so you look them up. If you are like most people, it's the everyday words that you misspell the most. Most of us are reluctant to lift the heavy dictionary off the shelf when we need it only for the spelling of a common word. We'd rather take our chances. All too often our confidence is misplaced. We suggest another approach. Most secretaries own small books, easily carried in a pocket, that list without definition twenty to thirty thousand of the most commonly used words. These books also divide words into syllables, so they are useful for breaking a word at the end of a line. Any bookseller will be happy to find one for you. If you own one, you'll find it convenient to use, and you'll improve your spelling.

To give you some immediate help with these common words, we have provided a list of 544 words that college students frequently misspell. See also the entries for Abbreviations and Word Division.

Commonly Misspelled Words

absence	affect *(verb)*	answer	awful
absorption	against	antiseptic	balance
accessible	aggravate	apparatus	basically
accommodate	aisle *(of theater)*	apparent	before
accompanied	alcohol	appear	beginning
accomplish	all ready	appearance	believe
accustomed	*(all prepared)*	appetite	benefit
ache	all right	appropriate	benefited
achieve	almost	arguing	breathe *(verb)*
achievement	already *(so soon)*	argument	brilliant
acquaint	although	around	buried
acquire	altogether	arouse	business
across	always	arrangement	busy
actual	amateur	article	cafeteria
actually	among	ascend	calculate
address	amount	assistant	calculator
advice *(noun)*	analysis	athlete	calendar
advise *(verb)*	analyze	athletic	captain
adviser	annual	author	carburetor
aerial	anoint	auxiliary	careful

carrying
category
ceiling
cemetery
certain
changeable
changing
characteristic
chief
choose
   (present tense)
chose
   (past tense)
climbed
clothes
collegiate
column
coming
commit
committed
committee
common
comparatively
competition
complement
   (to complete)
compliment
   (to praise)
conceivable
conceive
concentration
concern
conquer
conscience
conscientious
conscious
consider
consistent
continually
continuous
control
controlled
convenience
conversation
coolly
copies
corroborate
countries
course
courteous
criticism

criticize
crowd
crystal
curiosity
cylinder
dealt
decide
decision
definite
degree
dependent
describe
description
desirable
despair
desperate
destroy
determine
develop
development
device
didn't
diesel
dietitian
difference
different
dilemma
dining
disappear
disappoint
disapprove
disastrous
discipline
discoveries
discriminate
discussed
disease
dissatisfied
dissection
distinction
divide
divine
division
doesn't
dormitories
drunkenness
easily
ecstasy
effect
   (usually a noun)
efficiency

efficient
eighth
electricity
electronics
eligible
eliminate
embarrass
embarrassment
emphasize
enemy
engines
environment
equipment
equipped
especially
essential
etc.
exaggerate
exceed
excellent
except
exercise
exhausted
exhilaration
existence
expense
experience
experiment
explanation
extremely
familiar
fascinate
fascinating
February
finally
financial
flourish
forcibly
foreign
foresee
formally
   (in a formal way)
formerly *(earlier)*
forth *(forward)*
forty
forward
fourth *(4th)*
friend
frightening
fundamental
further

gardener
gauge
generally
government
governor
grammar
grateful
grievous
guarantee
guard
guidance
hadn't
handle
hear *(sound)*
height
here *(place)*
heroes
heroine
holiday
hoping
humorous
hungry
hurriedly
hurrying
identify
imaginary
imagination
imitation
immediately
incidentally
increase
incredible
independence
independent
indispensable
inevitably
influential
initiate
inoculate
insistent
intellectual
intelligence
intelligent
interest
interfere
interpret
interrupt
invitation
irrelevant
irresistible
irritable

island
it's *(it is)*
its *(possessive)*
jealous
judgment
knew
knowledge
laboratory
laid
larynx
later
led
leisure
length
library
license
lightening
   (removing weight)
lightning
   (and thunder)
liable
likelihood
likely
literally
literature
loneliness
losing
loyalty
lying
machine
magazine
maintenance
manageable
management
maneuver
manual
many
marriage
married
mathematics
meant
mechanics
medicine
merely
miniature
minutes
mischievous
misdemeanor
misspelled
morale
mortgage

mournful
muscle
mysterious
naturally
necessarily
necessary
neighbor
neither
nickel
niece
ninety
ninth
noticeable
obstacle
occasion
occasionally
occur
occurred
occurrence
o'clock
official
omission
omit
omitted
operate
opinion
opportunity
optimism
optimist
optimistic
origin
original
oscillate
paid
panicky
parallel
particularly
partner
pastime
peaceable
peculiar
perceive
perform
perhaps
permanent
perseverance
persistent
personal
personally
perspiration
persuade

pertain
piece
plain
planned
planning
pleasant
poison
politician
possess
possesses
possession
possible
potato
potatoes
practicability
practical
practically
prairie
precede
preceding
predictable
prefer
preferable
preference
preferred
prejudice
preparation
prepare
presence
prevalent
primitive
principal *(main)*
principle *(a rule)*
privilege
probably
procedure
proceed
professional
professor
prominent
pronunciation
propeller
protein
prove
psychology
publicly
pursue
quantity
quarter
quiet
realize

really
receipt
receive
recognize
recommend
referred
relevant
relieve
religious
repetition
representative
resemblance
resistance
respectability
restaurant
rhythm
rhythmical
ridiculous
safety
salary
scarcely
scene
schedule
science
secretarial
secretary
seize
sense
separate
sergeant
several
severe
shepherd
shining
shoulder
sight *(seeing)*
signal
similar
simile
sincerely
site *(location)*
sophomore
speak
specimen
speech
statement
stationary
   (not moving)
stationery *(paper)*
stopped
straight

strategy	temperament	truly	weather *(climate)*
strength	temperature	Tuesday	Wednesday
strenuous	tendency	twelfth	weird
stretch	than *(bigger than)*	two *(2)*	where
striking	their *(possessive)*	undoubtedly	whether
studying	then *(at that time)*	university	*(conjunction)*
succeed	there *(location)*	unnecessary	wholly
successful	therefore	until	who's *(who is)*
suddenness	they're *(they are)*	unusual	whose
superintendent	thorough	using	*(possessive)*
suppress	thought	usually	woman
surely	through	vacuum	women
surprise	to *(toward)*	vegetable	won't
syllable	together	vengeance	writing
symmetrical	too *(also)*	vertical	written
technical	toward	villain	you're *(you are)*
technician	transferred	vitamin	your *(possessive)*
technique	tries		

TRANSITION

Transitions move the reader from one idea to the next. More importantly they show the relationships among ideas as shown in the relationship of one sentence to the next or of one paragraph to a previous paragraph. You may need a transition to tie a sentence or paragraph into the overall purpose of a report.

There are many ways to provide transition. You can do it with words such as *however, therefore,* and *consequently,* as in this sentence:

> Generally, the system adapts best to large operations; *however,* it is a flexible system and may, in some instances, fit the needs of small operations.

You can provide transition by repeating key words from one paragraph or sentence to the next. Read the first sentence in this paragraph and in the previous two paragraphs, and you'll see that we have done exactly that with the key word *transition.* Sometimes you will need a more obvious transition to get you from one part of a report to the next, as in this example:

> Before making specific recommendations for design and management of natural-air drying systems, we will describe the principles involved.

The use of headings, particularly when combined with a good lead-in, can provide excellent transition:

FILLING SCHEDULES

Three types of filling schedules can be used when operating a natural-air drying bin: fast-fill, layer-fill, and weekly-fill.

Fast-fill Schedule
    With the fast-fill schedule . . . .

Layer-fill Schedule
    If filled in layers . . . .

Weekly-fill Schedule
    The weekly-fill schedule . . . .

Notice in these last examples the repetition of the key words in the sentences that follow the headings.

However you provide them, transitions are a key to the coherent and logical presentation of your material. Don't leave your readers without them.

UNDERLINING

See Italics.

VERB AGREEMENT

Make the verb agree with its subject. Normally, this won't be a problem for you, but some trouble spots do exist.

Intervening Prepositional Phrases

When a prepositional phrase with a plural object—for example, *of the women*—comes between a singular noun or pronoun and its verb, writers often go astray and use a plural verb:

Incorrect The *stack* of letters *are* . . . .
Correct The *stack* of letters *is* . . . .

The pronouns most likely to cause difficulty in this construction are *each, either, neither,* and *none,* all of which take singular verbs. Grammar is often at war with meaning here, but grammar decides the verb:

Incorrect If *each* of the group members *have* . . . .
Correct If *each* of the group members *has* . . . .

Compound Subjects

Compound subjects connected by *and* take a plural verb:

Hydrogen and oxygen are . . . .

When you have a compound subject in an *either . . . or* construction, the noun closest to the verb decides the form of the verb. Note the reversal in the two examples:

> Either the group members or the *leader is* . . . .
> Either the leader or the group *members are* . . . .

Collective Nouns

We have a good many collective nouns in English, nouns like *audience, band, committee, group, company,* and *class.* Collective nouns can take either singular or plural verbs, depending on the meaning of the sentence:

> The *committee is* having *its* last meeting tonight.
> The *committee are* arguing intensely among *themselves.*

However, most Americans feel uncomfortable using a plural verb after a collective noun. (The British do it naturally.) We're more likely to say, "The *committee members are* arguing intensely among *themselves.*" (See also the entry for Pronouns.)

Plural-Sounding Nouns

Some nouns sound plural but are not—for instance, *electronics, economics, mathematics, physics,* and *measles.* Despite their sound, such nouns take singular verbs:

> *Mathematics is* necessary in . . . .

Nouns of Measurement, Time, and Money

Plural nouns that express measurement, time, or money take singular verbs:

> *One hundred yards is* the distance from goal line to goal line.
> *Ten years was* the sentence.
> *Five thousand dollars is* a lot of money.

WORD DIVISION

When you have to carry part of a word over to another line, break it between syllables and hyphenate it:

> Even more important than the dormitory pro-
> gram is the . . . .

Your dictionary will show the syllabic division of words:

> croc·o·dile
> gum·my
> gra·cious

A few standard rules cover the proper way of dividing words:

- When a vowel ends a syllable or stands by itself, break after the vowel:

  paro-chial
  esti-mate (*not* est-imate)

- Break between double consonants, unless the double consonant appears in the root of the word:

  occur-ring
  bril-liant

but

  spell-ing
  toll-ing

- Don't carry over single letters or *-ed* when the *e* is silent. For instance, you would not carry over the *-y* of *bushy* or the *-ed* of *bucked*. You could break *darted* before the *-ed* because the *-ed* is pronounced. (However, usually it is better not to carry over only two letters. Leave them on the line above or carry the whole word over.)

METRIC CONVERSION TABLES

The metric system of measurement is used in virtually every country outside the United States and is increasingly used, especially in technical contexts, in the United States. In research and writing it is often necessary, therefore, to be able to convert readily from the metric system to the U.S. system and vice versa. The following tables provide multipliers for converting both ways; the multipliers have been rounded to the third decimal place and thus yield an approximate equivalent.

METRIC TO U.S.			U.S. TO METRIC		
to convert from	to	multiply the metric unit by	to convert from	to	multiply the U.S. unit by
Length					
kilometers (km)	miles	.621	miles	kilometers	1.609
meters (m)	yards	1.093	yards	meters	.914
meters	feet	3.280	feet	meters	.305
meters	inches	39.370	inches	meters	.025
centimeters (cm)	inches	.394	inches	centimeters	2.540
millimeters (mm)	inches	.039	inches	millimeters	25.400
Area and Volume					
square meters (m^2)	square yards	1.196	square yards	square meters	.836
square meters	square feet	10.764	square feet	square meters	.093
square centimeters (cm^2)	square inches	.155	square inches	square centimeters	6.451
cubic centimeters (cm^3)	cubic inches	.061	cubic inches	cubic centimeters	16.387
Liquid Measure					
liters (L)	cubic inches	61.020	cubic inches	liters	.016
liters	cubic feet	.035	cubic feet	liters	28.339
liters	U.S. gallons*	.264	U.S. gallons*	liters	3.785
liters	U.S. quarts*	1.057	U.S. quarts*	liters	.946
milliliters (mL)	fluid ounces	.034	fluid ounces	milliliters	29.573
Weight and Mass					
kilograms (kg)	pounds	2.205	pounds	kilograms	.453
grams (g)	ounces	.035	ounces	grams	28.349
grams	grains	15.430	grains	grams	.065

*The British imperial gallon equals approximately 1.2 U.S. gallons or 4.54 liters. Similarly, the British imperial quart equals 1.2 U.S. quarts, and so on.

CHAPTER NOTES

Preface

1. James Britton, Tony Burgess, Nancy Martin, Alex McLeod, and Harold Rosen, *The Development of Writing Abilities (11–18)* (London: Macmillan Education Ltd., 1975), 88.
2. Both phrase and passage are from "Teaching Writing for the World's Work," *Teaching English in the Two-Year College* 2, no. 1 (1975): 7–14.
3. "Confessions of a Teacher of Technical Writing," *The Technical Writing Teacher* 1, no. 1 (1973): 5.

Chapter 1: The Process of Transactional Writing

1. *What They Think of Higher Education,* Educational Relations Informational Bulletin (New York: General Electric Company, 1957).
2. Richard M. Davis, "How Important Is Technical Writing? A Survey of the Opinions of Successful Engineers," *Journal of Technical Writing and Communication* 4, no. 3 (1977): 83–88.
3. Victoria M. Winkler, Earl E. McDowell, and Ronaele Hoffman, "Communication Needs of Agriculture, Home Economics, and Forestry Alumni: Implications for Technical and Professional Communication Courses" (University of Minnesota: Department of Rhetoric, 1980), 9.
4. This passage and Figure 1 are from Jet Propulsion Laboratory, "Improved Coal-Slurry Pipeline," *NASA Tech Briefs,* Spring 1979, 47.

Chapter 2: Persuasion and Scientific Argument

1. Knowing people will see in all this our debt to Aristotle, a debt that we cheerfully acknowledge.
2. Andrea Hinding, "The Invisible Women," *Research,* Fall 1980, 21.
3. U.S. Bureau of the Census, *Statistical Abstract of the United States 1984,* 104th ed. (Washington, D.C.: U.S. Government Printing Office, 1984), Tables 1064, 1073.
4. National Oceanic and Atmospheric Administration, *Environmental Assessment of the Alaskan Continental Shelf: Lower Cook Inlet Interim Synthesis Report* (Washington, D.C.: U.S. Department of Commerce, 1979), 16.
5. Table 1077.
6. Copyright 1975 by Consumers Union of the United States, Inc., Mount Vernon, NY 10550. Reprinted by permission from *Consumer Reports,* October 1975.
7. National Oceanic and Atmospheric Administration, 62.
8. Excerpted from the September 1980 issue of *The Harvard Medical School Health Letter.* © 1980 President and Fellows of Harvard College.
9. William Bennett, "The Cigarette Century," *Science 80,* 1 (September/ October 1980), 42.

Chapter 3: Style and Tone

1. This example and its rewrite are from "Treating the Whole Document: A Benefits Handbook," *Simply Stated,* no. 21 (1981): 3.
2. U.S. Department of Commerce, *How Plain English Works for Business* (Washington, D.C.: U.S. Government Printing Office, 1984), 2.
3. Porter G. Perrin and George H. Smith, *Handbook of Current English* (New York: Scott, Foresman and Company, 1955), 211.
4. "Clunker Blight: High Time to Stamp It Out," *M.O.,* October 1983, 1.
5. This example and its rewrite are from "Three Document Design Principles," *Simply Stated,* no. 29 (1982): 3.
6. Reprinted by permission; © *Washington Post.*
7. This example and its rewrite are from "Three Document Design Principles," 4.
8. Ibid., 3.
9. George Larson, "The Mandrell Magic," *Raytheon Magazine,* Summer 1984, 28.
10. Daniel B. Felker et al., *Document Design: A Review of the Relevant Research* (Washington, D.C.: American Institutes for Research, 1980), 89.

Chapter 8: Sales Letters

1. All excerpts from Gokey's reprinted by permission.

Chapter 9: Basic Principles of Reports

1. *Technical Report Writing*, 2nd ed. (New York: John Wiley & Sons, 1977), 40.
2. New York: John Wiley & Sons, 1969, v.
3. Typing Suggestions are based on an article by Anne Shelby, "How to Type Your Paper," *The Technical Writing Teacher* 1 (1974): 11–22.

Chapter 11: Bibliographic Reports and Literature Reviews

1. Jose B. Cuellar and E. Percil Standford, *A Guide to Minority Aging References* (Washington, D.C.: U.S. Government Printing Office, 1983).
2. From *Agricultural Economics Research* 32, no. 3 (1980): 8–20. Material excerpted from pages 8 and 9.

Chapter 12: Mechanism Description

1. From an unpublished student report, used with permission of the author, Don Bowles.
2. From an unpublished student report, used with permission of the author, Jim Johnson.

Chapter 13: Process Description

1. Reprinted by permission from M. Nonaka and M. L. Weaver, "Texturizing Process Improves Quality of Baked French Fried Potatoes," *Food Technology* 27 (March 1973): 50.
2. George A. Miller, "The Magical Number Seven, Plus or Minus Two: Some Limits on Our Capacity for Processing Information," *Psychological Review* 63 (March 1956): 81–97.

Chapter 14: Instructions

1. For additional material on writing training materials, see Robert F. Mager and Kenneth M. Beach, Jr., *Developing Vocational Instructions* (Palo Alto, Calif.: Fearon Publishers, 1967). We also wish to thank Gerry Cohen for helpful discussion on using a form to gather information for instructions.
2. From an unpublished student report, used with permission of the author, Jesus N. Martinez.

Chapter 16: Recommendation Reports

1. All excerpts from "The Feasibility of Using Embark Plant Growth Regulator Instead of Mowing to Maintain Grassy Areas Along Minnesota's Highways," an unpublished student report, printed with the permission of Scott Pahl, the author.
2. Embark® is a registered trademark of the 3M Company.

Chapter 17: Proposals

1. Frank R. Smith, "Engineering Proposals," in *Handbook of Technical Writing,* vol. 1, ed. Stello Jordon, Joseph M. Kleinman, and H. Lee Shimberg (New York: Wiley-Interscience, 1971), 494.

Chapter 18: Oral Reports

1. Annual Convention of Toastmasters International, New York, 1965.
2. This statement and the next two excerpts are from S. Martin Shelton, "The Influence of the Information Film," in *Proceedings, 31st International Technical Communication Conference* (Washington, D.C.: Society for Technical Communication, 1984), VC–5, 6.
3. Elaine Babcock Selle, "The Woman Manager: An Inside Picture," *Proceedings, 26th International Technical Communication Conference* (Washington, D.C.: Society for Technical Communication, 1979), M–160.
4. Mary Fran Buehler, "Rules That Shape the Technical Message: Fidelity, Completeness, Conciseness," *Proceedings, 31st International Technical Communication Conference* (Washington, D.C.: Society for Technical Communication, 1984), WE–9.
5. Stephen L. Pistner, "Tough Customers Mean Better Business," *Vital Speeches* 50, no. 21 (1984): 669.
6. James E. Connolly, *Making More Effective Technical Presentations* (Minneapolis: University of Minnesota, 1981), 21–30.
7. John Davenport, "Slurvian Self-Taught," *The New Yorker,* June 18, 1949, 24.

Writer's Guide

1. Francis Christensen, "Notes Toward a New Rhetoric," *College English,* October 1963, 7–18.

SELECTED BIBLIOGRAPHY

The lists that follow are suggested for further reading on various areas of transactional writing. The lists, of course, do not include all the books devoted to a particular area, but they do include those books we think are particularly helpful to beginning writers.

Technical Writing
Houp, K., and T. Pearsall. *Reporting Technical Information.* 5th ed. New York: Macmillan, 1984.

Mathes J. C., and D. W. Stevenson. *Designing Technical Reports: Writing for Audiences in Organizations.* Indianapolis: Bobbs-Merrill, 1976.

Michaelson, H. B. *How to Write and Publish Engineering Papers and Reports.* Philadelphia: ISI Press, 1982.

Mills, G., and J. Walter. *Technical Writing,* 4th ed. New York: Holt, Rinehart and Winston, 1978.

Pickett, N. A., and A. A. Laster. *Technical English: Writing, Reading, and Speaking.* 4th ed. New York: Harper & Row, 1984.

Souther, J. W., and M. L. White. *Technical Report Writing.* 2nd ed. New York: Wiley-Interscience, 1977.

Business Letters and Reports
Davis, K. *Better Business Writing: A Process Approach.* Columbus, Ohio: Charles E. Merrill, 1983.

Murphy, H. A., and C. E. Peck. *Effective Business Communications.* 3rd ed. New York: McGraw-Hill, 1980.

Sigband, N. B. *Communication for Management and Business.* 3rd ed. Glenview, Ill.: Scott, Foresman, 1982.

Treece, M. *Successful Business Writing*. Boston: Allyn and Bacon, 1980.

Wilkinson, C. W., P. B. Clark, and D. C. M. Wilkinson. *Communicating Through Letters and Reports*. 7th ed. Homewood, Ill.: Richard D. Irwin 1980.

Writing in General

Brusaw, C. T., G. J. Alred, and W. E. Oliu. *Handbook of Technical Writing*. 2nd ed. New York: St. Martin's Press, 1982.

Felker, D. B., et al. *Guidelines for Document Designers*. Washington, D.C.: American Institutes for Research, 1981.

Flesch, R. *The ABC of Style—A Guide to Plain English*. New York: Harper & Row, 1980.

Flower, L. *Problem-Solving Strategies for Writing*. 2nd ed. New York: Harcourt Brace Jovanovich, 1985.

The Manual of Style. 13th ed. Chicago: University of Chicago Press, 1982.

Strunk, W., and E. B. White. *The Elements of Style*. 3rd ed. New York: Macmillan, 1979.

Williams, J. M. *Style: Ten Lessons in Clarity and Grace*. Glenview, Ill.: Scott, Foresman, 1981.

Zinsser, W. *Writing with a Word Processor*. New York: Harper & Row, 1983.

Business and Technical Speaking

Connolly, J. *Effective Technical Presentations*. St. Paul, Minn.: 3M Business Press, 1968.

Ehninger, D., et al. *Principles of Speech Communication*. 8th ed. Glenview, Ill.: Scott, Foresman, 1980.

Frank, T., and D. Ray. *Basic Business and Professional Speech Communication*. Englewood Cliffs, N.J.: Prentice-Hall, 1979.

Timm, P. R. *Functional Business Presentations: Getting Across*. Englewood Cliffs, N.J.: Prentice-Hall, 1981.

Graphics

Hanks, K., and L. Belliston. *Draw! A Visual Approach to Thinking, Learning, and Communicating*. Los Altos, Calif.: William Kaufmann, 1977.

Lefferts, R. *How to Prepare Charts and Graphs for Effective Reports*. New York: Barnes & Noble Books, 1981.

MacGregor, A. J. *Graphics Simplified: How to Plan and Prepare Effective Charts, Graphs, Illustrations, and Other Visual Aids*. Toronto: University of Toronto Press, 1979.

Pocket Pal: A Graphic Arts Production Handbook. 12th ed. New York: International Paper Company, 1979.

Turnbull, A. T., and R. N. Baird. *The Graphics of Communication*. 4th ed. New York: Holt, Rinehart and Winston, 1980.

INDEX

Page numbers in boldface refer to illustrations and examples.

To the Student

Usually only instructors are asked about the quality of a text. Now, we would like to ask you about HOW TO WRITE FOR THE WORLD OF WORK, 3rd ed. Please return this questionnaire to the English Editor, College Department, Holt, Rinehart and Winston, 383 Madison Avenue, New York, N.Y. 10017

Name _____ **Date** _____

School _____ **Course Title** _____

Instructor _____

1. Did you find this book too easy? _____ too difficult?_____

   about right? _____

2. Which chapters did you find the most helpful? Which chapters did you find least helpful?

	Helpful	Not Helpful
Unit I: Basic Principles		
1. The Process of Transactional Writing	____	____
2. Persuasion and Scientific Argument	____	____
3. Style and Tone	____	____
Unit II: Correspondence		
4. Basic Principles of Correspondence	____	____
5. Inquiry and Response Letters	____	____
6. Employment Letters and Interviews	____	____
7. Customer Relations Letters	____	____
8. Sales Letters	____	____
Unit III: Reports		
9. Basic Principles of Reports	____	____
10. Library Research	____	____
11. Bibliographic Reports and Literature Reviews	____	____
12. Mechanism Description	____	____
13. Process Description	____	____
14. Instructions	____	____
15. Periodic Reports	____	____
16. Recommendation Reports	____	____
17. Proposals	____	____
18. Oral Reports	____	____
Unit IV: A Writer's Guide	____	____

3. Do you intend to keep this book? Yes _____ No _____

4. Any other comments or suggestions: